RA,
ZETSUBOU-SENSEI

The Power of Negative Thinking 3

Koji Kumeta

Translated and adapted by Joyce Aurino
Lettered by Foltz Design

BALLANTINE BOOKS • NEW YORK

A Del Rey Manga/Kodansha Trade Paperback Original

Sayonara, Zetsubou-sensei: The Power of Negative Thinking
volume 3 copyright © 2006 Koji Kumeta
English translation copyright © 2009 Koji Kumeta

Published in the United States by Del Rey, an imprint of The Random House
Publishing Group, a division of Random House, Inc., New York.

DEL REY is a registered trademark and the Del Rey colophon
is a trademark of Random House, Inc.

Publication rights arranged through Kodansha Ltd.

First published in Japan in 2006 by Kodansha Ltd., Tokyo

ISBN 978-0-345-51024-2

Printed in the United States of America

www.delreymanga.com

2 3 4 5 6 7 8 9

Translator/Adapter: Joyce Aurino
Lettering: Foltz Design

SAYONARA, ZETSUBOU-SENSEI

The Power of Negative Thinking ❸

CONTENTS

Honorifics Explained

Throughout the Del Rey Manga books, you will find Japanese honorifics left intact in the translations. For those not familiar with how the Japanese use honorifics and, more important, how they differ from American honorifics, we present this brief overview.

Politeness has always been a critical facet of Japanese culture. Ever since the feudal era, when Japan was a highly stratified society, use of honorifics—which can be defined as polite speech that indicates relationship or status—has played an essential role in the Japanese language. When addressing someone in Japanese, an honorific usually takes the form of a suffix attached to one's name (example: "Asuna-san"), is used as a title at the end of one's name, or appears in place of the name itself (example: "Negi-sensei," or simply "Sensei").

Honorifics can be expressions of respect or endearment. In the context of manga and anime, honorifics give insight into the nature of the relationship between characters. Many English translations leave out these important honorifics and therefore distort the feel of the original Japanese. Because Japanese honorifics contain nuances that English honorifics lack, it is our policy at Del Rey not to translate them. Here, instead, is a guide to some of the honorifics you may encounter in Del Rey Manga.

-san: This is the most common honorific and is equivalent to Mr., Miss, Ms., or Mrs. It is the all-purpose honorific and can be used in any situation where politeness is required.

-sama: This is one level higher than "-san" and is used to confer great respect.

-dono: This comes from the word "tono," which means "lord." It is an even higher level than "-sama" and confers utmost respect.

-kun: This suffix is used at the end of boys' names to express familiarity or endearment. It is also sometimes used by men among friends, or when addressing someone younger or of a lower station.

-chan: This is used to express endearment, mostly toward girls. It is also used for little boys, pets, and even among lovers. It gives a sense of childish cuteness.

Bozu: This is an informal way to refer to a boy, similar to the English terms "kid" and "squirt."

Sempai/
Senpai: This title suggests that the addressee is one's senior in a group or organization. It is most often used in a school setting, where underclassmen refer to their upperclassmen as "sempai." It can also be used in the workplace, such as when a newer employee addresses an employee who has seniority in the company.

Kohai: This is the opposite of "sempai" and is used toward underclassmen in school or newcomers in the workplace. It connotes that the addressee is of a lower station.

Sensei: Literally meaning "one who has come before," this title is used for teachers, doctors, or masters of any profession or art.

-[blank]: This is usually forgotten in these lists, but it is perhaps the most significant difference between Japanese and English. The lack of honorific means that the speaker has permission to address the person in a very intimate way. Usually, only family, spouses, or very close friends have this kind of permission. Known as *yobisute,* it can be gratifying when someone who has earned the intimacy starts to call one by one's name without an honorific. But when that intimacy hasn't been earned, it can be very insulting.

Koji Kumeta

SAYONARA, ZETSUBOU-SENSEI 3

The Power of Negative Thinking

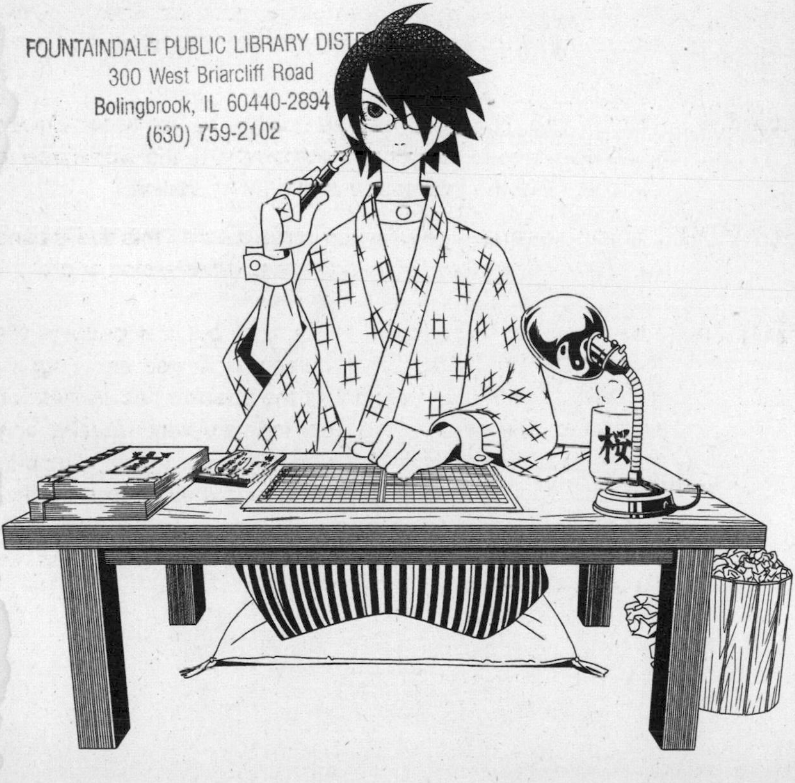
桜

Contents

Cast of Characters

ATTENDANCE LIST
CLASS 2-F

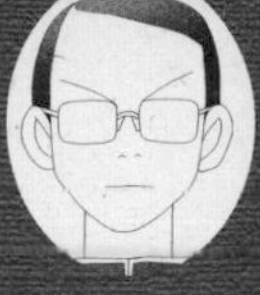

KAGER USUI
CHAIRMAN

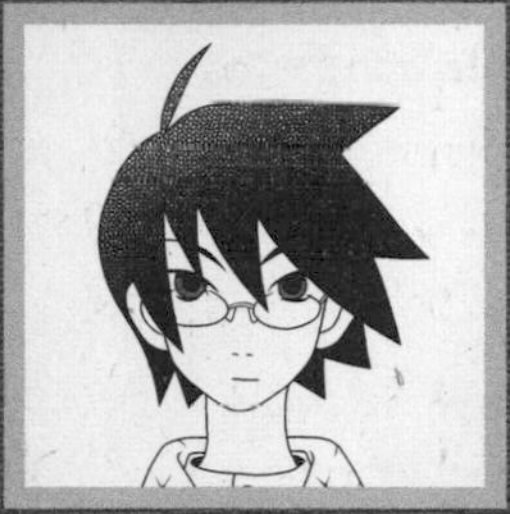

TEACHER-IN-CHARGE
NOZOMU ITOSHIKI
SUPER-NEGATIVE MAN

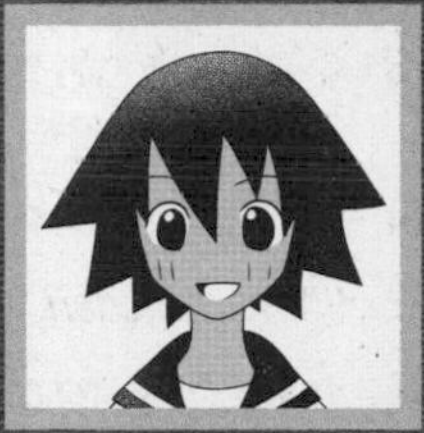

TARO MARIA SEKIUTSU
ILLEGAL IMMIGRANT; REFUGEE GIRL

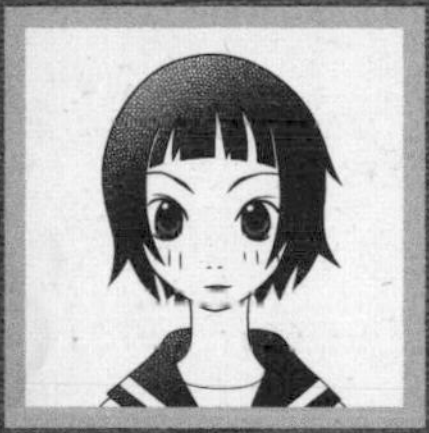

MATOI TSUNETSUKI
SUPER-LOVE-OBSESSED STALKER GIRL

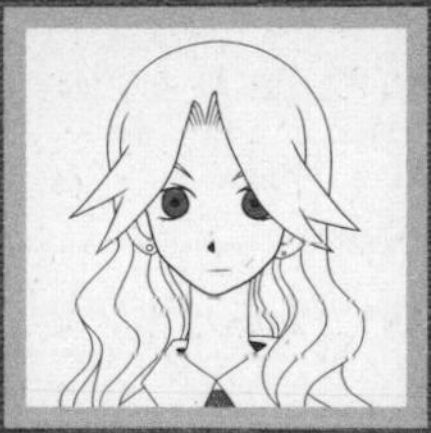

KAERE KIMURA
(ALSO KAEDE)
BILINGUAL GIRL

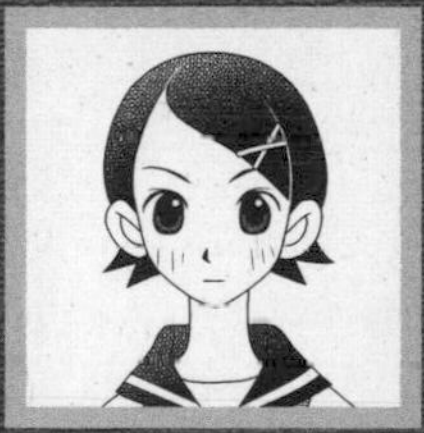

KAFUKA FUURA
SUPER-POSITIVE GIRL

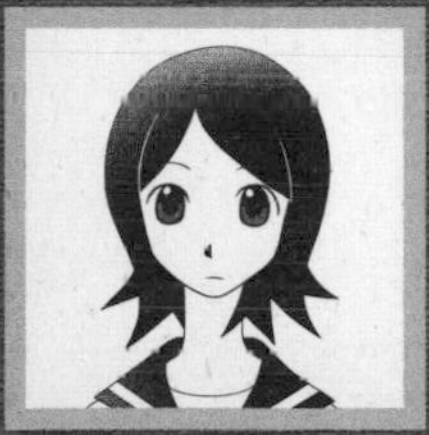

NAMI HITOU
ORDINARY GIRL

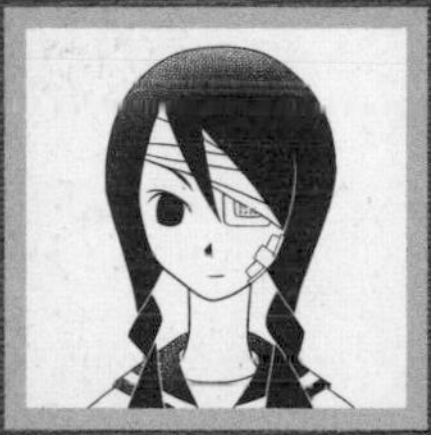

ABIRU KOBUSHI
TAIL FETISH GIRL; THOUGHT TO BE VICTIM OF DOMESTIC VIOLENCE

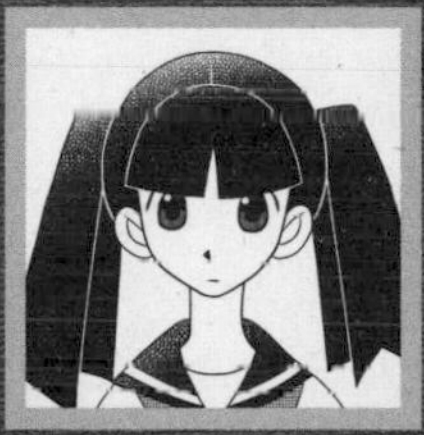

MERU OTONASHI
POISON EMAIL GIRL

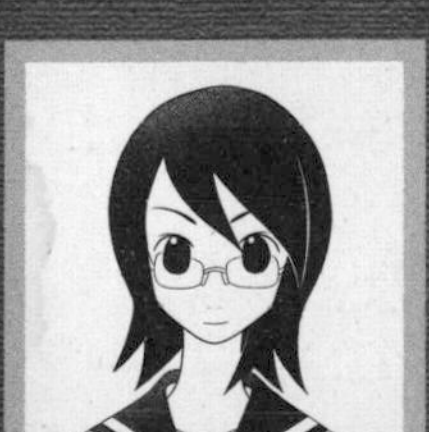

HARUMI FUJIYOSHI
EAR FETISH GIRL; ADDICTED TO COUPLING

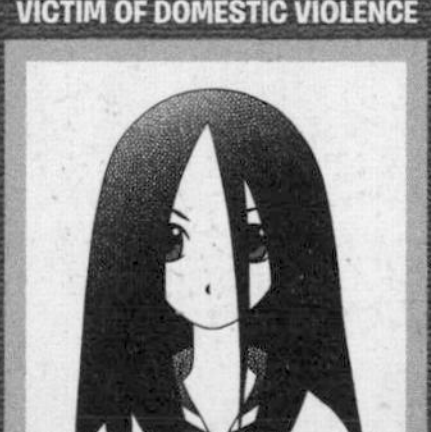

KIRI KOMORI
HIKIKOMORI GIRL

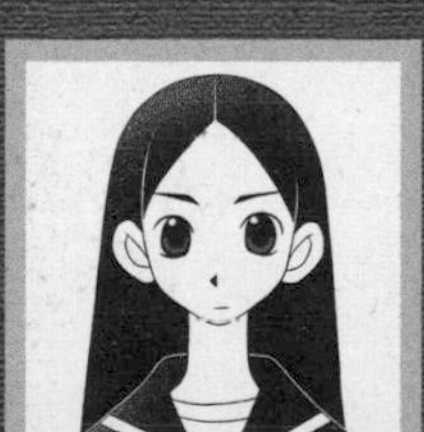

CHIRI KITSU
METHODICAL AND PRECISE GIRL

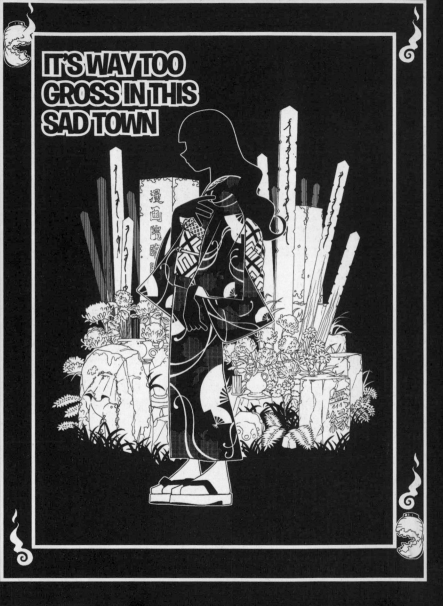

IT'S WAY TOO GROSS IN THIS SAD TOWN

CHAPTER 21

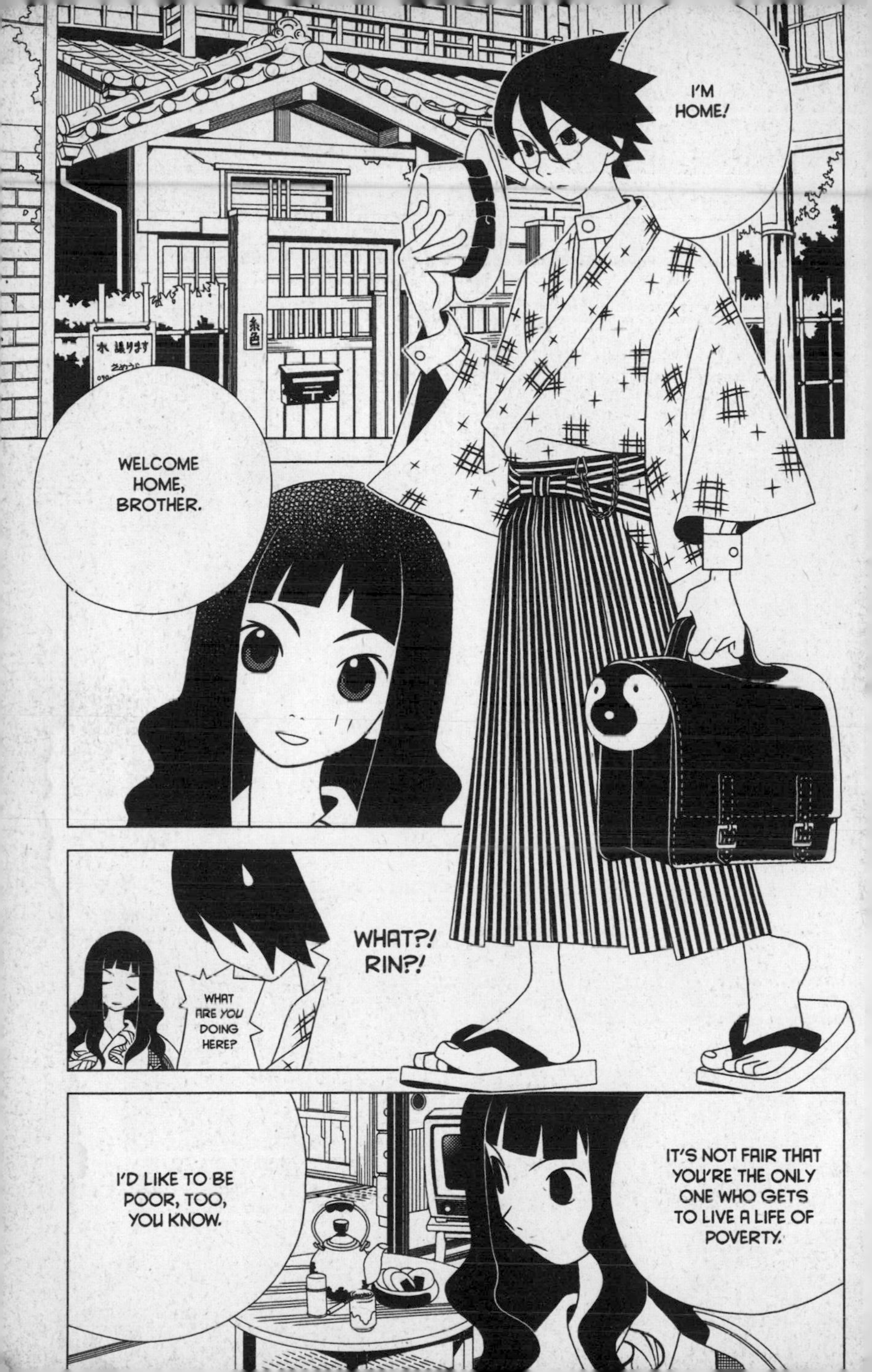
I'M HOME!
WELCOME HOME, BROTHER.
WHAT?! RIN?!
WHAT ARE YOU DOING HERE?
IT'S NOT FAIR THAT YOU'RE THE ONLY ONE WHO GETS TO LIVE A LIFE OF POVERTY.
I'D LIKE TO BE POOR, TOO, YOU KNOW.

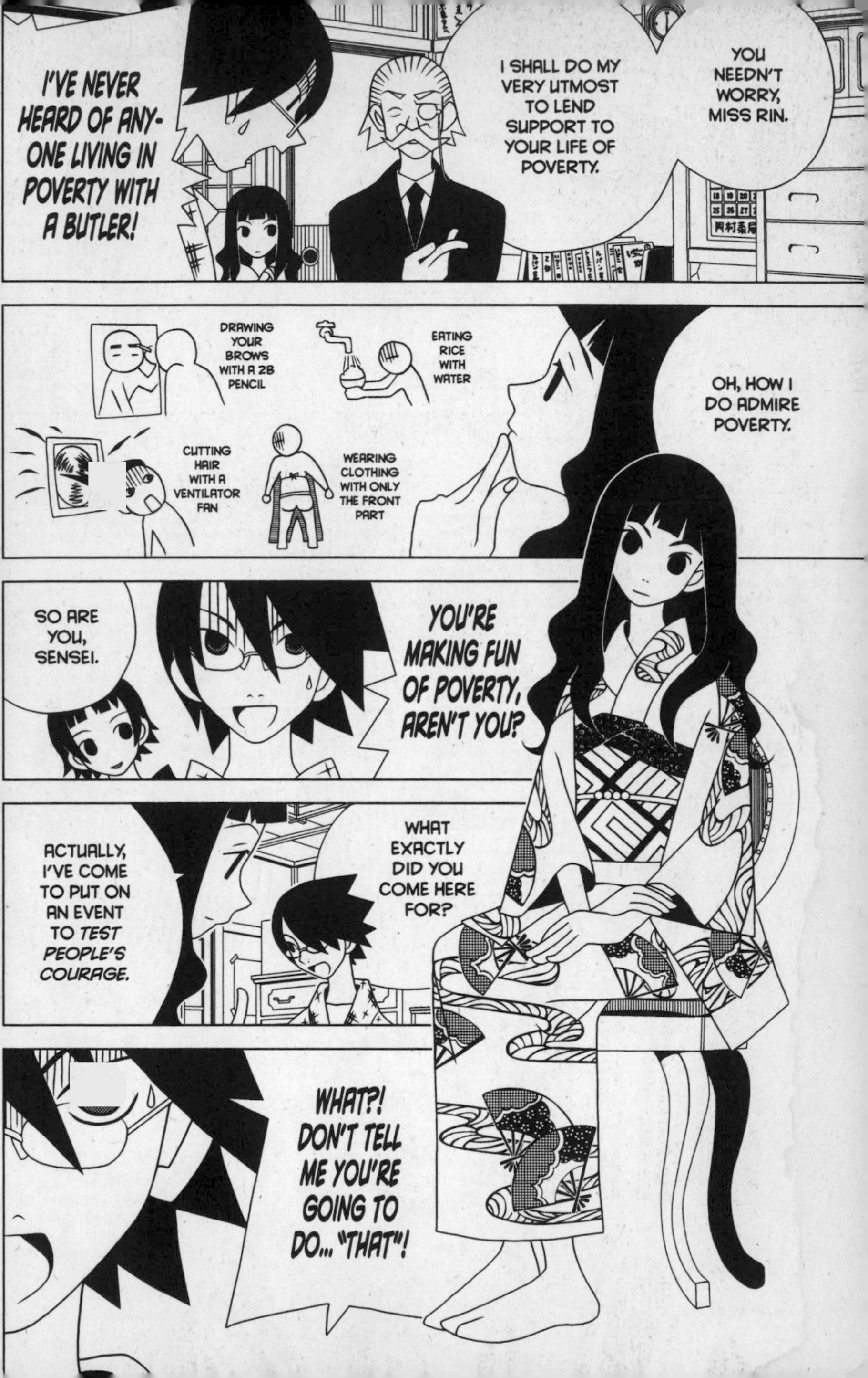
YOU NEEDN'T WORRY, MISS RIN.
I SHALL DO MY VERY UTMOST TO LEND SUPPORT TO YOUR LIFE OF POVERTY.
I'VE NEVER HEARD OF ANY-ONE LIVING IN POVERTY WITH A BUTLER!
OH, HOW I DO ADMIRE POVERTY.
EATING RICE WITH WATER
DRAWING YOUR BROWS WITH A 2B PENCIL
WEARING CLOTHING WITH ONLY THE FRONT PART
CUTTING HAIR WITH A VENTILATOR FAN
YOU'RE MAKING FUN OF POVERTY, AREN'T YOU?
SO ARE YOU, SENSEI.
WHAT EXACTLY DID YOU COME HERE FOR?
ACTUALLY, I'VE COME TO PUT ON AN EVENT TO TEST PEOPLE'S COURAGE.
WHAT?! DON'T TELL ME YOU'RE GOING TO DO... "THAT"!

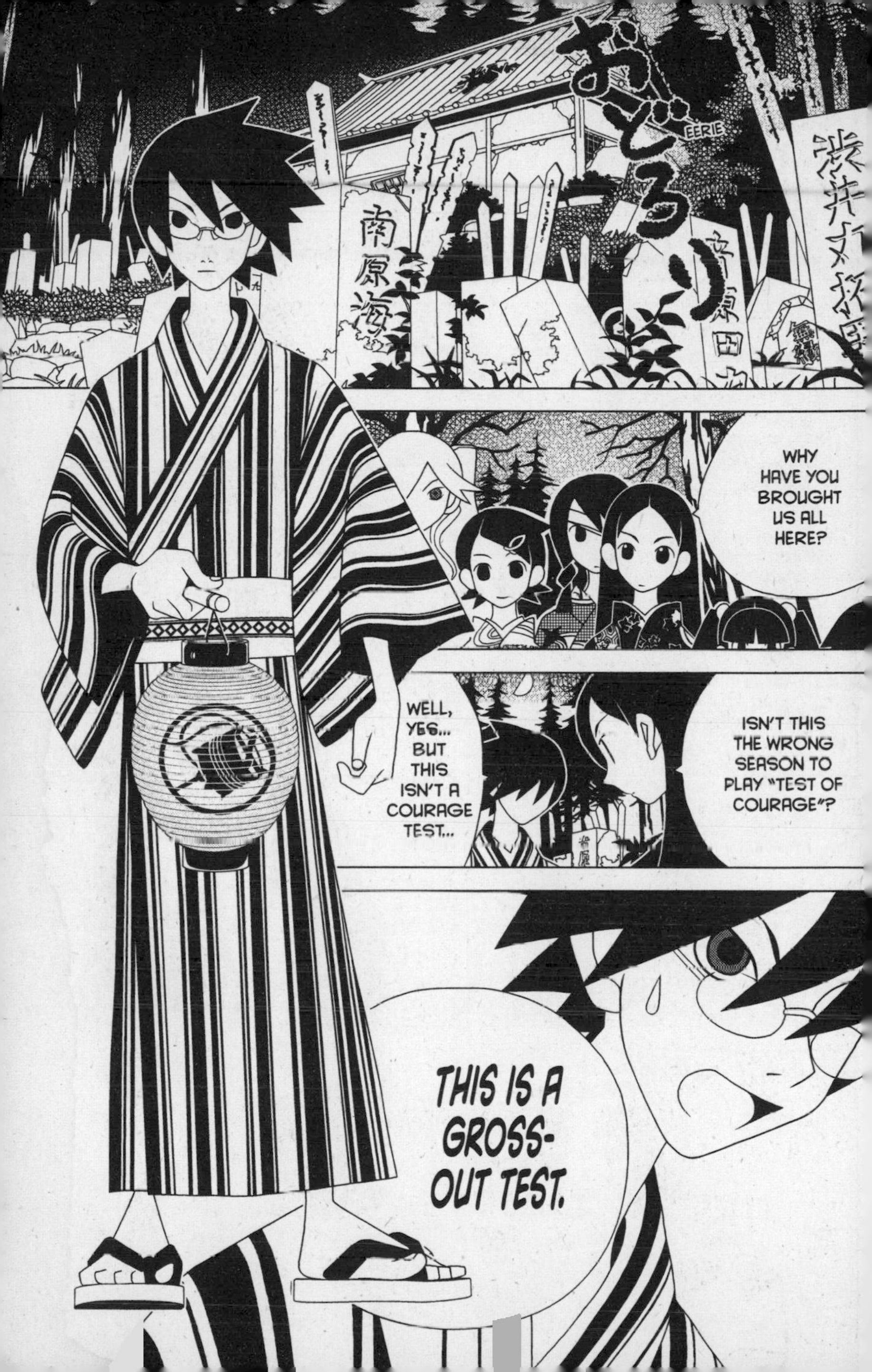
EERIE
WHY HAVE YOU BROUGHT US ALL HERE?
ISN'T THIS THE WRONG SEASON TO PLAY "TEST OF COURAGE"?
WELL, YES... BUT THIS ISN'T A COURAGE TEST...
THIS IS A GROSS-OUT TEST.

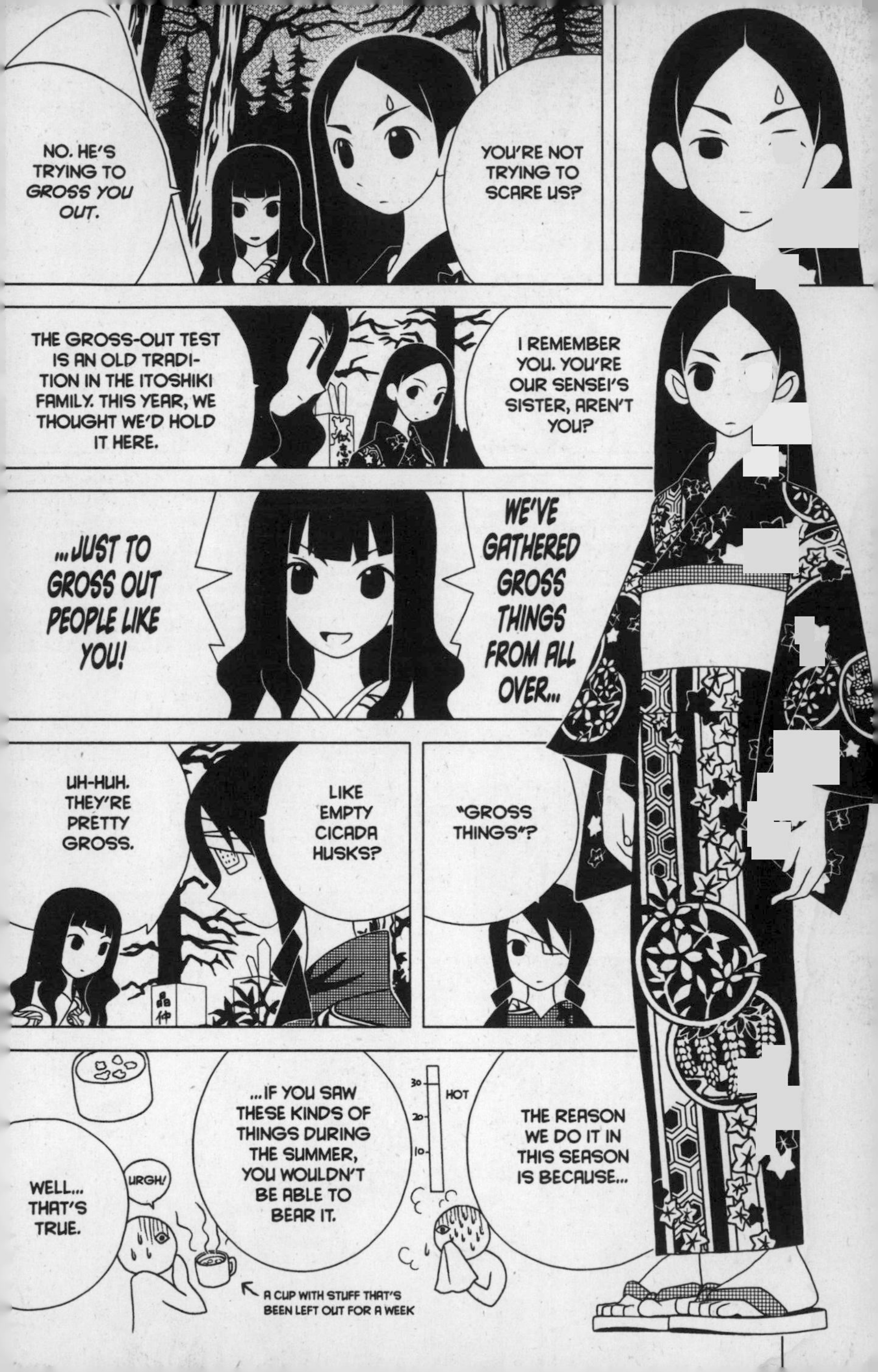
YOU'RE NOT TRYING TO SCARE US?
NO. HE'S TRYING TO *GROSS YOU OUT.*
I REMEMBER YOU. YOU'RE OUR SENSEI'S SISTER, AREN'T YOU?
THE GROSS-OUT TEST IS AN OLD TRADITION IN THE ITOSHIKI FAMILY. THIS YEAR, WE THOUGHT WE'D HOLD IT HERE.
WE'VE GATHERED GROSS THINGS FROM ALL OVER...
...JUST TO GROSS OUT PEOPLE LIKE YOU!
"GROSS THINGS"?
LIKE EMPTY CICADA HUSKS?
UH-HUH. THEY'RE PRETTY GROSS.
THE REASON WE DO IT IN THIS SEASON IS BECAUSE...
30
20
10
HOT
...IF YOU SAW THESE KINDS OF THINGS DURING THE SUMMER, YOU WOULDN'T BE ABLE TO BEAR IT.
URGH!
WELL... THAT'S TRUE.
A CUP WITH STUFF THAT'S BEEN LEFT OUT FOR A WEEK

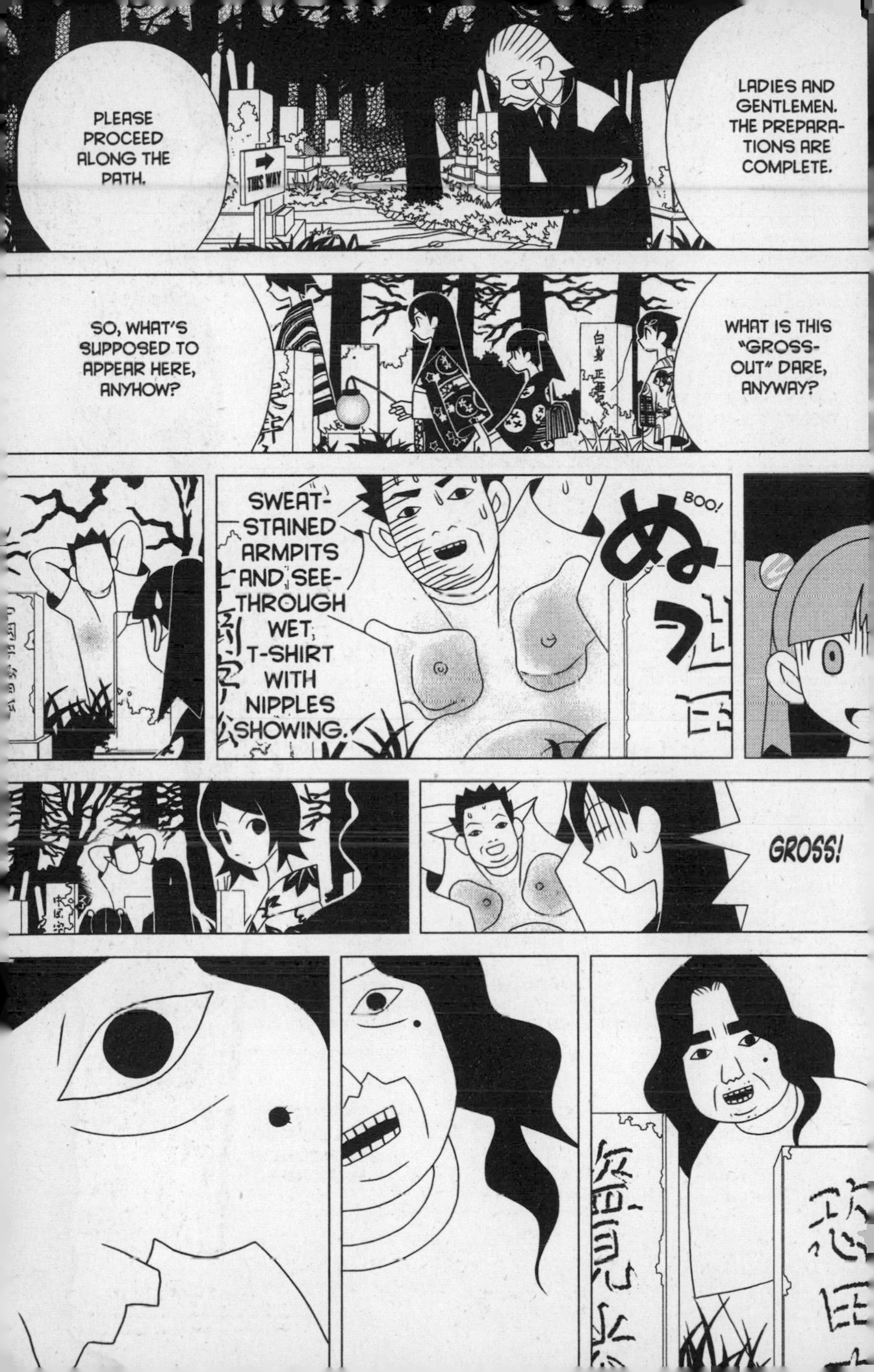
LADIES AND GENTLEMEN. THE PREPARATIONS ARE COMPLETE.
THIS WAY
PLEASE PROCEED ALONG THE PATH.
WHAT IS THIS "GROSS-OUT" DARE, ANYWAY?
SO, WHAT'S SUPPOSED TO APPEAR HERE, ANYHOW?
ぬっ
BOO!
SWEAT-STAINED ARMPITS AND SEE-THROUGH WET T-SHIRT WITH NIPPLES SHOWING.
GROSS!

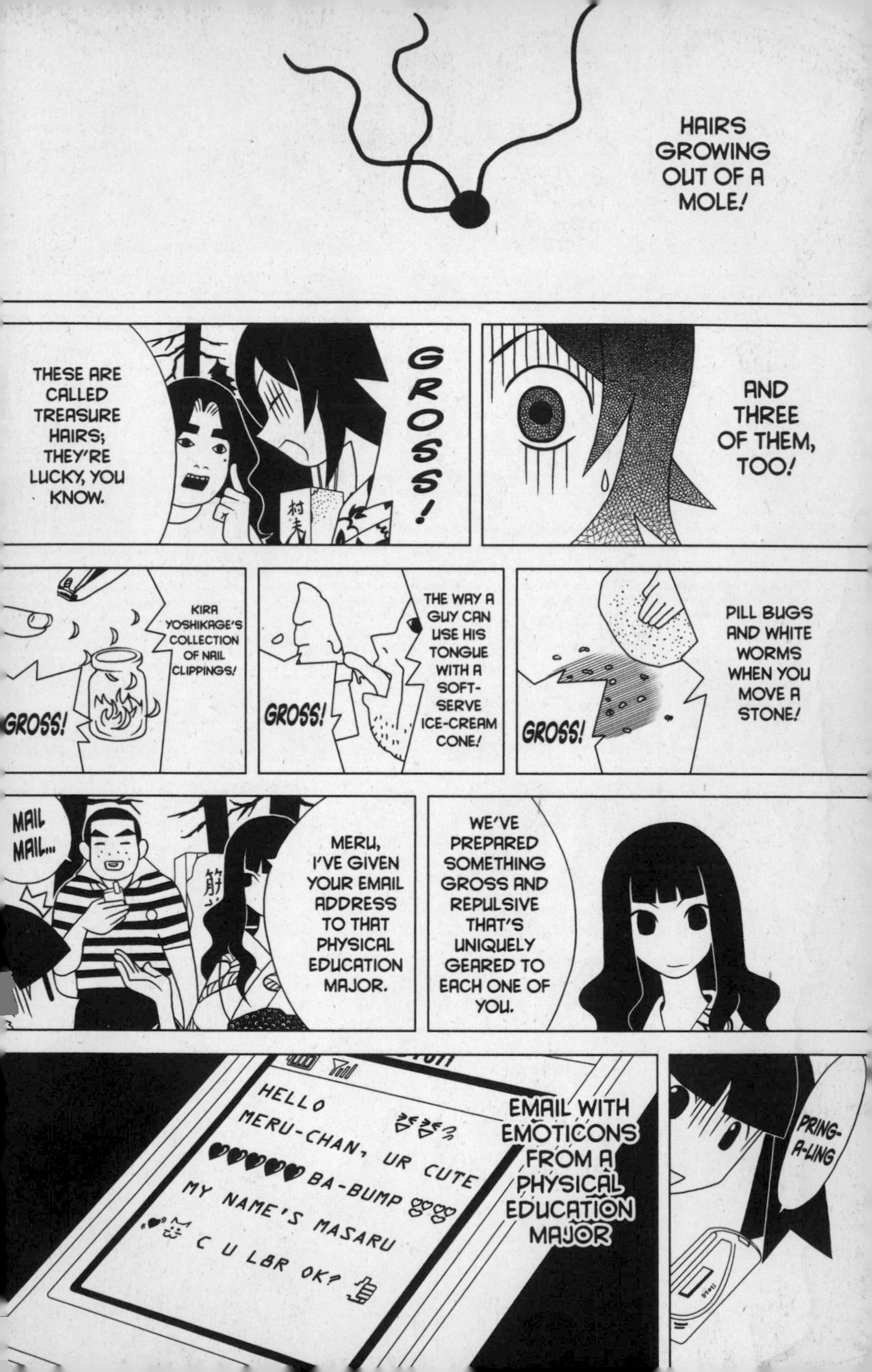
HAIRS GROWING OUT OF A MOLE!
AND THREE OF THEM, TOO!
GROSS!
THESE ARE CALLED TREASURE HAIRS; THEY'RE LUCKY, YOU KNOW.
PILL BUGS AND WHITE WORMS WHEN YOU MOVE A STONE!
GROSS!
THE WAY A GUY CAN USE HIS TONGUE WITH A SOFT-SERVE ICE-CREAM CONE!
GROSS!
KIRA YOSHIKAGE'S COLLECTION OF NAIL CLIPPINGS!
GROSS!
WE'VE PREPARED SOMETHING GROSS AND REPULSIVE THAT'S UNIQUELY GEARED TO EACH ONE OF YOU.
MERU, I'VE GIVEN YOUR EMAIL ADDRESS TO THAT PHYSICAL EDUCATION MAJOR.
MAIL MAIL...
PRING-A-LING
EMAIL WITH EMOTICONS FROM A PHYSICAL EDUCATION MAJOR
HELLO
MERU-CHAN, UR CUTE
BA-BUMP
MY NAME'S MASARU
C U L8R OK?

SH251;

YR DISGUSTING. A PHYS ED MAJOR SHOULDN'T USE EMOTICONS, MORON.

PRING-A-PING PING

MAIL MAIL

GROSS!

D7011

AWW SO SAD...ROTFC ♥♥♥

PRING-A-PING PING

WELL, RAW GARBAGE IS ALWAYS PRETTY DISGUSTING...

THIS IS DISGUST-ING!

GROSS!

SO THAT'S WHAT YOU MEANT...

IT'S DISGUST-ING!

I CAN'T BELIEVE THEY'D THROW OUT BURNABLE GARBAGE ON WEDNESDAY!

MON	NON-BURNABLES
TUES	BURNABLE
WED	NON-BURNABLE
THURS	RECYCLABLE
FRI	BURNABLE

TODAY IS NON-BURNABLES DAY, ISN'T IT?!

GROSS, GROSS!

HEY! HOLD ON A MINUTE!

I'M TAKING IT HOME TO THROW IT OUT ON FRIDAY!

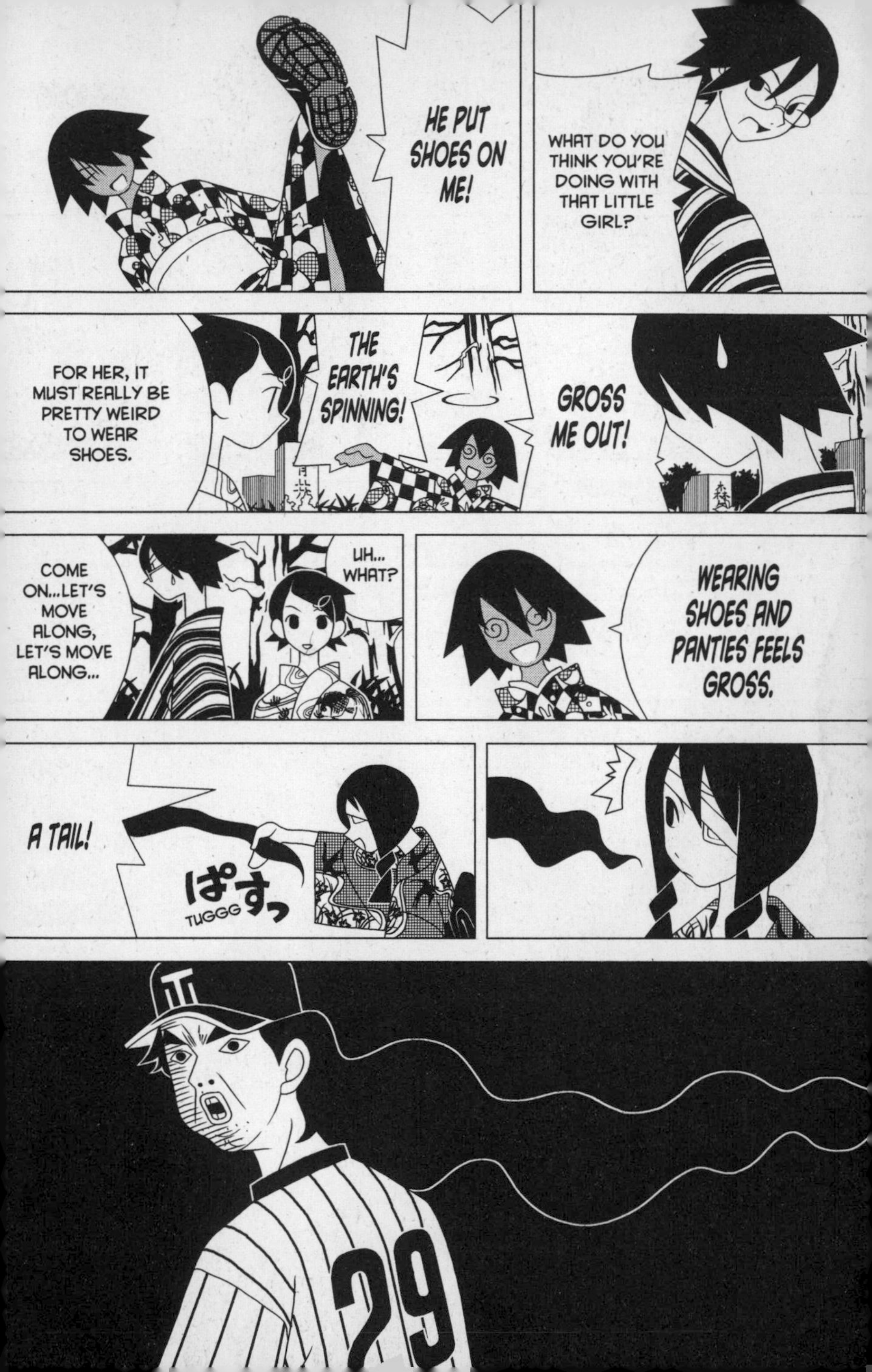
WHAT DO YOU THINK YOU'RE DOING WITH THAT LITTLE GIRL?
HE PUT SHOES ON ME!
GROSS ME OUT!
THE EARTH'S SPINNING!
FOR HER, IT MUST REALLY BE PRETTY WEIRD TO WEAR SHOES.
WEARING SHOES AND PANTIES FEELS GROSS.
UH... WHAT?
COME ON...LET'S MOVE ALONG, LET'S MOVE ALONG...
A TAIL!
ぱすっ
TUGGG
29

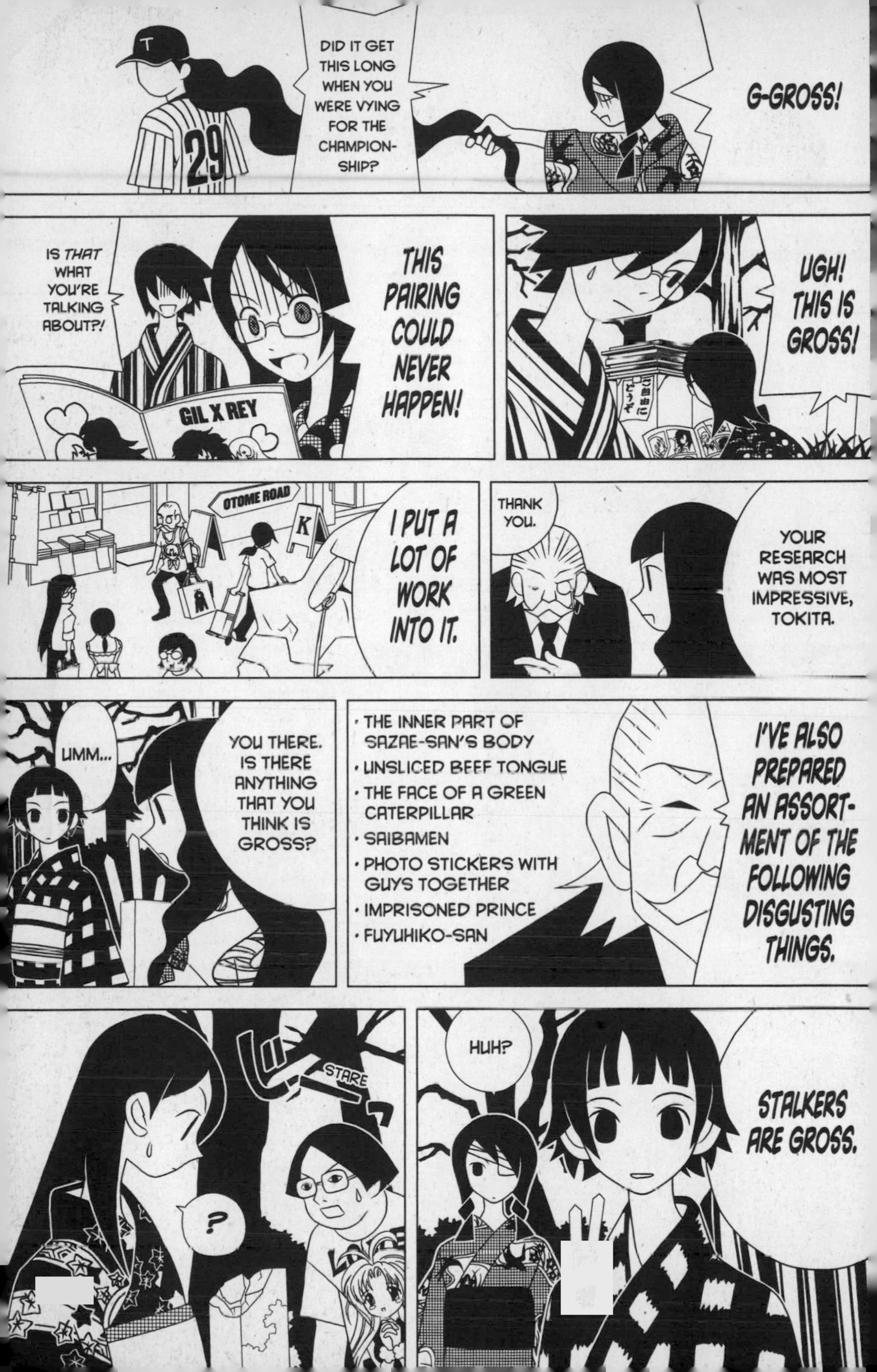
DID IT GET THIS LONG WHEN YOU WERE VYING FOR THE CHAMPIONSHIP?
G-GROSS!
UGH! THIS IS GROSS!
THIS PAIRING COULD NEVER HAPPEN!
IS *THAT* WHAT YOU'RE TALKING ABOUT?!
GIL X REY
YOUR RESEARCH WAS MOST IMPRESSIVE, TOKITA.
THANK YOU.
I PUT A LOT OF WORK INTO IT.
OTOME ROAD
K
I'VE ALSO PREPARED AN ASSORTMENT OF THE FOLLOWING DISGUSTING THINGS.
• THE INNER PART OF SAZAE-SAN'S BODY
• UNSLICED BEEF TONGUE
• THE FACE OF A GREEN CATERPILLAR
• SAIBAMEN
• PHOTO STICKERS WITH GUYS TOGETHER
• IMPRISONED PRINCE
• FUYUHIKO-SAN
YOU THERE. IS THERE ANYTHING THAT YOU THINK IS GROSS?
UMM...
STALKERS ARE GROSS.
HUH?
STARE
?

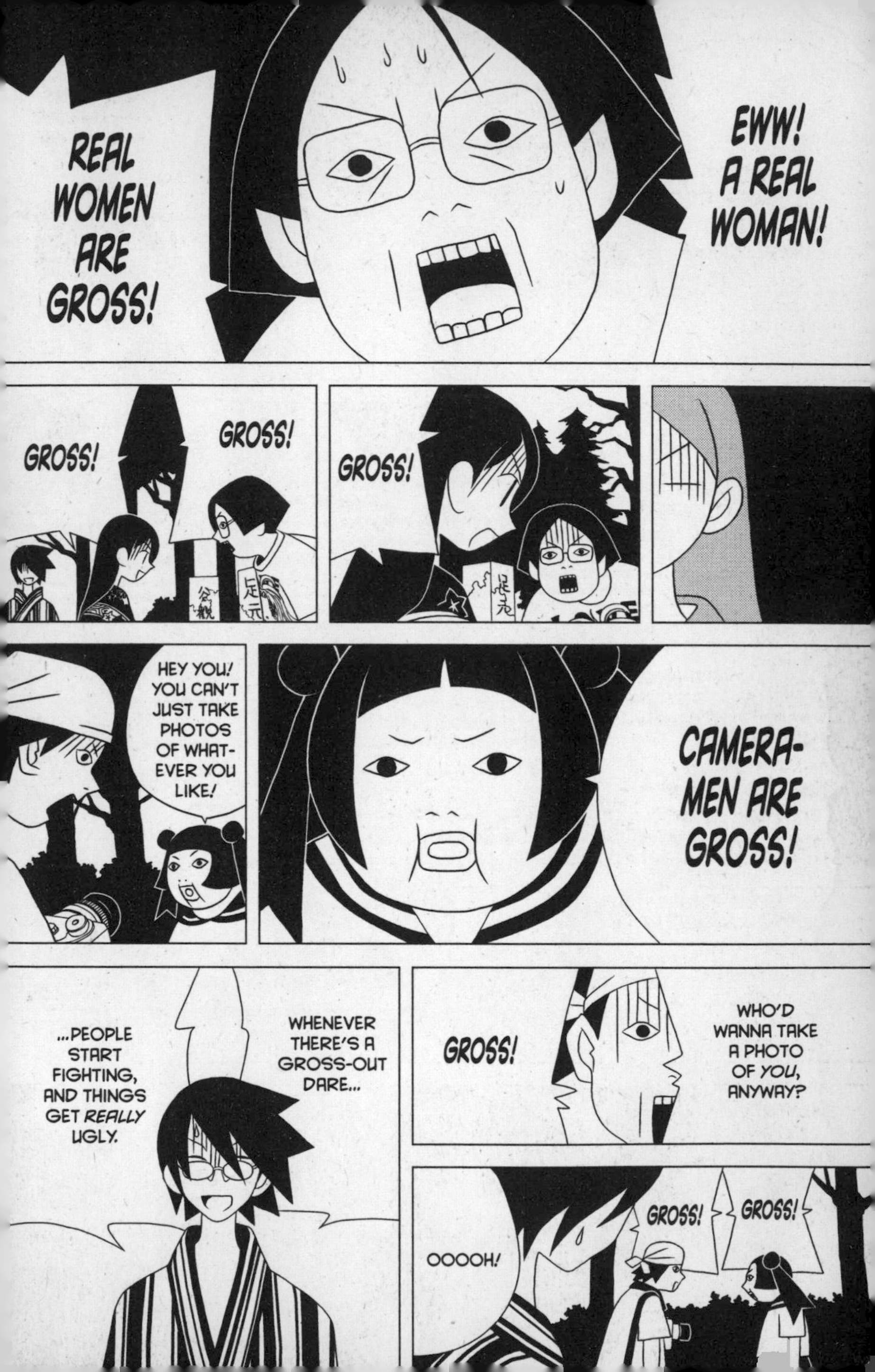

EWW! A REAL WOMAN!
REAL WOMEN ARE GROSS!
GROSS!
GROSS!
GROSS!
CAMERA-MEN ARE GROSS!
HEY YOU! YOU CAN'T JUST TAKE PHOTOS OF WHATEVER YOU LIKE!
WHO'D WANNA TAKE A PHOTO OF *YOU*, ANYWAY?
GROSS!
GROSS!
GROSS!
OOOOH!
WHENEVER THERE'S A GROSS-OUT DARE...
...PEOPLE START FIGHTING, AND THINGS GET *REALLY* UGLY.

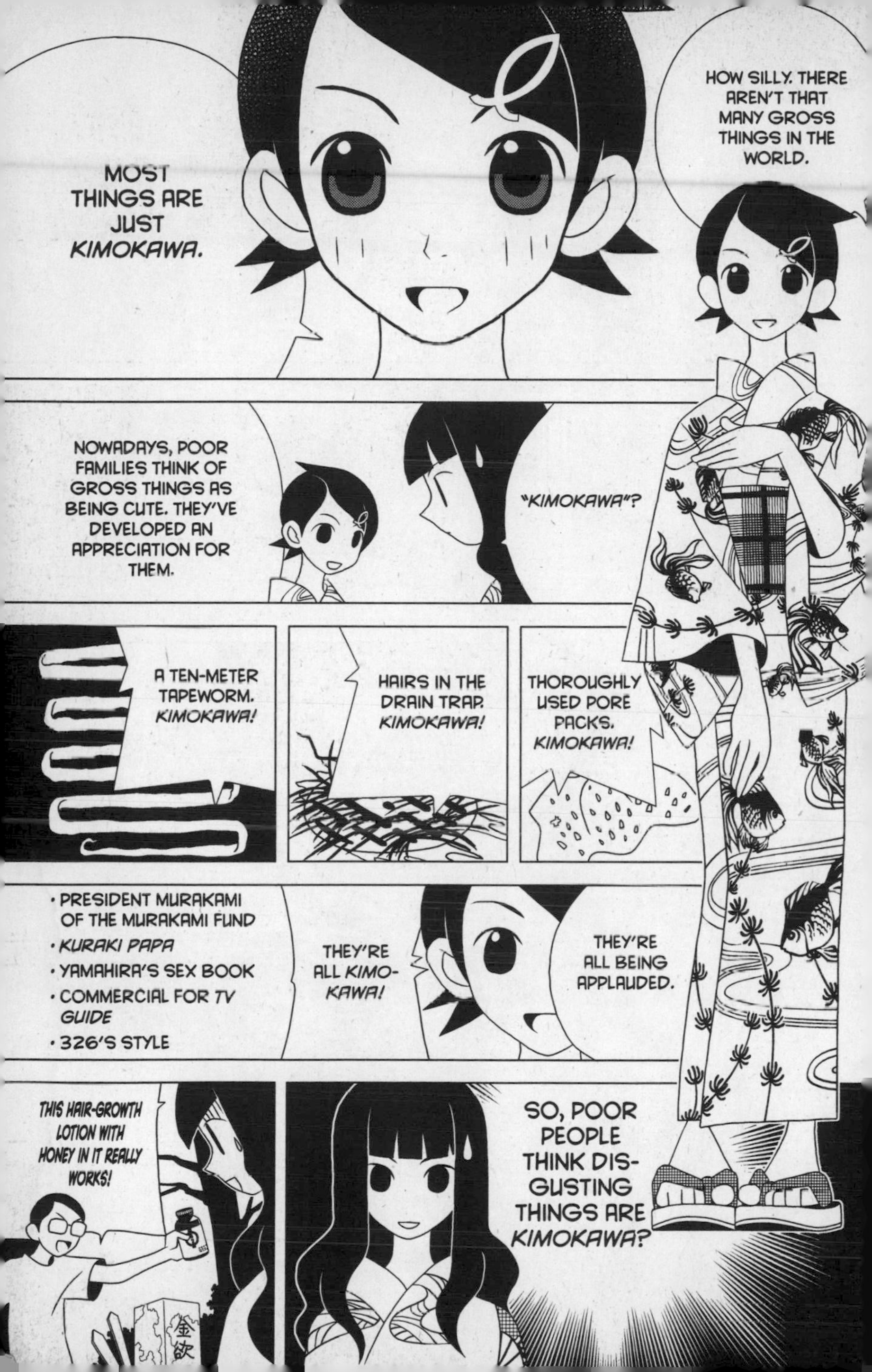
HOW SILLY. THERE AREN'T THAT MANY GROSS THINGS IN THE WORLD.
MOST THINGS ARE JUST *KIMOKAWA.*
"*KIMOKAWA*"?
NOWADAYS, POOR FAMILIES THINK OF GROSS THINGS AS BEING CUTE. THEY'VE DEVELOPED AN APPRECIATION FOR THEM.
THOROUGHLY USED PORE PACKS. *KIMOKAWA!*
HAIRS IN THE DRAIN TRAP. *KIMOKAWA!*
A TEN-METER TAPEWORM. *KIMOKAWA!*
THEY'RE ALL BEING APPLAUDED.
THEY'RE ALL *KIMO-KAWA!*
• PRESIDENT MURAKAMI OF THE MURAKAMI FUND
• *KURAKI PAPA*
• YAMAHIRA'S SEX BOOK
• COMMERCIAL FOR *TV GUIDE*
• 326'S STYLE
SO, POOR PEOPLE THINK DIS-GUSTING THINGS ARE *KIMOKAWA?*
THIS HAIR-GROWTH LOTION WITH HONEY IN IT REALLY WORKS!

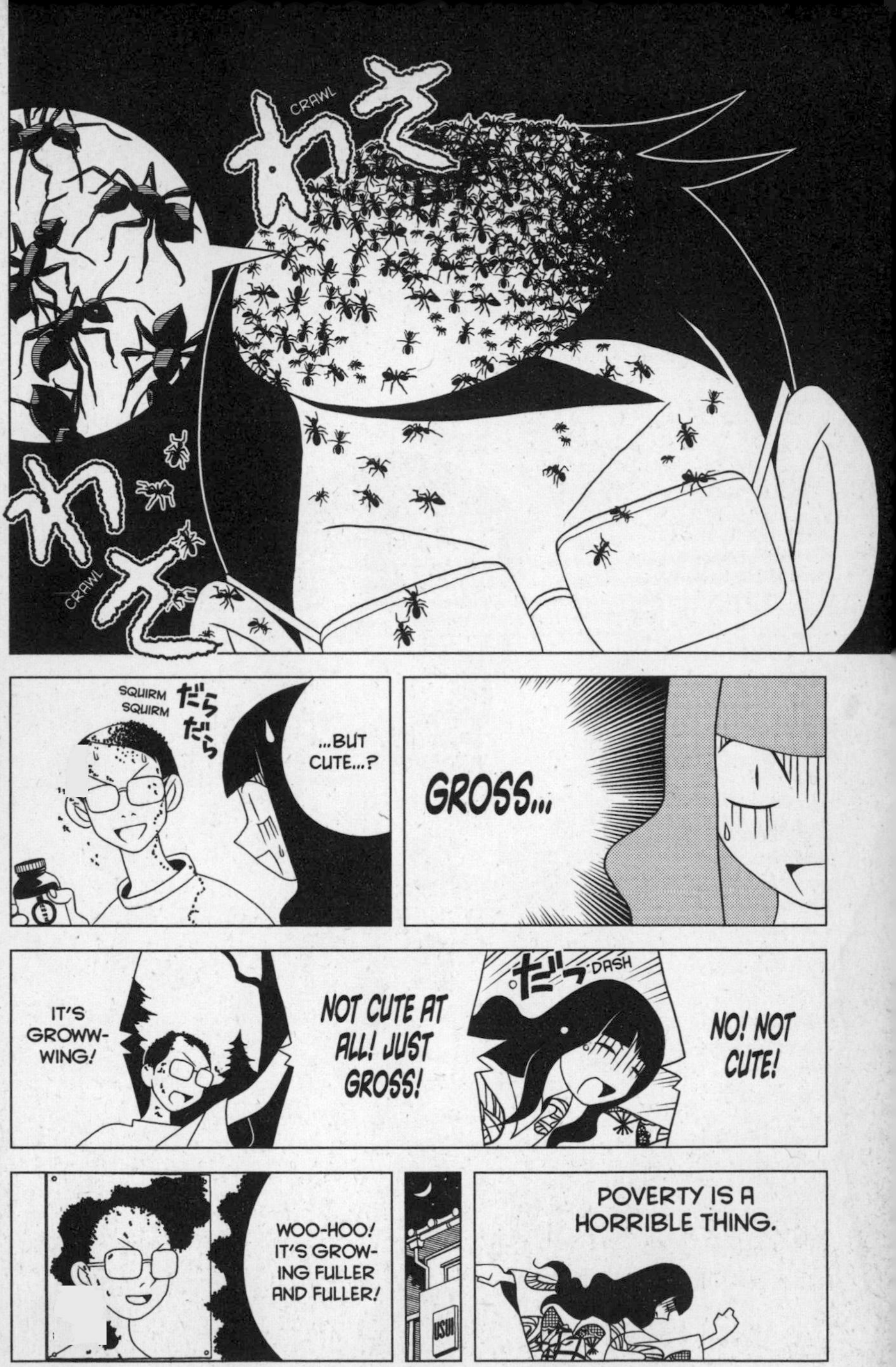

わさ
CRAWL
わさ
CRAWL
GROSS...
...BUT CUTE...?
SQUIRM SQUIRM
だらだら
NO! NOT CUTE!
だっ
DASH
NOT CUTE AT ALL! JUST GROSS!
IT'S GROWW-WING!
POVERTY IS A HORRIBLE THING.
USUI
WOO-HOO! IT'S GROW-ING FULLER AND FULLER!

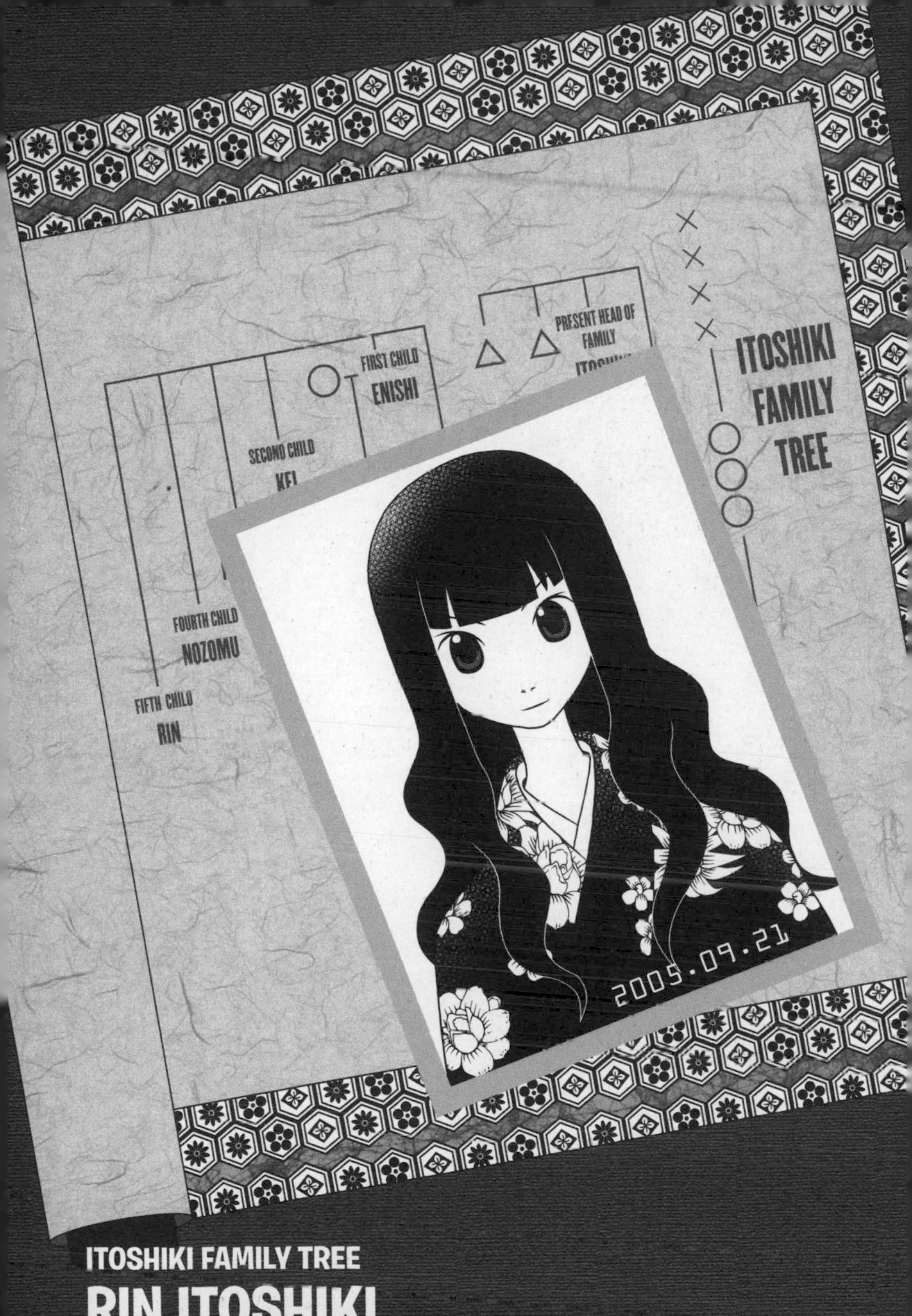
PRESENT HEAD OF FAMILY
FIRST CHILD
ENISHI
SECOND CHILD
KEI
FOURTH CHILD
NOZOMU
FIFTH CHILD
RIN
ITOSHIKI FAMILY TREE
2005.09.21

ITOSHIKI FAMILY TREE

RIN ITOSHIKI

INSTRUCTOR IN THE ITOSHIKI SCHOOL OF FLOWER ARRANGEMENT

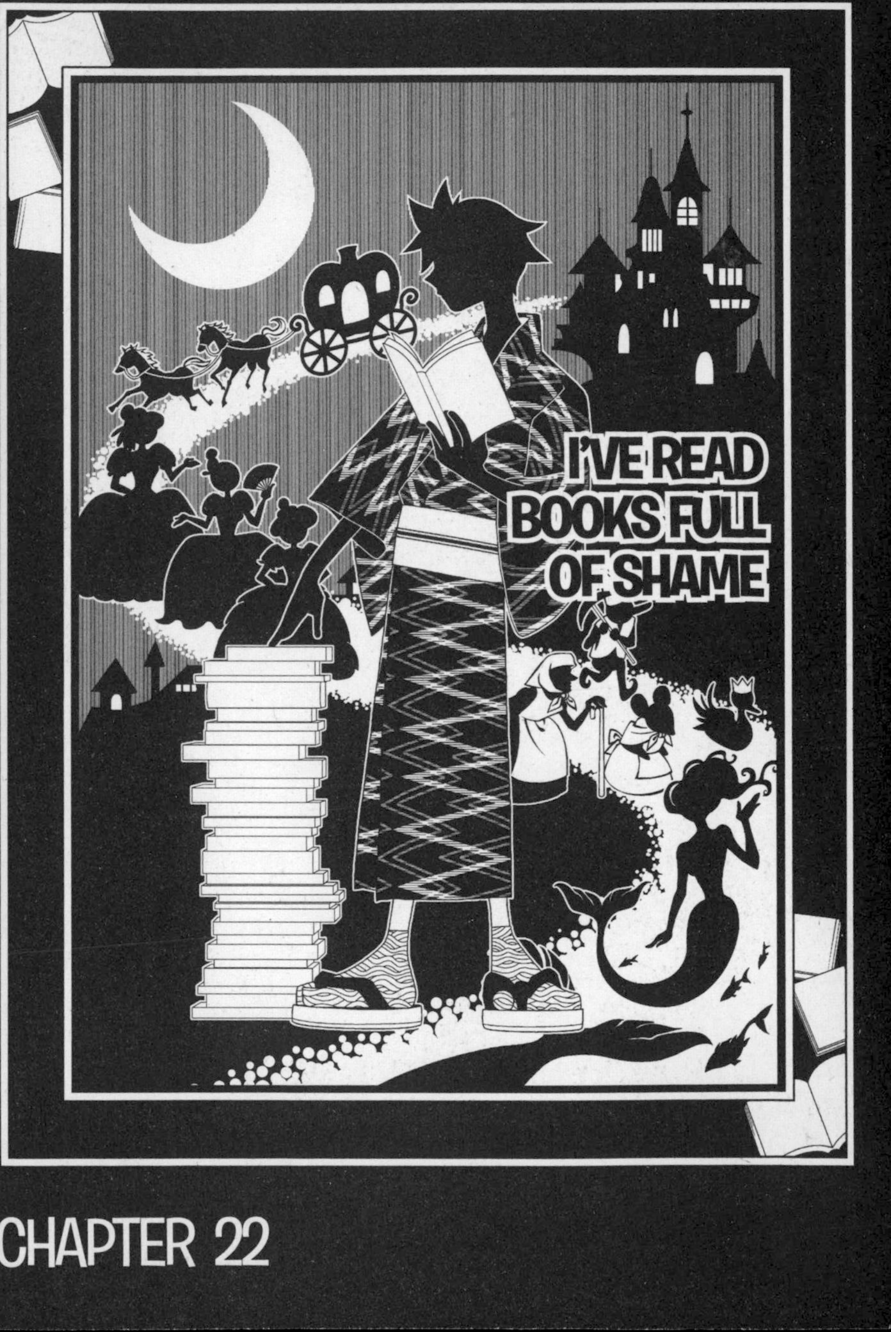
I'VE READ BOOKS FULL OF SHAME

CHAPTER 22

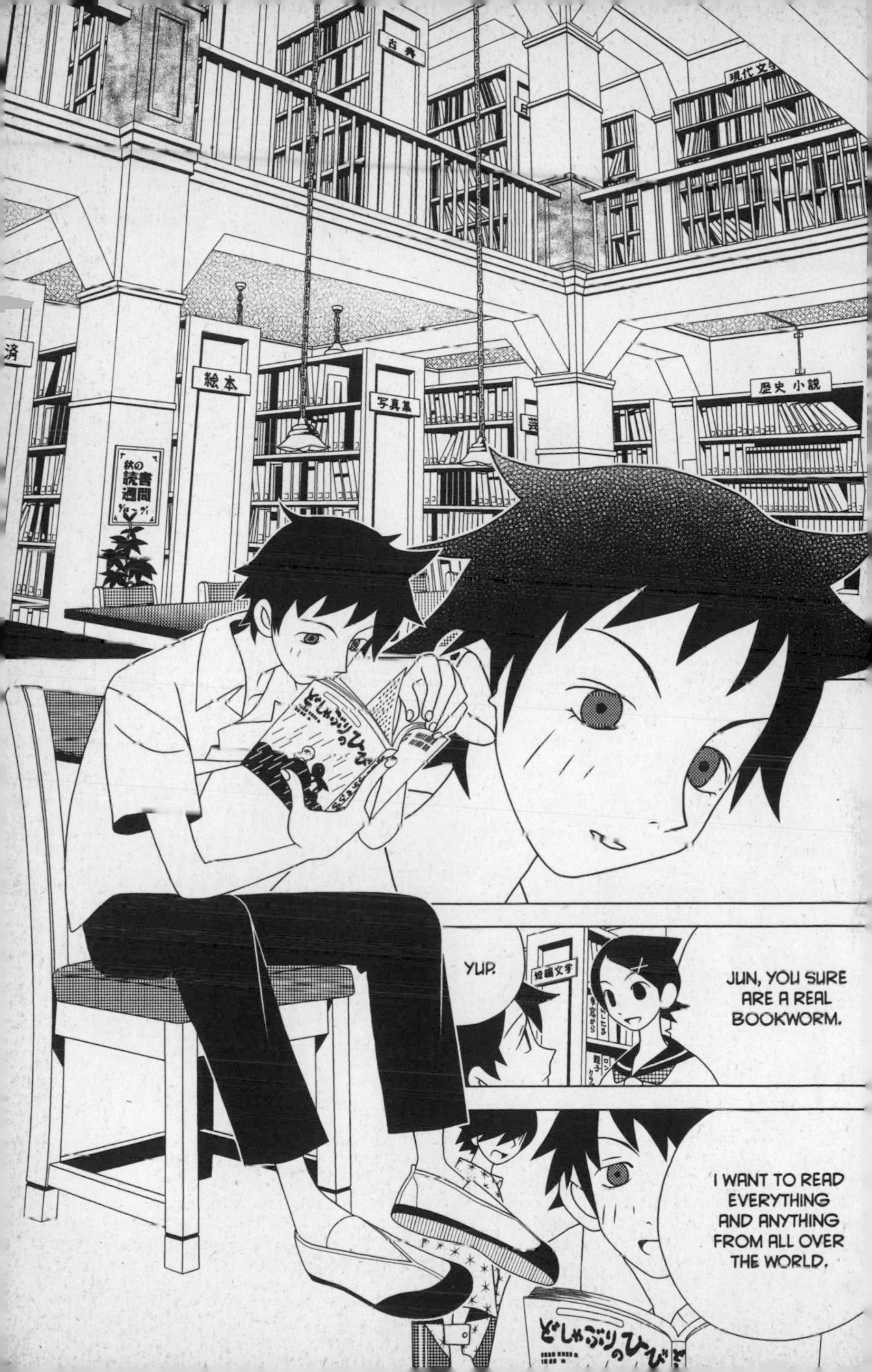
現代文学
古典
歴史小説
写真集
絵本
秋の読書週間
どしゃぶりのひび
JUN, YOU SURE ARE A REAL BOOKWORM.
YUP.
I WANT TO READ EVERYTHING AND ANYTHING FROM ALL OVER THE WORLD.

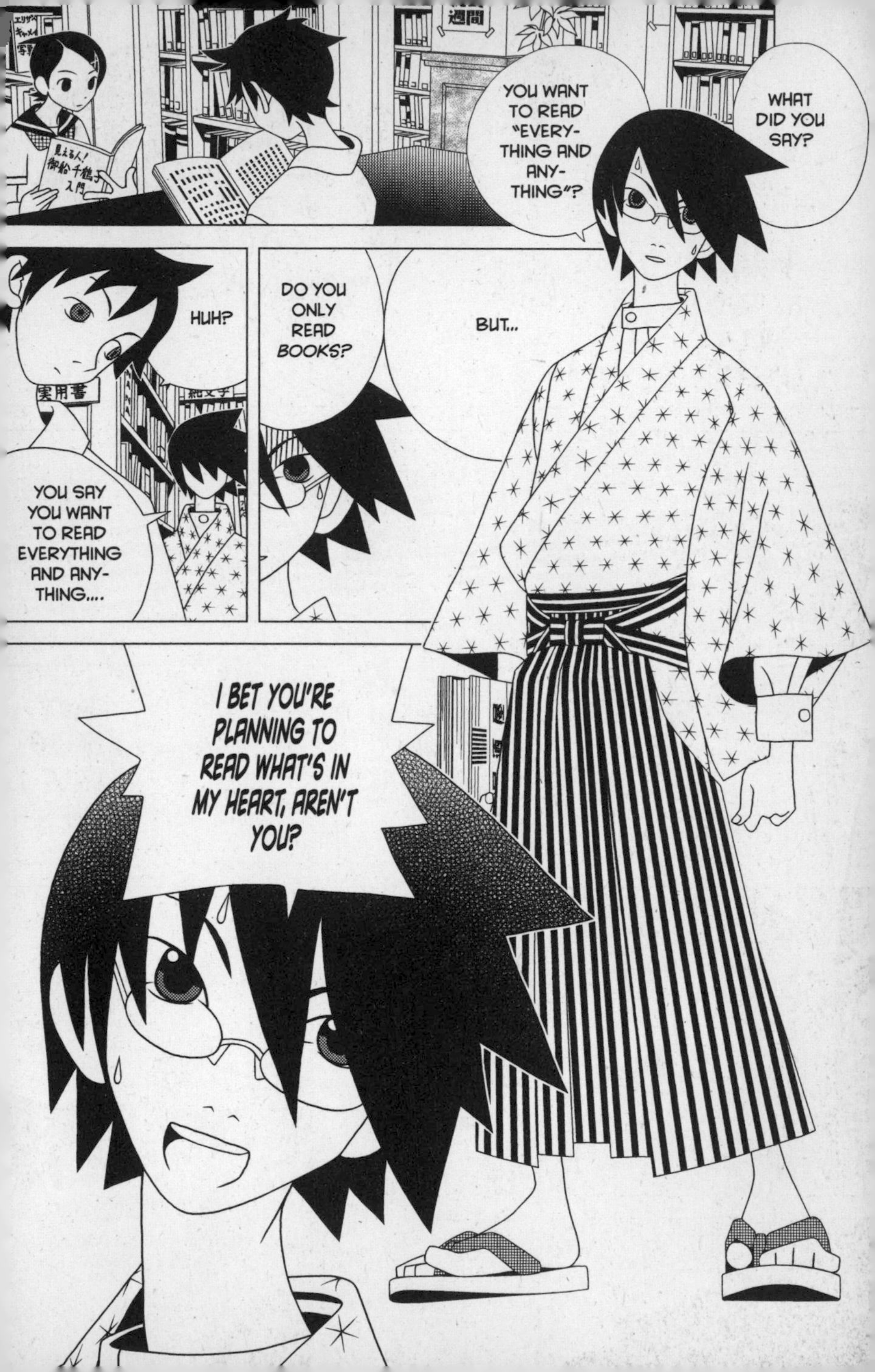
週間
WHAT DID YOU SAY?
YOU WANT TO READ "EVERY-THING AND ANY-THING"?
BUT...
DO YOU ONLY READ BOOKS?
HUH?
実用書
YOU SAY YOU WANT TO READ EVERYTHING AND ANY-THING....
I BET YOU'RE PLANNING TO READ WHAT'S IN MY HEART, AREN'T YOU?

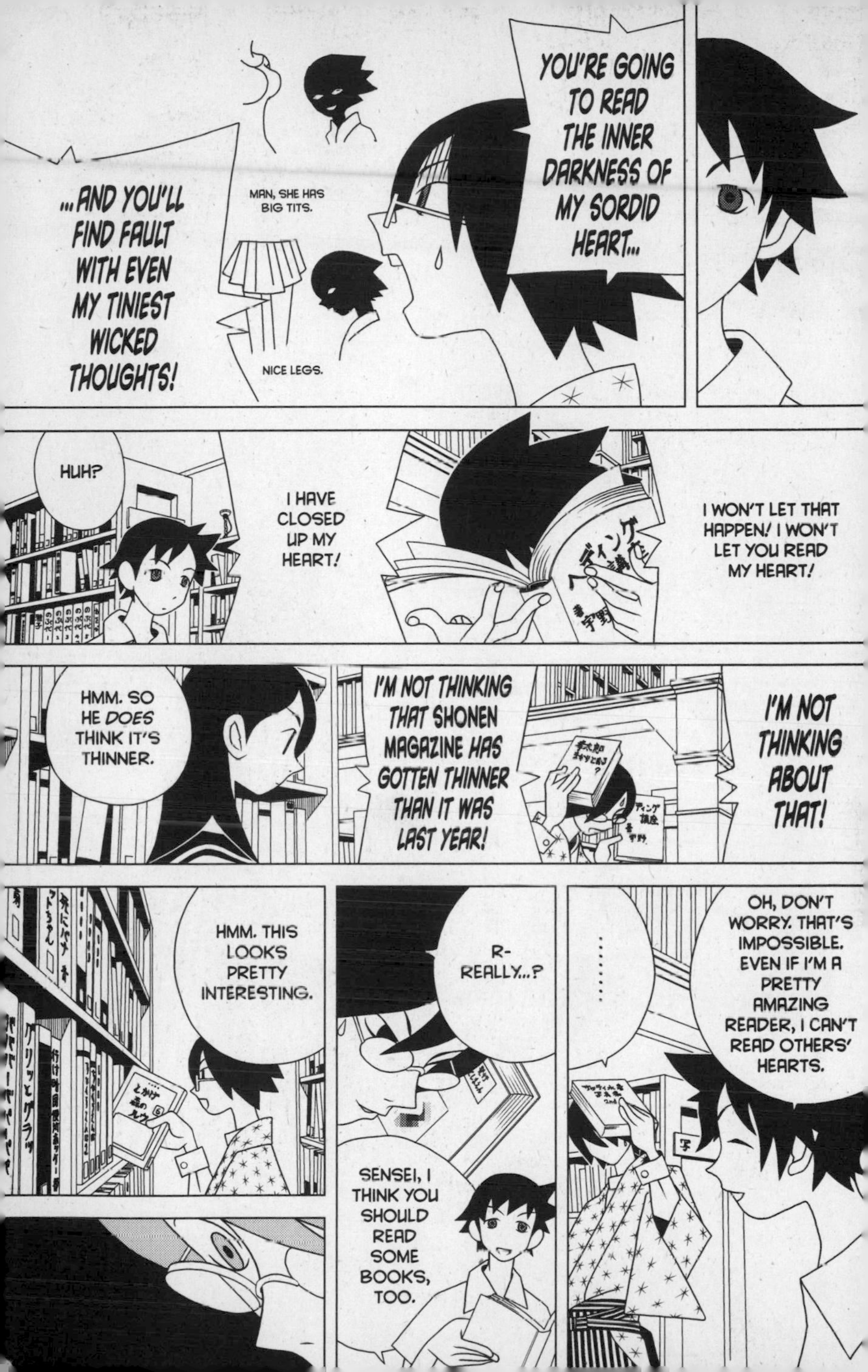
YOU'RE GOING TO READ THE INNER DARKNESS OF MY SORDID HEART...
...AND YOU'LL FIND FAULT WITH EVEN MY TINIEST WICKED THOUGHTS!
MAN, SHE HAS BIG TITS.
NICE LEGS.
I WON'T LET THAT HAPPEN! I WON'T LET YOU READ MY HEART!
I HAVE CLOSED UP MY HEART!
HUH?
I'M NOT THINKING ABOUT THAT!
I'M NOT THINKING THAT SHONEN MAGAZINE HAS GOTTEN THINNER THAN IT WAS LAST YEAR!
HMM. SO HE *DOES* THINK IT'S THINNER.
OH, DON'T WORRY. THAT'S IMPOSSIBLE. EVEN IF I'M A PRETTY AMAZING READER, I CAN'T READ OTHERS' HEARTS.
......
R- REALLY...?
SENSEI, I THINK YOU SHOULD READ SOME BOOKS, TOO.
HMM. THIS LOOKS PRETTY INTERESTING.

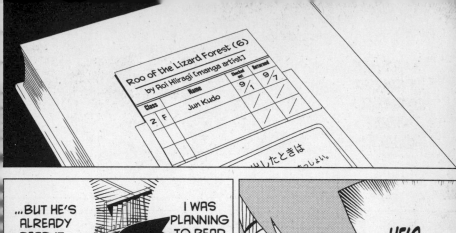

Roo of the Lizard Forest (6)

by Roi Hiiragi (manga artist)

Class		Name	Checked out	Returned
2	F	Jun Kudo	9/1	9/7
			/	/
			/	/
			/	/

...出したときは　　　　　　　っしょい。

...BUT HE'S ALREADY READ IT...

I WAS PLANNING TO READ THIS BOOK...

HE'S READ IT!

AND THIS ONE!

Battle of Flames

AND THIS ONE!

THIS ONE, TOO!

...EACH AND EVERY BOOK I WANTED TO READ!

Fairy tales

HE'S ALREADY READ...

THAT ONE, TOO...

JUST AS I THOUGHT...

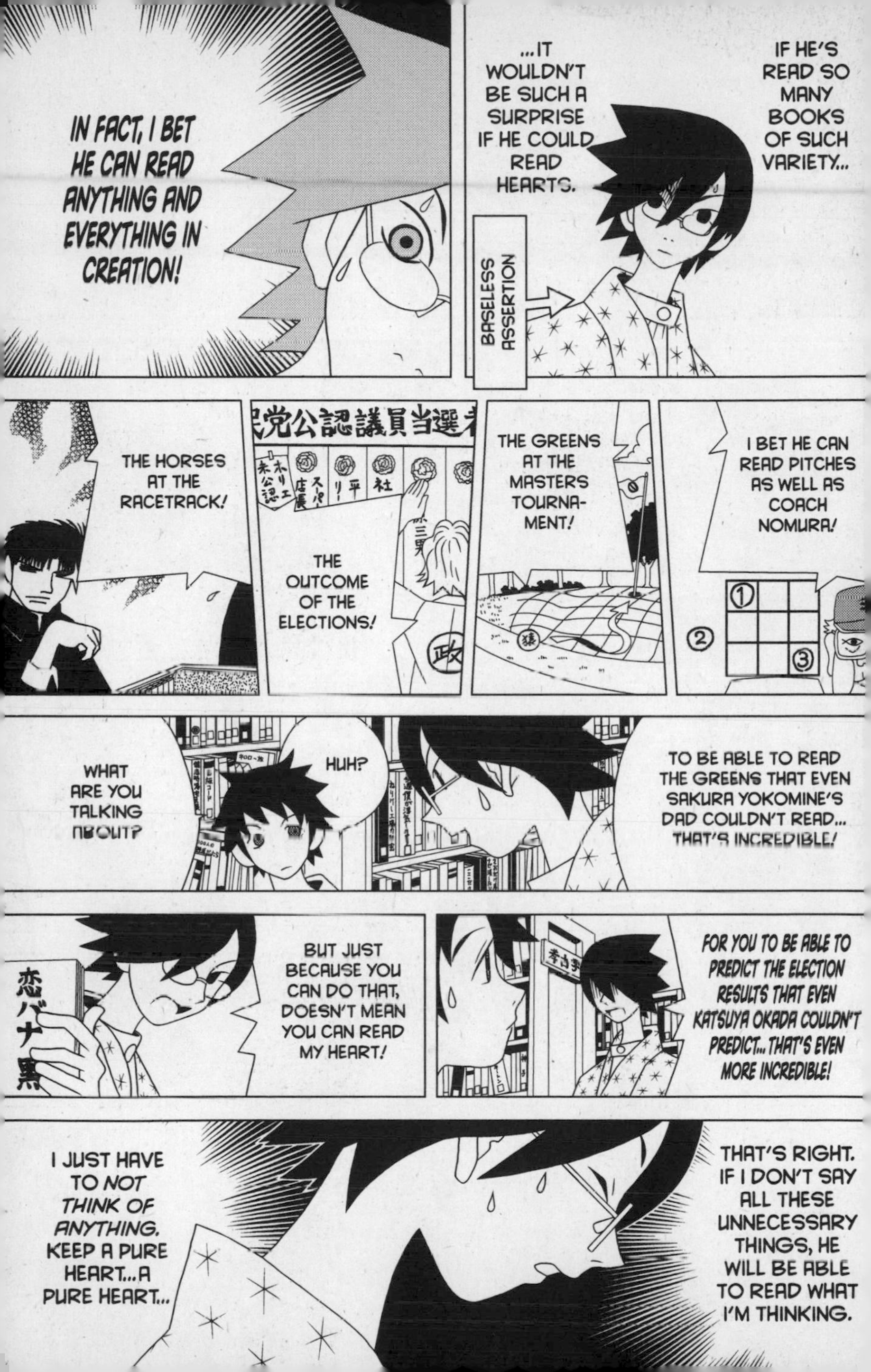
IF HE'S READ SO MANY BOOKS OF SUCH VARIETY...
...IT WOULDN'T BE SUCH A SURPRISE IF HE COULD READ HEARTS.
BASELESS ASSERTION
IN FACT, I BET HE CAN READ ANYTHING AND EVERYTHING IN CREATION!
I BET HE CAN READ PITCHES AS WELL AS COACH NOMURA!
THE GREENS AT THE MASTERS TOURNAMENT!
党公認議員当選者
THE OUTCOME OF THE ELECTIONS!
THE HORSES AT THE RACETRACK!
TO BE ABLE TO READ THE GREENS THAT EVEN SAKURA YOKOMINE'S DAD COULDN'T READ... THAT'S INCREDIBLE!
HUH?
WHAT ARE YOU TALKING ABOUT?
FOR YOU TO BE ABLE TO PREDICT THE ELECTION RESULTS THAT EVEN KATSUYA OKADA COULDN'T PREDICT... THAT'S EVEN MORE INCREDIBLE!
BUT JUST BECAUSE YOU CAN DO THAT, DOESN'T MEAN YOU CAN READ MY HEART!
THAT'S RIGHT. IF I DON'T SAY ALL THESE UNNECESSARY THINGS, HE WILL BE ABLE TO READ WHAT I'M THINKING.
I JUST HAVE TO *NOT* THINK OF ANYTHING. KEEP A PURE HEART...A PURE HEART...

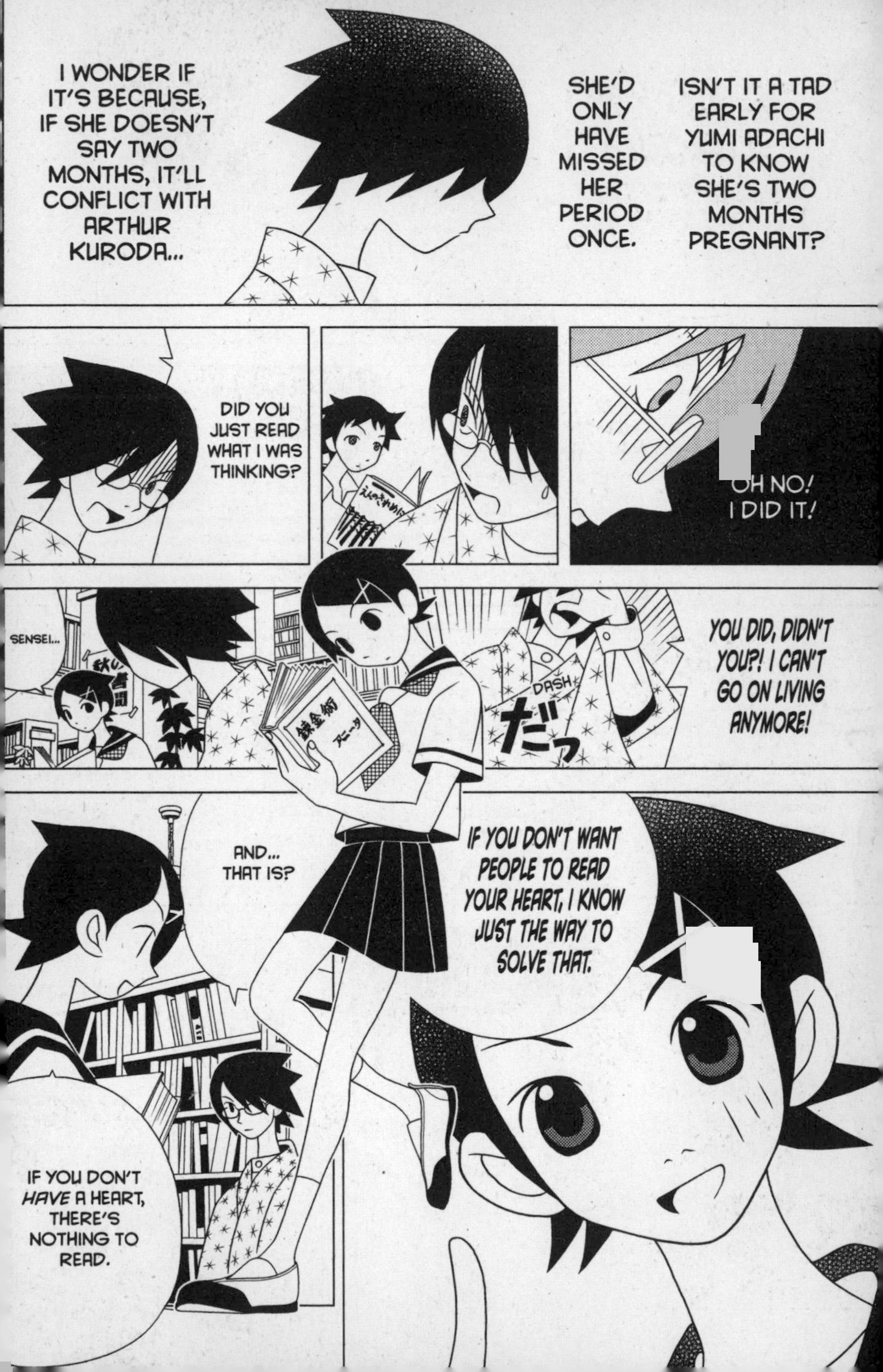
ISN'T IT A TAD EARLY FOR YUMI ADACHI TO KNOW SHE'S TWO MONTHS PREGNANT?
SHE'D ONLY HAVE MISSED HER PERIOD ONCE.
I WONDER IF IT'S BECAUSE, IF SHE DOESN'T SAY TWO MONTHS, IT'LL CONFLICT WITH ARTHUR KURODA...
OH NO! I DID IT!
DID YOU JUST READ WHAT I WAS THINKING?
YOU DID, DIDN'T YOU?! I CAN'T GO ON LIVING ANYMORE!
DASH
だっ
SENSEI...
IF YOU DON'T WANT PEOPLE TO READ YOUR HEART, I KNOW JUST THE WAY TO SOLVE THAT.
AND... THAT IS?
IF YOU DON'T *HAVE* A HEART, THERE'S NOTHING TO READ.

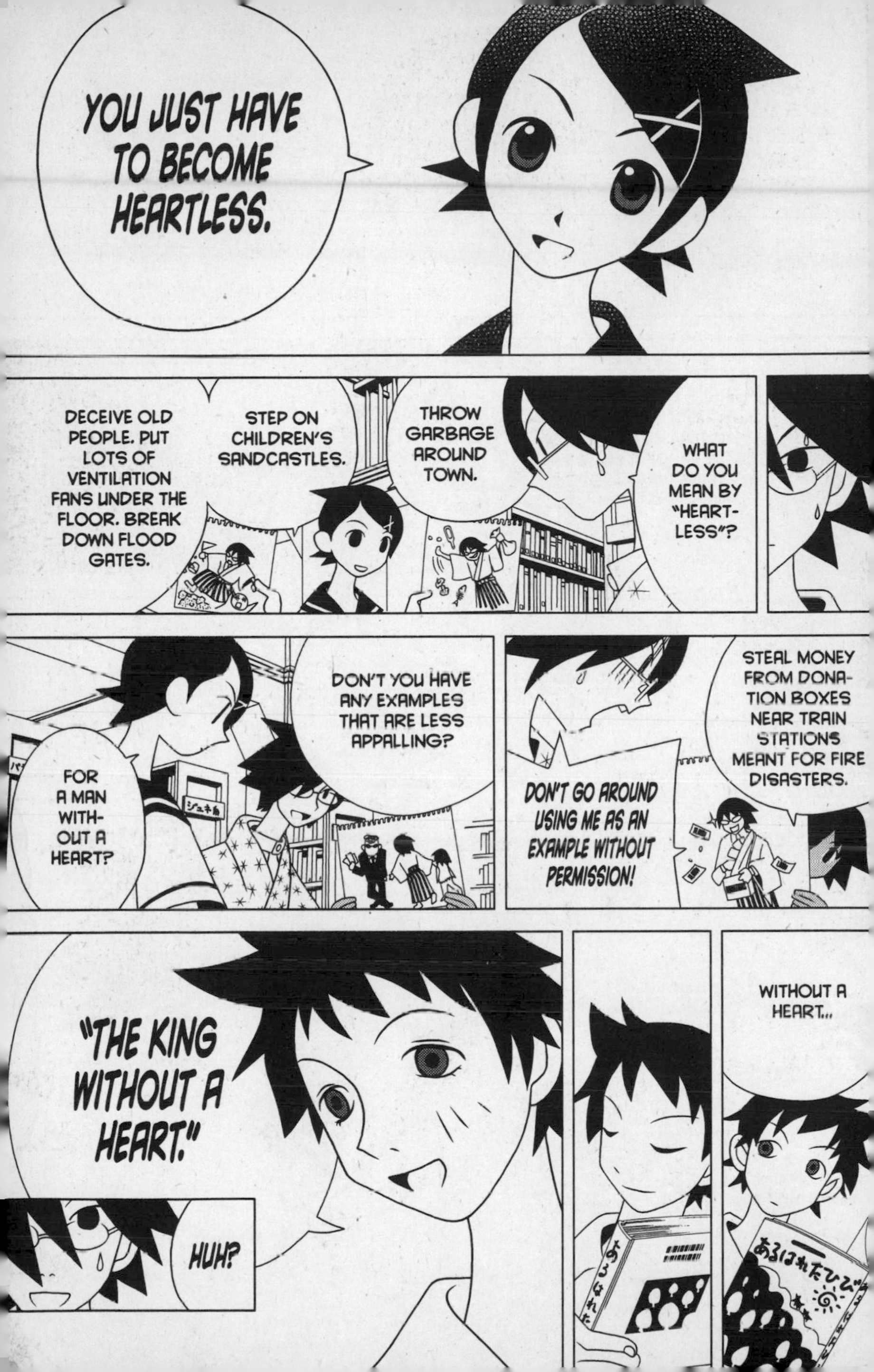
YOU JUST HAVE TO BECOME HEARTLESS.
WHAT DO YOU MEAN BY "HEART-LESS"?
THROW GARBAGE AROUND TOWN.
STEP ON CHILDREN'S SANDCASTLES.
DECEIVE OLD PEOPLE. PUT LOTS OF VENTILATION FANS UNDER THE FLOOR. BREAK DOWN FLOOD GATES.
STEAL MONEY FROM DONA-TION BOXES NEAR TRAIN STATIONS MEANT FOR FIRE DISASTERS.
DON'T GO AROUND USING ME AS AN EXAMPLE WITHOUT PERMISSION!
DON'T YOU HAVE ANY EXAMPLES THAT ARE LESS APPALLING?
FOR A MAN WITH-OUT A HEART?
WITHOUT A HEART...
"THE KING WITHOUT A HEART."
HUH?

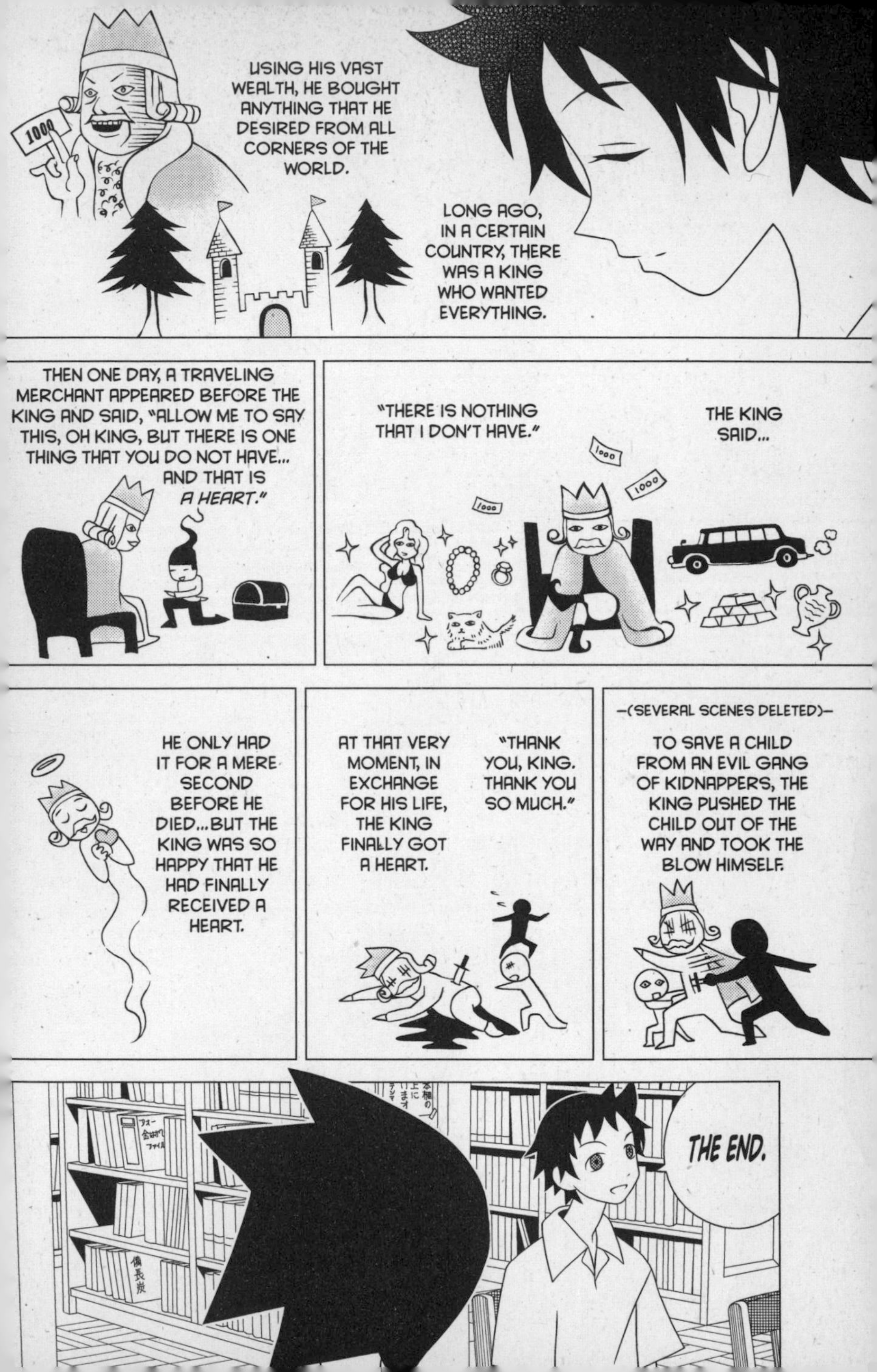
LONG AGO, IN A CERTAIN COUNTRY, THERE WAS A KING WHO WANTED EVERYTHING.
USING HIS VAST WEALTH, HE BOUGHT ANYTHING THAT HE DESIRED FROM ALL CORNERS OF THE WORLD.
THE KING SAID...
"THERE IS NOTHING THAT I DON'T HAVE."
THEN ONE DAY, A TRAVELING MERCHANT APPEARED BEFORE THE KING AND SAID, "ALLOW ME TO SAY THIS, OH KING, BUT THERE IS ONE THING THAT YOU DO NOT HAVE... AND THAT IS A HEART."
—(SEVERAL SCENES DELETED)—
TO SAVE A CHILD FROM AN EVIL GANG OF KIDNAPPERS, THE KING PUSHED THE CHILD OUT OF THE WAY AND TOOK THE BLOW HIMSELF.
"THANK YOU, KING. THANK YOU SO MUCH."
AT THAT VERY MOMENT, IN EXCHANGE FOR HIS LIFE, THE KING FINALLY GOT A HEART.
HE ONLY HAD IT FOR A MERE SECOND BEFORE HE DIED...BUT THE KING WAS SO HAPPY THAT HE HAD FINALLY RECEIVED A HEART.
THE END.

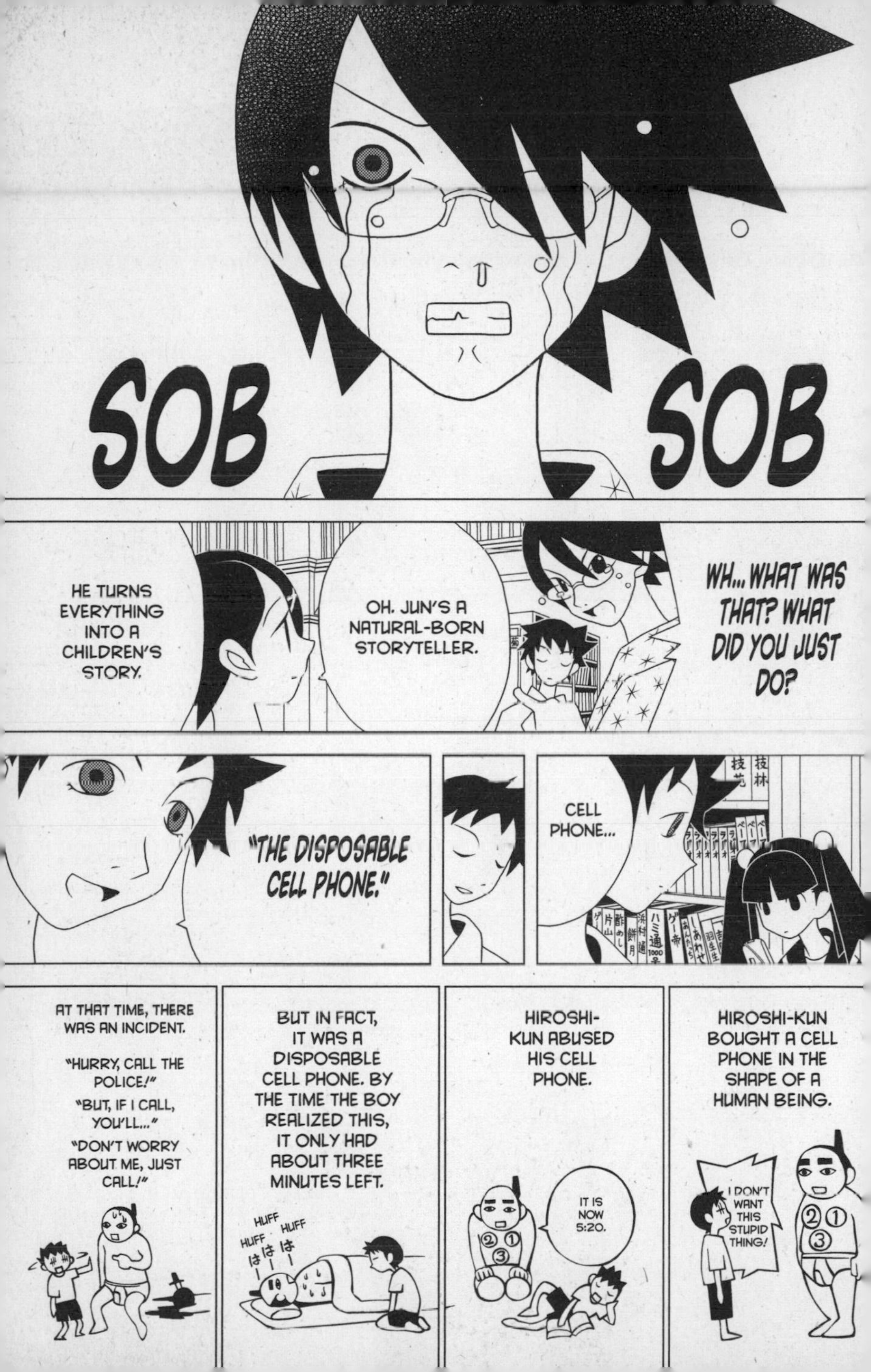
SOB SOB
WH... WHAT WAS THAT? WHAT DID YOU JUST DO?
OH. JUN'S A NATURAL-BORN STORYTELLER.
HE TURNS EVERYTHING INTO A CHILDREN'S STORY.
CELL PHONE...
"THE DISPOSABLE CELL PHONE."
HIROSHI-KUN BOUGHT A CELL PHONE IN THE SHAPE OF A HUMAN BEING.
I DON'T WANT THIS STUPID THING!
HIROSHI-KUN ABUSED HIS CELL PHONE.
IT IS NOW 5:20.
BUT IN FACT, IT WAS A DISPOSABLE CELL PHONE. BY THE TIME THE BOY REALIZED THIS, IT ONLY HAD ABOUT THREE MINUTES LEFT.
HUFF HUFF HUFF
AT THAT TIME, THERE WAS AN INCIDENT.
"HURRY, CALL THE POLICE!"
"BUT, IF I CALL, YOU'LL..."
"DON'T WORRY ABOUT ME, JUST CALL!"

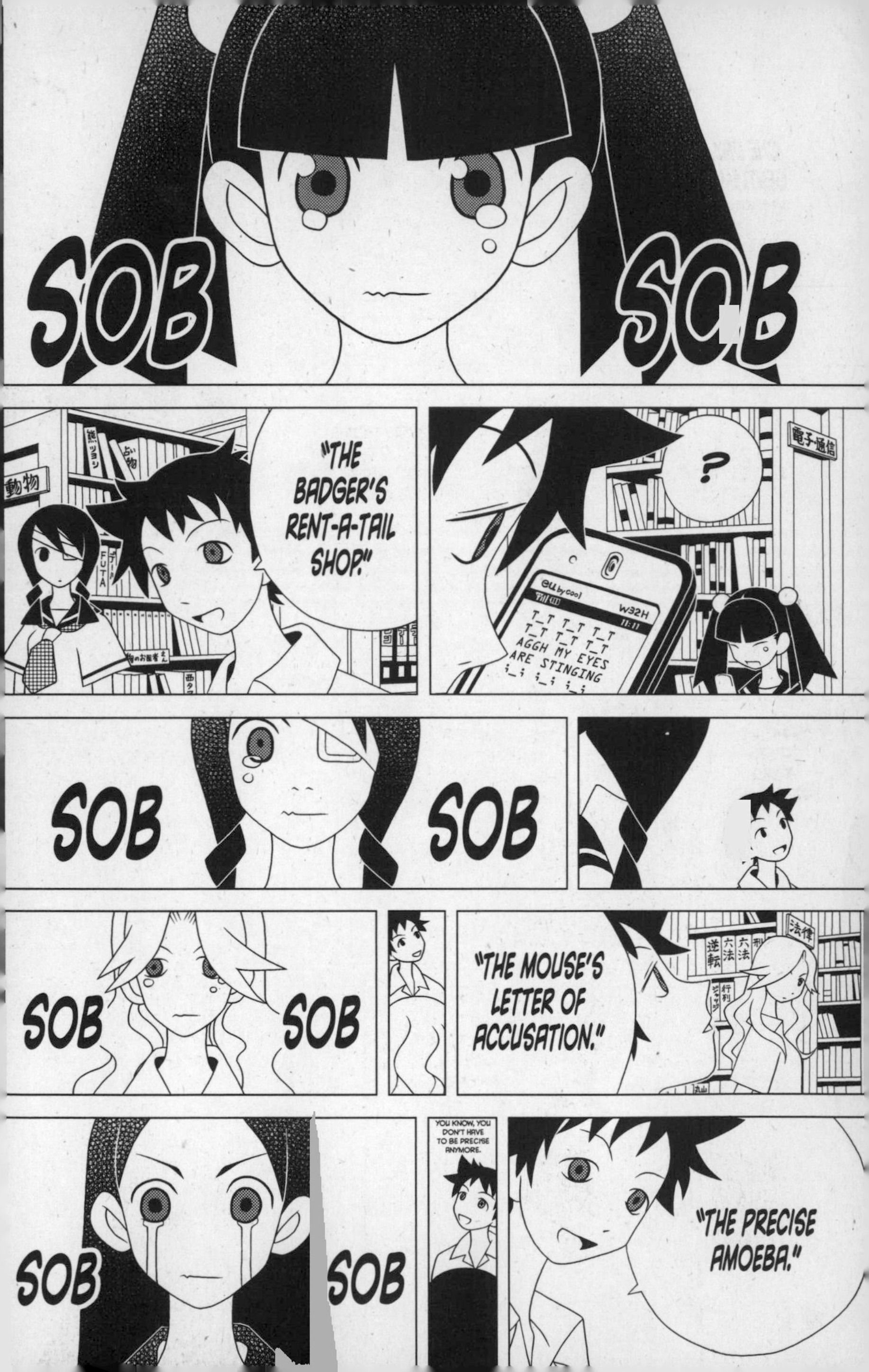
SOB
SOB
?
@u by cool
W32H
11:11
T_T T_T T_T
T_T T_T T_T
AGGH MY EYES
ARE STINGING
"THE BADGER'S RENT-A-TAIL SHOP."
SOB
SOB
"THE MOUSE'S LETTER OF ACCUSATION."
SOB
SOB
"THE PRECISE AMOEBA."
YOU KNOW, YOU DON'T HAVE TO BE PRECISE ANYMORE.
SOB
SOB

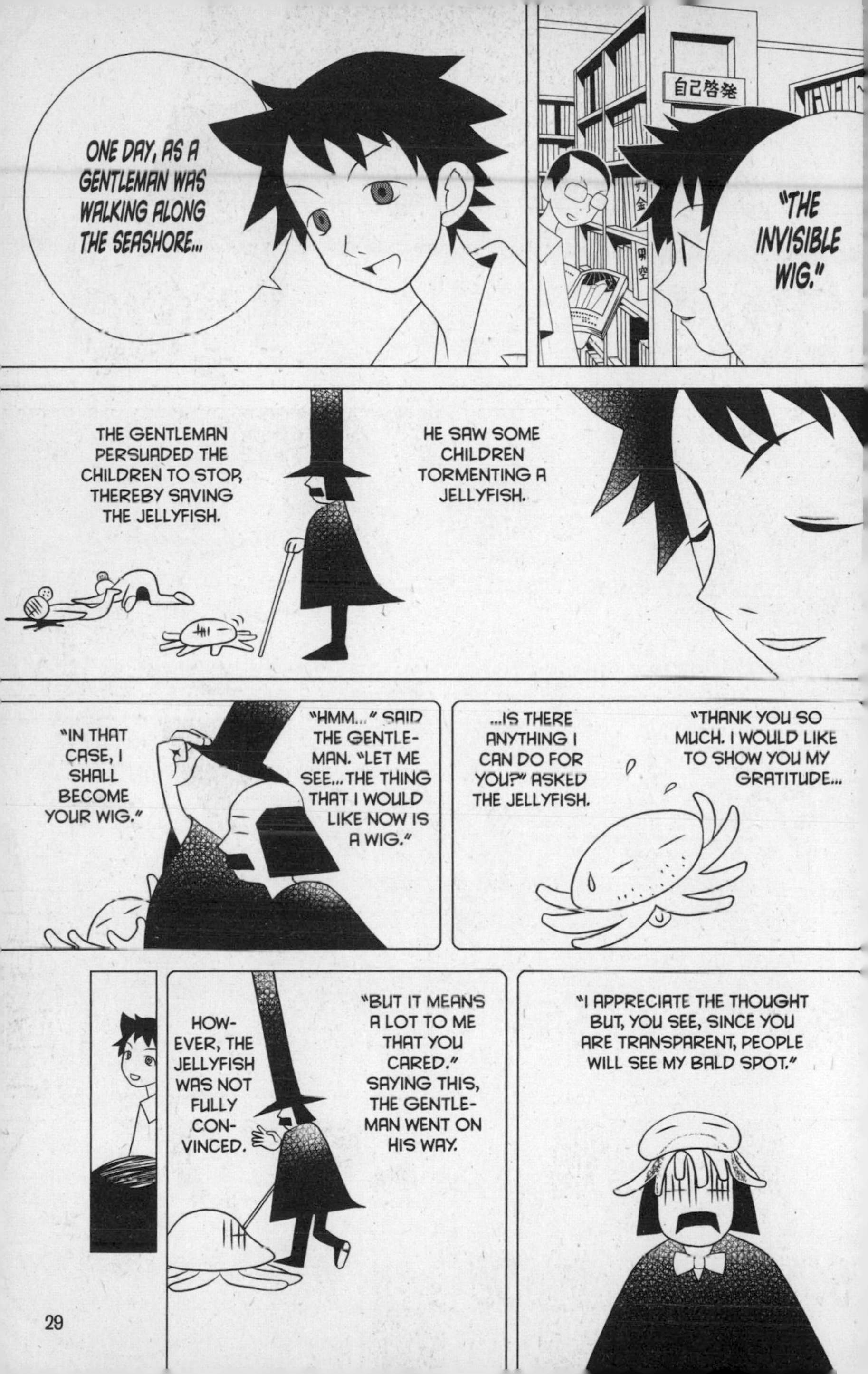
自己啓発
"THE INVISIBLE WIG."
ONE DAY, AS A GENTLEMAN WAS WALKING ALONG THE SEASHORE...
HE SAW SOME CHILDREN TORMENTING A JELLYFISH.
THE GENTLEMAN PERSUADED THE CHILDREN TO STOP, THEREBY SAVING THE JELLYFISH.
"THANK YOU SO MUCH. I WOULD LIKE TO SHOW YOU MY GRATITUDE...
...IS THERE ANYTHING I CAN DO FOR YOU?" ASKED THE JELLYFISH.
"HMM..." SAID THE GENTLE-MAN. "LET ME SEE... THE THING THAT I WOULD LIKE NOW IS A WIG."
"IN THAT CASE, I SHALL BECOME YOUR WIG."
"I APPRECIATE THE THOUGHT BUT, YOU SEE, SINCE YOU ARE TRANSPARENT, PEOPLE WILL SEE MY BALD SPOT."
"BUT IT MEANS A LOT TO ME THAT YOU CARED." SAYING THIS, THE GENTLE-MAN WENT ON HIS WAY.
HOW-EVER, THE JELLYFISH WAS NOT FULLY CON-VINCED.

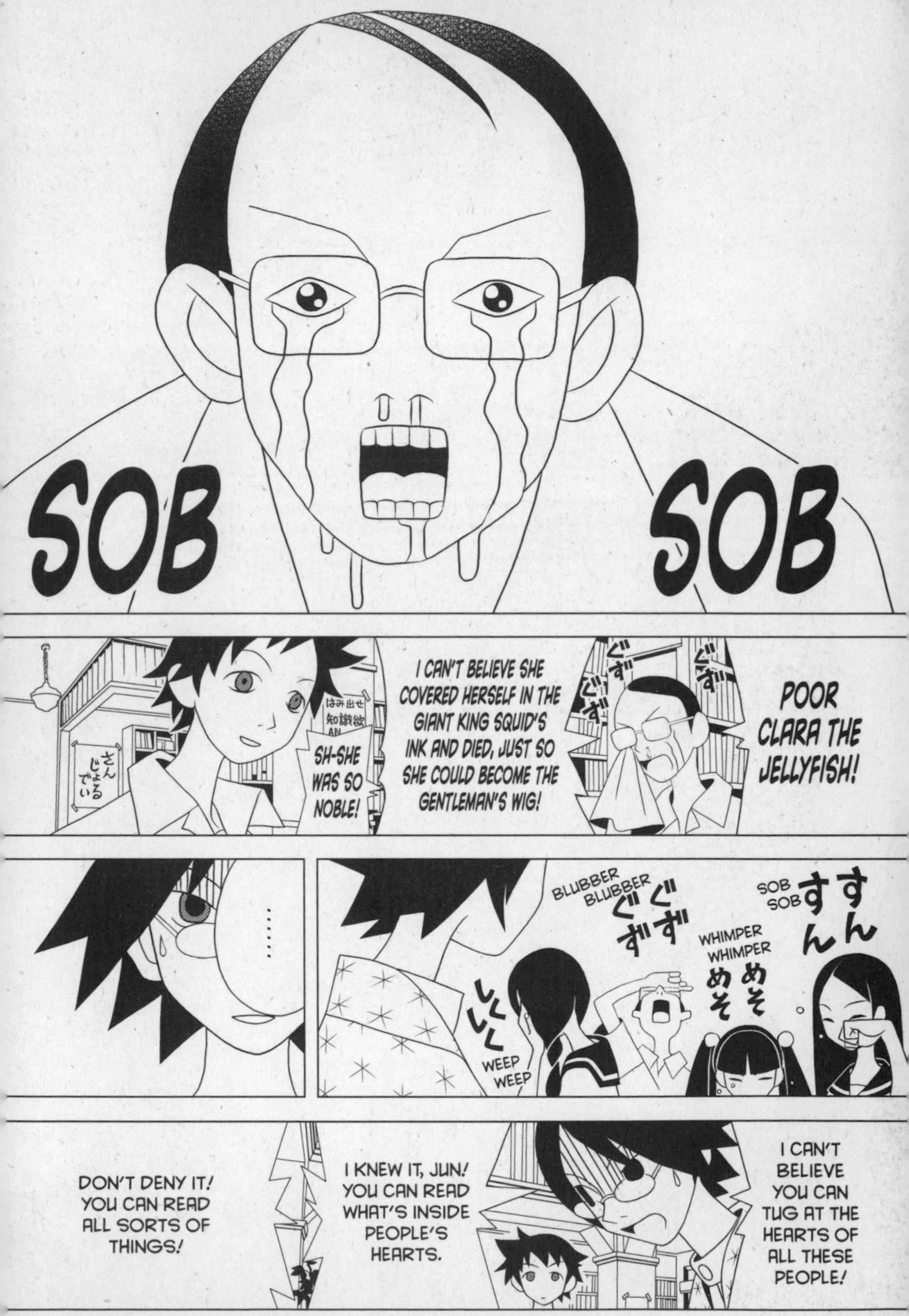
SOB SOB
POOR CLARA THE JELLYFISH!
ぐず ぐず
ぐず
I CAN'T BELIEVE SHE COVERED HERSELF IN THE GIANT KING SQUID'S INK AND DIED, JUST SO SHE COULD BECOME THE GENTLEMAN'S WIG!
SH-SHE WAS SO NOBLE!
はみ出せ 知識欲
さんじょるでい
SOB SOB すんすん
WHIMPER WHIMPER めそめそ
BLUBBER BLUBBER ぐずぐず
しくしく WEEP WEEP
......
I CAN'T BELIEVE YOU CAN TUG AT THE HEARTS OF ALL THESE PEOPLE!
I KNEW IT, JUN! YOU CAN READ WHAT'S INSIDE PEOPLE'S HEARTS.
DON'T DENY IT! YOU CAN READ ALL SORTS OF THINGS!

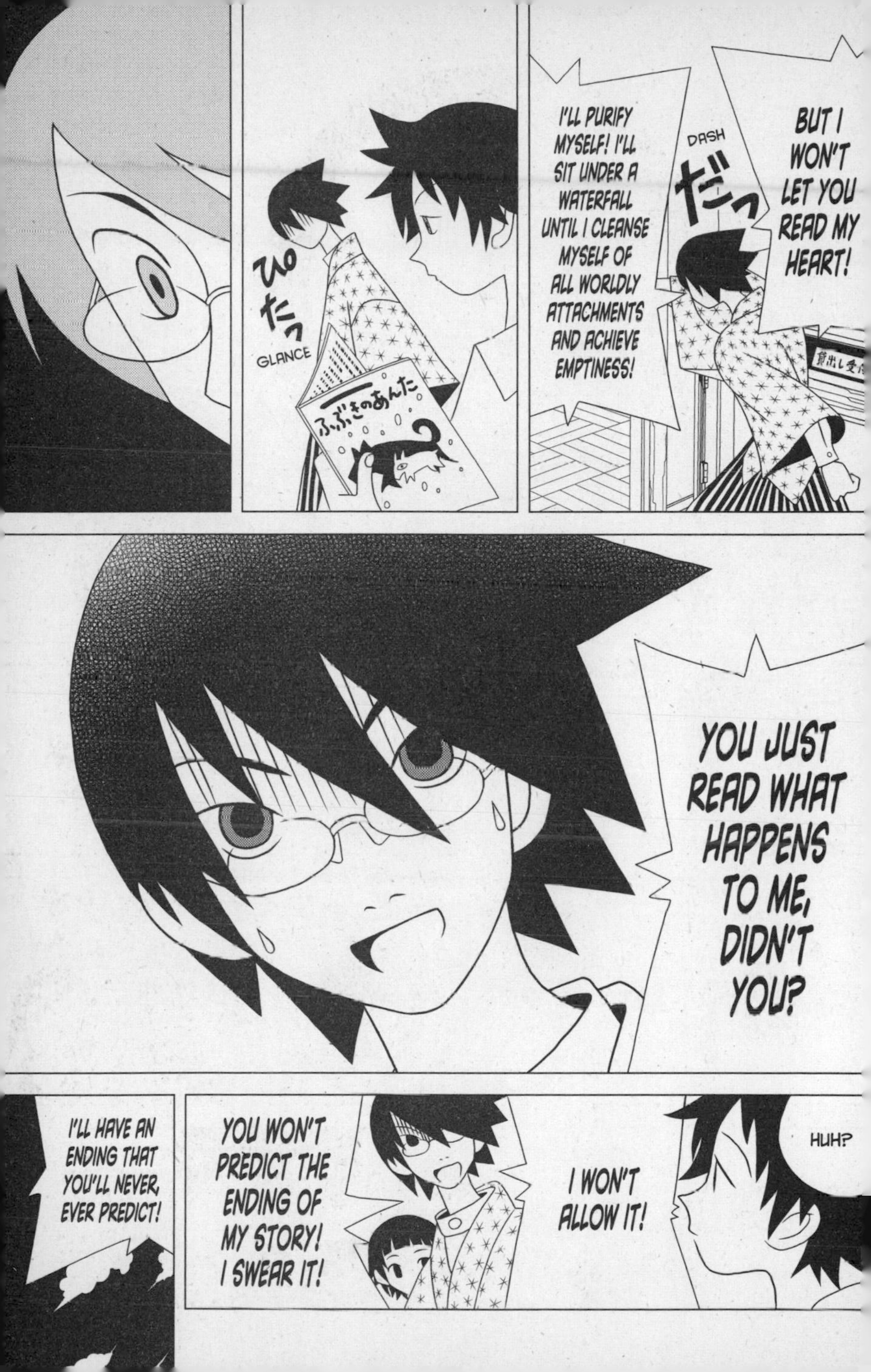
BUT I WON'T LET YOU READ MY HEART!
だっ
DASH
I'LL PURIFY MYSELF! I'LL SIT UNDER A WATERFALL UNTIL I CLEANSE MYSELF OF ALL WORLDLY ATTACHMENTS AND ACHIEVE EMPTINESS!
ひたっ
GLANCE
ふぶきのあんた
YOU JUST READ WHAT HAPPENS TO ME, DIDN'T YOU?
HUH?
I WON'T ALLOW IT!
YOU WON'T PREDICT THE ENDING OF MY STORY! I SWEAR IT!
I'LL HAVE AN ENDING THAT YOU'LL NEVER, EVER PREDICT!

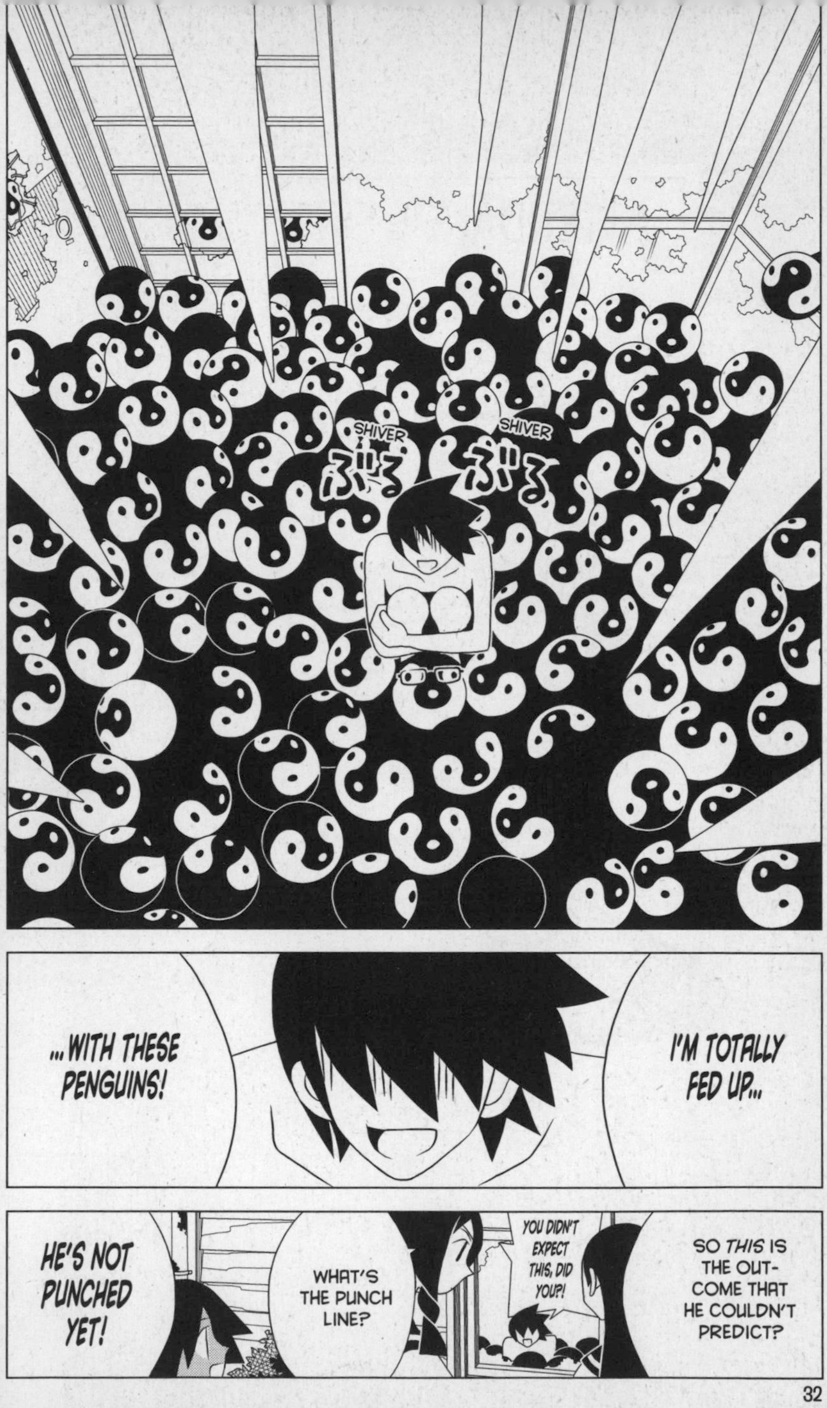
SHIVER
ぶる
SHIVER
ぶる
I'M TOTALLY FED UP...
...WITH THESE PENGUINS!
SO *THIS* IS THE OUT-COME THAT HE COULDN'T PREDICT?
YOU DIDN'T EXPECT THIS, DID YOU?!
WHAT'S THE PUNCH LINE?
HE'S NOT PUNCHED YET!

ATTENDANCE LIST
CLASS 2-F

2005.09.28

ATTENDANCE NO. 6
JUN KUTOU
GENIUS STORYTELLER

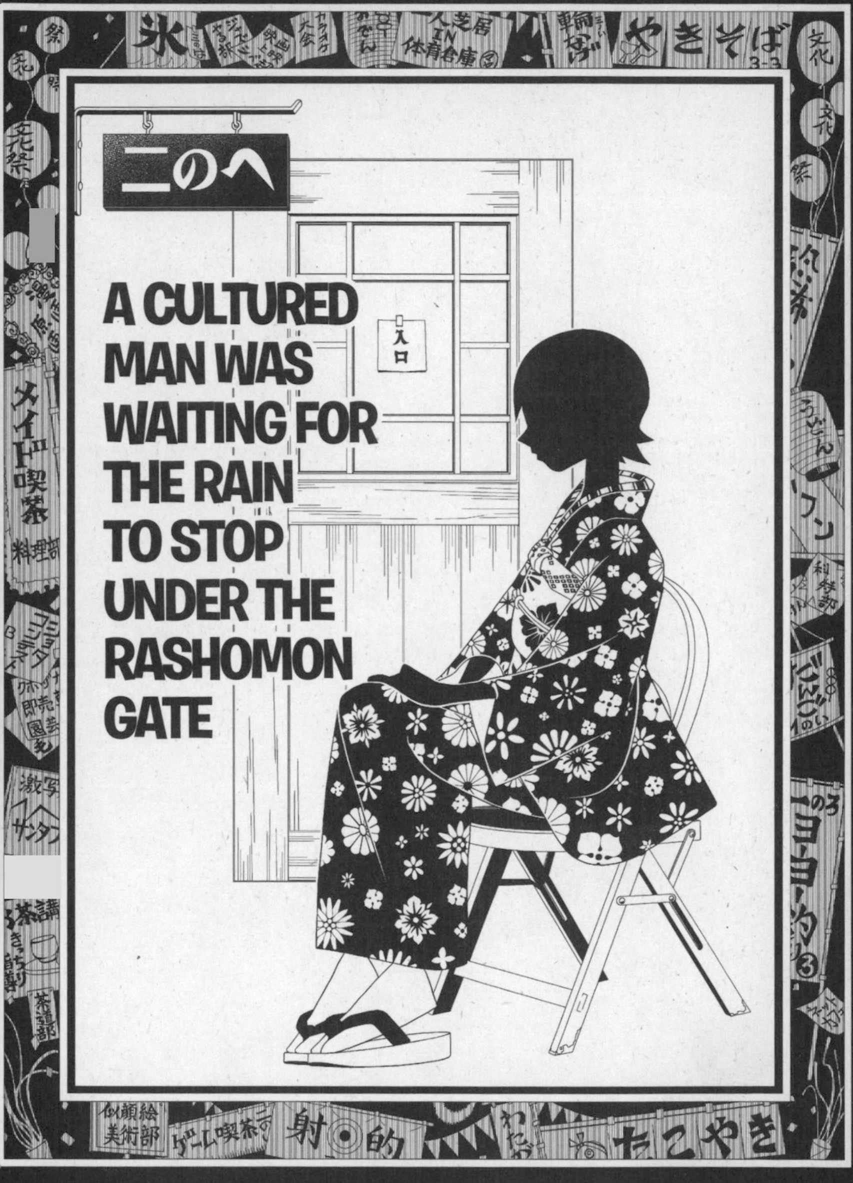
二のへ
入口
A CULTURED MAN WAS WAITING FOR THE RAIN TO STOP UNDER THE RASHOMON GATE
一人芝居 IN 体育倉庫
やきそば
氷
メイド喫茶
料理部
茶道部
美術部
ゲーム喫茶
射的
たこやき

CHAPTER 23

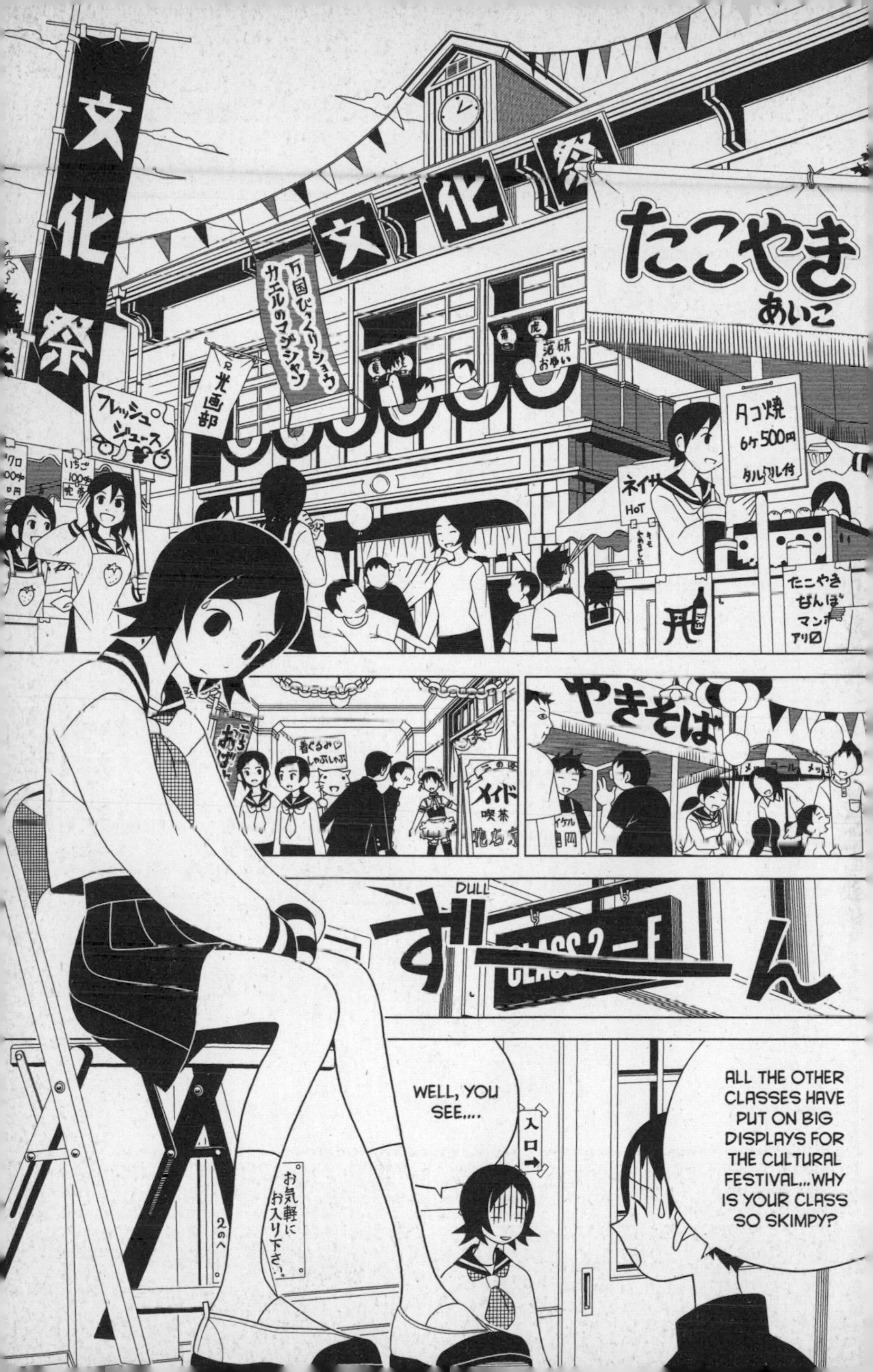
文化祭
たこやき
あいこ
文化祭
万国びっくりショウ
カエルのマジシャン
落研
おゆい
光画部
フレッシュジュース
タコ焼
6ケ500円
タルタル付
ネイサ
HoT
やきそば
メイド
喫茶
春ぐるみ♡
しゃぶしゃぶ
DULL
ず
CLASS 2 — F
ん
ALL THE OTHER CLASSES HAVE PUT ON BIG DISPLAYS FOR THE CULTURAL FESTIVAL...WHY IS YOUR CLASS SO SKIMPY?
入口→
WELL, YOU SEE....
お気軽にお入り下さい!
2のへ

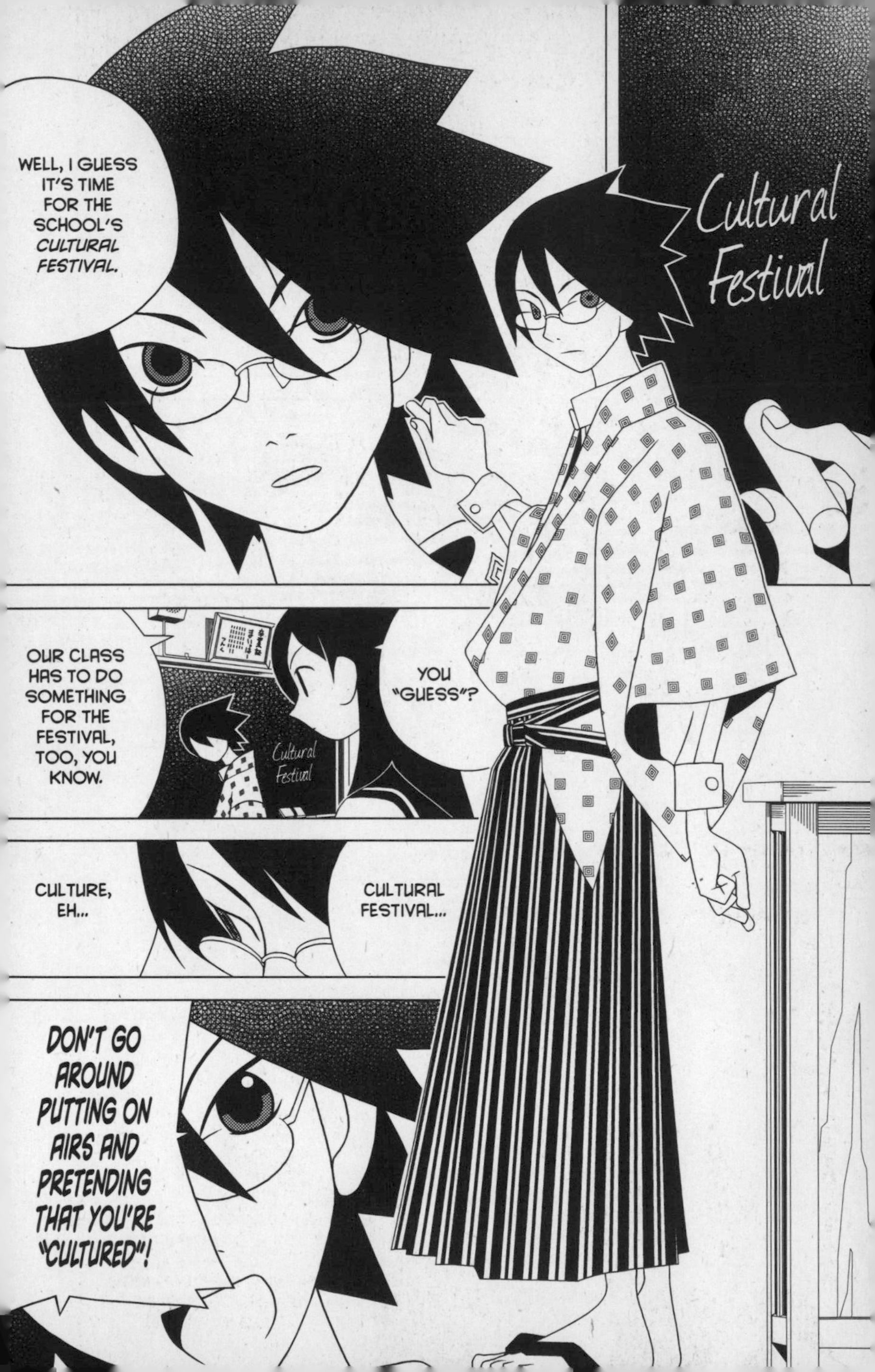
Cultural Festival
WELL, I GUESS IT'S TIME FOR THE SCHOOL'S CULTURAL FESTIVAL.
YOU "GUESS"?
OUR CLASS HAS TO DO SOMETHING FOR THE FESTIVAL, TOO, YOU KNOW.
Cultural Festival
CULTURAL FESTIVAL...
CULTURE, EH...
DON'T GO AROUND PUTTING ON AIRS AND PRETENDING THAT YOU'RE "CULTURED"!

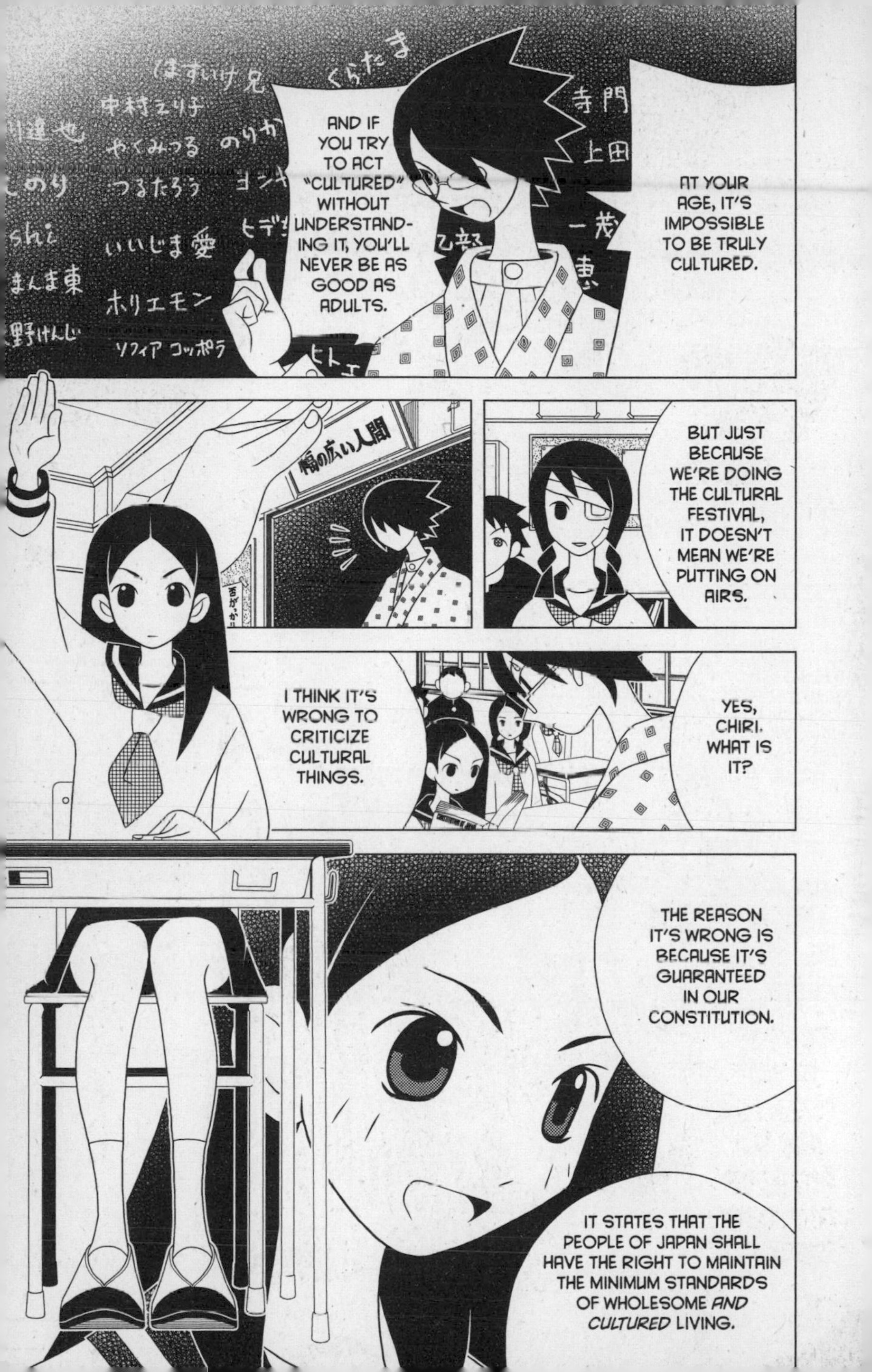
AT YOUR AGE, IT'S IMPOSSIBLE TO BE TRULY CULTURED.
AND IF YOU TRY TO ACT "CULTURED" WITHOUT UNDERSTANDING IT, YOU'LL NEVER BE AS GOOD AS ADULTS.
BUT JUST BECAUSE WE'RE DOING THE CULTURAL FESTIVAL, IT DOESN'T MEAN WE'RE PUTTING ON AIRS.
幅の広い人間
YES, CHIRI. WHAT IS IT?
I THINK IT'S WRONG TO CRITICIZE CULTURAL THINGS.
THE REASON IT'S WRONG IS BECAUSE IT'S GUARANTEED IN OUR CONSTITUTION.
IT STATES THAT THE PEOPLE OF JAPAN SHALL HAVE THE RIGHT TO MAINTAIN THE MINIMUM STANDARDS OF WHOLESOME *AND CULTURED* LIVING.

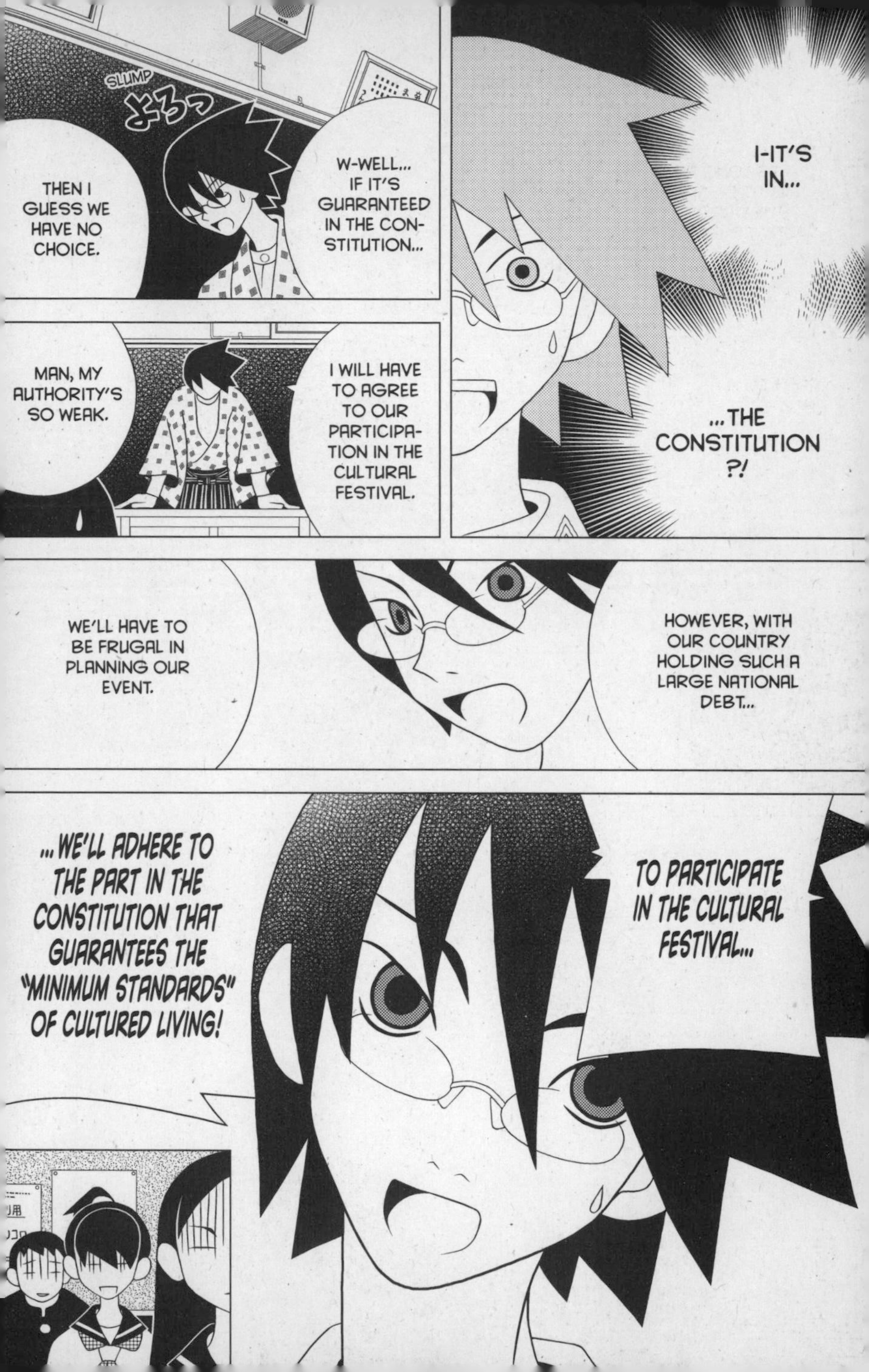
I-IT'S IN...
...THE CONSTITUTION ?!
W-WELL... IF IT'S GUARANTEED IN THE CONSTITUTION...
SLUMP
よろっ
THEN I GUESS WE HAVE NO CHOICE.
I WILL HAVE TO AGREE TO OUR PARTICIPATION IN THE CULTURAL FESTIVAL.
MAN, MY AUTHORITY'S SO WEAK.
HOWEVER, WITH OUR COUNTRY HOLDING SUCH A LARGE NATIONAL DEBT...
WE'LL HAVE TO BE FRUGAL IN PLANNING OUR EVENT.
TO PARTICIPATE IN THE CULTURAL FESTIVAL...
...WE'LL ADHERE TO THE PART IN THE CONSTITUTION THAT GUARANTEES THE "MINIMUM STANDARDS" OF CULTURED LIVING!

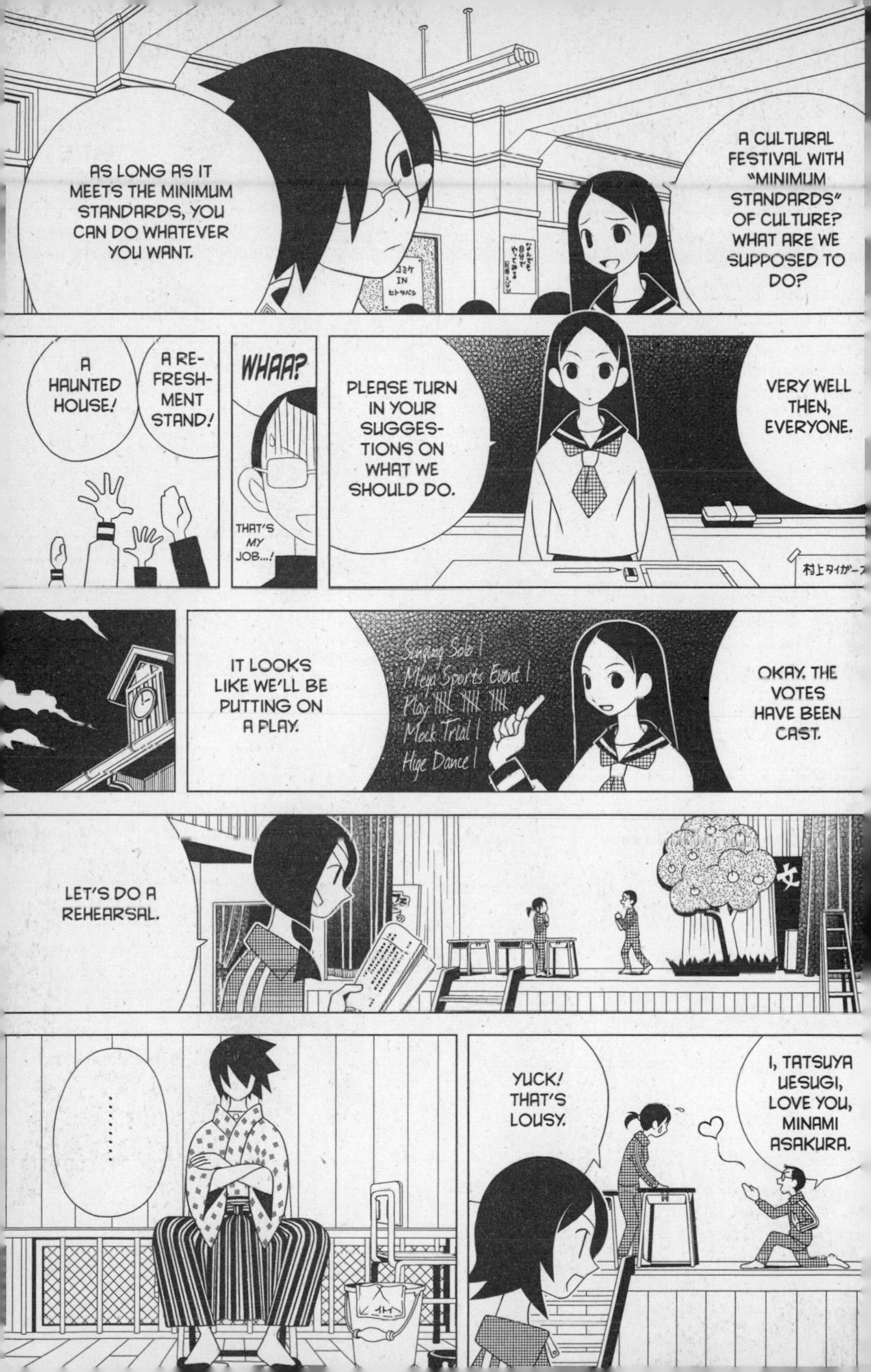
A CULTURAL FESTIVAL WITH "MINIMUM STANDARDS" OF CULTURE? WHAT ARE WE SUPPOSED TO DO?
AS LONG AS IT MEETS THE MINIMUM STANDARDS, YOU CAN DO WHATEVER YOU WANT.
VERY WELL THEN, EVERYONE.
PLEASE TURN IN YOUR SUGGESTIONS ON WHAT WE SHOULD DO.
WHAA?
THAT'S MY JOB...!
A REFRESHMENT STAND!
A HAUNTED HOUSE!
OKAY. THE VOTES HAVE BEEN CAST.
Singing Solo!
M'eya Sports Event!
Play
Mock Trial!
Hige Dance!
IT LOOKS LIKE WE'LL BE PUTTING ON A PLAY.
LET'S DO A REHEARSAL.
I, TATSUYA UESUGI, LOVE YOU, MINAMI ASAKURA.
YUCK! THAT'S LOUSY.
......

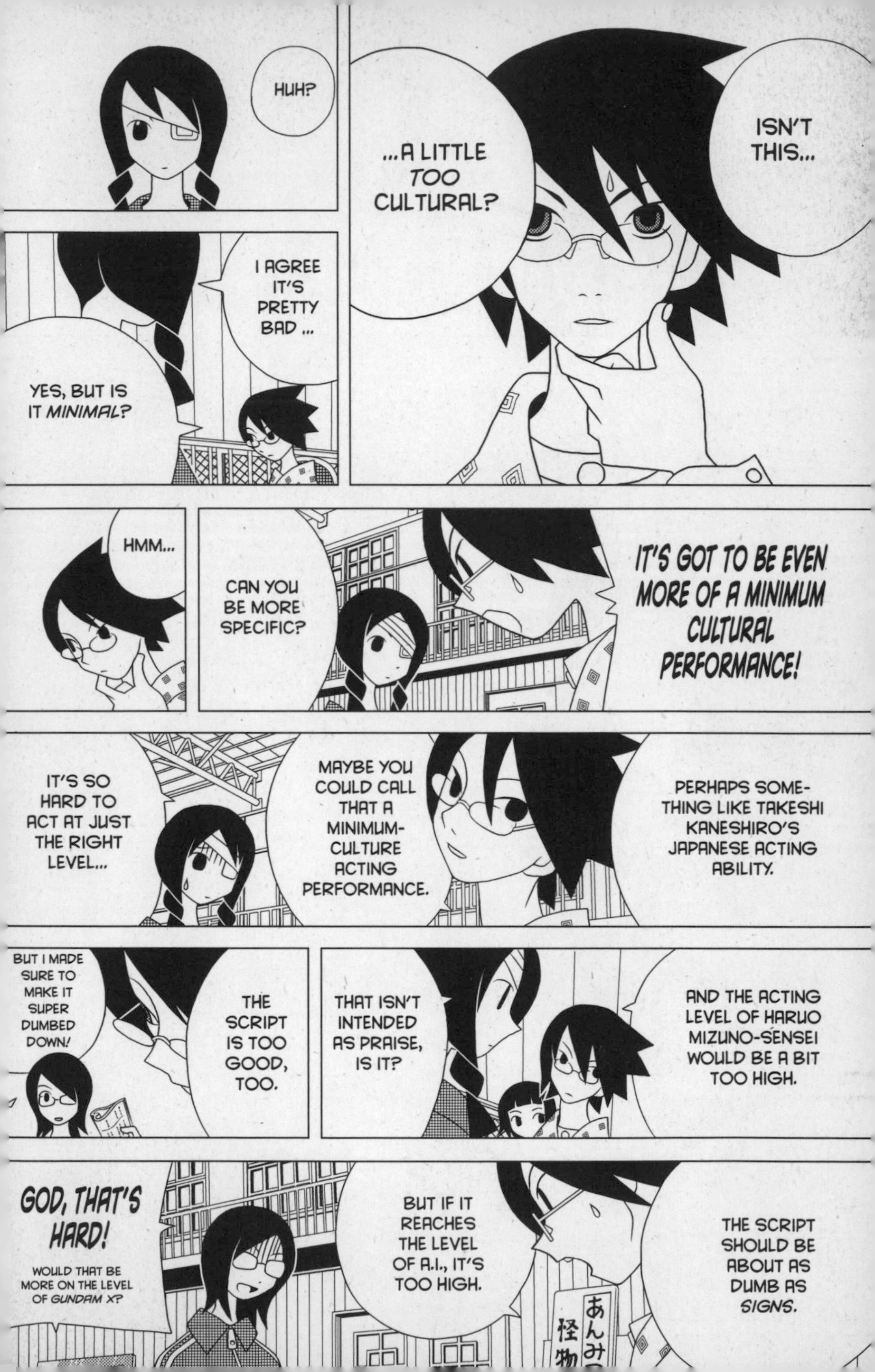
ISN'T THIS...
...A LITTLE *TOO* CULTURAL?
HUH?
I AGREE IT'S PRETTY BAD ...
YES, BUT IS IT *MINIMAL*?
IT'S GOT TO BE EVEN MORE OF A MINIMUM CULTURAL PERFORMANCE!
CAN YOU BE MORE SPECIFIC?
HMM...
PERHAPS SOME-THING LIKE TAKESHI KANESHIRO'S JAPANESE ACTING ABILITY.
MAYBE YOU COULD CALL THAT A MINIMUM-CULTURE ACTING PERFORMANCE.
IT'S SO HARD TO ACT AT JUST THE RIGHT LEVEL...
AND THE ACTING LEVEL OF HARUO MIZUNO-SENSEI WOULD BE A BIT TOO HIGH.
THAT ISN'T INTENDED AS PRAISE, IS IT?
THE SCRIPT IS TOO GOOD, TOO.
BUT I MADE SURE TO MAKE IT SUPER DUMBED DOWN!
THE SCRIPT SHOULD BE ABOUT AS DUMB AS *SIGNS*.
BUT IF IT REACHES THE LEVEL OF A.I., IT'S TOO HIGH.
GOD, THAT'S HARD!
WOULD THAT BE MORE ON THE LEVEL OF *GUNDAM X*?

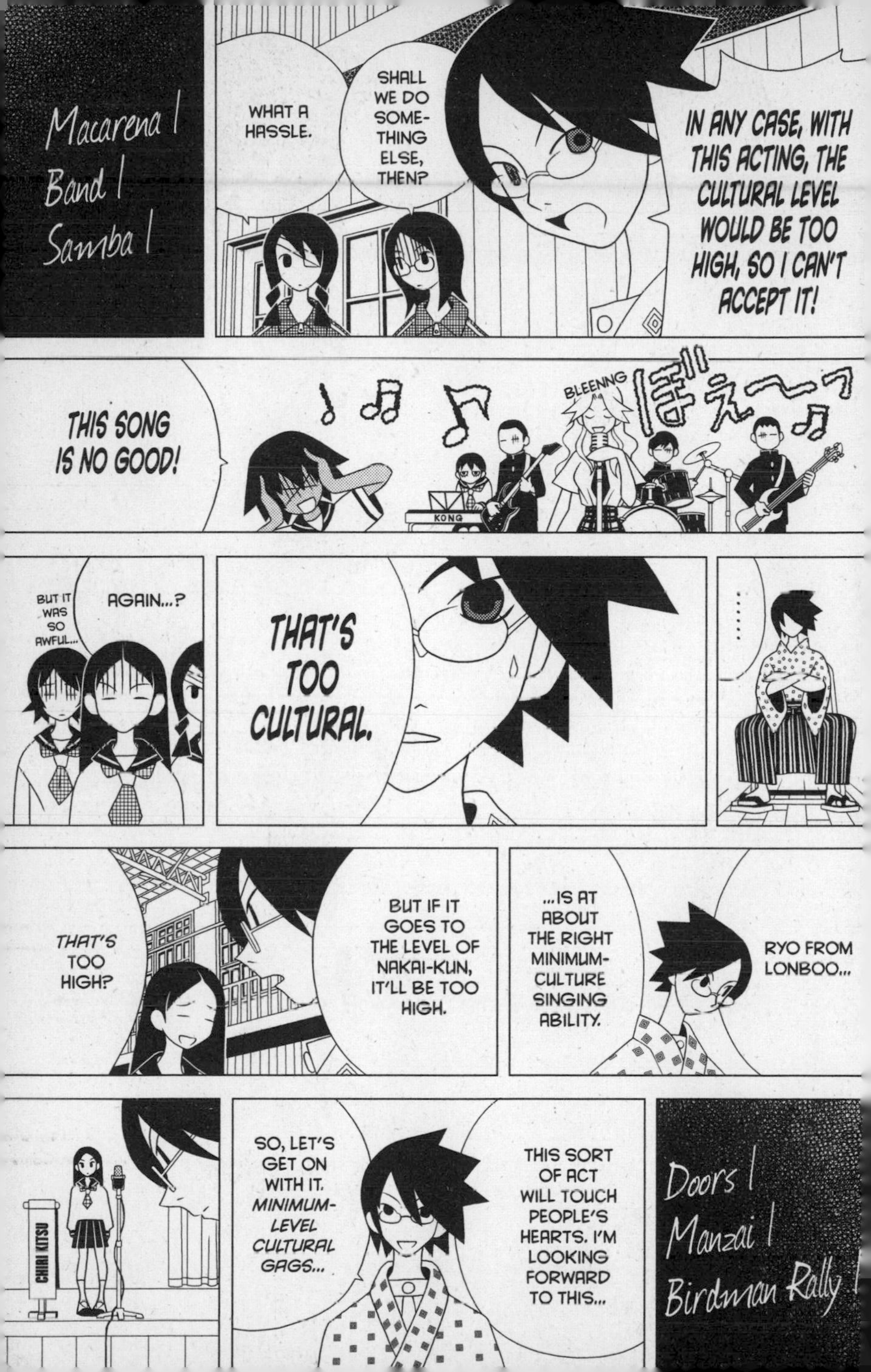
IN ANY CASE, WITH THIS ACTING, THE CULTURAL LEVEL WOULD BE TOO HIGH, SO I CAN'T ACCEPT IT!
SHALL WE DO SOMETHING ELSE, THEN?
WHAT A HASSLE.
Macarena! Band! Samba!
BLEENNG
ぼえ〜っ
KONG
THIS SONG IS NO GOOD!
......
THAT'S TOO CULTURAL.
AGAIN...?
BUT IT WAS SO AWFUL...
RYO FROM LONBOO...
...IS AT ABOUT THE RIGHT MINIMUM-CULTURE SINGING ABILITY.
BUT IF IT GOES TO THE LEVEL OF NAKAI-KUN, IT'LL BE TOO HIGH.
THAT'S TOO HIGH?
Doors! Manzai! Birdman Rally!
THIS SORT OF ACT WILL TOUCH PEOPLE'S HEARTS. I'M LOOKING FORWARD TO THIS...
SO, LET'S GET ON WITH IT. MINIMUM-LEVEL CULTURAL GAGS...
CHIRI KITSU

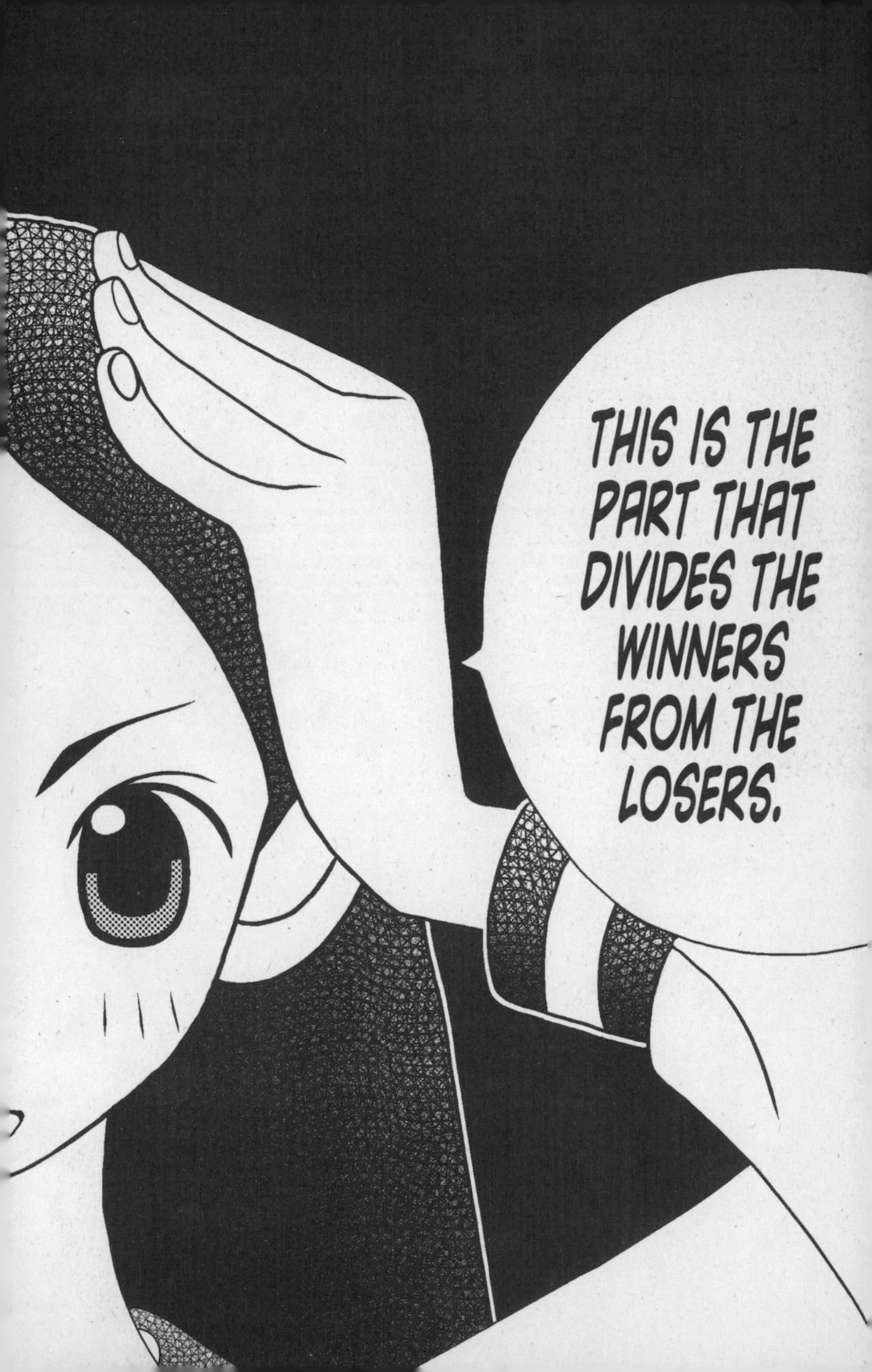
THIS IS THE PART THAT DIVIDES THE WINNERS FROM THE LOSERS.

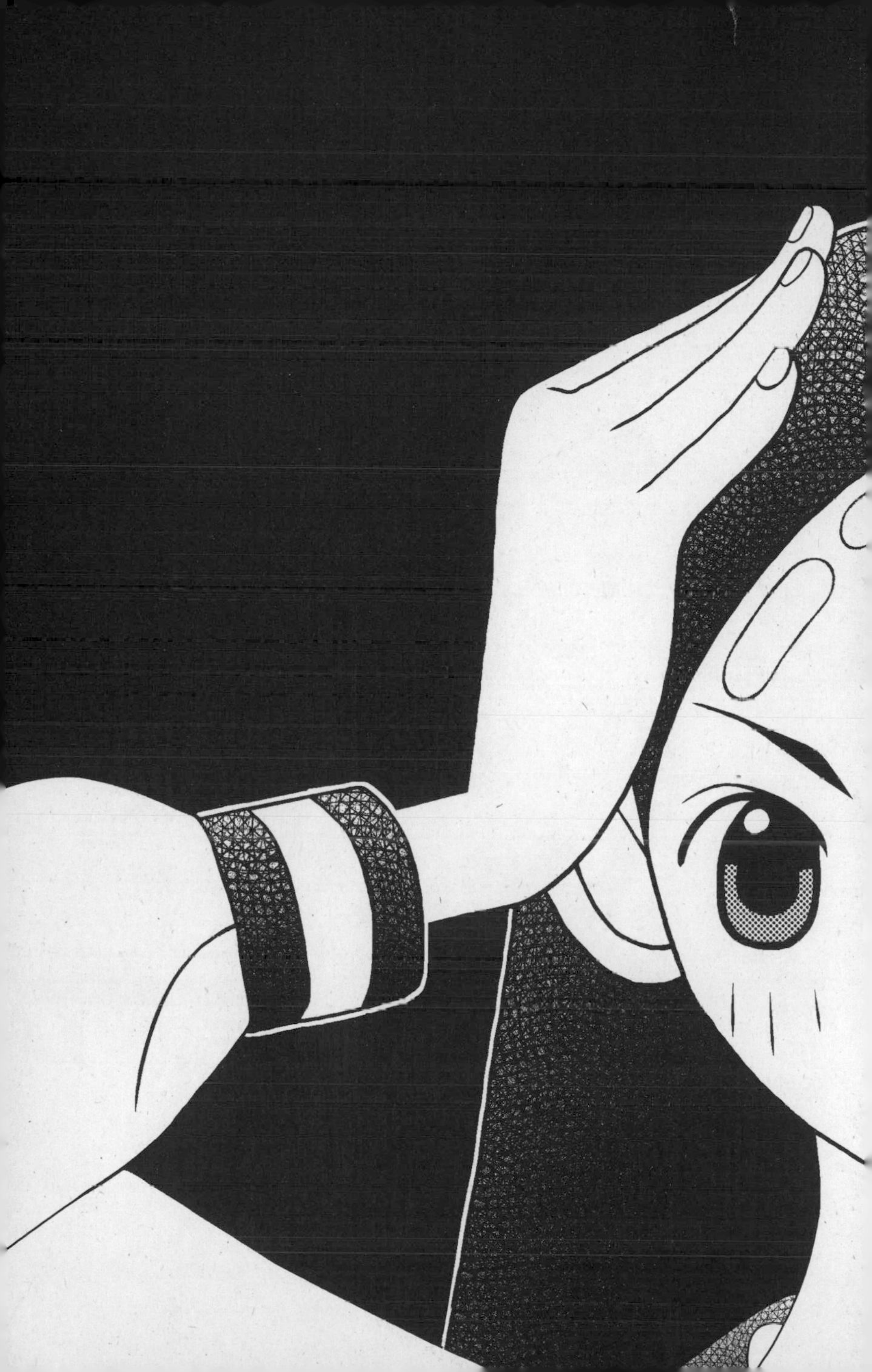

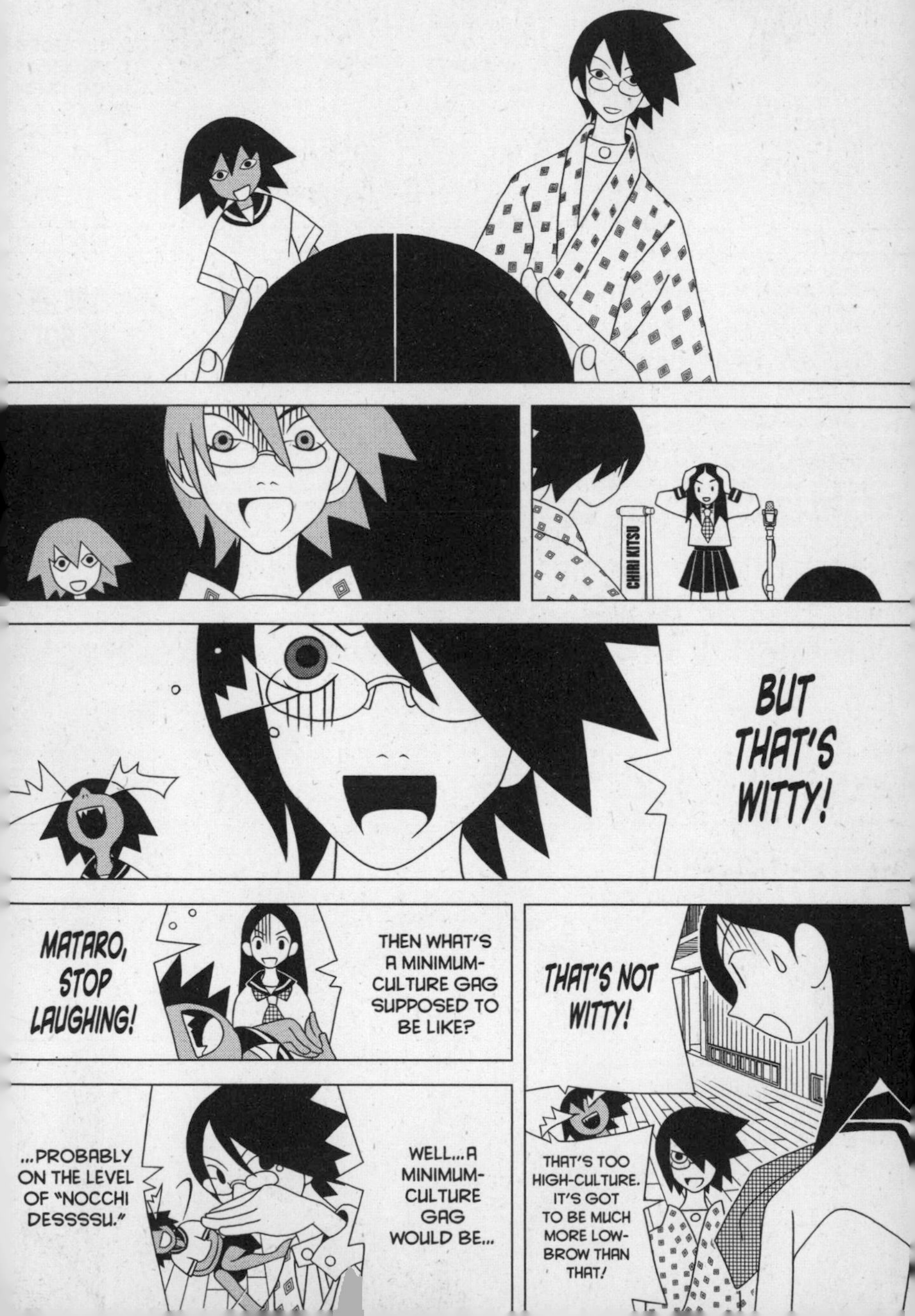
CHIRI KITSU
BUT THAT'S WITTY!
THAT'S NOT WITTY!
THAT'S TOO HIGH-CULTURE. IT'S GOT TO BE MUCH MORE LOW-BROW THAN THAT!
THEN WHAT'S A MINIMUM-CULTURE GAG SUPPOSED TO BE LIKE?
MATARO, STOP LAUGHING!
WELL...A MINIMUM-CULTURE GAG WOULD BE...
...PROBABLY ON THE LEVEL OF "NOCCHI DESSSSU."

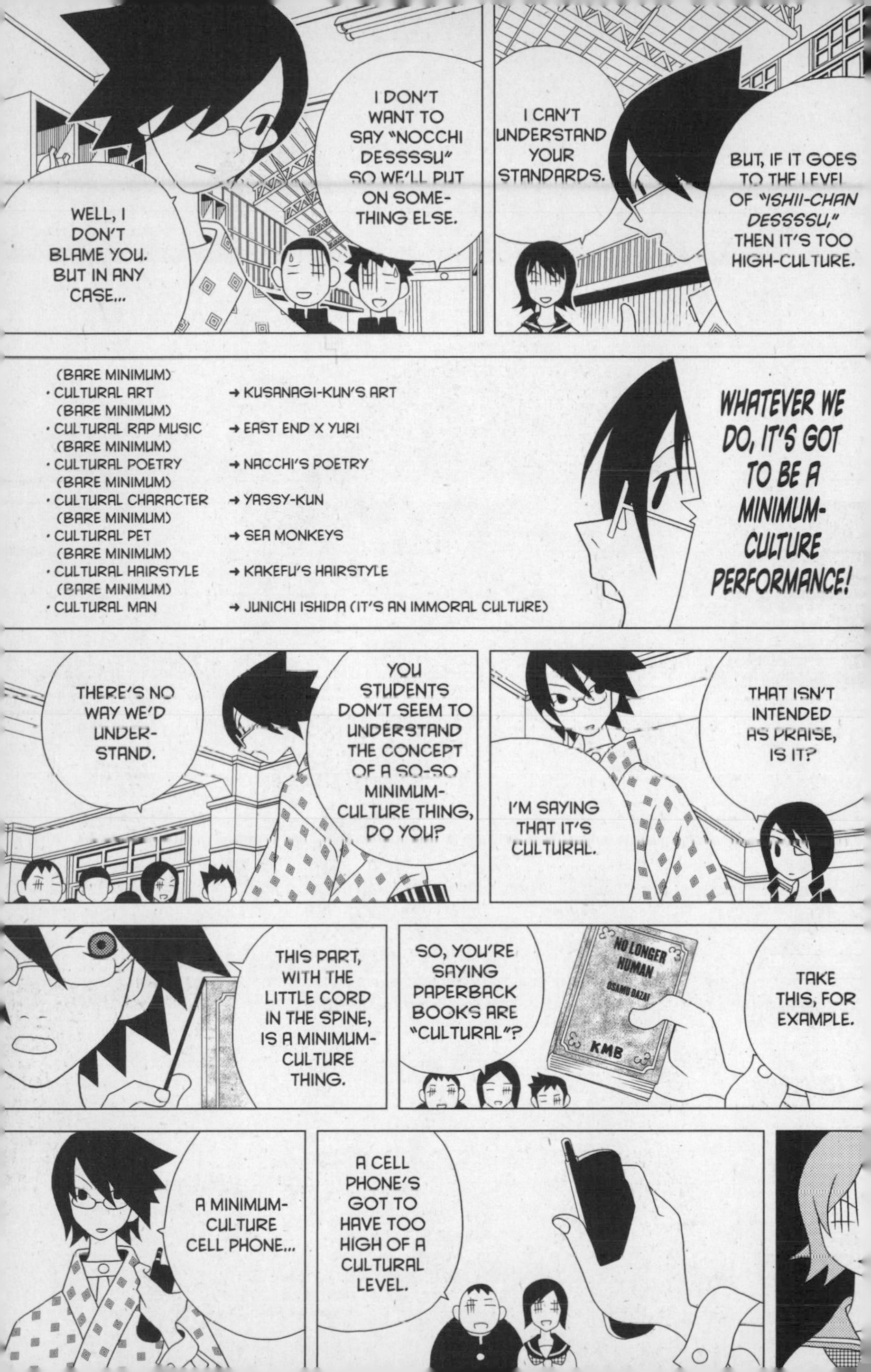
BUT, IF IT GOES TO THE LEVEL OF "ISHII-CHAN DESSSSU," THEN IT'S TOO HIGH-CULTURE.
I CAN'T UNDERSTAND YOUR STANDARDS.
I DON'T WANT TO SAY "NOCCHI DESSSSU" SO WE'LL PUT ON SOME-THING ELSE.
WELL, I DON'T BLAME YOU. BUT IN ANY CASE...
WHATEVER WE DO, IT'S GOT TO BE A MINIMUM-CULTURE PERFORMANCE!
(BARE MINIMUM) · CULTURAL ART → KUSANAGI-KUN'S ART
(BARE MINIMUM) · CULTURAL RAP MUSIC → EAST END X YURI
(BARE MINIMUM) · CULTURAL POETRY → NACCHI'S POETRY
(BARE MINIMUM) · CULTURAL CHARACTER → YASSY-KUN
(BARE MINIMUM) · CULTURAL PET → SEA MONKEYS
(BARE MINIMUM) · CULTURAL HAIRSTYLE → KAKEFU'S HAIRSTYLE
(BARE MINIMUM) · CULTURAL MAN → JUNICHI ISHIDA (IT'S AN IMMORAL CULTURE)
THAT ISN'T INTENDED AS PRAISE, IS IT?
I'M SAYING THAT IT'S CULTURAL.
YOU STUDENTS DON'T SEEM TO UNDERSTAND THE CONCEPT OF A SO-SO MINIMUM-CULTURE THING, DO YOU?
THERE'S NO WAY WE'D UNDER-STAND.
TAKE THIS, FOR EXAMPLE.
NO LONGER HUMAN
OSAMU DAZAI
KMB
SO, YOU'RE SAYING PAPERBACK BOOKS ARE "CULTURAL"?
THIS PART, WITH THE LITTLE CORD IN THE SPINE, IS A MINIMUM-CULTURE THING.
A CELL PHONE'S GOT TO HAVE TOO HIGH OF A CULTURAL LEVEL.
A MINIMUM-CULTURE CELL PHONE...

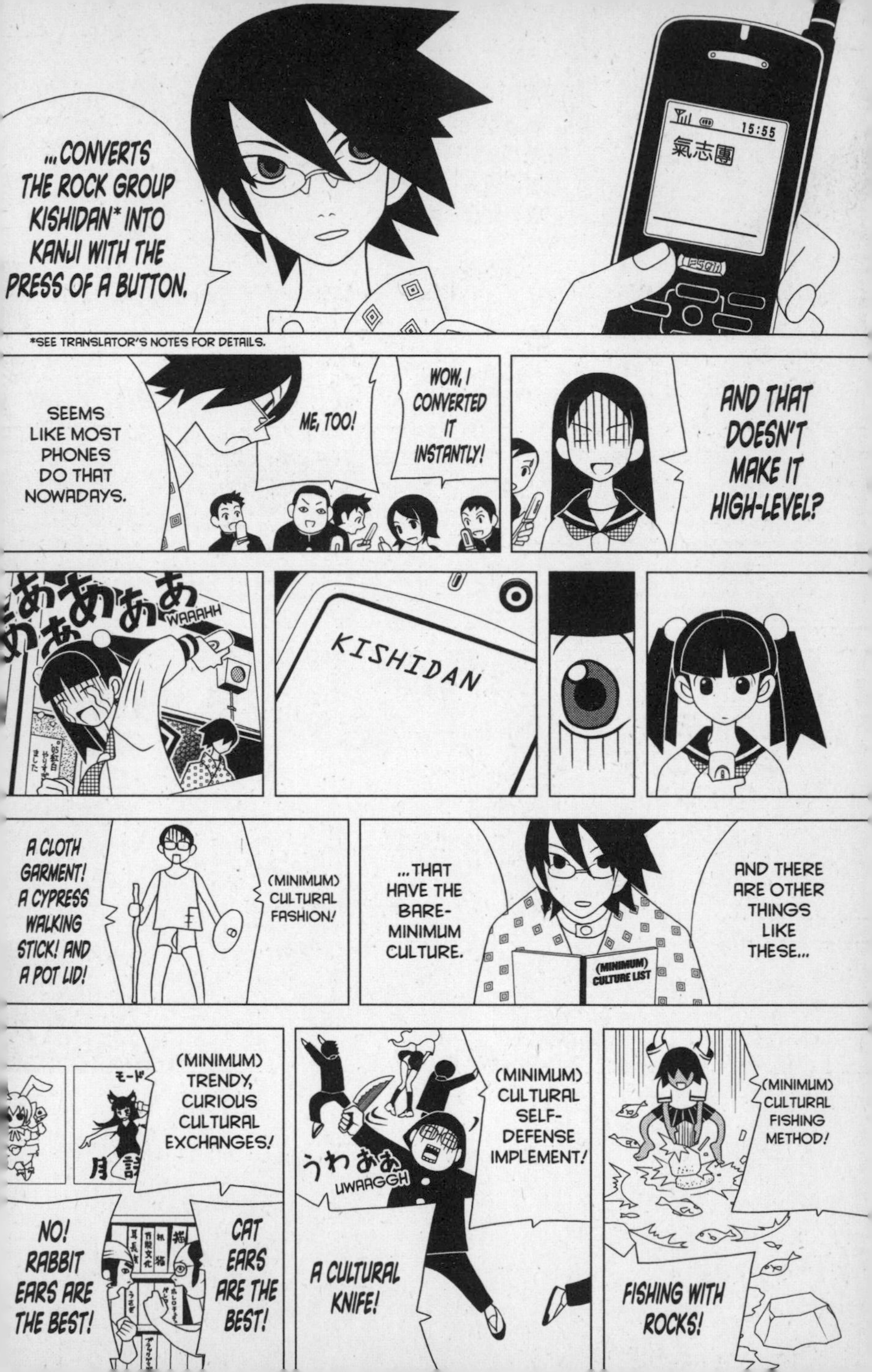
...CONVERTS THE ROCK GROUP KISHIDAN* INTO KANJI WITH THE PRESS OF A BUTTON.
15:55
氣志團
*SEE TRANSLATOR'S NOTES FOR DETAILS.
AND THAT DOESN'T MAKE IT HIGH-LEVEL?
WOW, I CONVERTED IT INSTANTLY!
ME, TOO!
SEEMS LIKE MOST PHONES DO THAT NOWADAYS.
KISHIDAN
あああああ
WAAAHH
AND THERE ARE OTHER THINGS LIKE THESE...
...THAT HAVE THE BARE-MINIMUM CULTURE.
(MINIMUM) CULTURE LIST
(MINIMUM) CULTURAL FASHION!
A CLOTH GARMENT! A CYPRESS WALKING STICK! AND A POT LID!
(MINIMUM) CULTURAL FISHING METHOD!
FISHING WITH ROCKS!
(MINIMUM) CULTURAL SELF-DEFENSE IMPLEMENT!
うわああ
UWAAGGH
A CULTURAL KNIFE!
(MINIMUM) TRENDY, CURIOUS CULTURAL EXCHANGES!
モード
CAT EARS ARE THE BEST!
NO! RABBIT EARS ARE THE BEST!

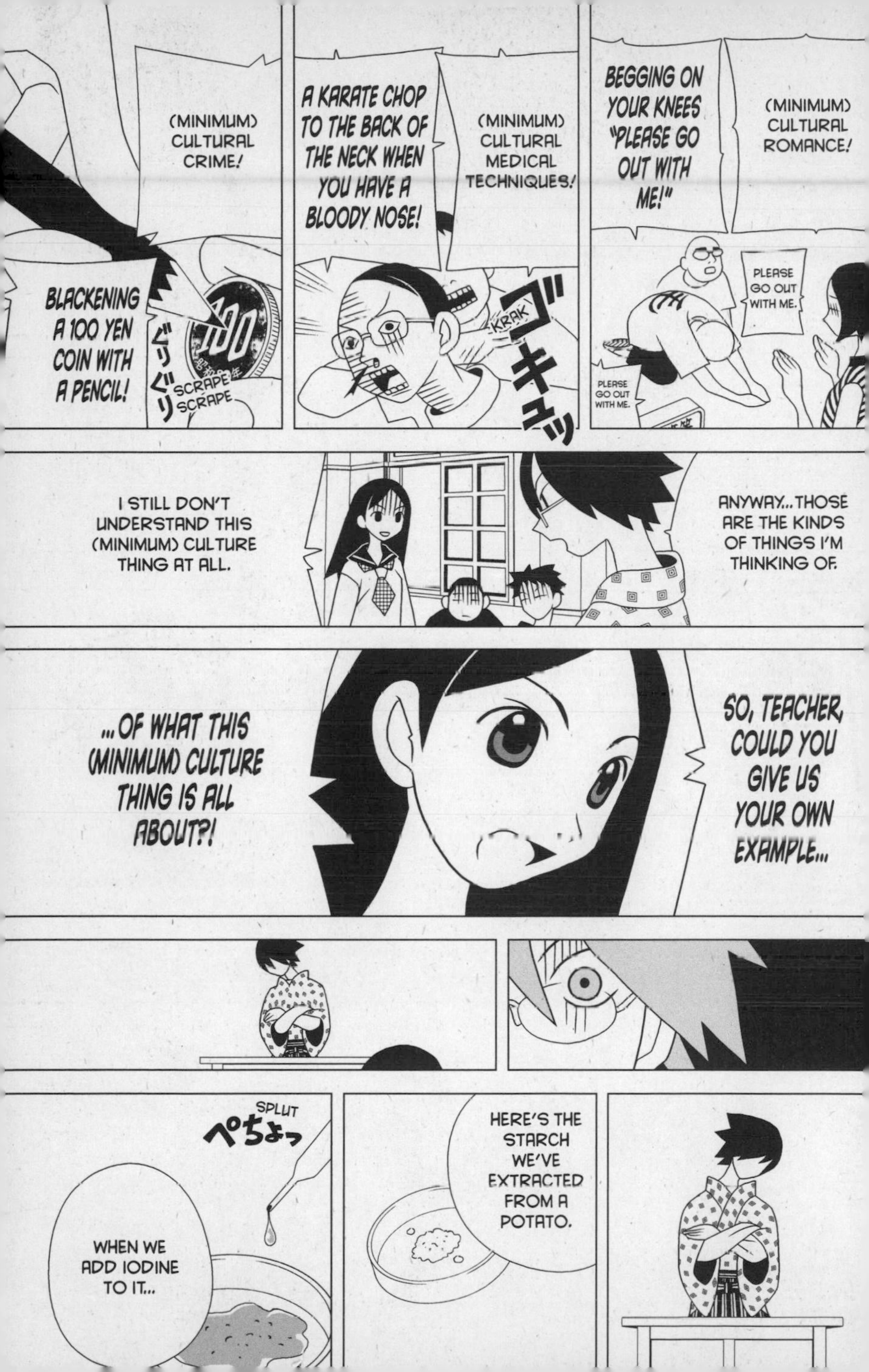
(MINIMUM) CULTURAL ROMANCE!
BEGGING ON YOUR KNEES "PLEASE GO OUT WITH ME!"
PLEASE GO OUT WITH ME.
PLEASE GO OUT WITH ME.
(MINIMUM) CULTURAL MEDICAL TECHNIQUES!
A KARATE CHOP TO THE BACK OF THE NECK WHEN YOU HAVE A BLOODY NOSE!
ゴキュッ
KRAK
(MINIMUM) CULTURAL CRIME!
BLACKENING A 100 YEN COIN WITH A PENCIL!
ぐりぐり
SCRAPE SCRAPE
ANYWAY...THOSE ARE THE KINDS OF THINGS I'M THINKING OF.
I STILL DON'T UNDERSTAND THIS (MINIMUM) CULTURE THING AT ALL.
SO, TEACHER, COULD YOU GIVE US YOUR OWN EXAMPLE...
...OF WHAT THIS (MINIMUM) CULTURE THING IS ALL ABOUT?!
HERE'S THE STARCH WE'VE EXTRACTED FROM A POTATO.
ぺちょっ
SPLUT
WHEN WE ADD IODINE TO IT...

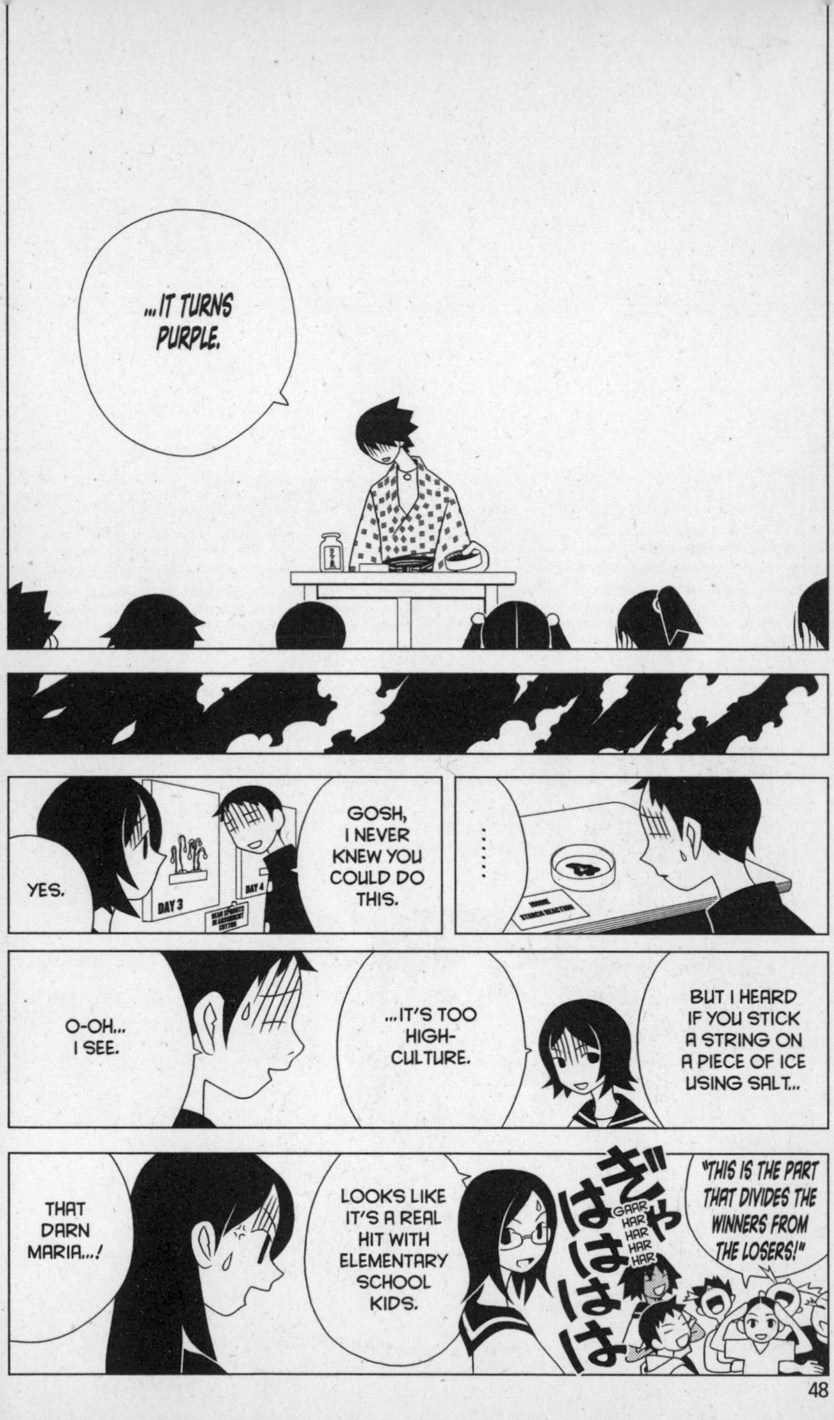
...IT TURNS PURPLE.
......
STARCH REACTION
GOSH, I NEVER KNEW YOU COULD DO THIS.
DAY 4
DAY 3
YES.
BUT I HEARD IF YOU STICK A STRING ON A PIECE OF ICE USING SALT...
...IT'S TOO HIGH-CULTURE.
O-OH... I SEE.
"THIS IS THE PART THAT DIVIDES THE WINNERS FROM THE LOSERS!"
ぎゃははははは
GAAR HAR HAR HAR HAR
LOOKS LIKE IT'S A REAL HIT WITH ELEMENTARY SCHOOL KIDS.
THAT DARN MARIA...!

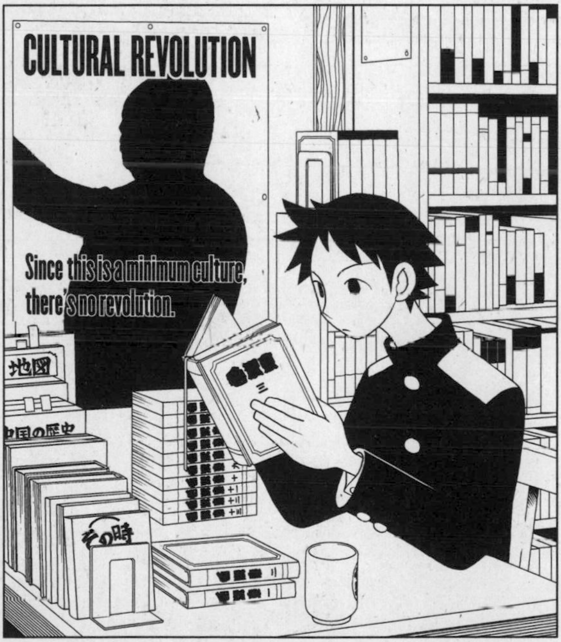
CULTURAL REVOLUTION
Since this is a minimum culture, there's no revolution.
地図
その時

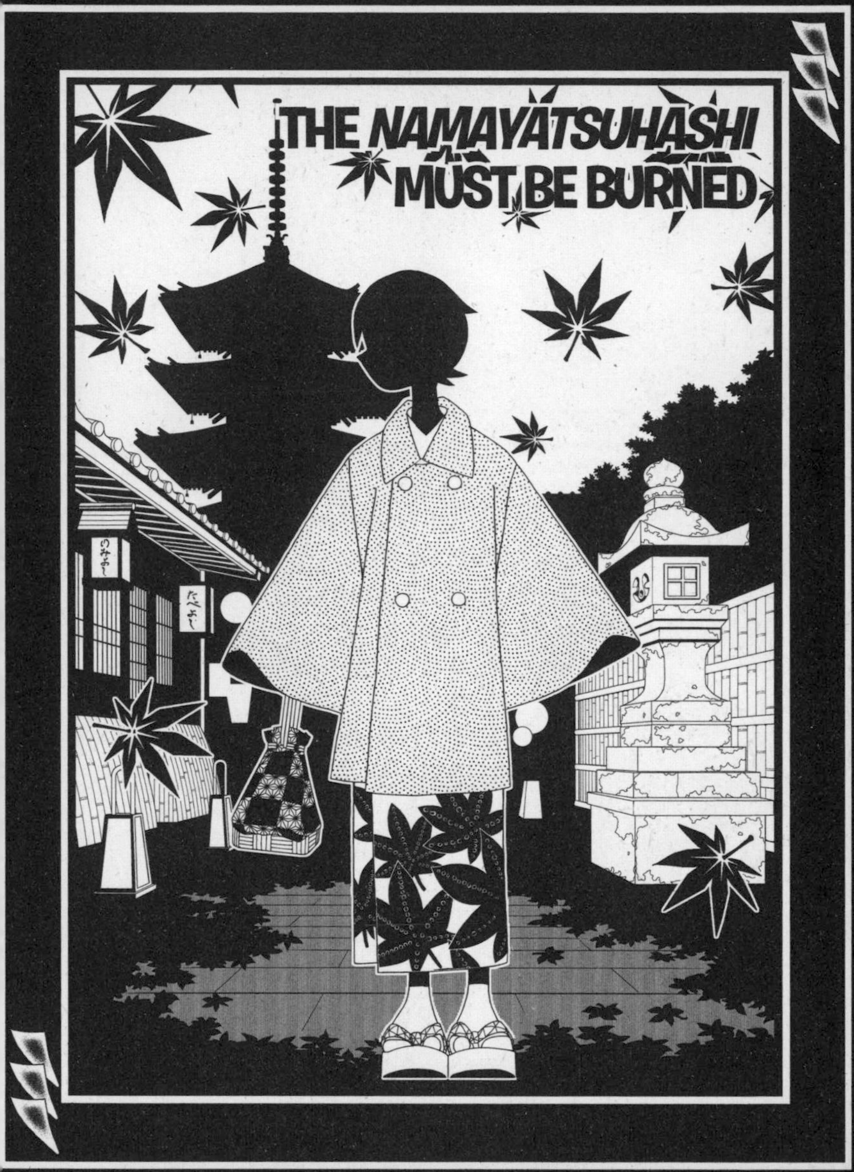
THE NAMAYATSUHASHI MUST BE BURNED

CHAPTER 24

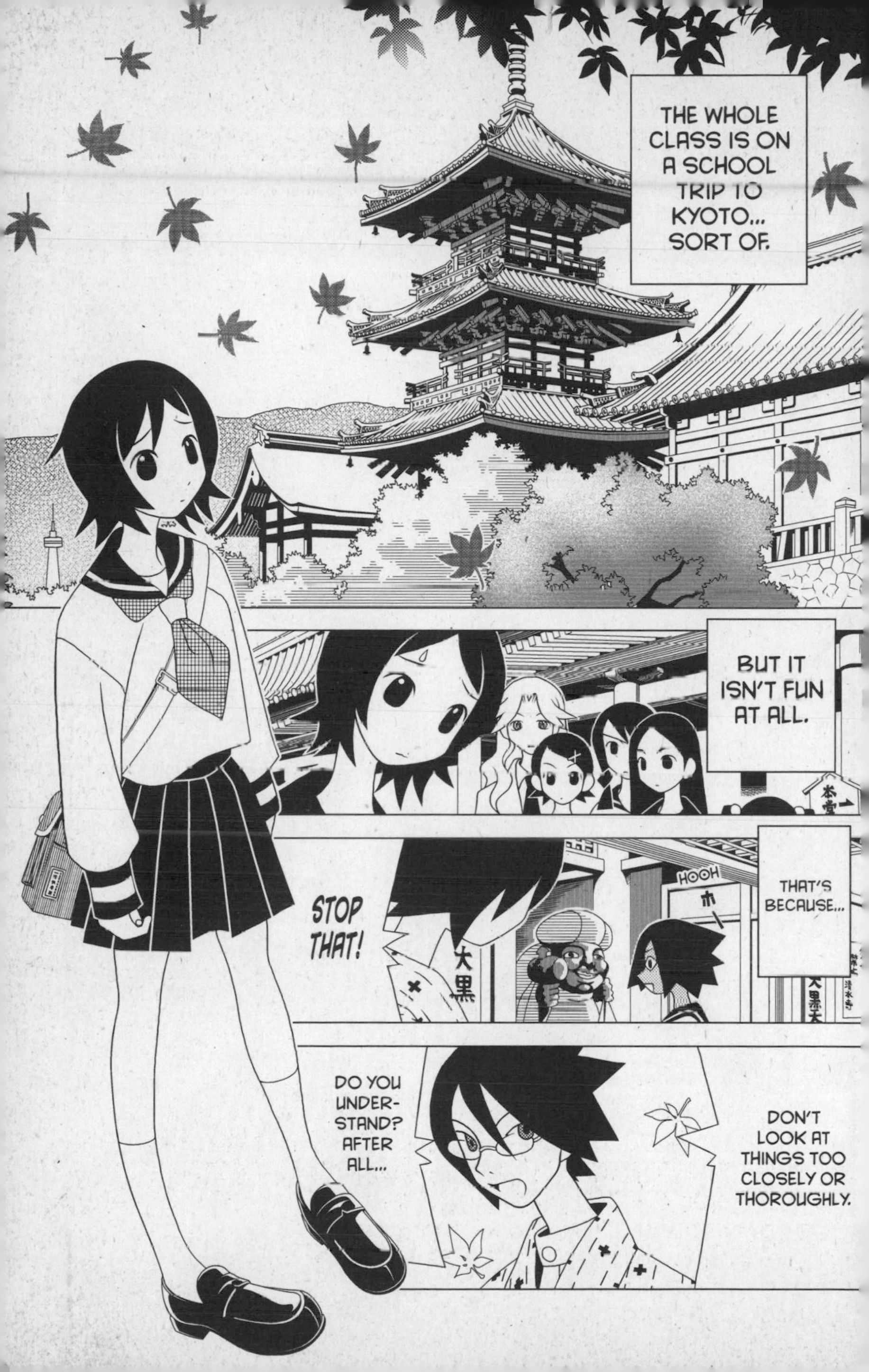
THE WHOLE CLASS IS ON A SCHOOL TRIP TO KYOTO... SORT OF.
BUT IT ISN'T FUN AT ALL.
本堂
THAT'S BECAUSE...
HOOH
ホー
大黒
STOP THAT!
DON'T LOOK AT THINGS TOO CLOSELY OR THOROUGHLY.
DO YOU UNDER-STAND? AFTER ALL...

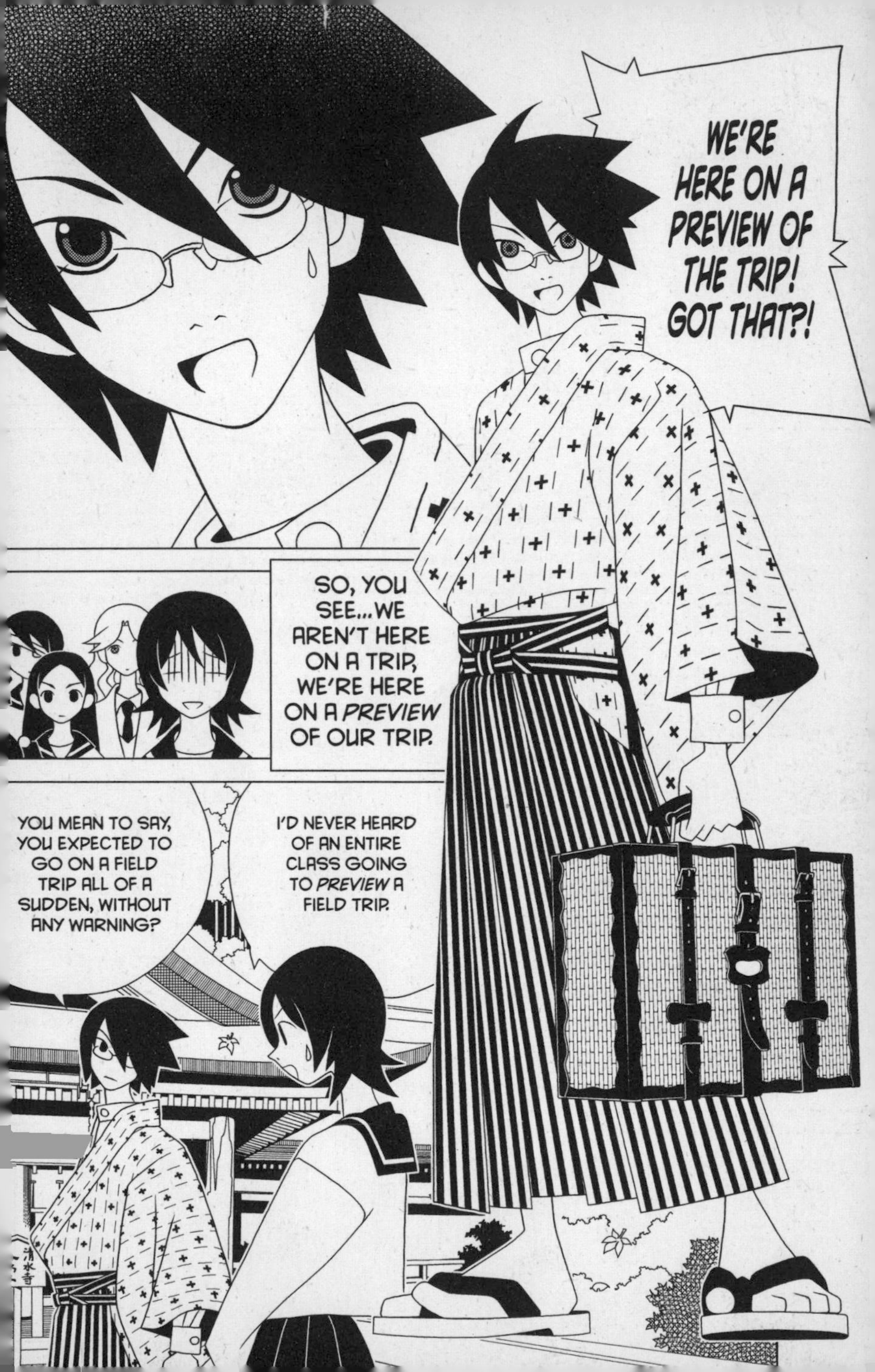
WE'RE HERE ON A PREVIEW OF THE TRIP! GOT THAT?!
SO, YOU SEE...WE AREN'T HERE ON A TRIP, WE'RE HERE ON A *PREVIEW* OF OUR TRIP.
I'D NEVER HEARD OF AN ENTIRE CLASS GOING TO *PREVIEW* A FIELD TRIP.
YOU MEAN TO SAY, YOU EXPECTED TO GO ON A FIELD TRIP ALL OF A SUDDEN, WITHOUT ANY WARNING?
清水寺

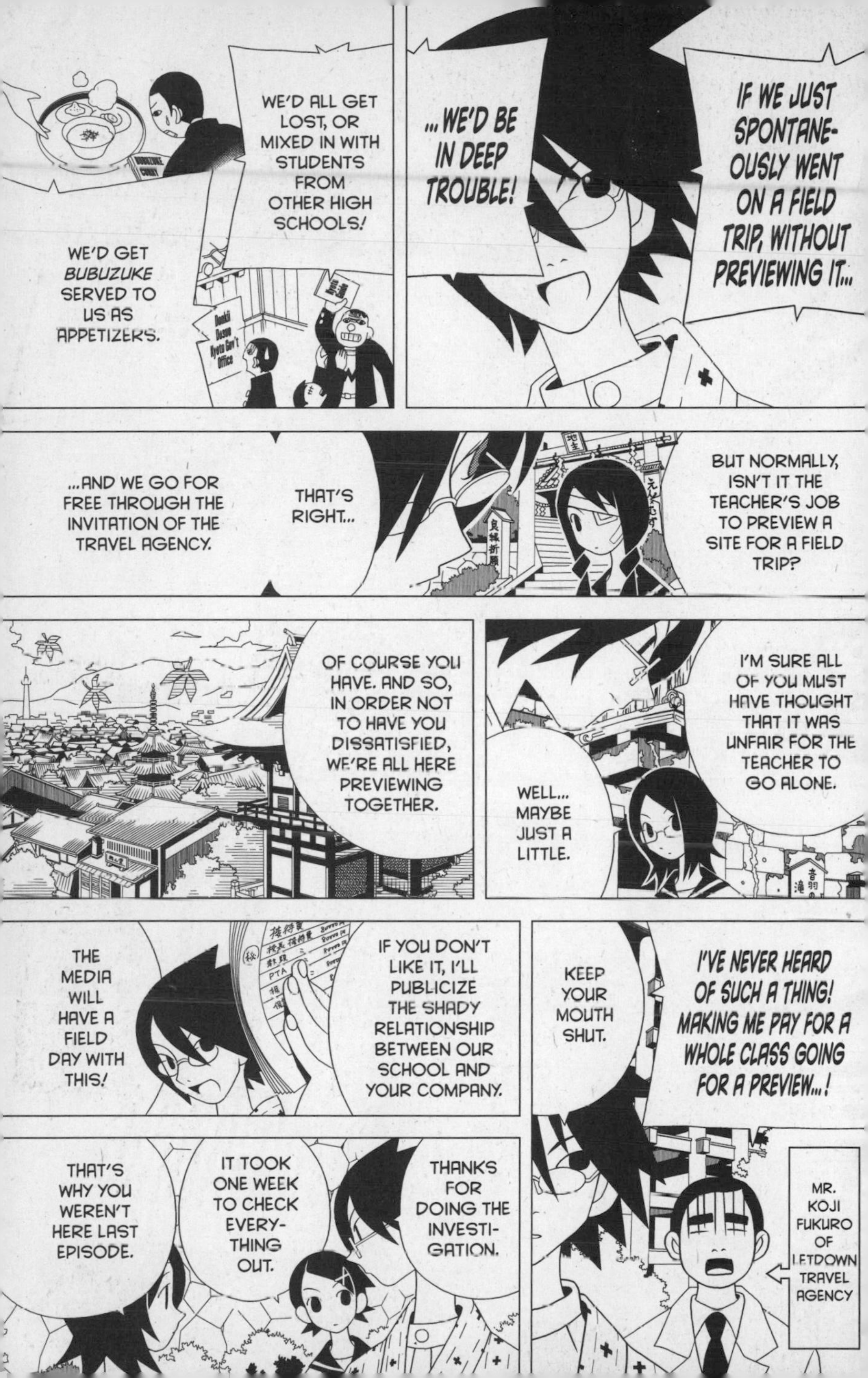
IF WE JUST SPONTANEOUSLY WENT ON A FIELD TRIP, WITHOUT PREVIEWING IT...
...WE'D BE IN DEEP TROUBLE!
WE'D ALL GET LOST, OR MIXED IN WITH STUDENTS FROM OTHER HIGH SCHOOLS!
WE'D GET *BUBUZUKE* SERVED TO US AS APPETIZERS.
BUT NORMALLY, ISN'T IT THE TEACHER'S JOB TO PREVIEW A SITE FOR A FIELD TRIP?
THAT'S RIGHT...
...AND WE GO FOR FREE THROUGH THE INVITATION OF THE TRAVEL AGENCY.
I'M SURE ALL OF YOU MUST HAVE THOUGHT THAT IT WAS UNFAIR FOR THE TEACHER TO GO ALONE.
WELL... MAYBE JUST A LITTLE.
OF COURSE YOU HAVE. AND SO, IN ORDER NOT TO HAVE YOU DISSATISFIED, WE'RE ALL HERE PREVIEWING TOGETHER.
I'VE NEVER HEARD OF SUCH A THING! MAKING ME PAY FOR A WHOLE CLASS GOING FOR A PREVIEW...!
KEEP YOUR MOUTH SHUT.
MR. KOJI FUKURO OF LETDOWN TRAVEL AGENCY
IF YOU DON'T LIKE IT, I'LL PUBLICIZE THE SHADY RELATIONSHIP BETWEEN OUR SCHOOL AND YOUR COMPANY.
THE MEDIA WILL HAVE A FIELD DAY WITH THIS!
THANKS FOR DOING THE INVESTIGATION.
IT TOOK ONE WEEK TO CHECK EVERYTHING OUT.
THAT'S WHY YOU WEREN'T HERE LAST EPISODE.

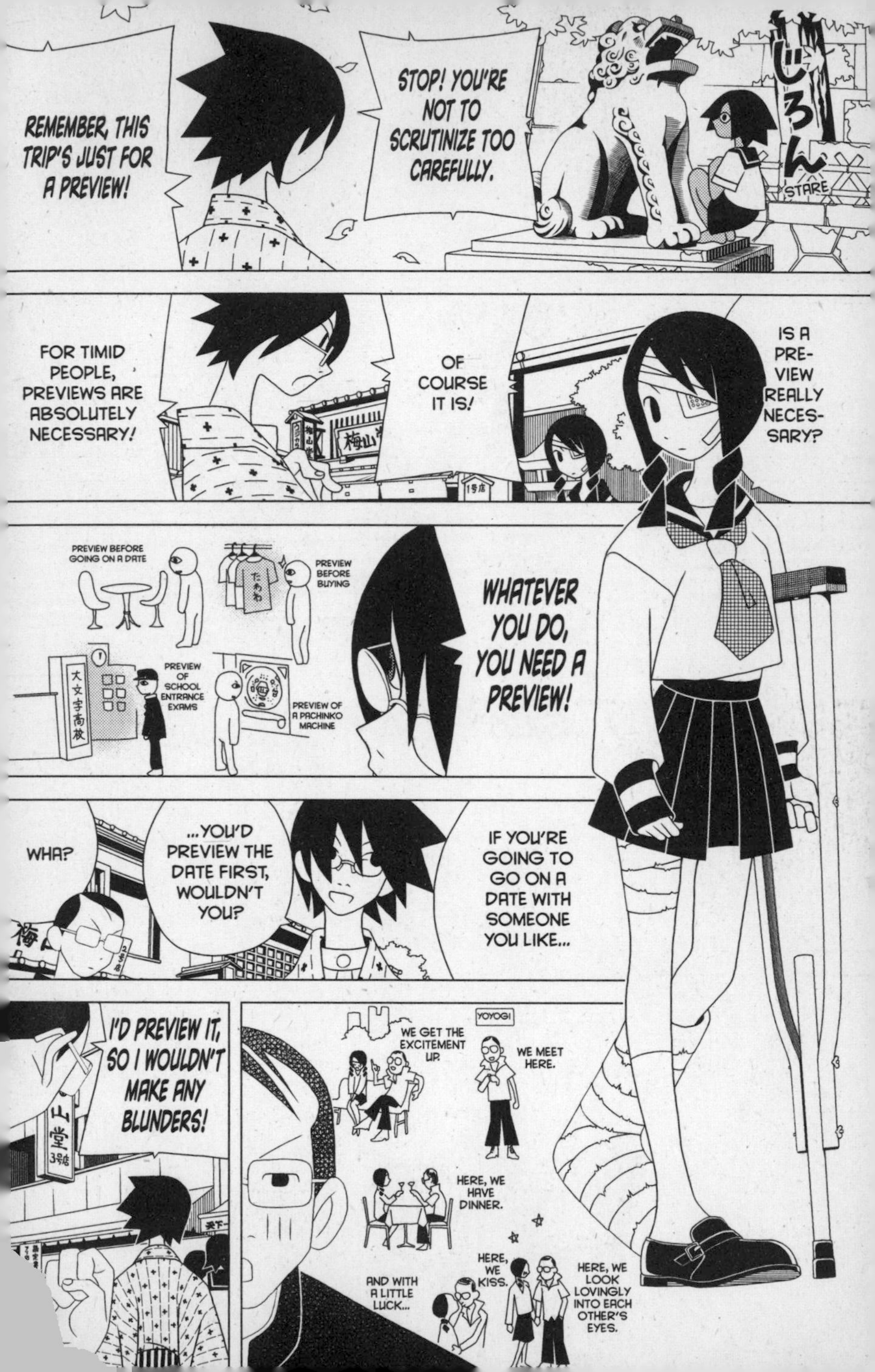
じろん
STARE
STOP! YOU'RE NOT TO SCRUTINIZE TOO CAREFULLY.
REMEMBER, THIS TRIP'S JUST FOR A PREVIEW!
IS A PRE-VIEW REALLY NECES-SARY?
1号店
OF COURSE IT IS!
梅山
FOR TIMID PEOPLE, PREVIEWS ARE ABSOLUTELY NECESSARY!
WHATEVER YOU DO, YOU NEED A PREVIEW!
PREVIEW BEFORE BUYING
たわわ
PREVIEW BEFORE GOING ON A DATE
PREVIEW OF A PACHINKO MACHINE
PREVIEW OF SCHOOL ENTRANCE EXAMS
大文字高校
IF YOU'RE GOING TO GO ON A DATE WITH SOMEONE YOU LIKE...
...YOU'D PREVIEW THE DATE FIRST, WOULDN'T YOU?
WHA?
YOYOGI
WE MEET HERE.
WE GET THE EXCITEMENT UP.
HERE, WE HAVE DINNER.
HERE, WE LOOK LOVINGLY INTO EACH OTHER'S EYES.
HERE, WE KISS.
AND WITH A LITTLE LUCK...
I'D PREVIEW IT, SO I WOULDN'T MAKE ANY BLUNDERS!
山堂 3号店

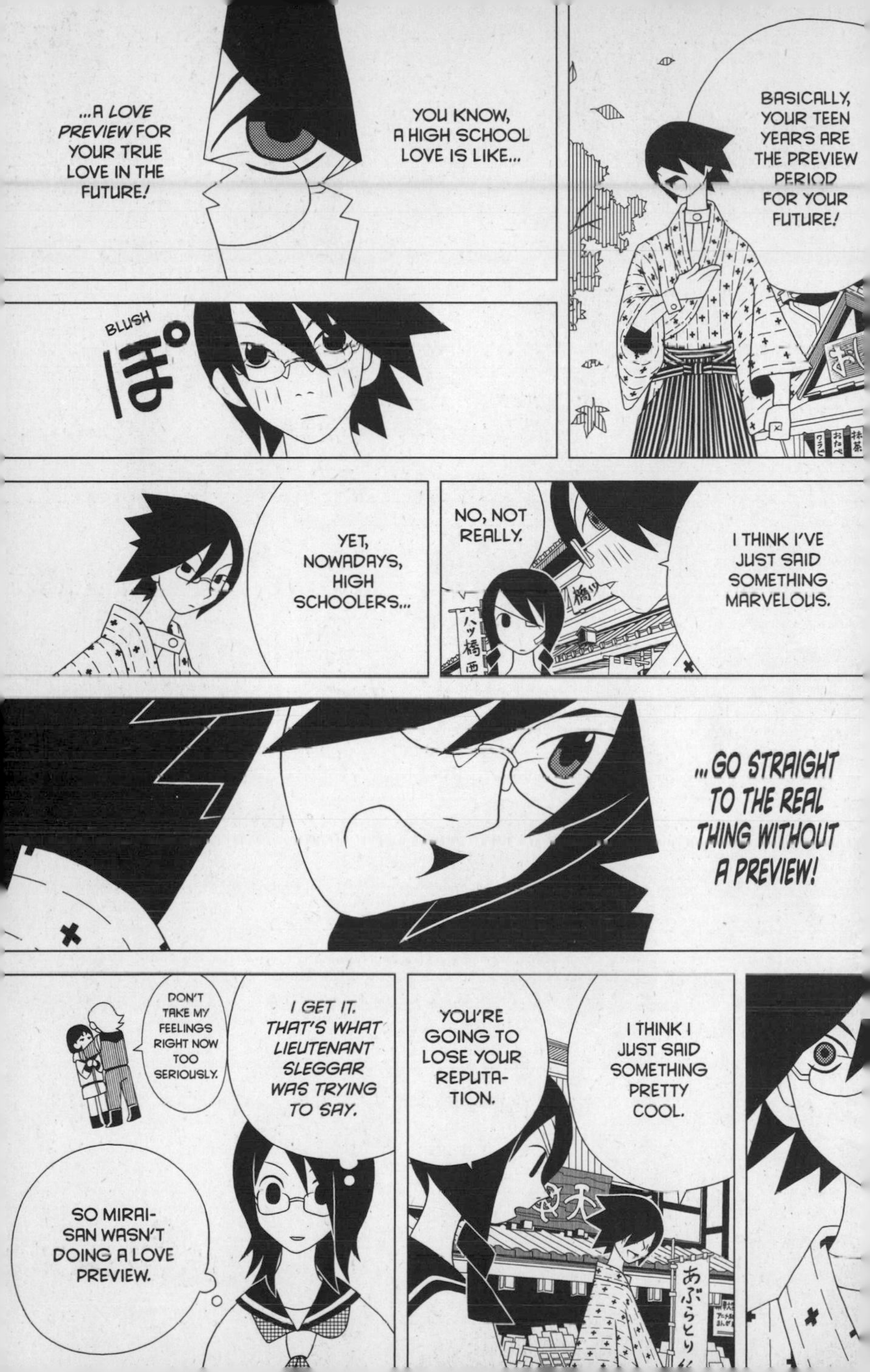
BASICALLY, YOUR TEEN YEARS ARE THE PREVIEW PERIOD FOR YOUR FUTURE!
YOU KNOW, A HIGH SCHOOL LOVE IS LIKE...
...A LOVE PREVIEW FOR YOUR TRUE LOVE IN THE FUTURE!
BLUSH
ぽ
I THINK I'VE JUST SAID SOMETHING MARVELOUS.
NO, NOT REALLY.
YET, NOWADAYS, HIGH SCHOOLERS...
...GO STRAIGHT TO THE REAL THING WITHOUT A PREVIEW!
I THINK I JUST SAID SOMETHING PRETTY COOL.
YOU'RE GOING TO LOSE YOUR REPUTA-TION.
I GET IT. THAT'S WHAT LIEUTENANT SLEGGAR WAS TRYING TO SAY.
DON'T TAKE MY FEELINGS RIGHT NOW TOO SERIOUSLY.
SO MIRAI-SAN WASN'T DOING A LOVE PREVIEW.

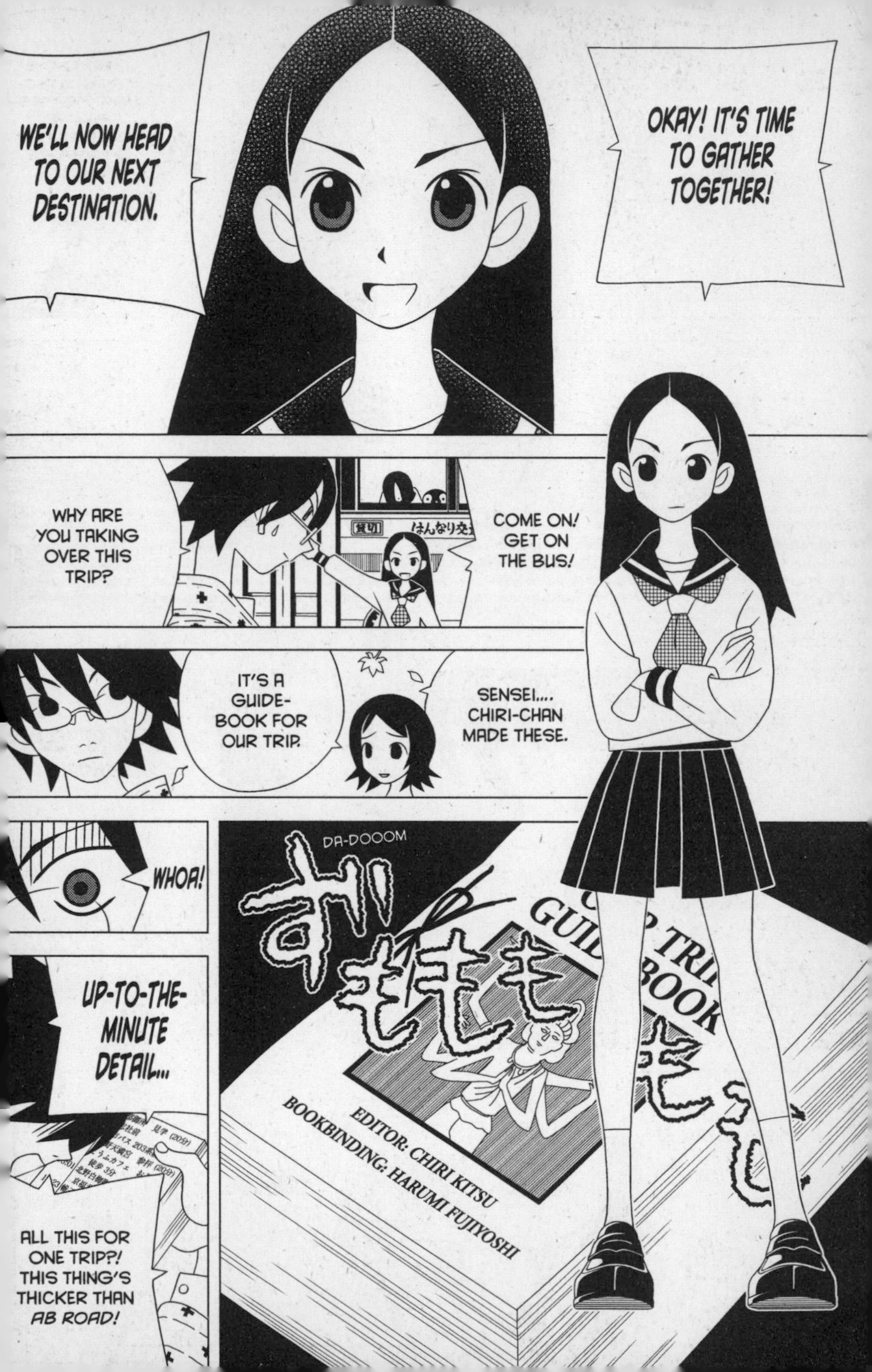
OKAY! IT'S TIME TO GATHER TOGETHER!
WE'LL NOW HEAD TO OUR NEXT DESTINATION.
COME ON! GET ON THE BUS!
WHY ARE YOU TAKING OVER THIS TRIP?
SENSEI.... CHIRI-CHAN MADE THESE.
IT'S A GUIDE-BOOK FOR OUR TRIP.
DA-DOOOM
EDITOR: CHIRI KITSU
BOOKBINDING: HARUMI FUJIYOSHI
WHOA!
UP-TO-THE-MINUTE DETAIL...
ALL THIS FOR ONE TRIP?! THIS THING'S THICKER THAN AB ROAD!

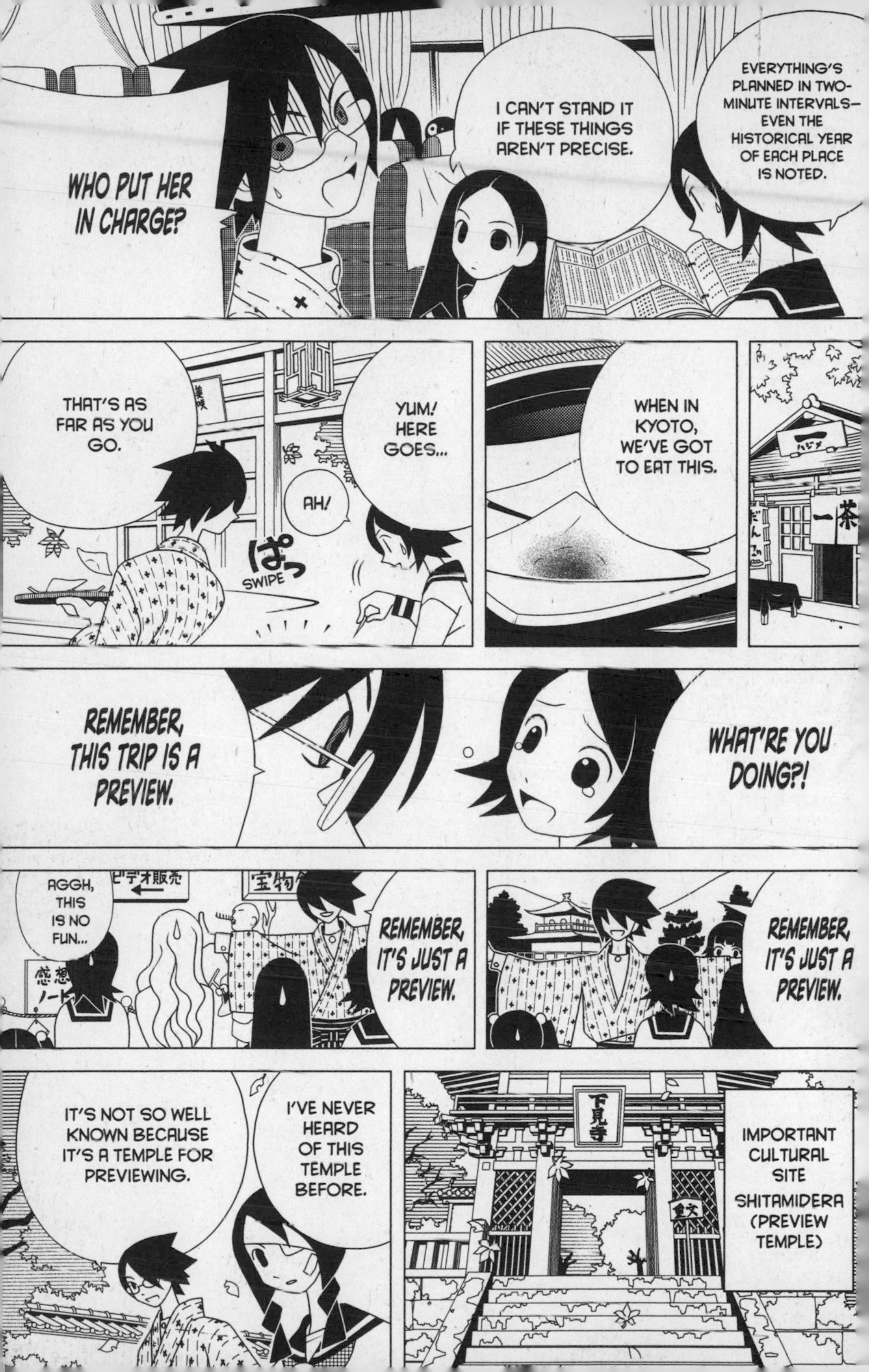

EVERYTHING'S PLANNED IN TWO-MINUTE INTERVALS—EVEN THE HISTORICAL YEAR OF EACH PLACE IS NOTED.
I CAN'T STAND IT IF THESE THINGS AREN'T PRECISE.
WHO PUT HER IN CHARGE?
一茶
WHEN IN KYOTO, WE'VE GOT TO EAT THIS.
YUM! HERE GOES...
AH!
ぱっ
SWIPE
THAT'S AS FAR AS YOU GO.
WHAT'RE YOU DOING?!
REMEMBER, THIS TRIP IS A PREVIEW.
REMEMBER, IT'S JUST A PREVIEW.
REMEMBER, IT'S JUST A PREVIEW.
ビデオ販売
AGGH, THIS IS NO FUN...
感想ノート
下見寺
IMPORTANT CULTURAL SITE SHITAMIDERA (PREVIEW TEMPLE)
I'VE NEVER HEARD OF THIS TEMPLE BEFORE.
IT'S NOT SO WELL KNOWN BECAUSE IT'S A TEMPLE FOR PREVIEWING.

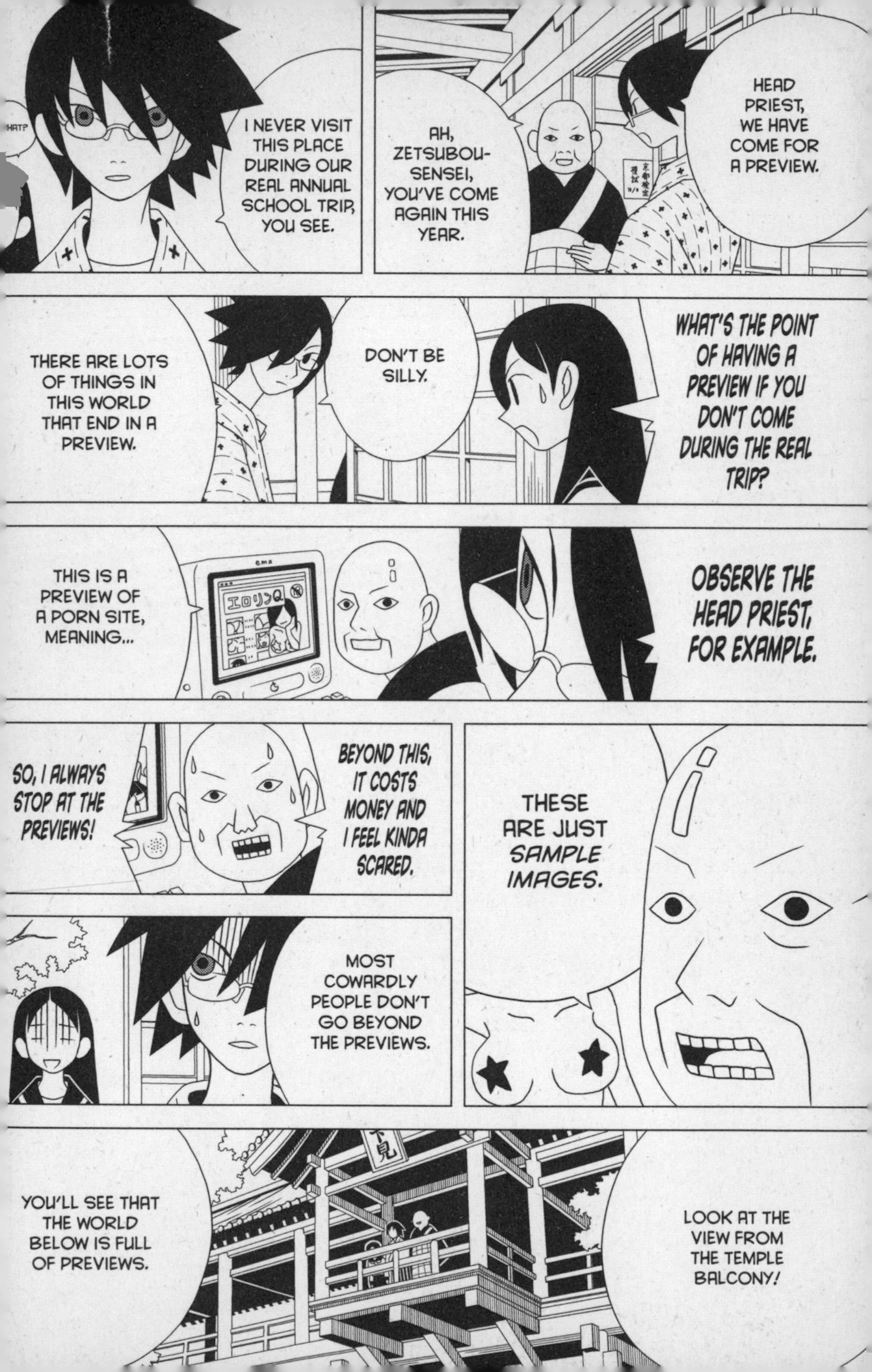
HEAD PRIEST, WE HAVE COME FOR A PREVIEW.
AH, ZETSUBOU-SENSEI, YOU'VE COME AGAIN THIS YEAR.
I NEVER VISIT THIS PLACE DURING OUR REAL ANNUAL SCHOOL TRIP, YOU SEE.
WHAT'S THE POINT OF HAVING A PREVIEW IF YOU DON'T COME DURING THE REAL TRIP?
DON'T BE SILLY.
THERE ARE LOTS OF THINGS IN THIS WORLD THAT END IN A PREVIEW.
OBSERVE THE HEAD PRIEST, FOR EXAMPLE.
THIS IS A PREVIEW OF A PORN SITE, MEANING...
THESE ARE JUST SAMPLE IMAGES.
BEYOND THIS, IT COSTS MONEY AND I FEEL KINDA SCARED.
SO, I ALWAYS STOP AT THE PREVIEWS!
MOST COWARDLY PEOPLE DON'T GO BEYOND THE PREVIEWS.
LOOK AT THE VIEW FROM THE TEMPLE BALCONY!
YOU'LL SEE THAT THE WORLD BELOW IS FULL OF PREVIEWS.

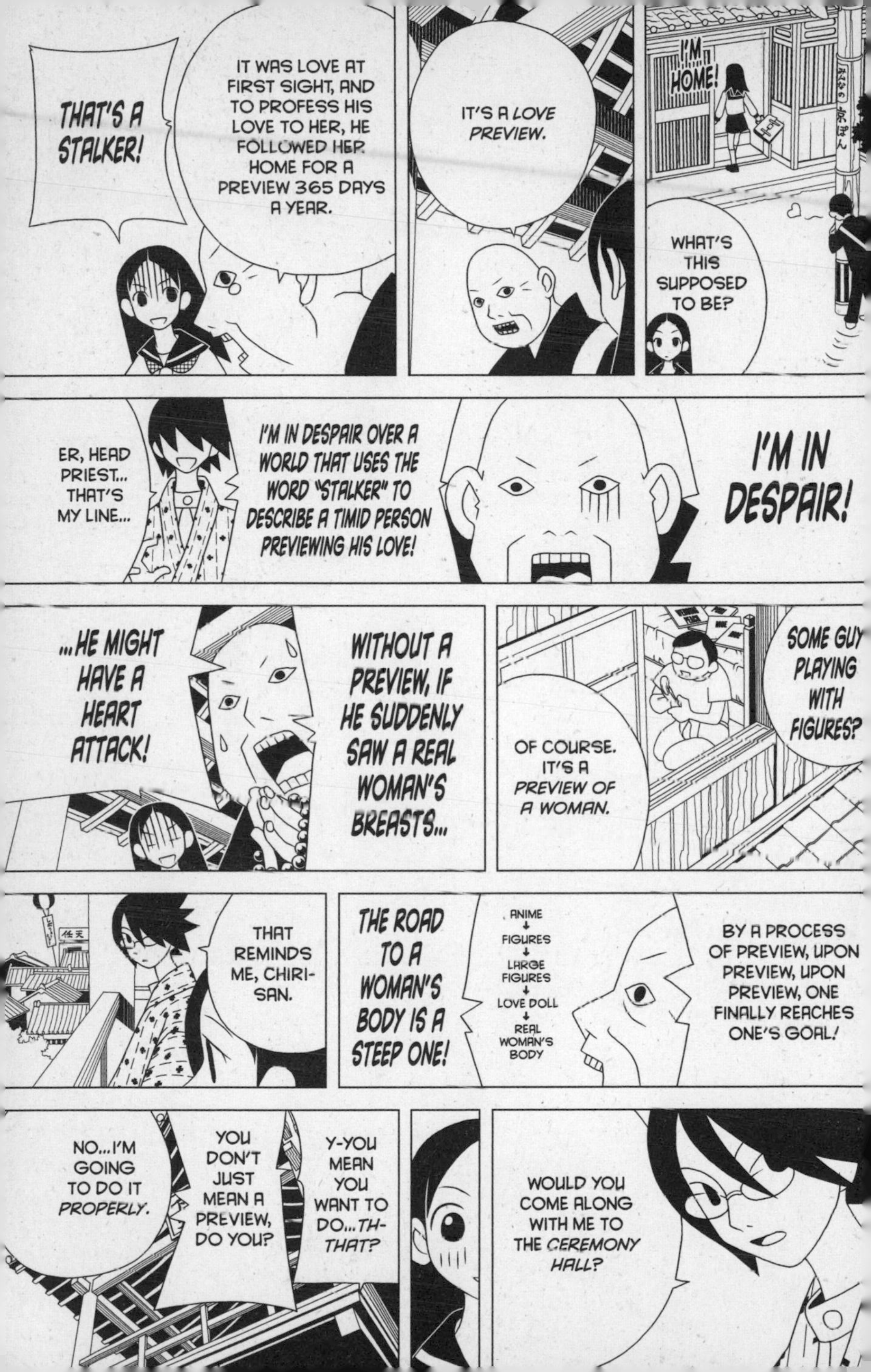
I'M HOME!
WHAT'S THIS SUPPOSED TO BE?
IT'S A *LOVE PREVIEW.*
IT WAS LOVE AT FIRST SIGHT, AND TO PROFESS HIS LOVE TO HER, HE FOLLOWED HER HOME FOR A PREVIEW 365 DAYS A YEAR.
THAT'S A STALKER!
I'M IN DESPAIR!
I'M IN DESPAIR OVER A WORLD THAT USES THE WORD "STALKER" TO DESCRIBE A TIMID PERSON PREVIEWING HIS LOVE!
ER, HEAD PRIEST... THAT'S MY LINE...
SOME GUY PLAYING WITH FIGURES?
OF COURSE. IT'S A *PREVIEW OF A WOMAN.*
WITHOUT A PREVIEW, IF HE SUDDENLY SAW A REAL WOMAN'S BREASTS...
...HE MIGHT HAVE A HEART ATTACK!
BY A PROCESS OF PREVIEW, UPON PREVIEW, UPON PREVIEW, ONE FINALLY REACHES ONE'S GOAL!
ANIME ↓ FIGURES ↓ LARGE FIGURES ↓ LOVE DOLL ↓ REAL WOMAN'S BODY
THE ROAD TO A WOMAN'S BODY IS A STEEP ONE!
THAT REMINDS ME, CHIRI-SAN.
WOULD YOU COME ALONG WITH ME TO THE *CEREMONY HALL?*
Y-YOU MEAN YOU WANT TO DO...*TH-THAT?*
YOU DON'T JUST MEAN A PREVIEW, DO YOU?
NO...I'M GOING TO DO IT *PROPERLY.*

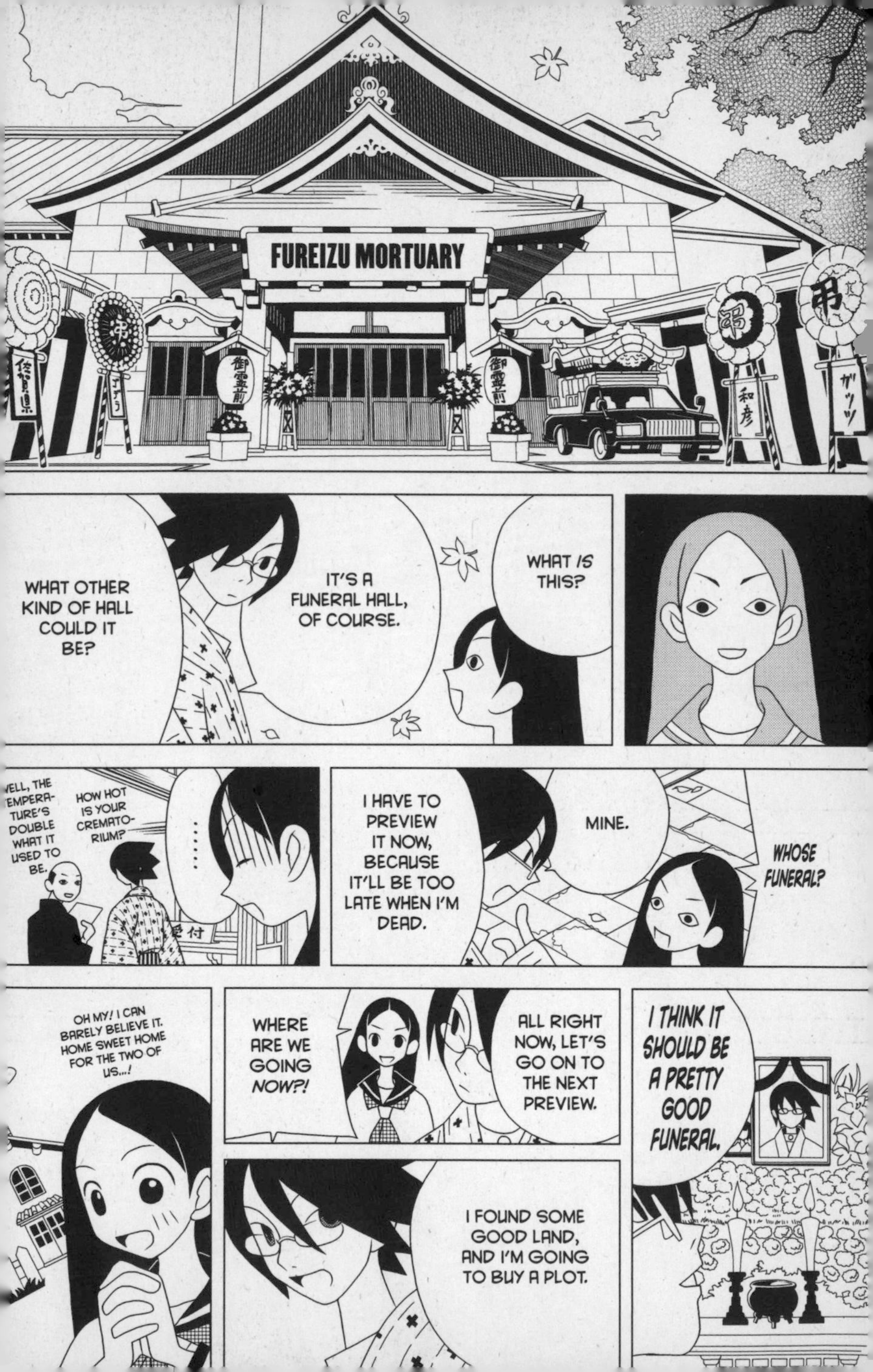
FUREIZU MORTUARY
御霊前
御霊前
佐賀県
和彦
ガッツ
WHAT *IS* THIS?
IT'S A FUNERAL HALL, OF COURSE.
WHAT OTHER KIND OF HALL COULD IT BE?
WHOSE FUNERAL?
MINE.
I HAVE TO PREVIEW IT NOW, BECAUSE IT'LL BE TOO LATE WHEN I'M DEAD.
......
受付
HOW HOT IS YOUR CREMATORIUM?
WELL, THE TEMPERATURE'S DOUBLE WHAT IT USED TO BE.
I THINK IT SHOULD BE A PRETTY GOOD FUNERAL.
ALL RIGHT NOW, LET'S GO ON TO THE NEXT PREVIEW.
WHERE ARE WE GOING *NOW?!*
I FOUND SOME GOOD LAND, AND I'M GOING TO BUY A PLOT.
OH MY! I CAN BARELY BELIEVE IT. HOME SWEET HOME FOR THE TWO OF US...!

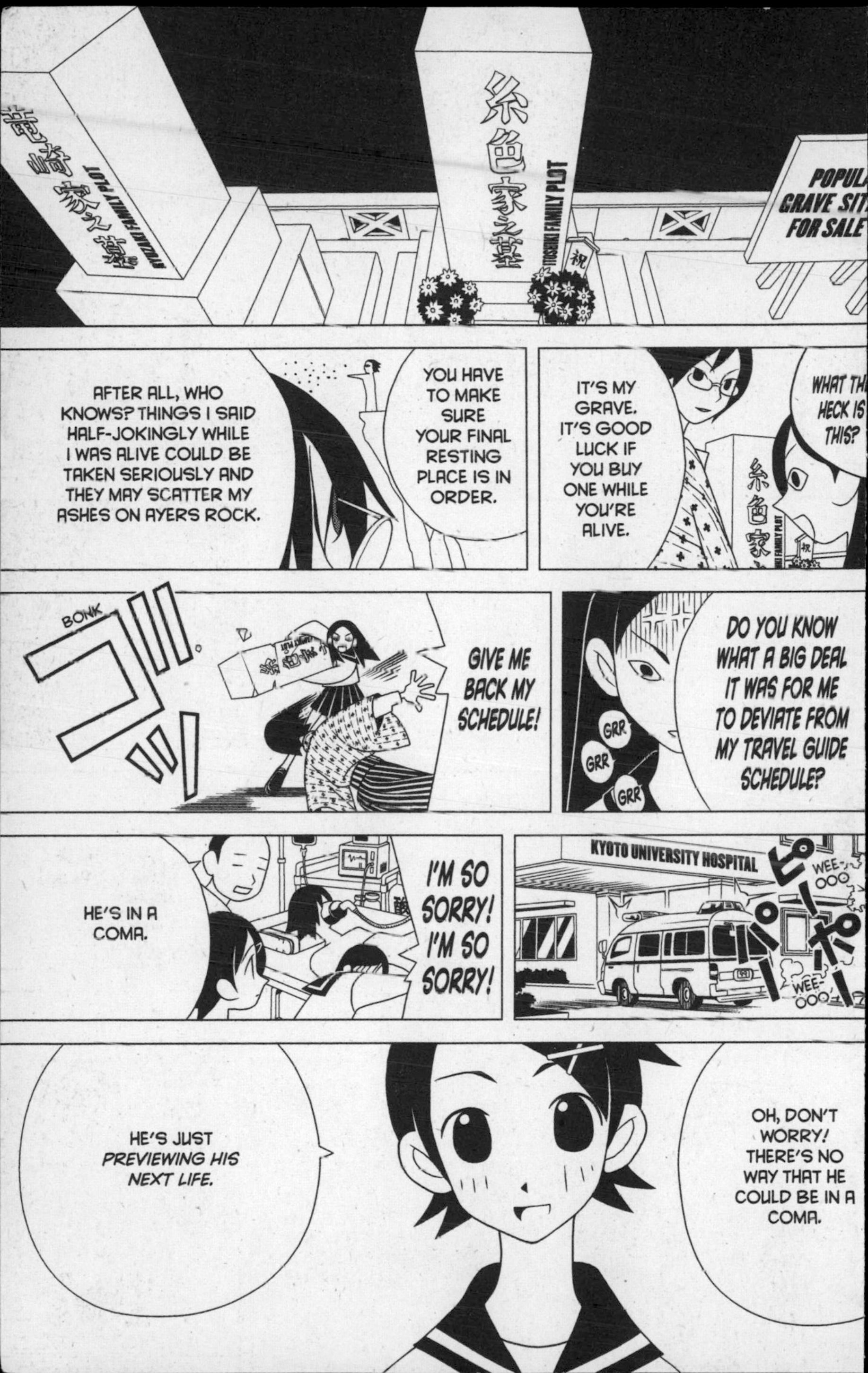
POPULA
GRAVE SIT
FOR SALE
糸色家之墓
ITOSHIKI FAMILY PLOT
竜崎家之墓
RYOZAKI FAMILY PLOT
WHAT TH
HECK IS THIS?
IT'S MY GRAVE. IT'S GOOD LUCK IF YOU BUY ONE WHILE YOU'RE ALIVE.
YOU HAVE TO MAKE SURE YOUR FINAL RESTING PLACE IS IN ORDER.
AFTER ALL, WHO KNOWS? THINGS I SAID HALF-JOKINGLY WHILE I WAS ALIVE COULD BE TAKEN SERIOUSLY AND THEY MAY SCATTER MY ASHES ON AYERS ROCK.
DO YOU KNOW WHAT A BIG DEAL IT WAS FOR ME TO DEVIATE FROM MY TRAVEL GUIDE SCHEDULE?
GRR
GRR
GRR
GIVE ME BACK MY SCHEDULE!
BONK
KYOTO UNIVERSITY HOSPITAL
WEE-OOO
WEE-OOO
I'M SO SORRY! I'M SO SORRY!
HE'S IN A COMA.
OH, DON'T WORRY! THERE'S NO WAY THAT HE COULD BE IN A COMA.
HE'S JUST *PREVIEWING HIS NEXT LIFE.*

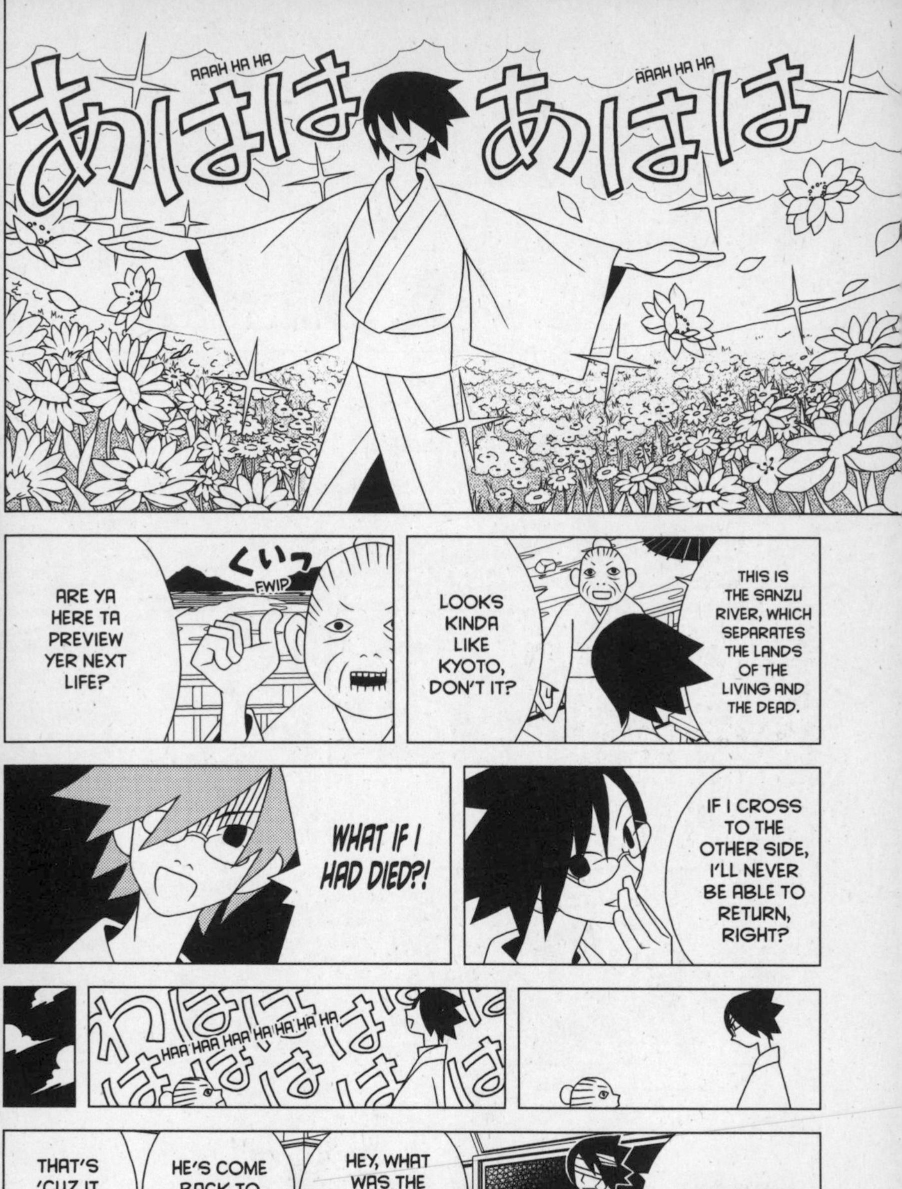
AAAH HA HA
あはは
AAAH HA HA
あはは
THIS IS THE SANZU RIVER, WHICH SEPARATES THE LANDS OF THE LIVING AND THE DEAD.
LOOKS KINDA LIKE KYOTO, DON'T IT?
くいっ
FWIP
ARE YA HERE TA PREVIEW YER NEXT LIFE?
IF I CROSS TO THE OTHER SIDE, I'LL NEVER BE ABLE TO RETURN, RIGHT?
WHAT IF I HAD DIED?!
わはははははははは
HAA HAA HAA HA HA HA HA
ANYWAY... THIS YEAR WE'LL BE GOING TO OKINAWA FOR OUR SCHOOL TRIP.
HEY, WHAT WAS THE MEANING OF ALL THAT?
HE'S COME BACK TO LIFE.
THAT'S 'CUZ IT WAS A PREVIEW.

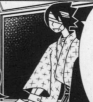

WRITE WRITE
チチチ
GLEAM
OUR TRIP GUIDEBOOK
EDITOR: CHIRI KITSU
BOOKBINDING & EMBOSSED PHOTOS: HARUMI FUJIYOSHI

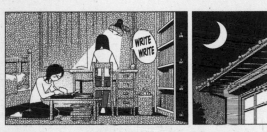

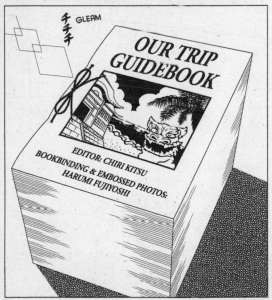

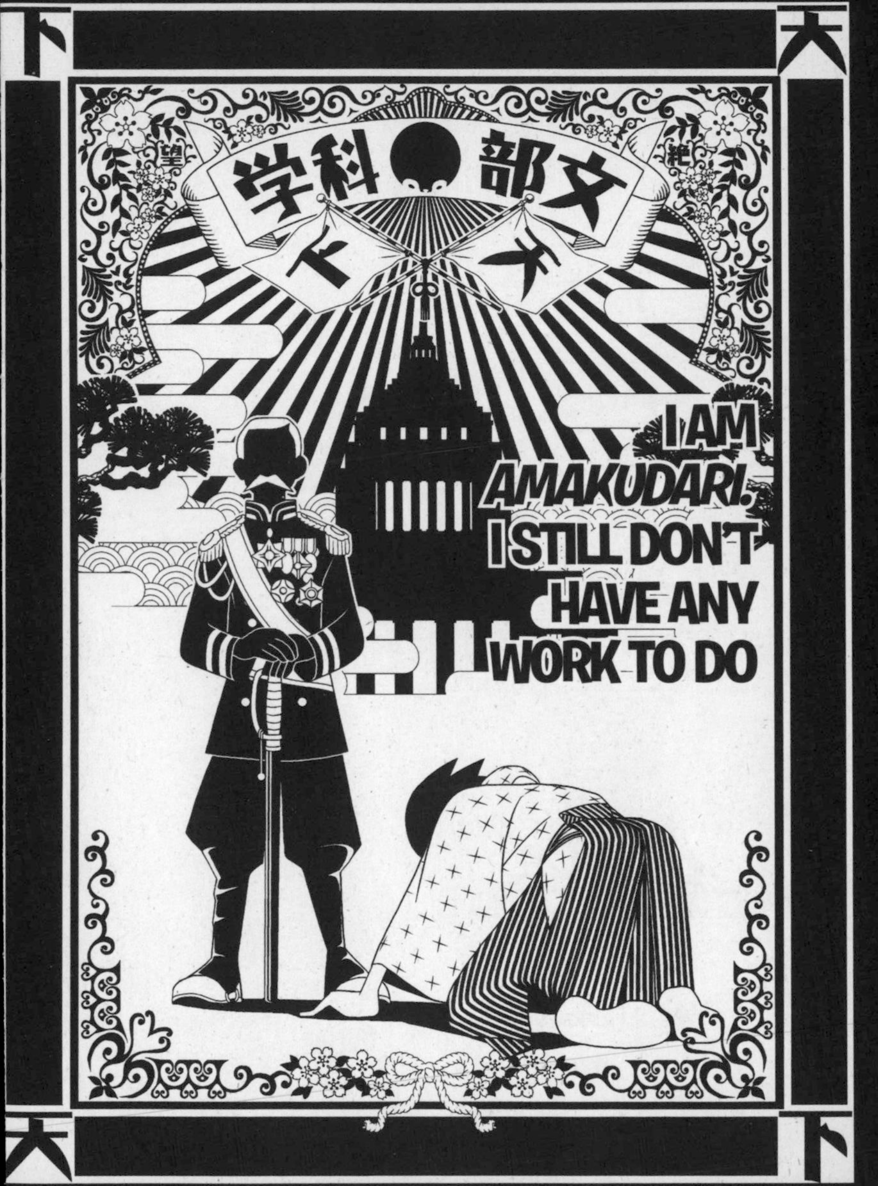

文部科学
I AM AMAKUDARI.
I STILL DON'T HAVE ANY WORK TO DO

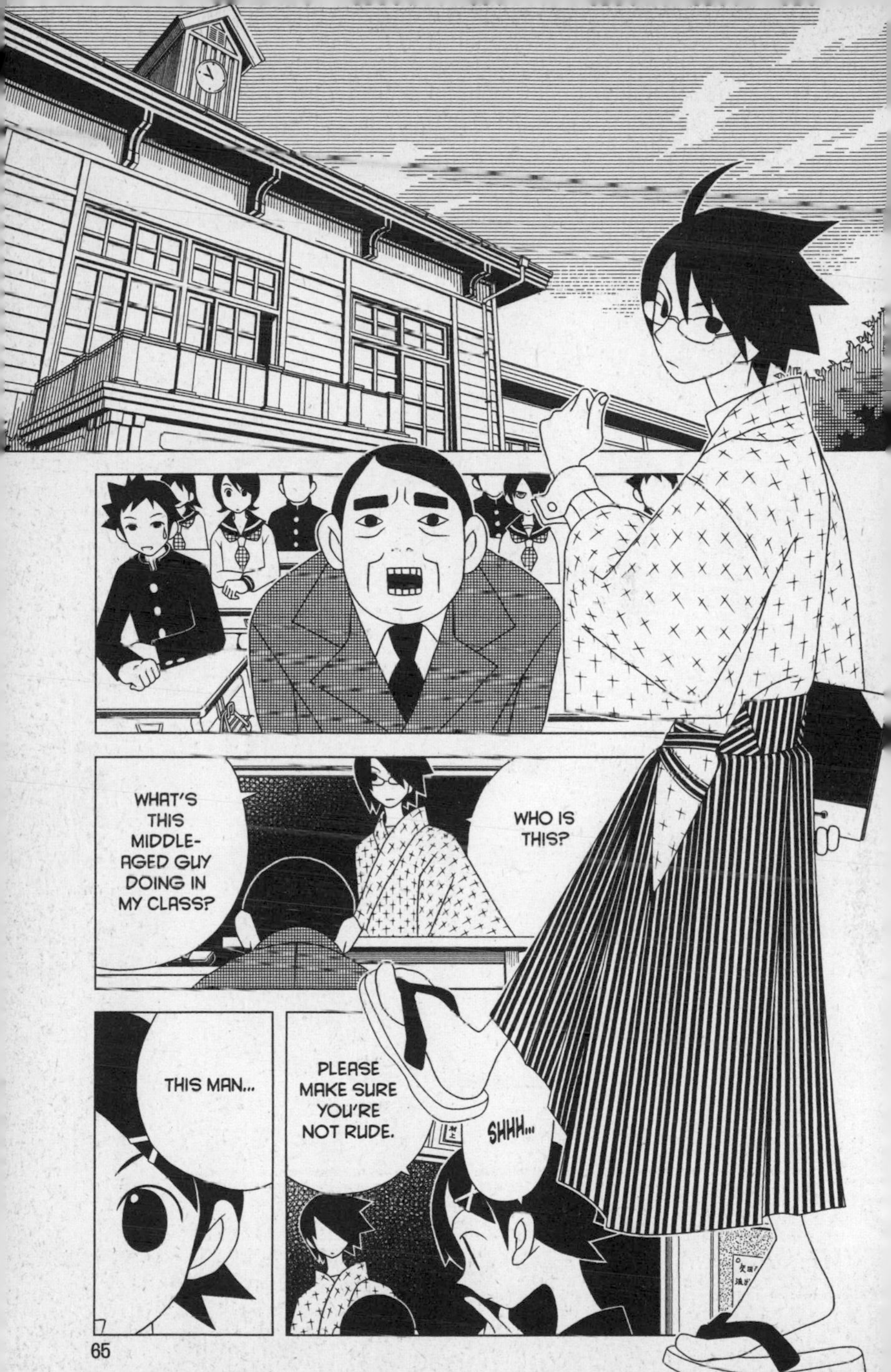
WHO IS THIS?
WHAT'S THIS MIDDLE-AGED GUY DOING IN MY CLASS?
SHHH...
PLEASE MAKE SURE YOU'RE NOT RUDE.
THIS MAN...

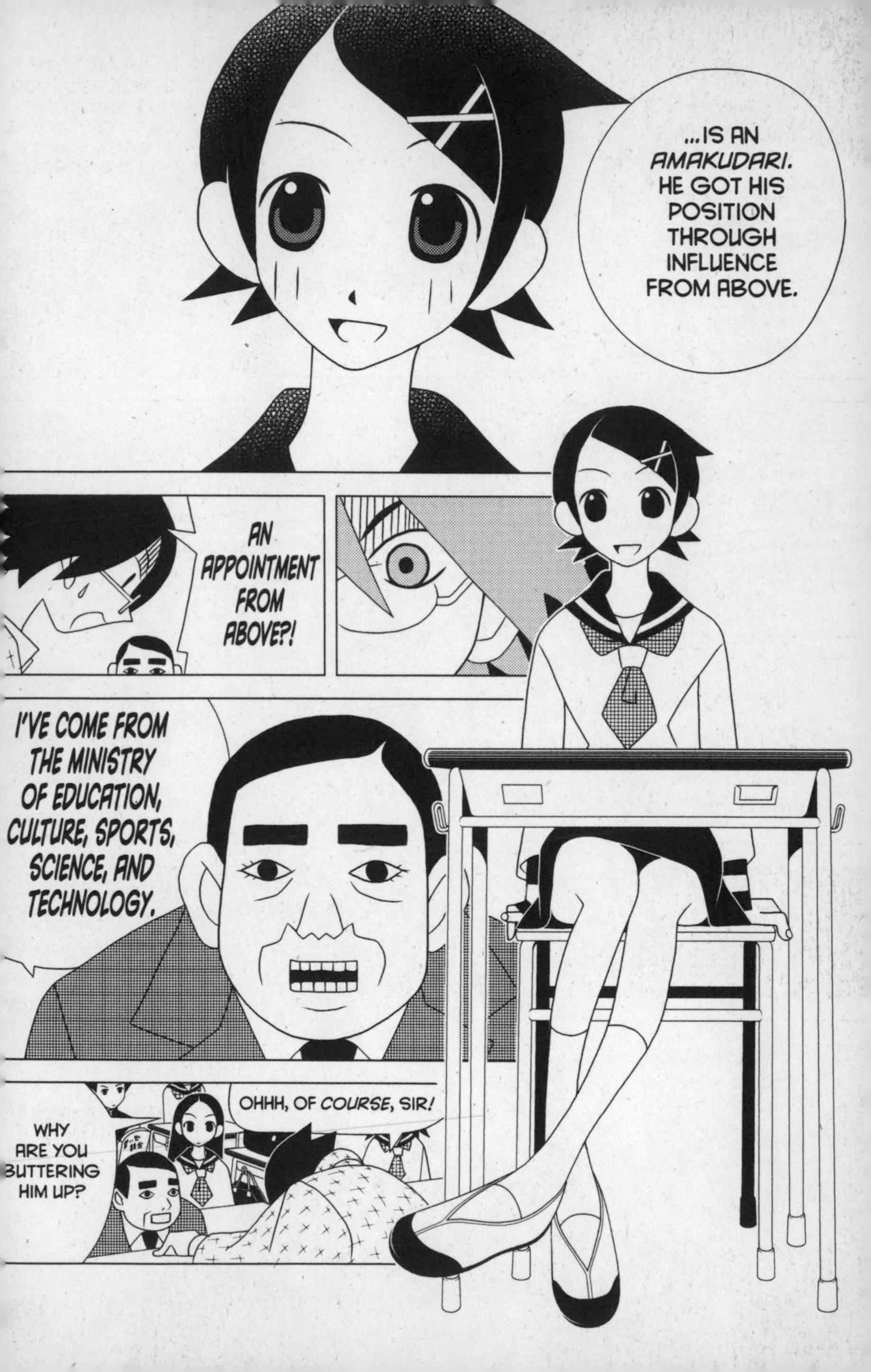
...IS AN *AMAKUDARI*. HE GOT HIS POSITION THROUGH INFLUENCE FROM ABOVE.
AN APPOINTMENT FROM ABOVE?!
I'VE COME FROM THE MINISTRY OF EDUCATION, CULTURE, SPORTS, SCIENCE, AND TECHNOLOGY.
OHHH, OF *COURSE*, SIR!
WHY ARE YOU BUTTERING HIM UP?

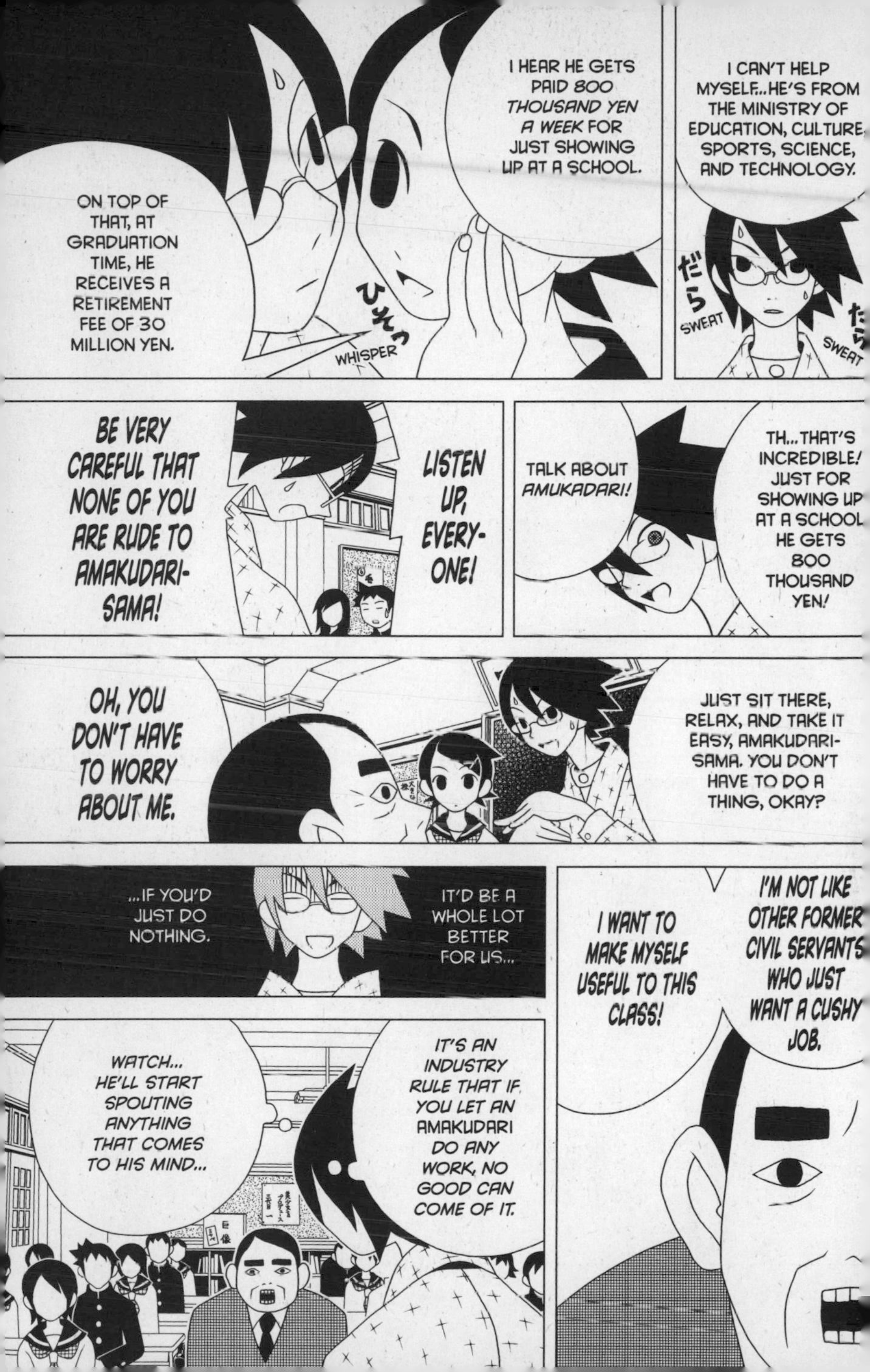
I CAN'T HELP MYSELF...HE'S FROM THE MINISTRY OF EDUCATION, CULTURE, SPORTS, SCIENCE, AND TECHNOLOGY.
だら SWEAT
だら SWEAT
I HEAR HE GETS PAID 800 THOUSAND YEN A WEEK FOR JUST SHOWING UP AT A SCHOOL.
ON TOP OF THAT, AT GRADUATION TIME, HE RECEIVES A RETIREMENT FEE OF 30 MILLION YEN.
ひそっ WHISPER
TH...THAT'S INCREDIBLE! JUST FOR SHOWING UP AT A SCHOOL HE GETS 800 THOUSAND YEN!
TALK ABOUT AMUKADARI!
LISTEN UP, EVERY-ONE!
BE VERY CAREFUL THAT NONE OF YOU ARE RUDE TO AMAKUDARI-SAMA!
JUST SIT THERE, RELAX, AND TAKE IT EASY, AMAKUDARI-SAMA. YOU DON'T HAVE TO DO A THING, OKAY?
OH, YOU DON'T HAVE TO WORRY ABOUT ME.
I'M NOT LIKE OTHER FORMER CIVIL SERVANTS WHO JUST WANT A CUSHY JOB.
I WANT TO MAKE MYSELF USEFUL TO THIS CLASS!
IT'D BE A WHOLE LOT BETTER FOR US...
...IF YOU'D JUST DO NOTHING.
IT'S AN INDUSTRY RULE THAT IF YOU LET AN AMAKUDARI DO ANY WORK, NO GOOD CAN COME OF IT.
WATCH... HE'LL START SPOUTING ANYTHING THAT COMES TO HIS MIND...

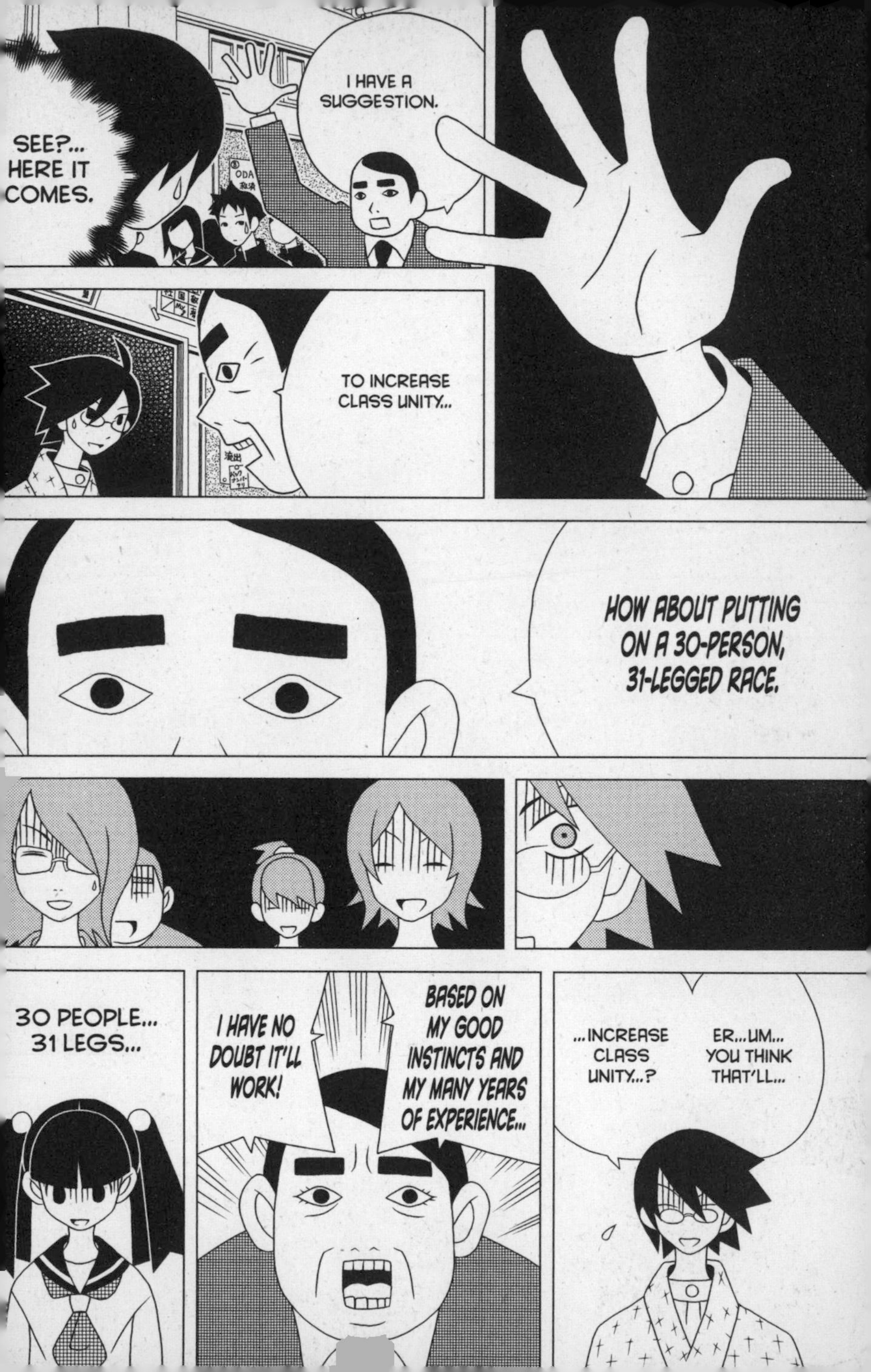
I HAVE A SUGGESTION.
SEE?... HERE IT COMES.
TO INCREASE CLASS UNITY...
HOW ABOUT PUTTING ON A 30-PERSON, 31-LEGGED RACE.
ER...UM... YOU THINK THAT'LL...
...INCREASE CLASS UNITY...?
BASED ON MY GOOD INSTINCTS AND MY MANY YEARS OF EXPERIENCE...
I HAVE NO DOUBT IT'LL WORK!
30 PEOPLE... 31 LEGS...

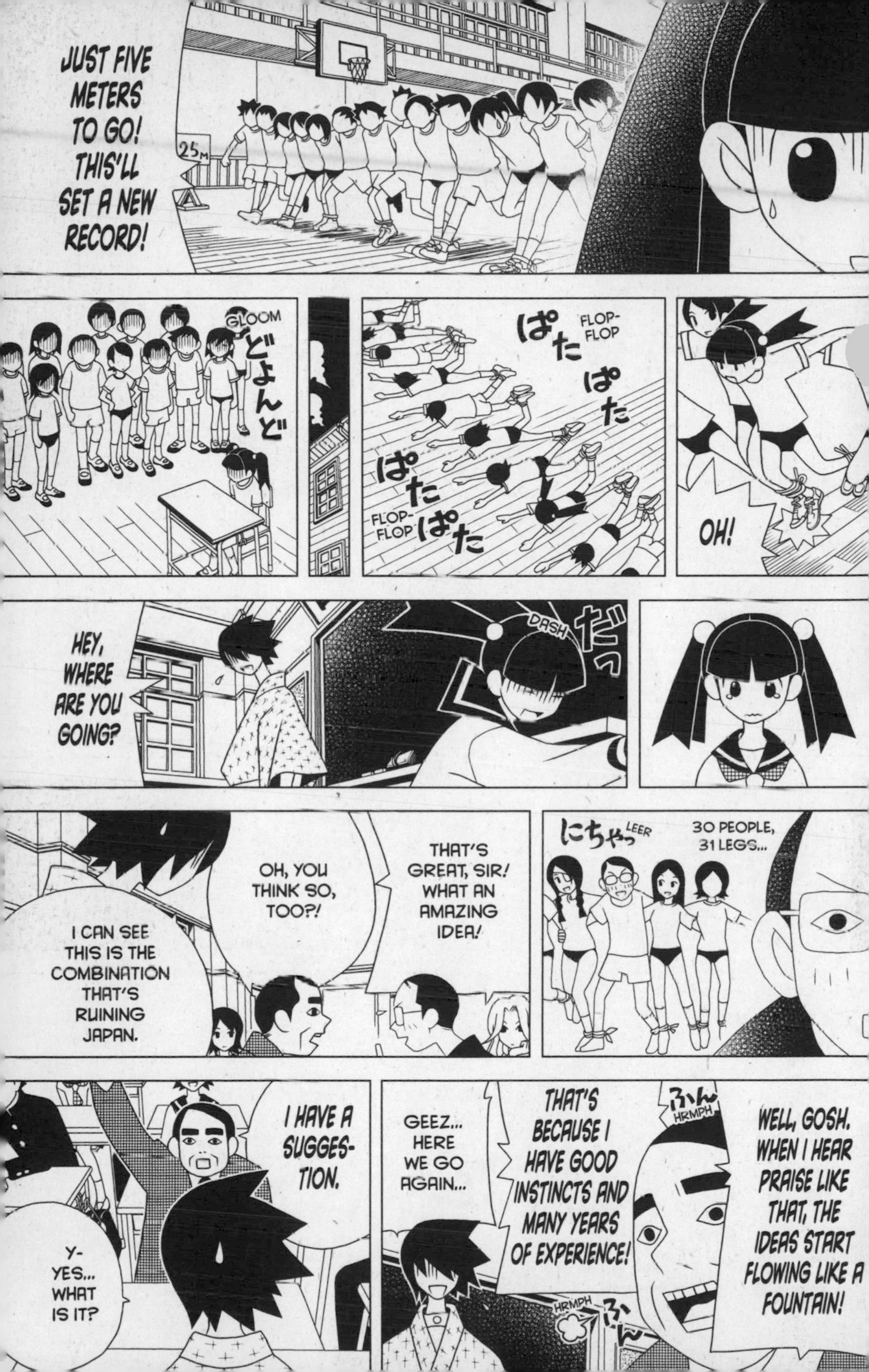
JUST FIVE METERS TO GO! THIS'LL SET A NEW RECORD!
25M
OH!
ぱたぱたぱたぱた FLOP-FLOP FLOP-FLOP
どよんど GLOOM
だっ DASH
HEY, WHERE ARE YOU GOING?
にちゃっ LEER
30 PEOPLE, 31 LEGS...
THAT'S GREAT, SIR! WHAT AN AMAZING IDEA!
OH, YOU THINK SO, TOO?!
I CAN SEE THIS IS THE COMBINATION THAT'S RUINING JAPAN.
ふん HRMPH
WELL, GOSH. WHEN I HEAR PRAISE LIKE THAT, THE IDEAS START FLOWING LIKE A FOUNTAIN!
THAT'S BECAUSE I HAVE GOOD INSTINCTS AND MANY YEARS OF EXPERIENCE!
HRMPH ふん
GEEZ... HERE WE GO AGAIN...
I HAVE A SUGGESTION.
Y-YES... WHAT IS IT?

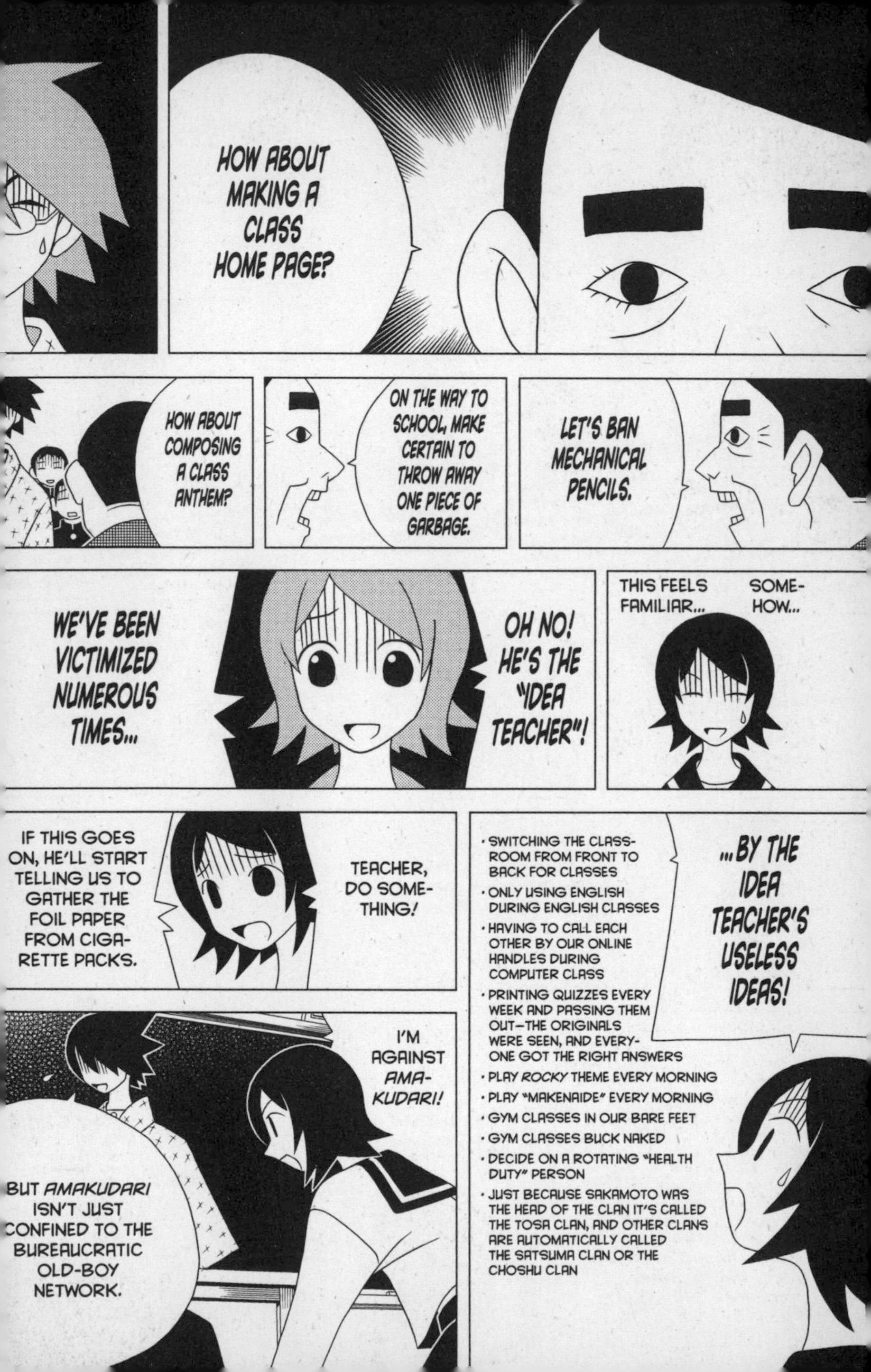
HOW ABOUT MAKING A CLASS HOME PAGE?
LET'S BAN MECHANICAL PENCILS.
ON THE WAY TO SCHOOL, MAKE CERTAIN TO THROW AWAY ONE PIECE OF GARBAGE.
HOW ABOUT COMPOSING A CLASS ANTHEM?
SOME-HOW...
THIS FEELS FAMILIAR...
OH NO! HE'S THE "IDEA TEACHER"!
WE'VE BEEN VICTIMIZED NUMEROUS TIMES...
...BY THE IDEA TEACHER'S USELESS IDEAS!
• SWITCHING THE CLASS-ROOM FROM FRONT TO BACK FOR CLASSES
• ONLY USING ENGLISH DURING ENGLISH CLASSES
• HAVING TO CALL EACH OTHER BY OUR ONLINE HANDLES DURING COMPUTER CLASS
• PRINTING QUIZZES EVERY WEEK AND PASSING THEM OUT—THE ORIGINALS WERE SEEN, AND EVERY-ONE GOT THE RIGHT ANSWERS
• PLAY *ROCKY* THEME EVERY MORNING
• PLAY "MAKENAIDE" EVERY MORNING
• GYM CLASSES IN OUR BARE FEET
• GYM CLASSES BUCK NAKED
• DECIDE ON A ROTATING "HEALTH DUTY" PERSON
• JUST BECAUSE SAKAMOTO WAS THE HEAD OF THE CLAN IT'S CALLED THE TOSA CLAN, AND OTHER CLANS ARE AUTOMATICALLY CALLED THE SATSUMA CLAN OR THE CHOSHU CLAN
TEACHER, DO SOME-THING!
IF THIS GOES ON, HE'LL START TELLING US TO GATHER THE FOIL PAPER FROM CIGA-RETTE PACKS.
I'M AGAINST *AMA-KUDARI!*
BUT *AMAKUDARI* ISN'T JUST CONFINED TO THE BUREAUCRATIC OLD-BOY NETWORK.

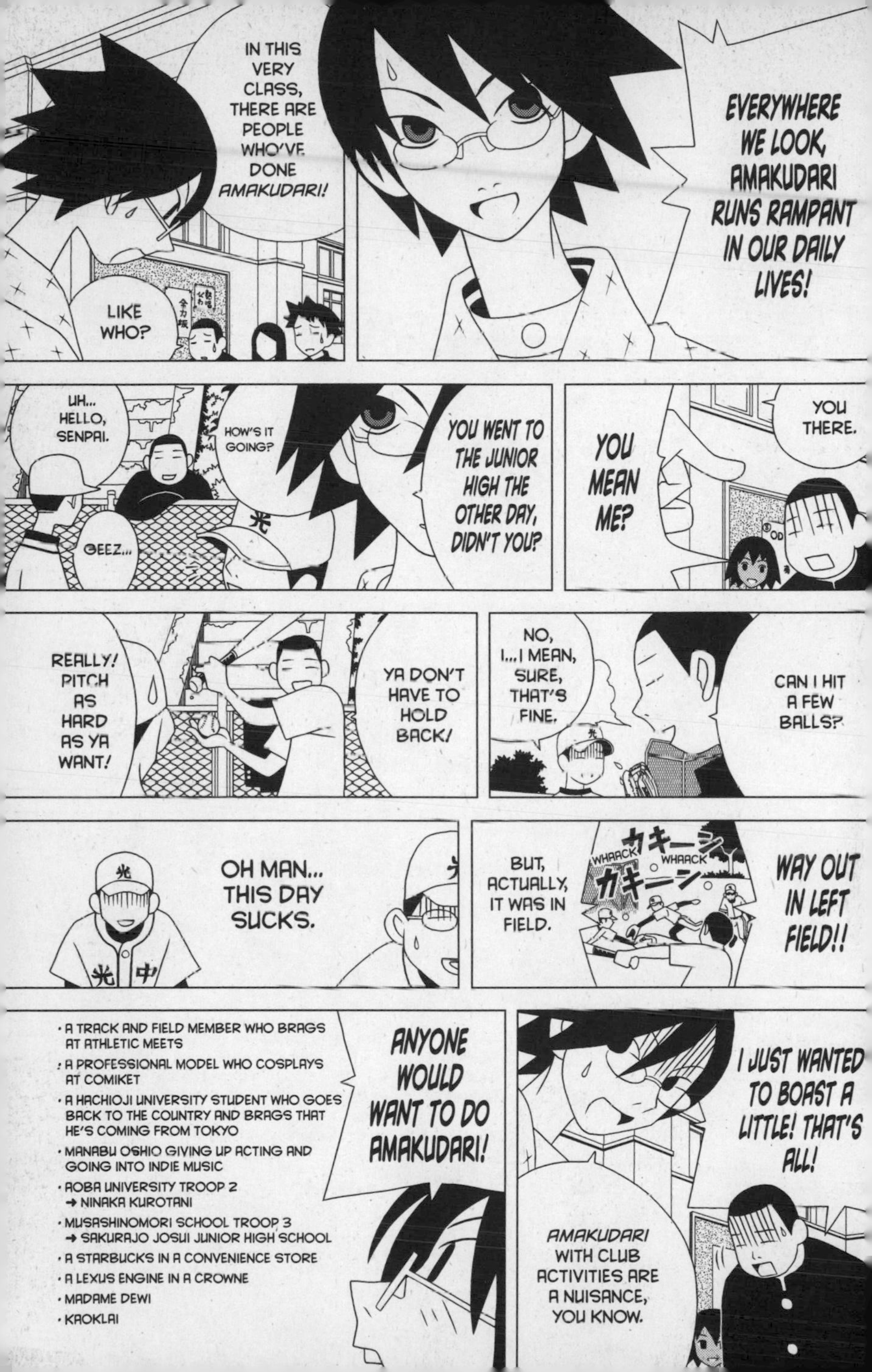
EVERYWHERE WE LOOK, AMAKUDARI RUNS RAMPANT IN OUR DAILY LIVES!
IN THIS VERY CLASS, THERE ARE PEOPLE WHO'VE DONE AMAKUDARI!
LIKE WHO?
YOU THERE.
YOU MEAN ME?
YOU WENT TO THE JUNIOR HIGH THE OTHER DAY, DIDN'T YOU?
HOW'S IT GOING?
UH... HELLO, SENPAI.
GEEZ...
CAN I HIT A FEW BALLS?
NO, I...I MEAN, SURE, THAT'S FINE.
YA DON'T HAVE TO HOLD BACK!
REALLY! PITCH AS HARD AS YA WANT!
WAY OUT IN LEFT FIELD!!
カキーン WHAACK
カキーン WHAACK
BUT, ACTUALLY, IT WAS IN FIELD.
OH MAN... THIS DAY SUCKS.
I JUST WANTED TO BOAST A LITTLE! THAT'S ALL!
AMAKUDARI WITH CLUB ACTIVITIES ARE A NUISANCE, YOU KNOW.
ANYONE WOULD WANT TO DO AMAKUDARI!
• A TRACK AND FIELD MEMBER WHO BRAGS AT ATHLETIC MEETS
• A PROFESSIONAL MODEL WHO COSPLAYS AT COMIKET
• A HACHIOJI UNIVERSITY STUDENT WHO GOES BACK TO THE COUNTRY AND BRAGS THAT HE'S COMING FROM TOKYO
• MANABU OSHIO GIVING UP ACTING AND GOING INTO INDIE MUSIC
• AOBA UNIVERSITY TROOP 2 → NINAKA KUROTANI
• MUSASHINOMORI SCHOOL TROOP 3 → SAKURAJO JOSUI JUNIOR HIGH SCHOOL
• A STARBUCKS IN A CONVENIENCE STORE
• A LEXUS ENGINE IN A CROWNE
• MADAME DEWI
• KAOKLAI

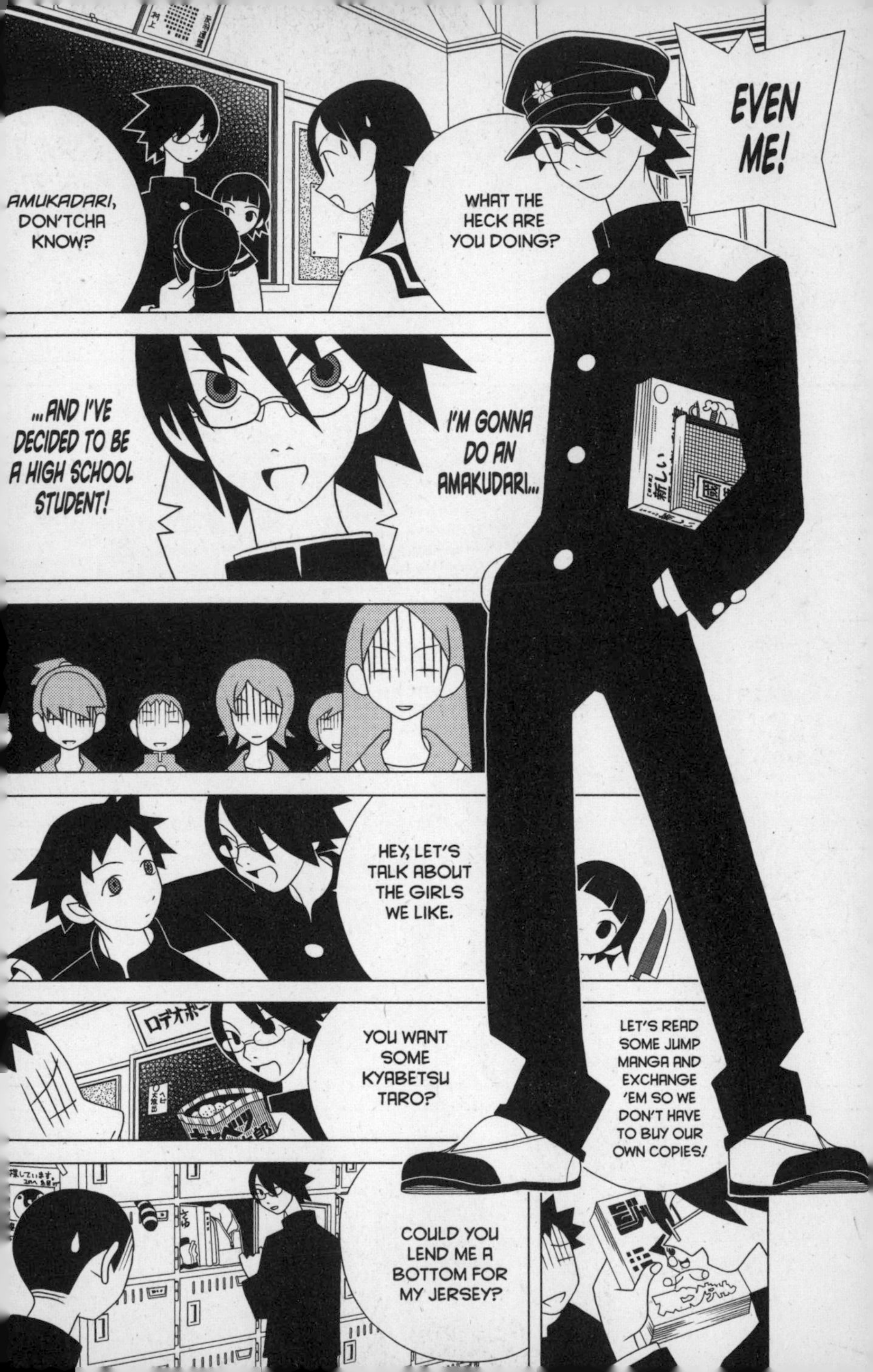
EVEN ME!
WHAT THE HECK ARE YOU DOING?
AMUKADARI, DON'TCHA KNOW?
I'M GONNA DO AN AMAKUDARI...
...AND I'VE DECIDED TO BE A HIGH SCHOOL STUDENT!
HEY, LET'S TALK ABOUT THE GIRLS WE LIKE.
LET'S READ SOME JUMP MANGA AND EXCHANGE 'EM SO WE DON'T HAVE TO BUY OUR OWN COPIES!
YOU WANT SOME KYABETSU TARO?
COULD YOU LEND ME A BOTTOM FOR MY JERSEY?

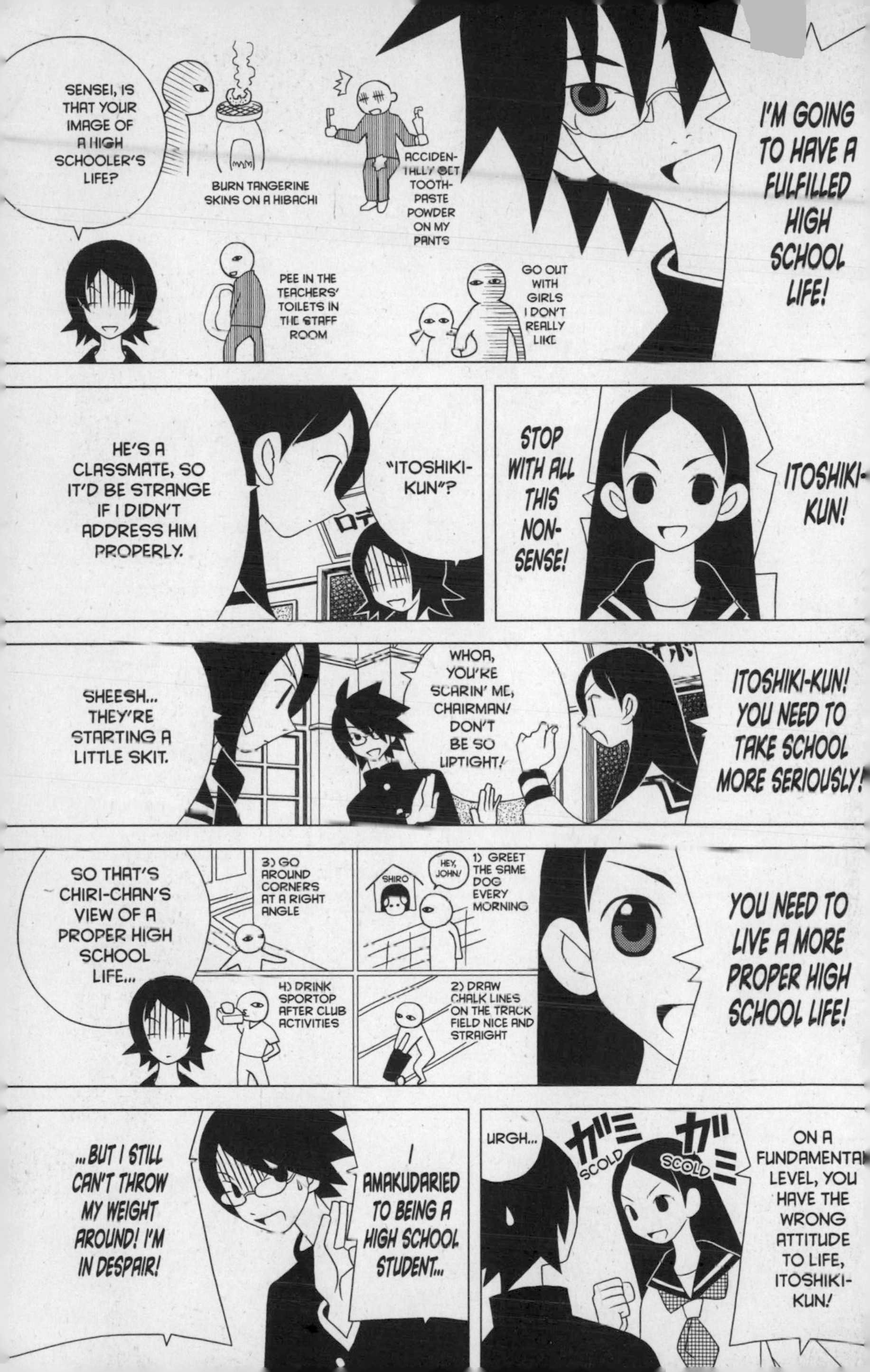
I'M GOING TO HAVE A FULFILLED HIGH SCHOOL LIFE!
ACCIDENTALLY GET TOOTHPASTE POWDER ON MY PANTS
BURN TANGERINE SKINS ON A HIBACHI
GO OUT WITH GIRLS I DON'T REALLY LIKE
PEE IN THE TEACHERS' TOILETS IN THE STAFF ROOM
SENSEI, IS THAT YOUR IMAGE OF A HIGH SCHOOLER'S LIFE?
ITOSHIKI-KUN!
STOP WITH ALL THIS NONSENSE!
"ITOSHIKI-KUN"?
HE'S A CLASSMATE, SO IT'D BE STRANGE IF I DIDN'T ADDRESS HIM PROPERLY.
ITOSHIKI-KUN! YOU NEED TO TAKE SCHOOL MORE SERIOUSLY!
WHOA, YOU'RE SCARIN' ME, CHAIRMAN! DON'T BE SO UPTIGHT!
SHEESH... THEY'RE STARTING A LITTLE SKIT.
YOU NEED TO LIVE A MORE PROPER HIGH SCHOOL LIFE!
1) GREET THE SAME DOG EVERY MORNING
HEY, JOHN!
SHIRO
2) DRAW CHALK LINES ON THE TRACK FIELD NICE AND STRAIGHT
3) GO AROUND CORNERS AT A RIGHT ANGLE
4) DRINK SPORTOP AFTER CLUB ACTIVITIES
SO THAT'S CHIRI-CHAN'S VIEW OF A PROPER HIGH SCHOOL LIFE...
ON A FUNDAMENTA LEVEL, YOU HAVE THE WRONG ATTITUDE TO LIFE, ITOSHIKI-KUN!
SCOLD
SCOLD
URGH...
I AMAKUDARIED TO BEING A HIGH SCHOOL STUDENT...
...BUT I STILL CAN'T THROW MY WEIGHT AROUND! I'M IN DESPAIR!

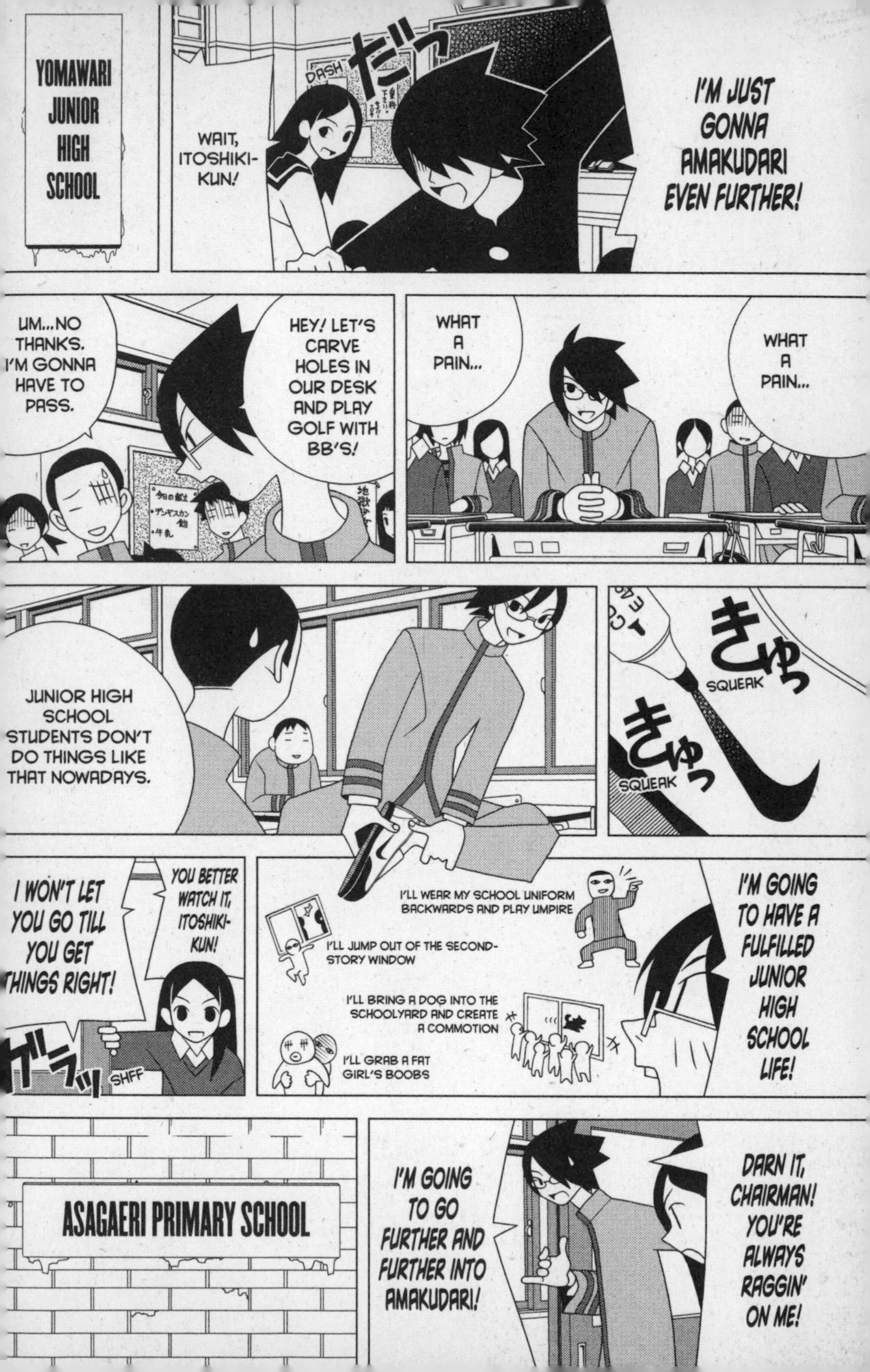
I'M JUST GONNA AMAKUDARI EVEN FURTHER!
だっ
DASH
WAIT, ITOSHIKI-KUN!
YOMAWARI JUNIOR HIGH SCHOOL
WHAT A PAIN...
WHAT A PAIN...
HEY! LET'S CARVE HOLES IN OUR DESK AND PLAY GOLF WITH BB'S!
UM...NO THANKS. I'M GONNA HAVE TO PASS.
きゅっ
SQUEAK
きゅっ
SQUEAK
JUNIOR HIGH SCHOOL STUDENTS DON'T DO THINGS LIKE THAT NOWADAYS.
I'M GOING TO HAVE A FULFILLED JUNIOR HIGH SCHOOL LIFE!
I'LL WEAR MY SCHOOL UNIFORM BACKWARDS AND PLAY UMPIRE
I'LL JUMP OUT OF THE SECOND-STORY WINDOW
I'LL BRING A DOG INTO THE SCHOOLYARD AND CREATE A COMMOTION
I'LL GRAB A FAT GIRL'S BOOBS
YOU BETTER WATCH IT, ITOSHIKI-KUN!
I WON'T LET YOU GO TILL YOU GET THINGS RIGHT!
ガラッ
SHFF
DARN IT, CHAIRMAN! YOU'RE ALWAYS RAGGIN' ON ME!
I'M GOING TO GO FURTHER AND FURTHER INTO AMAKUDARI!
ASAGAERI PRIMARY SCHOOL

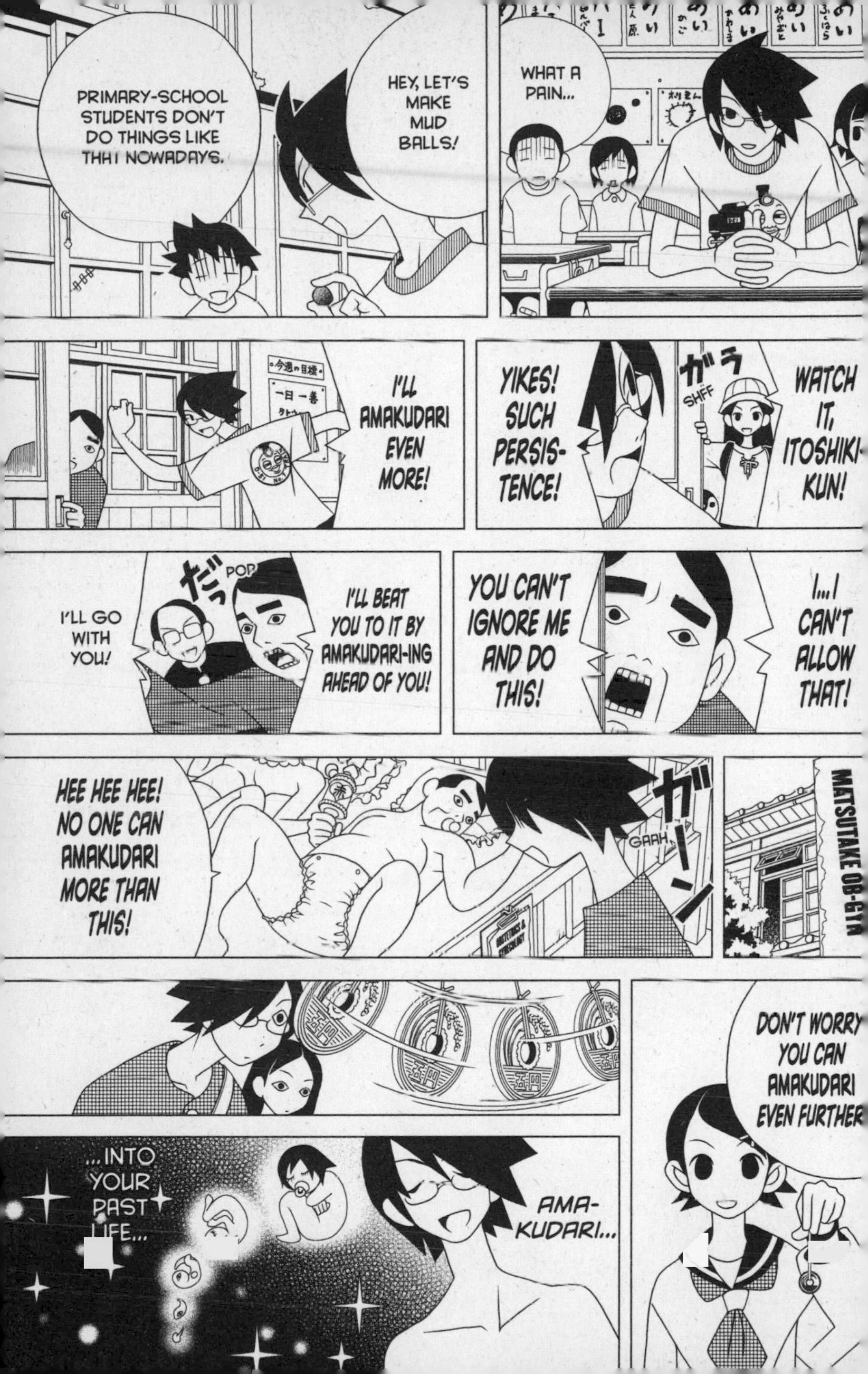
WHAT A PAIN...
HEY, LET'S MAKE MUD BALLS!
PRIMARY-SCHOOL STUDENTS DON'T DO THINGS LIKE THAT NOWADAYS.
ガラ
SHFF
WATCH IT, ITOSHIKI-KUN!
YIKES! SUCH PERSISTENCE!
今週の目標
一日一善
I'LL AMAKUDARI EVEN MORE!
I...I CAN'T ALLOW THAT!
YOU CAN'T IGNORE ME AND DO THIS!
だっ
POP
I'LL BEAT YOU TO IT BY AMAKUDARI-ING AHEAD OF YOU!
I'LL GO WITH YOU!
MATSUTAKE OB-GYN
ガーン
GAAH
HEE HEE HEE! NO ONE CAN AMAKUDARI MORE THAN THIS!
DON'T WORRY YOU CAN AMAKUDARI EVEN FURTHER
AMA-KUDARI...
...INTO YOUR PAST LIFE...

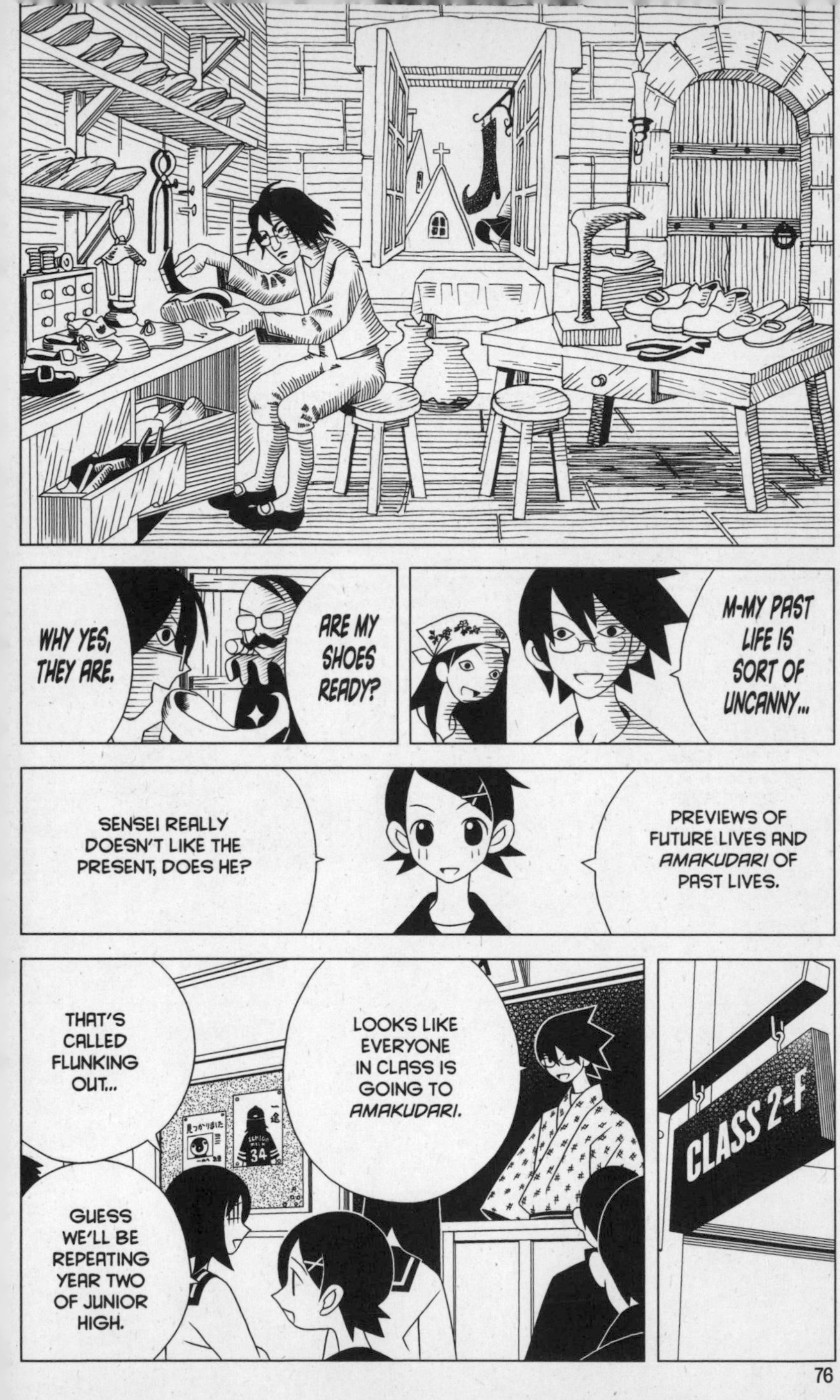
M-MY PAST LIFE IS SORT OF UNCANNY...
ARE MY SHOES READY?
WHY YES, THEY ARE.
PREVIEWS OF FUTURE LIVES AND *AMAKUDARI* OF PAST LIVES.
SENSEI REALLY DOESN'T LIKE THE PRESENT, DOES HE?
CLASS 2-F
LOOKS LIKE EVERYONE IN CLASS IS GOING TO *AMAKUDARI*.
THAT'S CALLED FLUNKING OUT...
GUESS WE'LL BE REPEATING YEAR TWO OF JUNIOR HIGH.

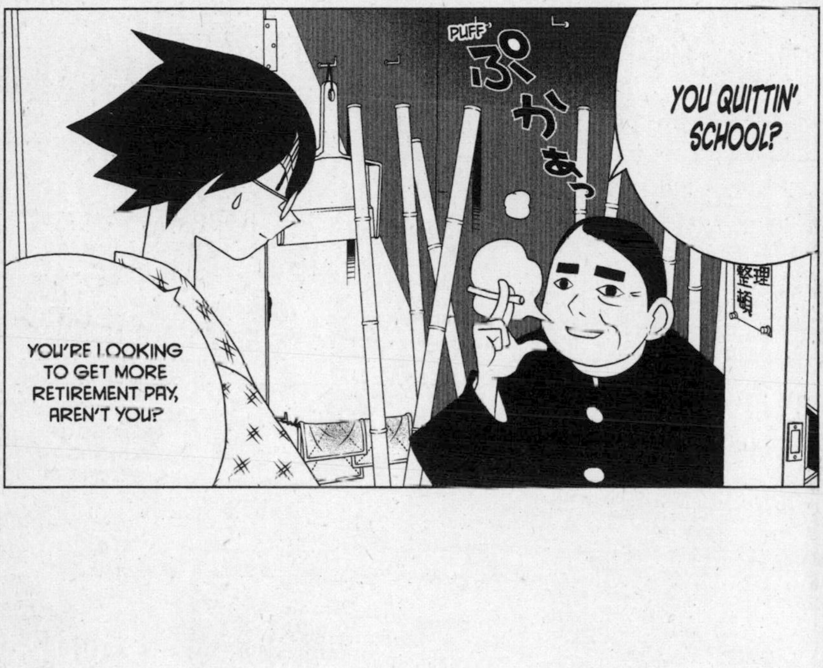
YOU QUITTIN' SCHOOL?
PUFF
ぷかあっ
YOU'RE LOOKING TO GET MORE RETIREMENT PAY, AREN'T YOU?

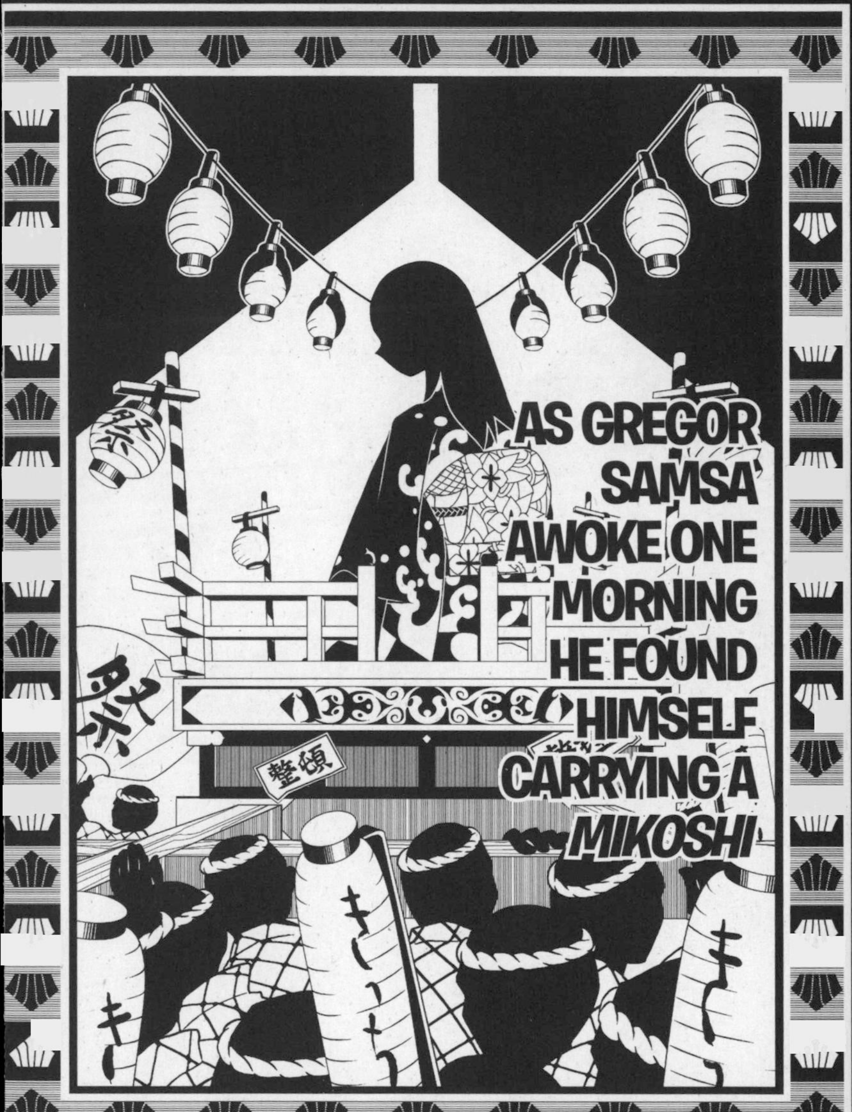
AS GREGOR SAMSA AWOKE ONE MORNING HE FOUND HIMSELF CARRYING A MIKOSHI
祭
整頓

CHAPTER 26

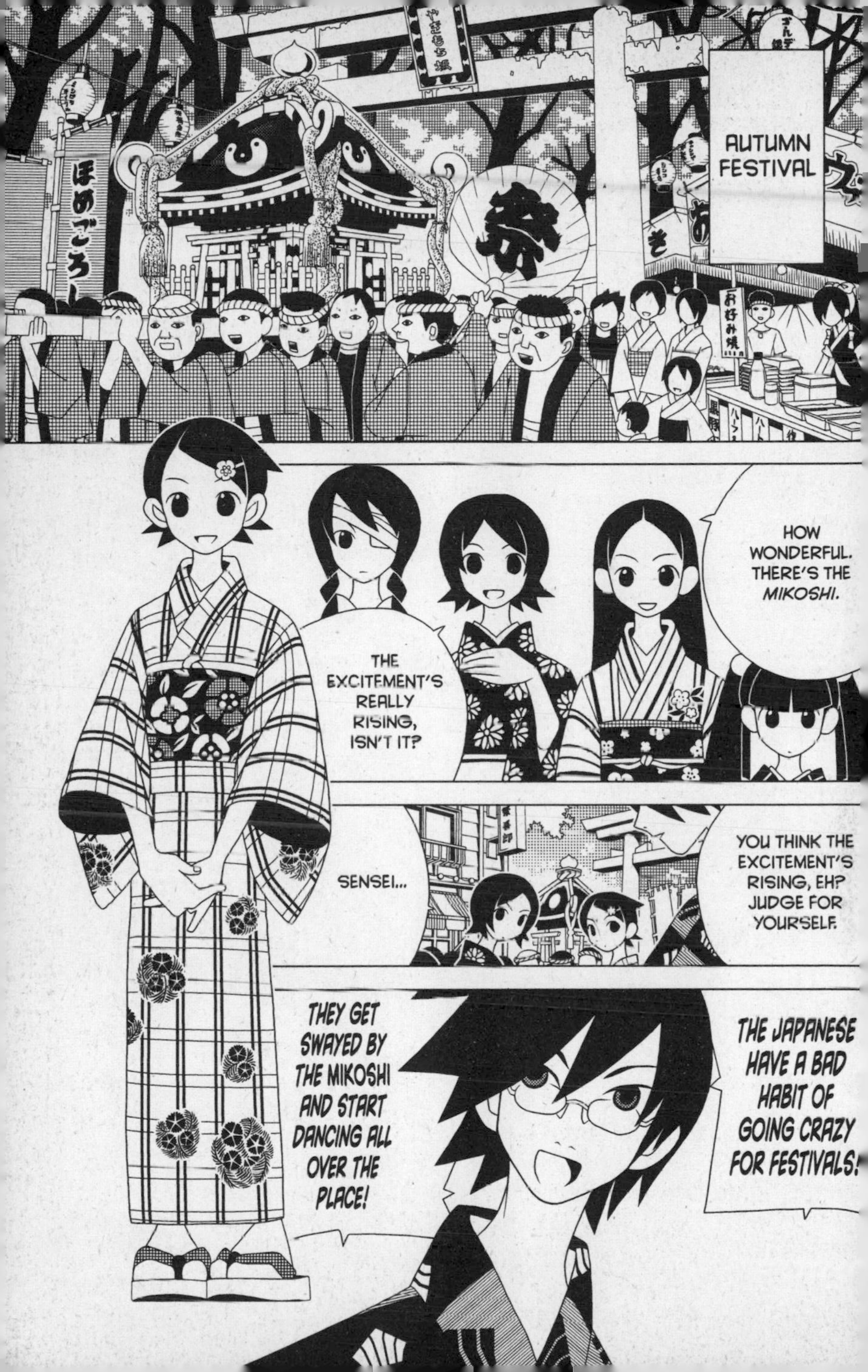
AUTUMN FESTIVAL
お好み焼
祭
ほめごろし
HOW WONDERFUL. THERE'S THE *MIKOSHI*.
THE EXCITEMENT'S REALLY RISING, ISN'T IT?
YOU THINK THE EXCITEMENT'S RISING, EH? JUDGE FOR YOURSELF.
SENSEI...
THE JAPANESE HAVE A BAD HABIT OF GOING CRAZY FOR FESTIVALS!
THEY GET SWAYED BY THE MIKOSHI AND START DANCING ALL OVER THE PLACE!

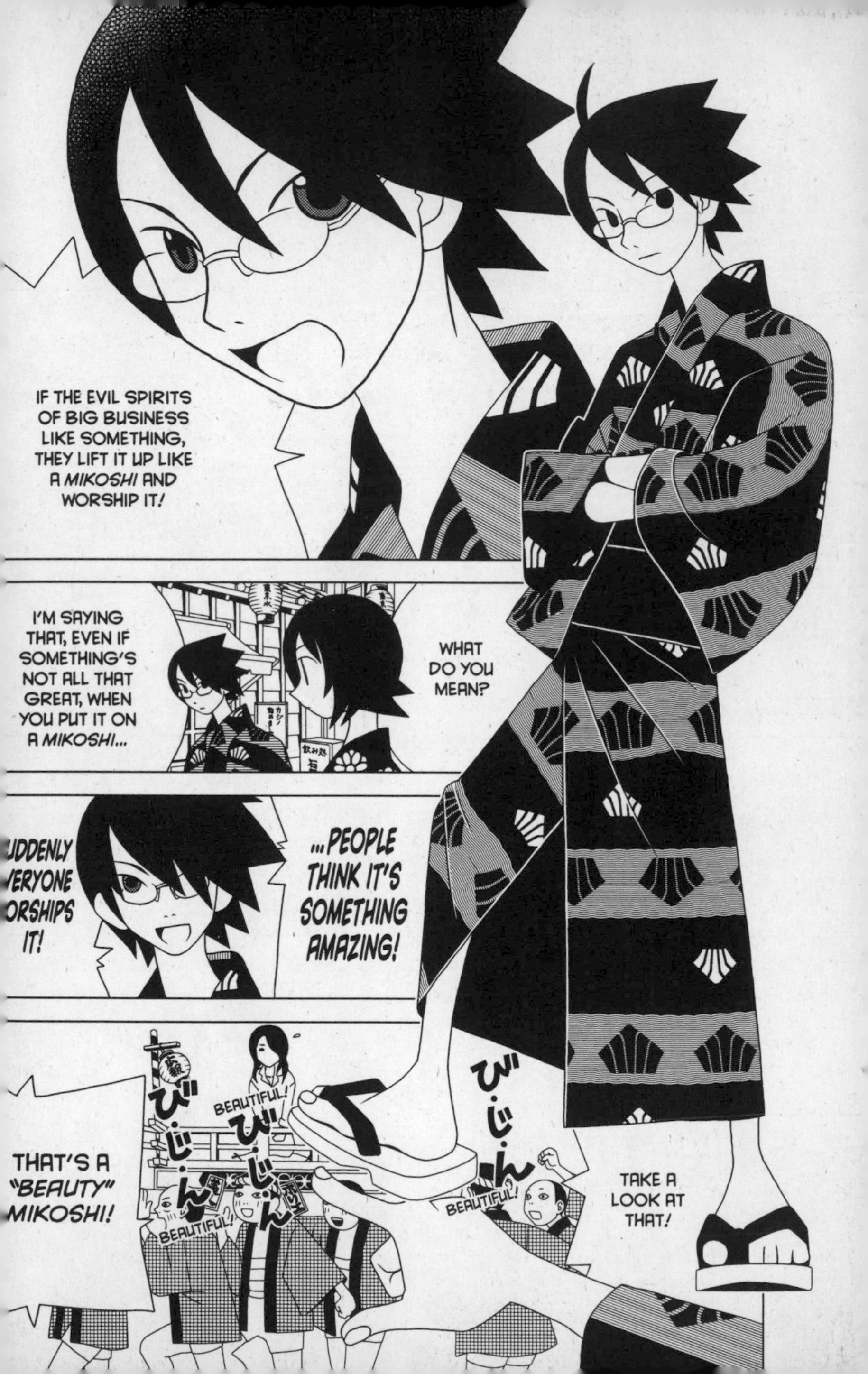
IF THE EVIL SPIRITS OF BIG BUSINESS LIKE SOMETHING, THEY LIFT IT UP LIKE A *MIKOSHI* AND WORSHIP IT!
WHAT DO YOU MEAN?
I'M SAYING THAT, EVEN IF SOMETHING'S NOT ALL THAT GREAT, WHEN YOU PUT IT ON A *MIKOSHI*...
...PEOPLE THINK IT'S SOMETHING AMAZING!
UDDENLY VERYONE ORSHIPS IT!
TAKE A LOOK AT THAT!
びじん
BEAUTIFUL!
びじん
BEAUTIFUL!
びじん
BEAUTIFUL!
びじん
BEAUTIFUL!
THAT'S A "BEAUTY" MIKOSHI!

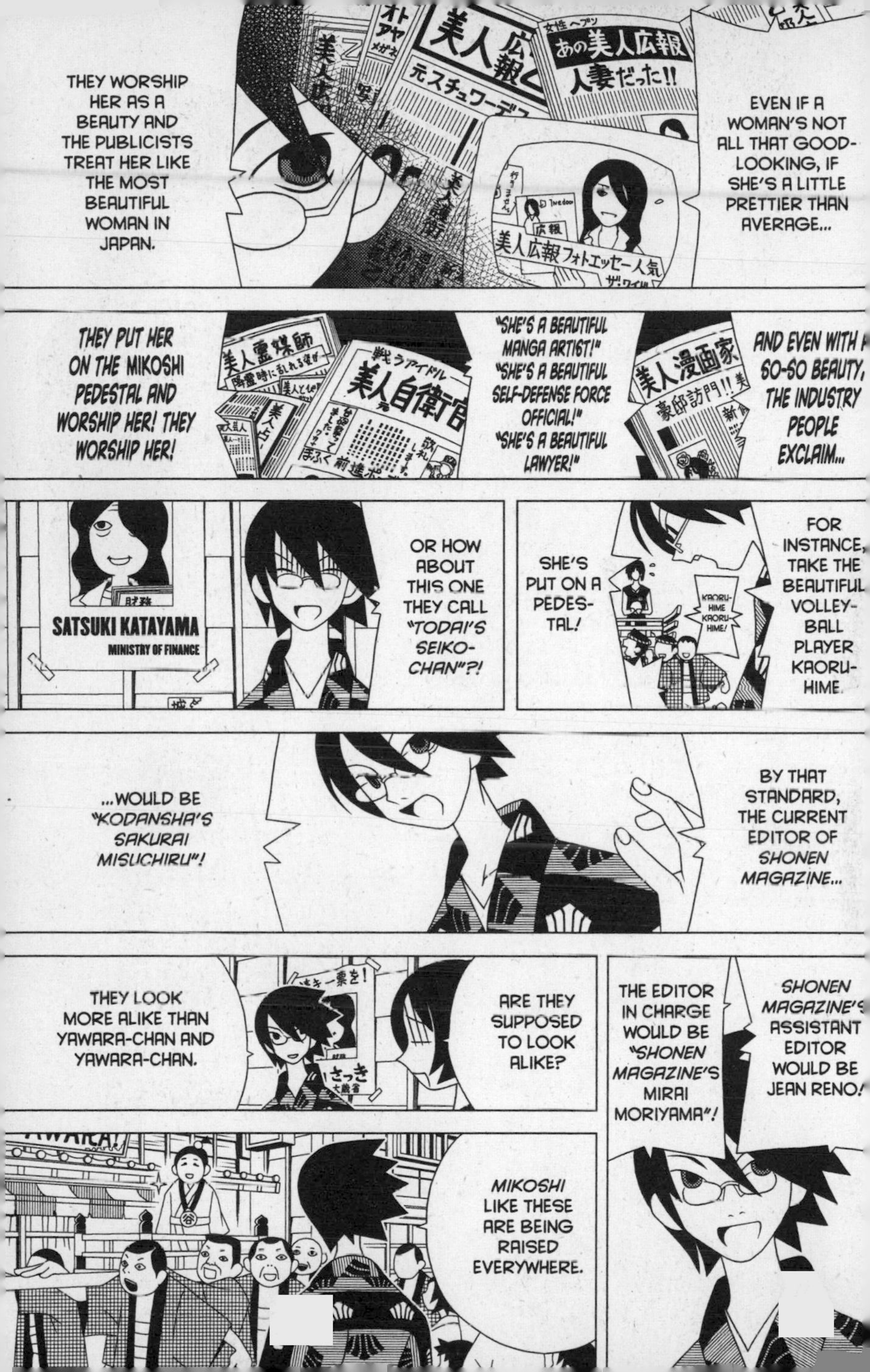
EVEN IF A WOMAN'S NOT ALL THAT GOOD-LOOKING, IF SHE'S A LITTLE PRETTIER THAN AVERAGE...
あの美人広報 人妻だった!!
美人広報
元スチュワーデス
美人広報フォトエッセー人気
THEY WORSHIP HER AS A BEAUTY AND THE PUBLICISTS TREAT HER LIKE THE MOST BEAUTIFUL WOMAN IN JAPAN.
AND EVEN WITH
SO-SO BEAUTY, THE INDUSTRY PEOPLE EXCLAIM...
美人漫画家
豪邸訪問!!
"SHE'S A BEAUTIFUL MANGA ARTIST!" "SHE'S A BEAUTIFUL SELF-DEFENSE FORCE OFFICIAL!" "SHE'S A BEAUTIFUL LAWYER!"
戦うアイドル
美人自衛官
美人霊媒師
THEY PUT HER ON THE MIKOSHI PEDESTAL AND WORSHIP HER! THEY WORSHIP HER!
FOR INSTANCE, TAKE THE BEAUTIFUL VOLLEY-BALL PLAYER KAORU-HIME.
SHE'S PUT ON A PEDES-TAL!
KAORU-HIME KAORU-HIME!
OR HOW ABOUT THIS ONE THEY CALL "TODAI'S SEIKO-CHAN"?!
SATSUKI KATAYAMA
MINISTRY OF FINANCE
BY THAT STANDARD, THE CURRENT EDITOR OF SHONEN MAGAZINE...
...WOULD BE "KODANSHA'S SAKURAI MISUCHIRU"!
SHONEN MAGAZINE'S ASSISTANT EDITOR WOULD BE JEAN RENO!
THE EDITOR IN CHARGE WOULD BE "SHONEN MAGAZINE'S MIRAI MORIYAMA"!
ARE THEY SUPPOSED TO LOOK ALIKE?
さっき
THEY LOOK MORE ALIKE THAN YAWARA-CHAN AND YAWARA-CHAN.
MIKOSHI LIKE THESE ARE BEING RAISED EVERYWHERE.

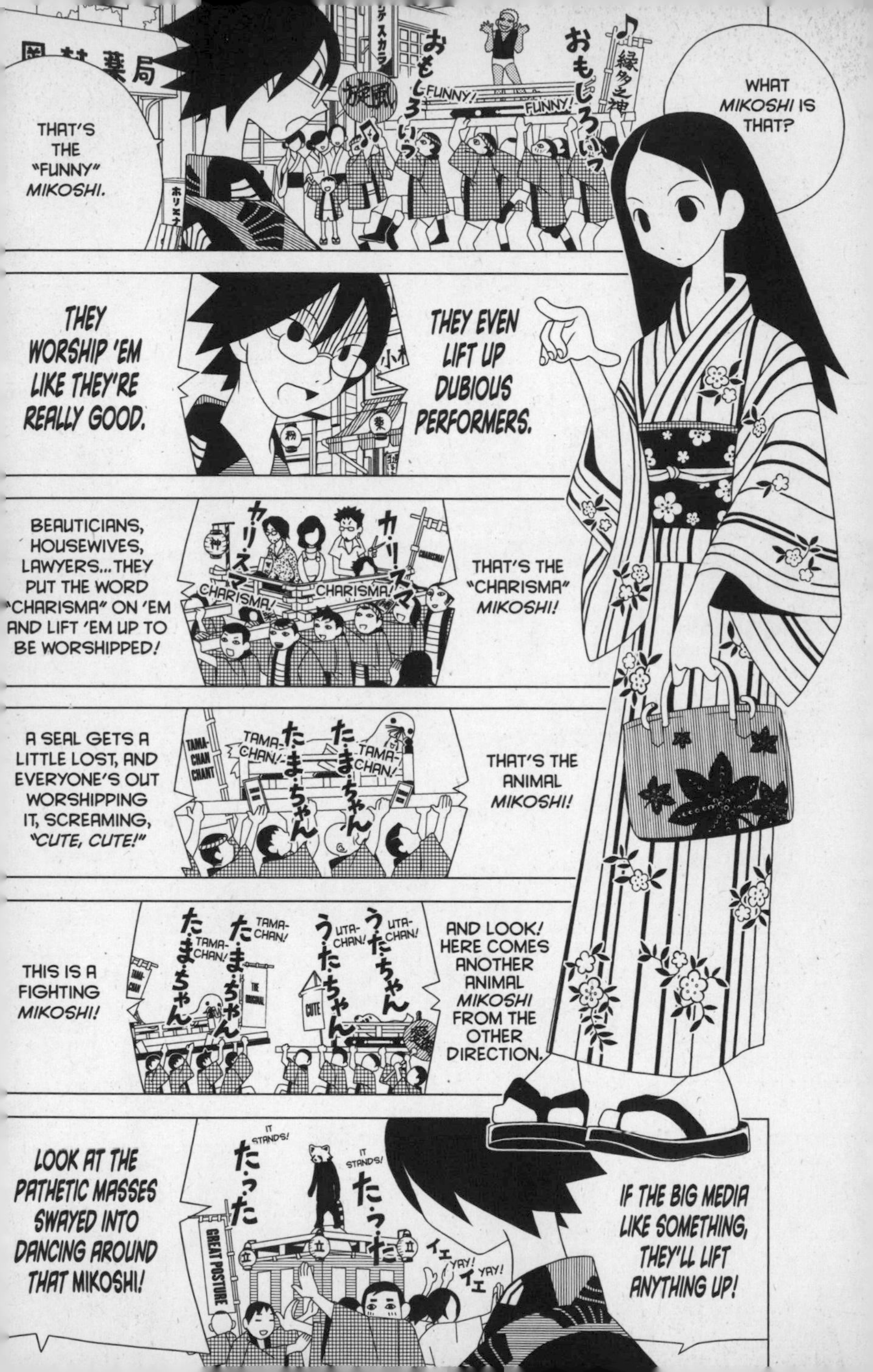
WHAT MIKOSHI IS THAT?
おもしろいっ
縁多之神
FUNNY!
FUNNY!
おもしろいっ
旋風
THAT'S THE "FUNNY" MIKOSHI.
THEY EVEN LIFT UP DUBIOUS PERFORMERS.
THEY WORSHIP 'EM LIKE THEY'RE REALLY GOOD.
THAT'S THE "CHARISMA" MIKOSHI!
カリスマ
CHARISMA!
CHARISMA!
カリスマ
CHARISMA!
BEAUTICIANS, HOUSEWIVES, LAWYERS...THEY PUT THE WORD "CHARISMA" ON 'EM AND LIFT 'EM UP TO BE WORSHIPPED!
THAT'S THE ANIMAL MIKOSHI!
たまちゃん
TAMA-CHAN!
たまちゃん
TAMA-CHAN!
TAMA-CHAN CHANT
A SEAL GETS A LITTLE LOST, AND EVERYONE'S OUT WORSHIPPING IT, SCREAMING, "CUTE, CUTE!"
AND LOOK! HERE COMES ANOTHER ANIMAL MIKOSHI FROM THE OTHER DIRECTION.
UTA-CHAN!
うたちゃん
UTA-CHAN!
うたちゃん
CUTE
TAMA-CHAN!
たまちゃん
TAMA-CHAN!
たまちゃん
THE ORIGINAL
TAMA-CHAN
THIS IS A FIGHTING MIKOSHI!
IF THE BIG MEDIA LIKE SOMETHING, THEY'LL LIFT ANYTHING UP!
YAY!
イエ
YAY!
イエ
IT STANDS!
たった
IT STANDS!
たった
GREAT POSTURE
LOOK AT THE PATHETIC MASSES SWAYED INTO DANCING AROUND THAT MIKOSHI!

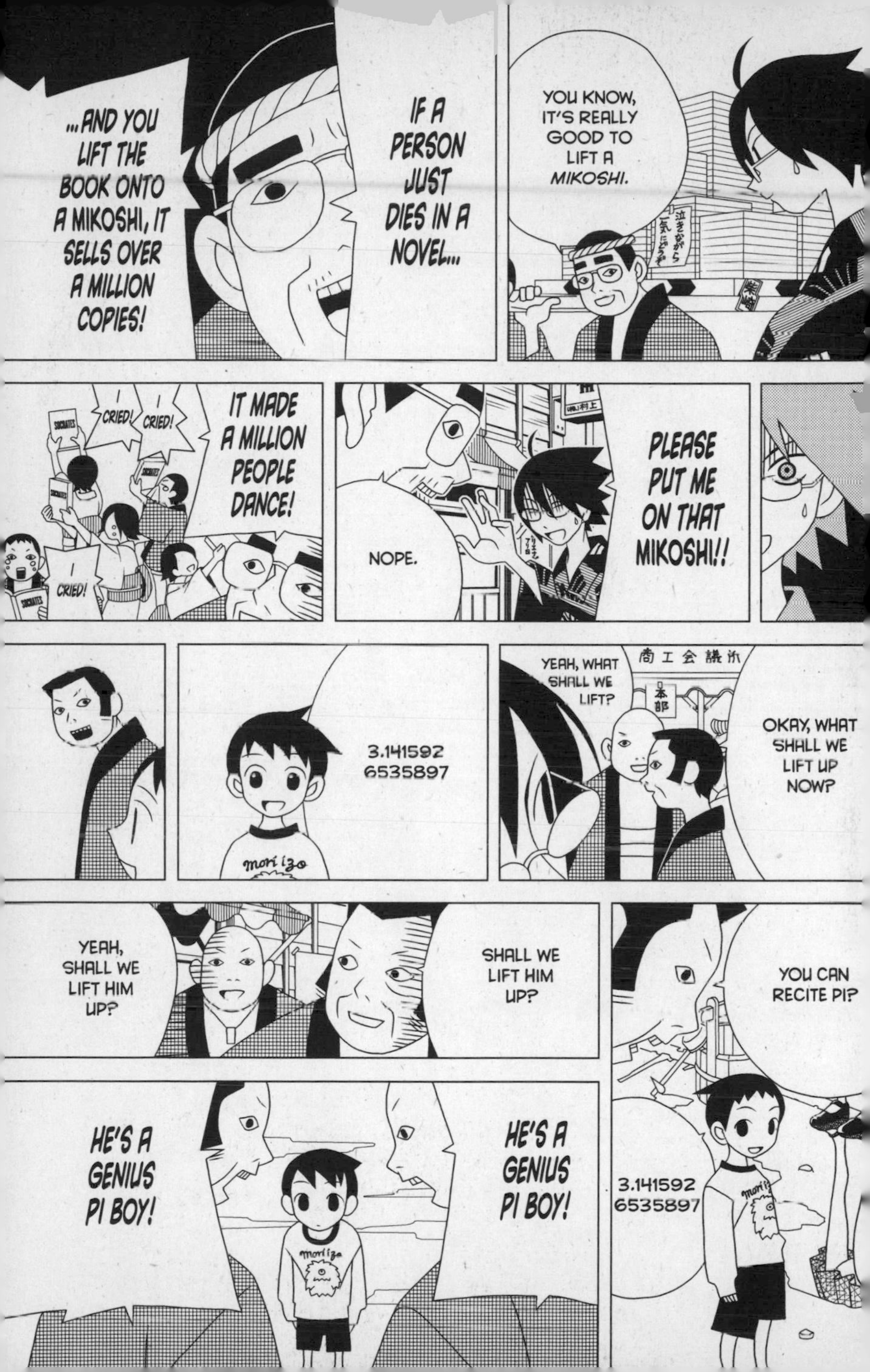
YOU KNOW, IT'S REALLY GOOD TO LIFT A MIKOSHI.
泣きながら一気にどうぞ
IF A PERSON JUST DIES IN A NOVEL...
...AND YOU LIFT THE BOOK ONTO A MIKOSHI, IT SELLS OVER A MILLION COPIES!
PLEASE PUT ME ON THAT MIKOSHI!!
NOPE.
IT MADE A MILLION PEOPLE DANCE!
I CRIED!
I CRIED!
I CRIED!
SOCRATES
OKAY, WHAT SHALL WE LIFT UP NOW?
商工会議所
本部
YEAH, WHAT SHALL WE LIFT?
3.141592 6535897
mori izo
YOU CAN RECITE PI?
3.141592 6535897
SHALL WE LIFT HIM UP?
YEAH, SHALL WE LIFT HIM UP?
HE'S A GENIUS PI BOY!
HE'S A GENIUS PI BOY!
mori izo

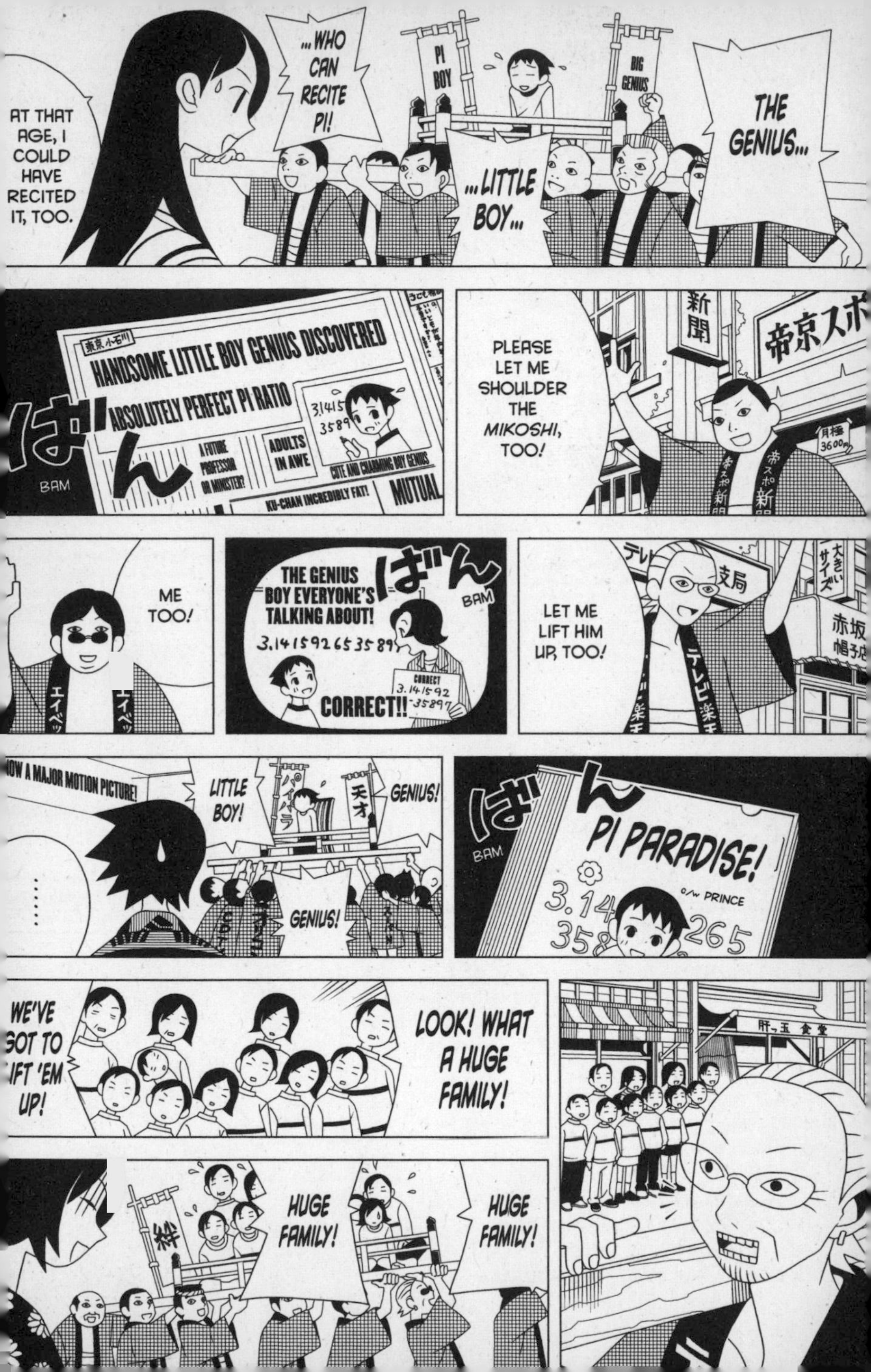
THE GENIUS...
BIG GENIUS
...LITTLE BOY...
PI BOY
...WHO CAN RECITE PI!
AT THAT AGE, I COULD HAVE RECITED IT, TOO.
新聞
帝京スポ
月極 3600円
PLEASE LET ME SHOULDER THE MIKOSHI, TOO!
帝スポ新聞
東京 小石川
HANDSOME LITTLE BOY GENIUS DISCOVERED
ABSOLUTELY PERFECT PI RATIO
3.1415 3589
A FUTURE PROFESSOR OR MINISTER?
ADULTS IN AWE
CUTE AND CHARMING BOY GENIUS
KU-CHAN INCREDIBLY FAT!
MUTUAL
ばん
BAM
テレ
支局
大きいサイズ
赤坂 帽子店
LET ME LIFT HIM UP, TOO!
テレビ楽天
THE GENIUS BOY EVERYONE'S TALKING ABOUT!
ばん
BAM
3.14159265358
CORRECT 3.141592-35897
CORRECT!!
ME TOO!
エイベッ
ばん
BAM
PI PARADISE!
C/W PRINCE
3.14 358 265
NOW A MAJOR MOTION PICTURE!
LITTLE BOY!
パイパラ
天才
GENIUS!
GENIUS!
......
肝っ玉食堂
LOOK! WHAT A HUGE FAMILY!
WE'VE GOT TO LIFT 'EM UP!
HUGE FAMILY!
HUGE FAMILY!
絆

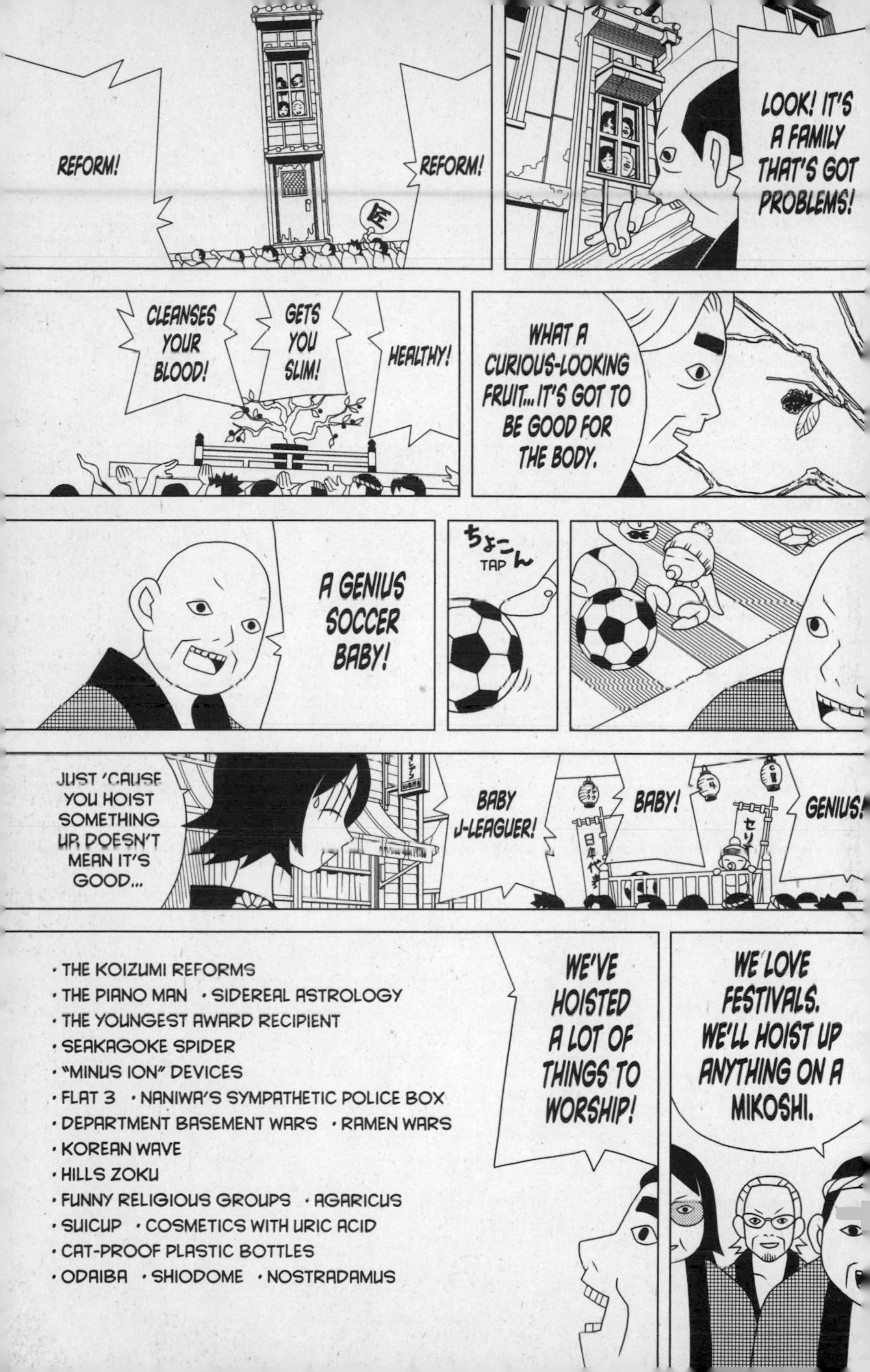
LOOK! IT'S A FAMILY THAT'S GOT PROBLEMS!
REFORM!
REFORM!
WHAT A CURIOUS-LOOKING FRUIT...IT'S GOT TO BE GOOD FOR THE BODY.
HEALTHY!
GETS YOU SLIM!
CLEANSES YOUR BLOOD!
ちょこん
TAP
A GENIUS SOCCER BABY!
GENIUS!
BABY!
BABY J-LEAGUER!
JUST 'CAUSE YOU HOIST SOMETHING UP DOESN'T MEAN IT'S GOOD...
WE LOVE FESTIVALS. WE'LL HOIST UP ANYTHING ON A MIKOSHI.
WE'VE HOISTED A LOT OF THINGS TO WORSHIP!
• THE KOIZUMI REFORMS
• THE PIANO MAN • SIDEREAL ASTROLOGY
• THE YOUNGEST AWARD RECIPIENT
• SEAKAGOKE SPIDER
• "MINUS ION" DEVICES
• FLAT 3 • NANIWA'S SYMPATHETIC POLICE BOX
• DEPARTMENT BASEMENT WARS • RAMEN WARS
• KOREAN WAVE
• HILLS ZOKU
• FUNNY RELIGIOUS GROUPS • AGARICUS
• SUICUP • COSMETICS WITH URIC ACID
• CAT-PROOF PLASTIC BOTTLES
• ODAIBA • SHIODOME • NOSTRADAMUS

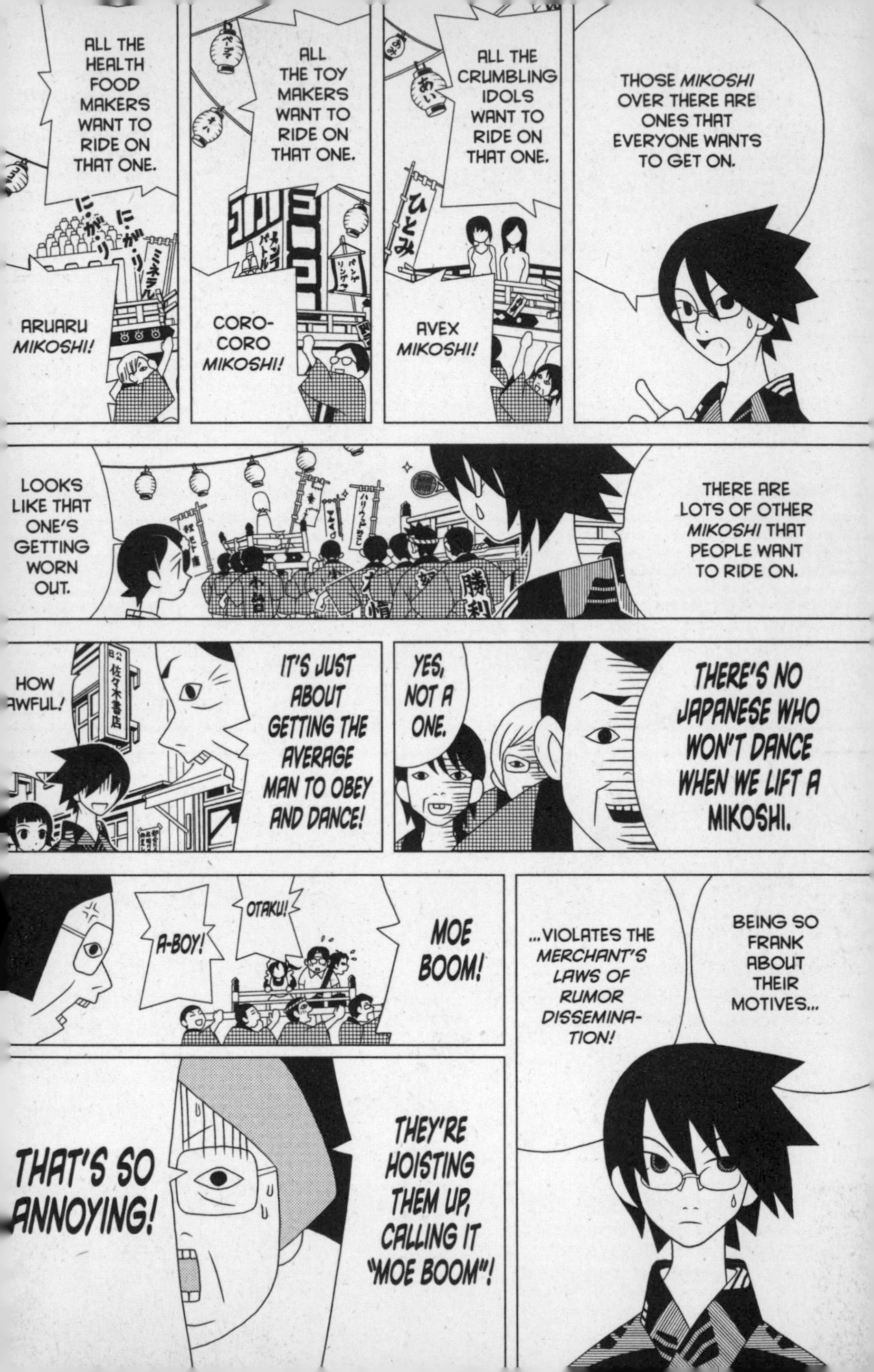
THOSE MIKOSHI OVER THERE ARE ONES THAT EVERYONE WANTS TO GET ON.
ALL THE CRUMBLING IDOLS WANT TO RIDE ON THAT ONE.
AVEX MIKOSHI!
ALL THE TOY MAKERS WANT TO RIDE ON THAT ONE.
CORO-CORO MIKOSHI!
ALL THE HEALTH FOOD MAKERS WANT TO RIDE ON THAT ONE.
ARUARU MIKOSHI!
THERE ARE LOTS OF OTHER MIKOSHI THAT PEOPLE WANT TO RIDE ON.
LOOKS LIKE THAT ONE'S GETTING WORN OUT.
THERE'S NO JAPANESE WHO WON'T DANCE WHEN WE LIFT A MIKOSHI.
YES, NOT A ONE.
IT'S JUST ABOUT GETTING THE AVERAGE MAN TO OBEY AND DANCE!
HOW AWFUL!
BEING SO FRANK ABOUT THEIR MOTIVES...
...VIOLATES THE MERCHANT'S LAWS OF RUMOR DISSEMINATION!
MOE BOOM!
OTAKU!
A-BOY!
THEY'RE HOISTING THEM UP, CALLING IT "MOE BOOM"!
THAT'S SO ANNOYING!

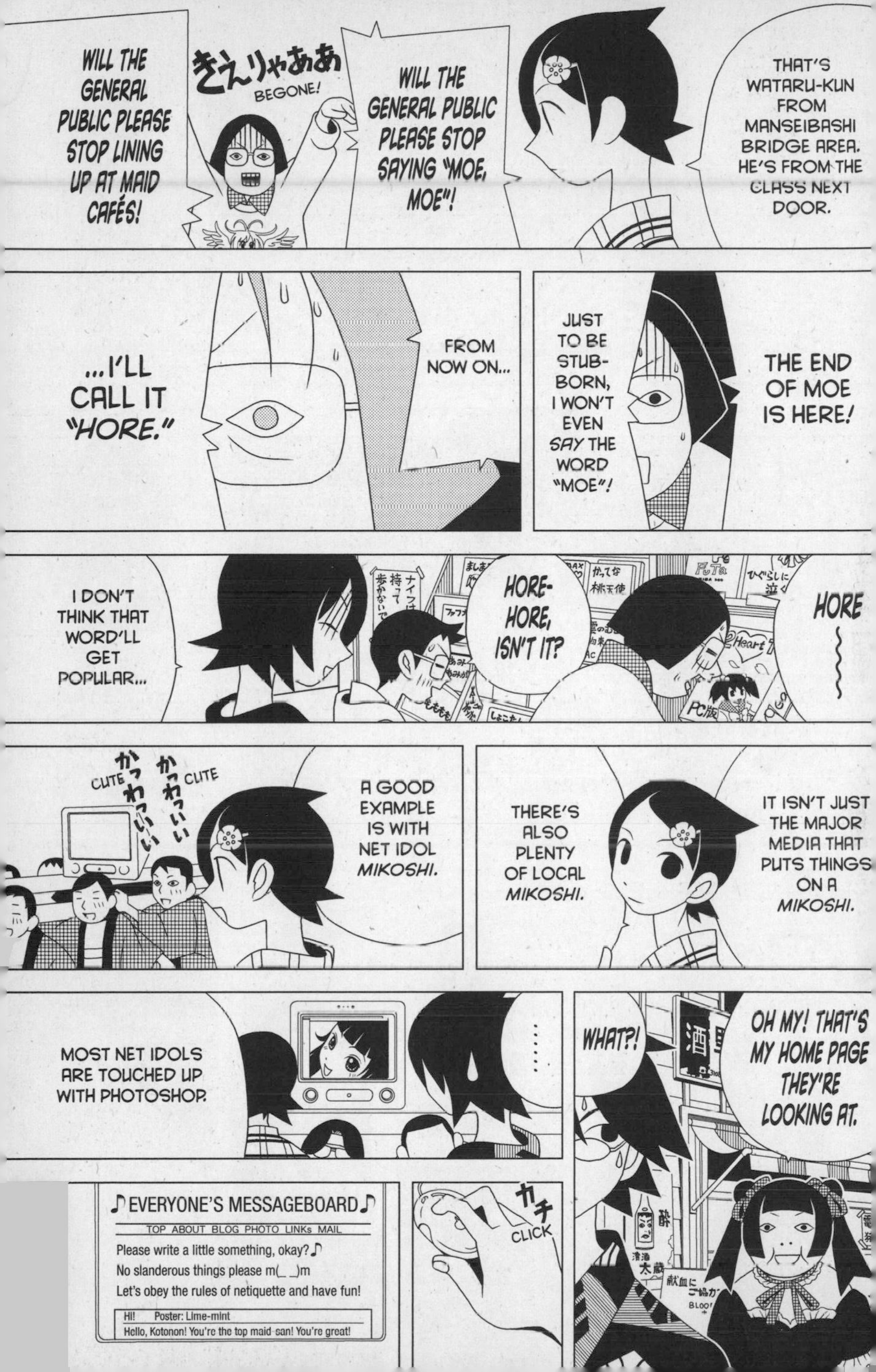
THAT'S WATARU-KUN FROM MANSEIBASHI BRIDGE AREA. HE'S FROM THE CLASS NEXT DOOR.
WILL THE GENERAL PUBLIC PLEASE STOP SAYING "MOE, MOE"!
きえりゃあああ
BEGONE!
WILL THE GENERAL PUBLIC PLEASE STOP LINING UP AT MAID CAFÉS!
THE END OF MOE IS HERE!
JUST TO BE STUBBORN, I WON'T EVEN SAY THE WORD "MOE"!
FROM NOW ON...
...I'LL CALL IT "HORE."
HORE~~
HORE-HORE, ISN'T IT?
I DON'T THINK THAT WORD'LL GET POPULAR...
IT ISN'T JUST THE MAJOR MEDIA THAT PUTS THINGS ON A MIKOSHI.
THERE'S ALSO PLENTY OF LOCAL MIKOSHI.
A GOOD EXAMPLE IS WITH NET IDOL MIKOSHI.
かっわいい
CUTE
かっわいい
CUTE
OH MY! THAT'S MY HOME PAGE THEY'RE LOOKING AT.
WHAT?!
酒
献血にご協力
BLOOD
......
MOST NET IDOLS ARE TOUCHED UP WITH PHOTOSHOP.
カチ
CLICK
♪EVERYONE'S MESSAGEBOARD♪
TOP ABOUT BLOG PHOTO LINKs MAIL
Please write a little something, okay?♪
No slanderous things please m(_ _)m
Let's obey the rules of netiquette and have fun!
Hi! Poster: Lime-mint
Hello, Kotonon! You're the top maid-san! You're great!

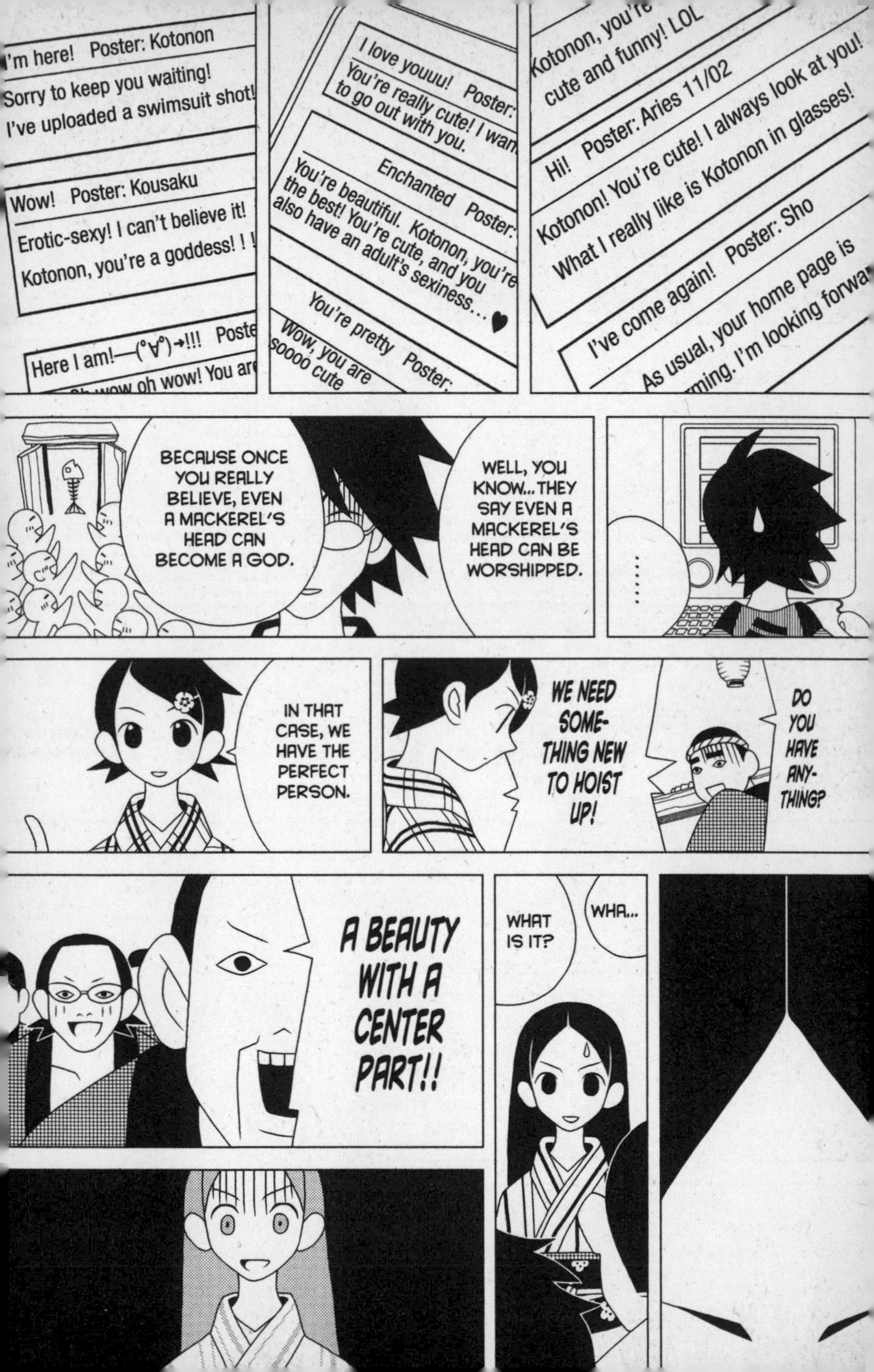

Kotonon, you're
cute and funny! LOL
Hi! Poster: Aries 11/02
Kotonon! You're cute! I always look at you!
What I really like is Kotonon in glasses!
I've come again! Poster: Sho
As usual, your home page is
rming. I'm looking forwa
I love youuu! Poster:
You're really cute! I wan
to go out with you.
Enchanted Poster:
You're beautiful. Kotonon, you're the best! You're cute, and you also have an adult's sexiness…♥
You're pretty Poster:
Wow, you are soooo cute
I'm here! Poster: Kotonon
Sorry to keep you waiting!
I've uploaded a swimsuit shot!
Wow! Poster: Kousaku
Erotic-sexy! I can't believe it!
Kotonon, you're a goddess! ! !
Here I am!—(°∀°)→!!! Poste
oh wow! You are
......
WELL, YOU KNOW... THEY SAY EVEN A MACKEREL'S HEAD CAN BE WORSHIPPED.
BECAUSE ONCE YOU REALLY BELIEVE, EVEN A MACKEREL'S HEAD CAN BECOME A GOD.
DO YOU HAVE ANYTHING?
WE NEED SOMETHING NEW TO HOIST UP!
IN THAT CASE, WE HAVE THE PERFECT PERSON.
WHA...
WHAT IS IT?
A BEAUTY WITH A CENTER PART!!

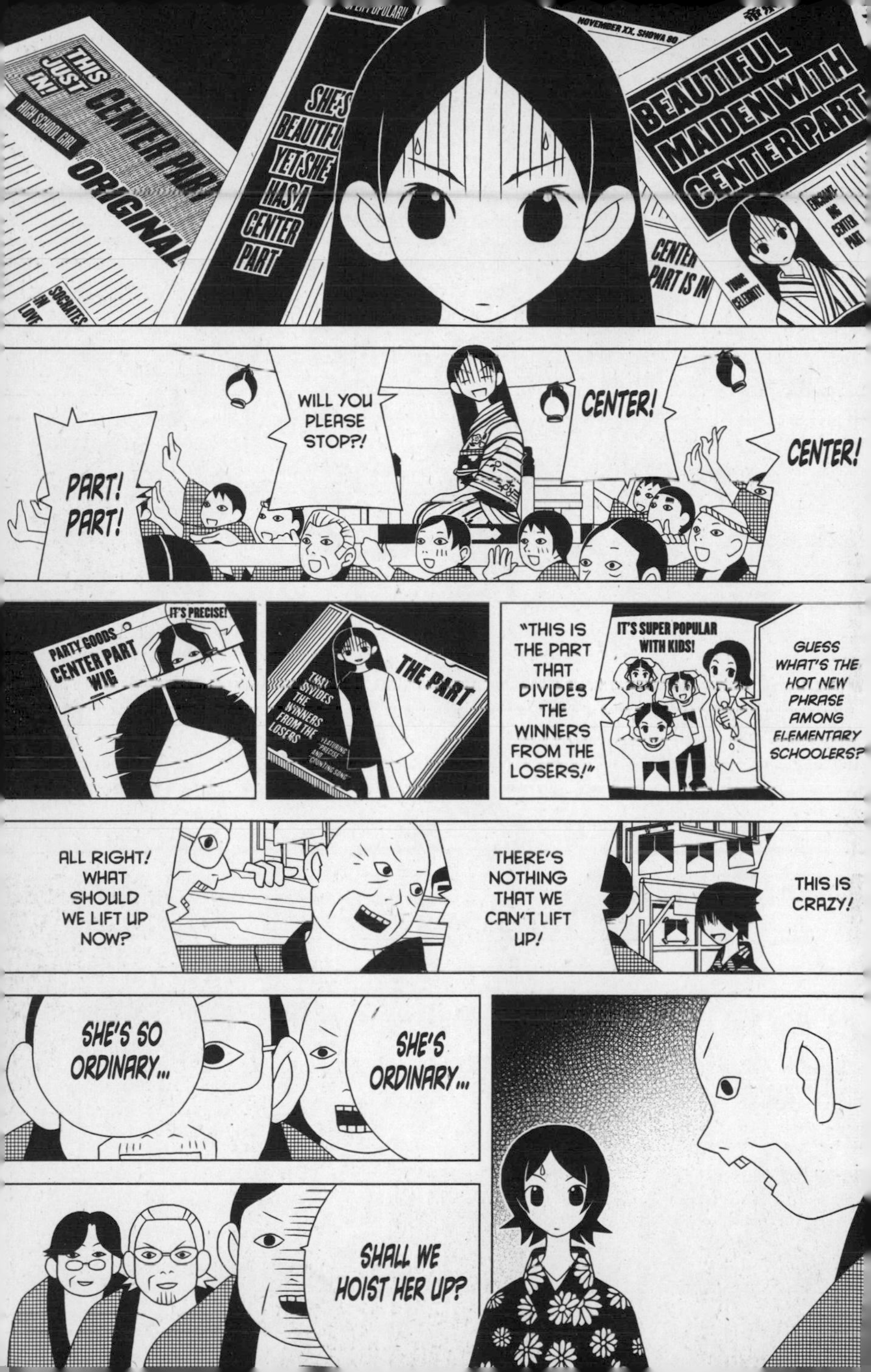
NOVEMBER XX, SHOWA 60
BEAUTIFUL MAIDEN WITH CENTER PART
ENCHANTING CENTER PART
CENTER PART IS IN
YOUNG CELEBRITY
SHE'S BEAUTIFUL YET SHE HAS A CENTER PART
THIS JUST IN!
CENTER PART ORIGINAL
HIGH SCHOOL GIRL
SOCRATES IN LOVE
CENTER!
CENTER!
WILL YOU PLEASE STOP?!
PART! PART!
GUESS WHAT'S THE HOT NEW PHRASE AMONG ELEMENTARY SCHOOLERS?
IT'S SUPER POPULAR WITH KIDS!
"THIS IS THE PART THAT DIVIDES THE WINNERS FROM THE LOSERS!"
THE PART
THAT DIVIDES THE WINNERS FROM THE LOSERS
FEATURING "PRECISE" AND "COUNTING SONG"
IT'S PRECISE!
PARTY GOODS
CENTER PART WIG
THIS IS CRAZY!
THERE'S NOTHING THAT WE CAN'T LIFT UP!
ALL RIGHT! WHAT SHOULD WE LIFT UP NOW?
SHE'S ORDINARY...
SHE'S SO ORDINARY...
SHALL WE HOIST HER UP?

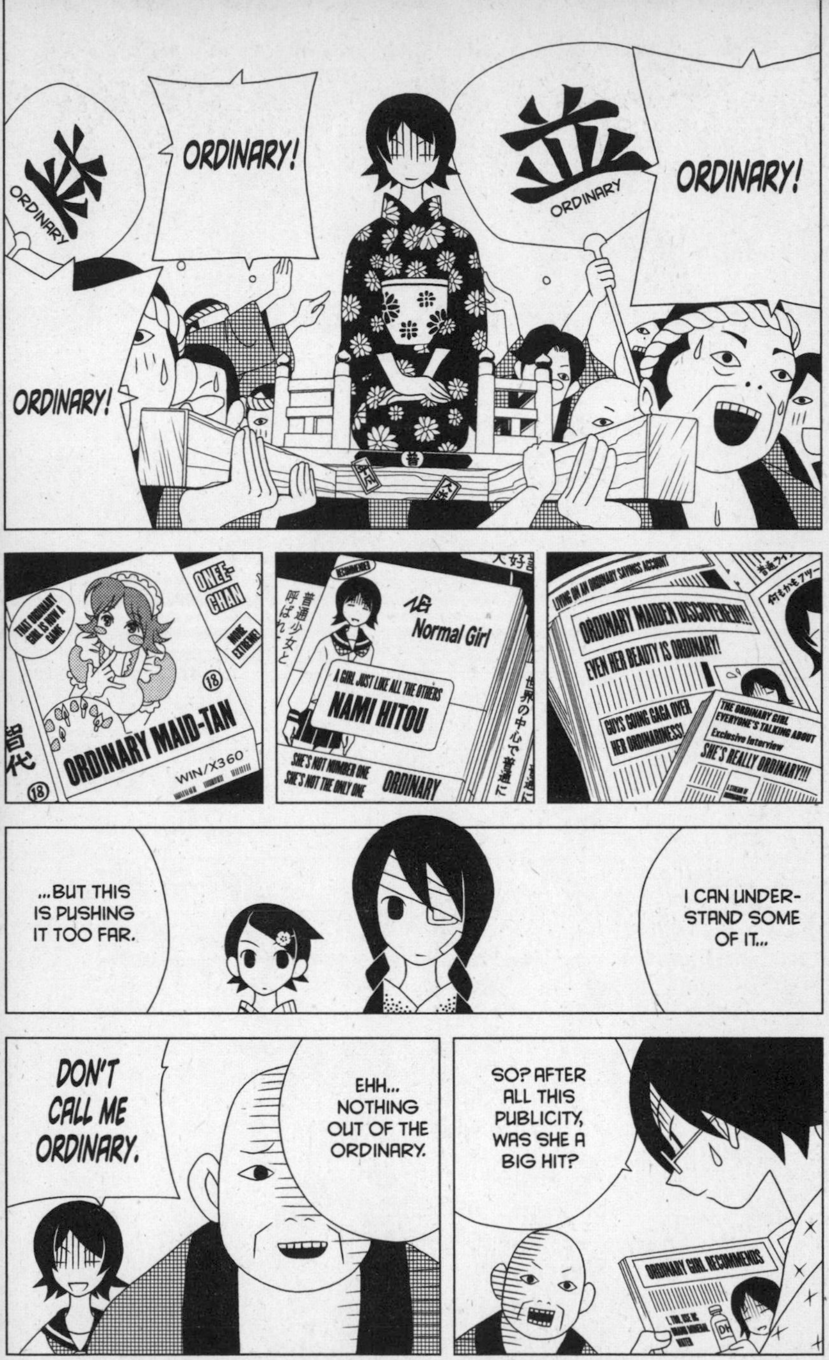
ORDINARY!
並 ORDINARY
ORDINARY!
ORDINARY
ORDINARY!
LIVING ON AN ORDINARY SAVINGS ACCOUNT
ORDINARY MAIDEN DISCOVERED!!!
EVEN HER BEAUTY IS ORDINARY!
GUYS GOING GAGA OVER HER ORDINARINESS!
THE ORDINARY GIRL EVERYONE'S TALKING ABOUT
Exclusive Interview
SHE'S REALLY ORDINARY!!!
RECOMMENDED
普通少女と呼ばれ
Normal Girl
A GIRL JUST LIKE ALL THE OTHERS
NAMI HITOU
SHE'S NOT NUMBER ONE
SHE'S NOT THE ONLY ONE
ORDINARY
世界の中心で普通に
ONEE-CHAN
THAT ORDINARY GIRL IS NOW A GAME
MORE EXTREME!
ORDINARY MAID-TAN
WIN/X360
I CAN UNDER-STAND SOME OF IT...
...BUT THIS IS PUSHING IT TOO FAR.
SO? AFTER ALL THIS PUBLICITY, WAS SHE A BIG HIT?
ORDINARY GIRL RECOMMENDS
EHH... NOTHING OUT OF THE ORDINARY.
DON'T CALL ME ORDINARY.

EXCLUSIVE KOTONON INFO

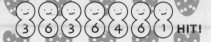

3636461 HIT!

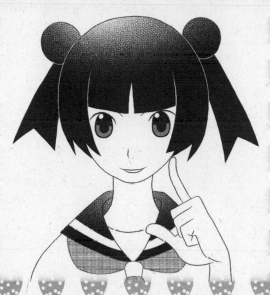

HN: KOTONON ✉ ← EMAIL ME HERE

SEX: MAIDEN

BIRTHDAY: THE DAY I MET YOU

BLOOD TYPE: RH + - O

ADDRESS: IN YOUR HEART

BIRTHPLACE: HOKKAIDO

PROFESSION: APPRENTICE NET IDOL

HEIGHT: 158 CM (ABOUT 5'2")

WEIGHT: AS MUCH AS THREE CRATES OF APPLES

HOBBIES: ATTENDING CAT SHOWS

SPECIAL TALENT: NOTHING SPECIAL

CIGARETTES: ~~VIRGINIA SLIM LIGHTS~~

SKILLS: LICENSED FOR PHOTOSHOP

FAVORITE FOODS: VEGGIES

FOODS I DISLIKE: MEAT...I JUST CAN'T TAKE IT

WHERE I WANT TO TRAVEL: NEW CALEDONIA ISLAND

ROUTE YOU TRAVEL THE MOST: OFF THE BEATEN TRACK

FIRST CD I BOUGHT: PLAYBACK PART 2

IF I WERE REINCARNATED: I'D BE AN EVEN CUTER ME

♥ **ENTRY JUST FOR KOTO:** ♥

THERE'LL BE MUSIC FROM THE NEXT PAGE ON.
BE CAREFUL WITH THE VOLUME, OKAY?

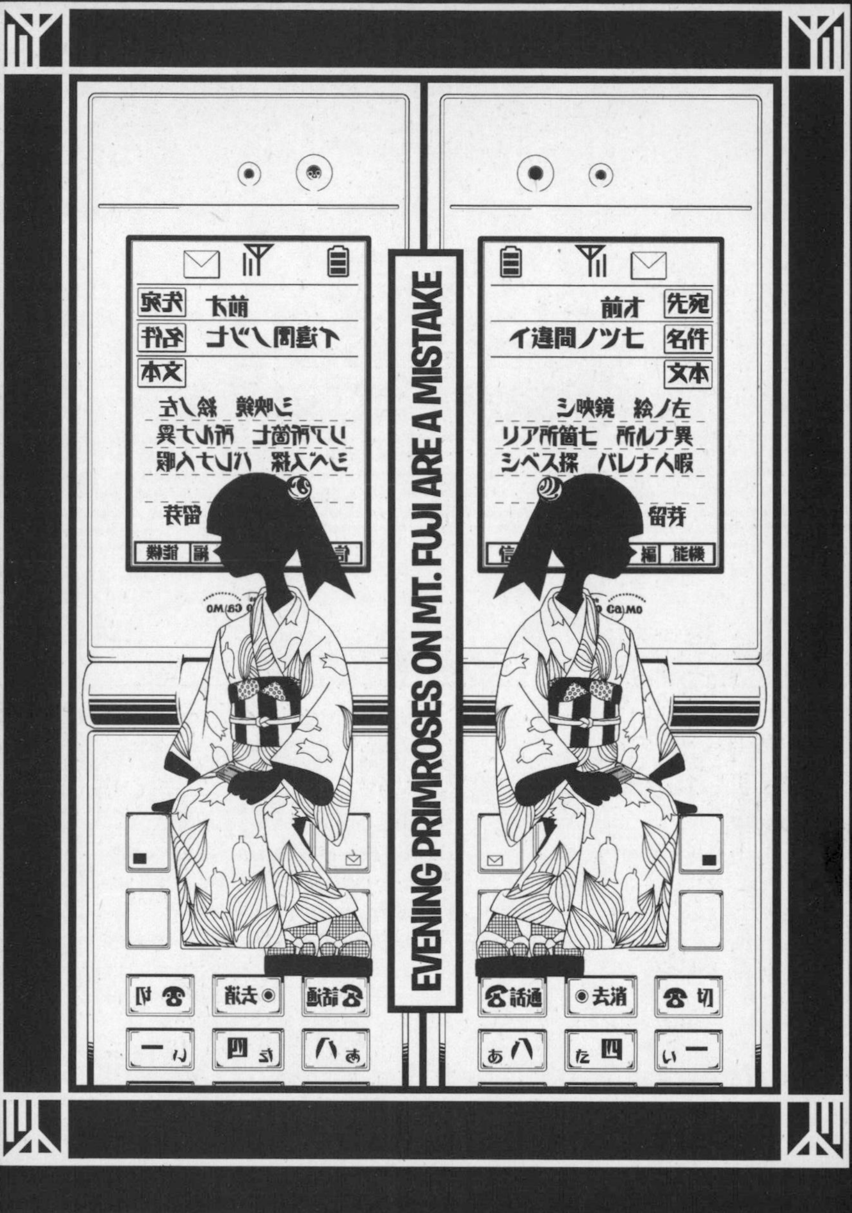
EVENING PRIMROSES ON MT. FUJI ARE A MISTAKE
宛先 オ前
件名 七ツノ間違イ
本文
左ノ絵 鏡映シ
異ナル所 七箇所アリ
暇人ナレバ 探スベシ

CHAPTER 27

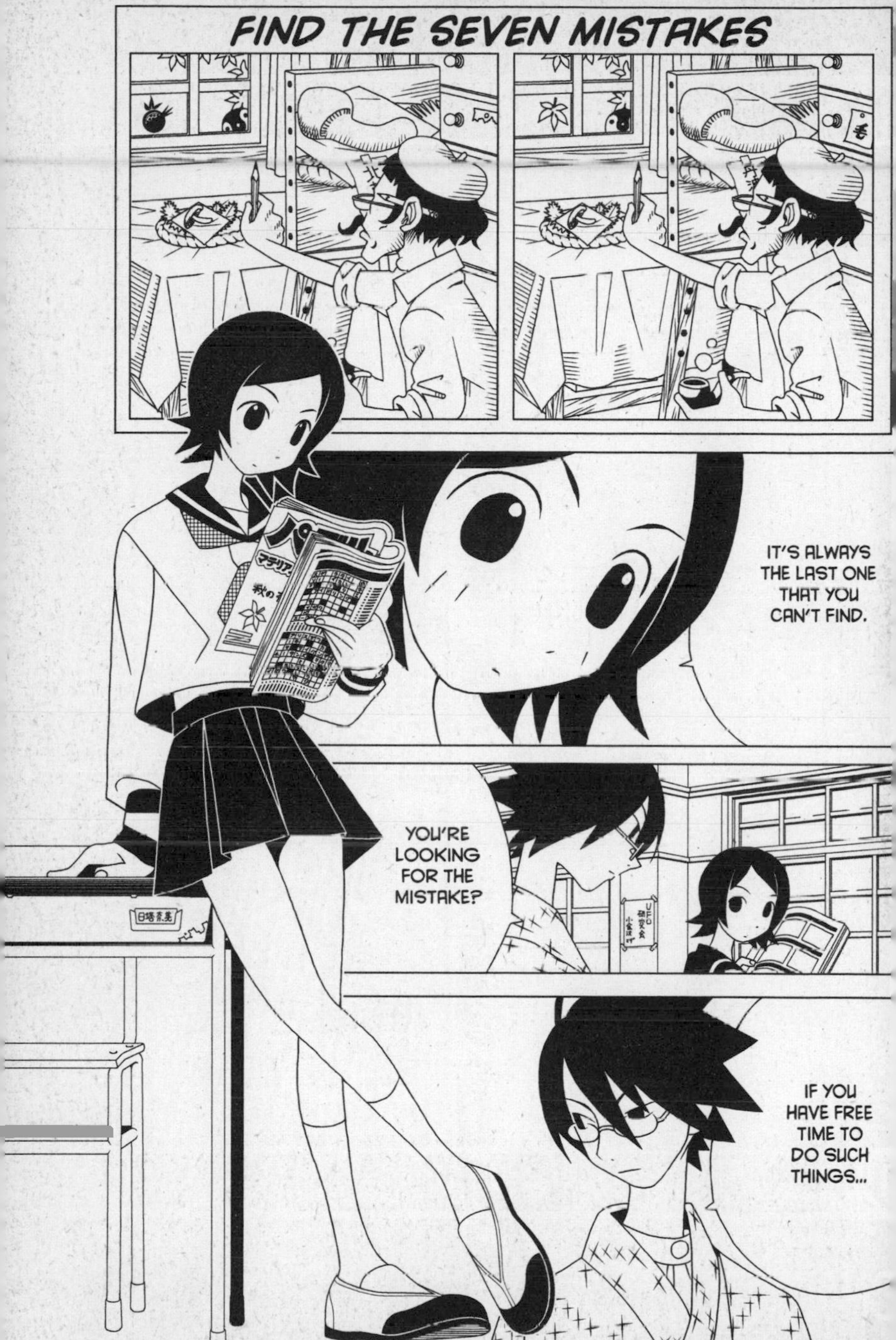
FIND THE SEVEN MISTAKES
IT'S ALWAYS THE LAST ONE THAT YOU CAN'T FIND.
YOU'RE LOOKING FOR THE MISTAKE?
IF YOU HAVE FREE TIME TO DO SUCH THINGS...

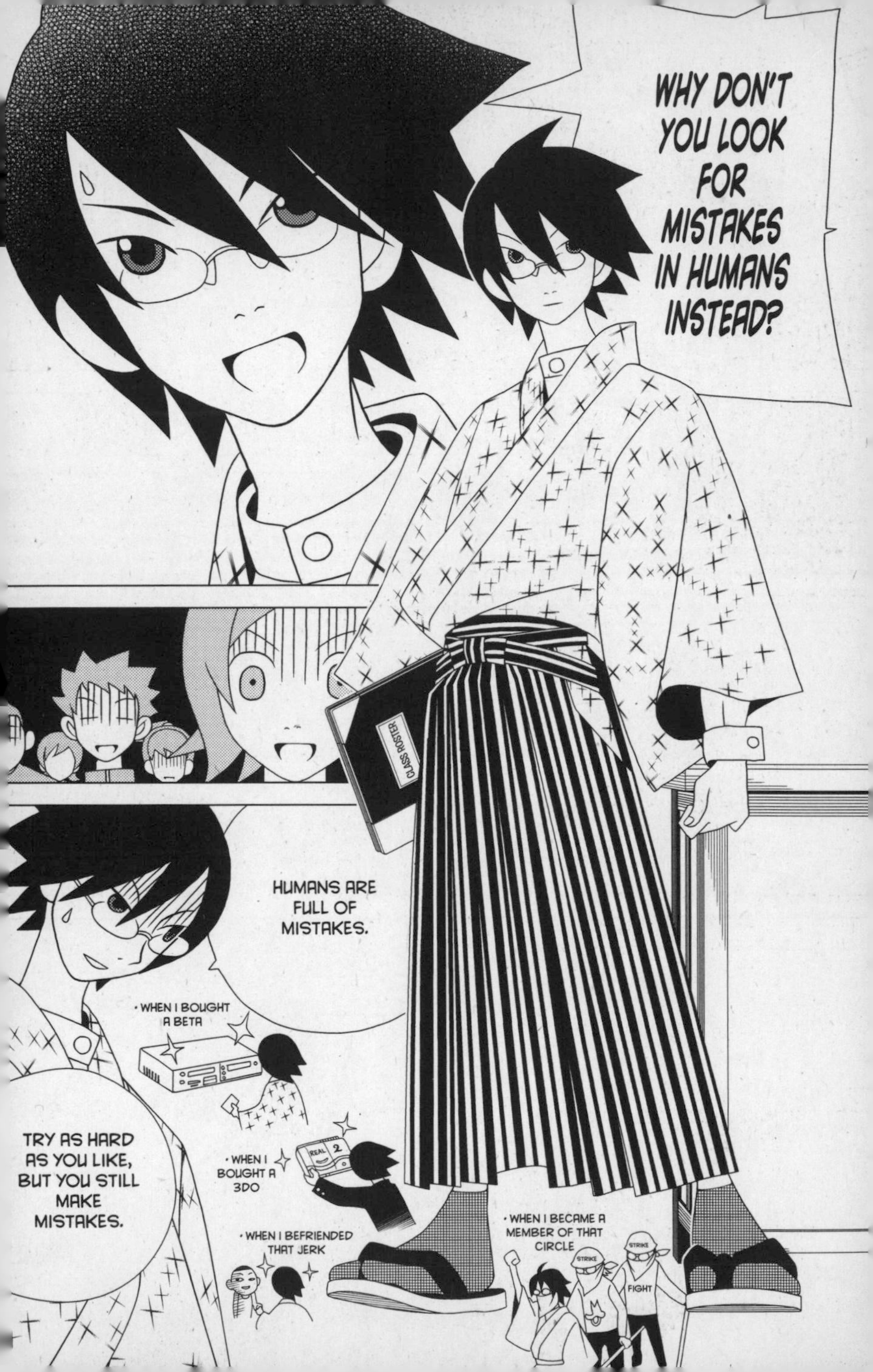
WHY DON'T YOU LOOK FOR MISTAKES IN HUMANS INSTEAD?
CLASS ROSTER
HUMANS ARE FULL OF MISTAKES.
• WHEN I BOUGHT A BETA
• WHEN I BOUGHT A 3DO
REAL 2
• WHEN I BECAME A MEMBER OF THAT CIRCLE
STRIKE
STRIKE
FIGHT
• WHEN I BEFRIENDED THAT JERK
TRY AS HARD AS YOU LIKE, BUT YOU STILL MAKE MISTAKES.

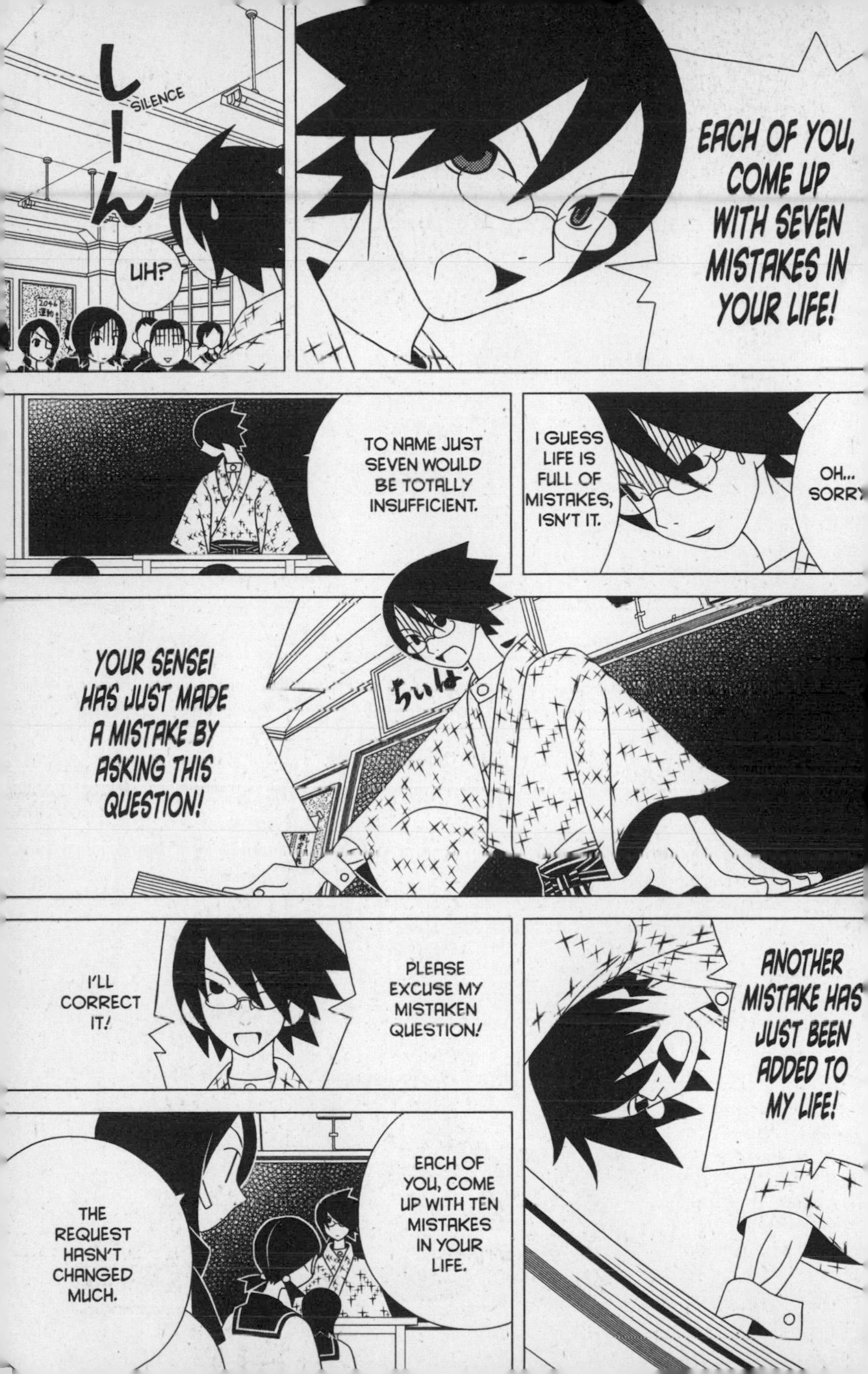
EACH OF YOU, COME UP WITH SEVEN MISTAKES IN YOUR LIFE!
しーん
SILENCE
UH?
OH... SORRY
I GUESS LIFE IS FULL OF MISTAKES, ISN'T IT.
TO NAME JUST SEVEN WOULD BE TOTALLY INSUFFICIENT.
YOUR SENSEI HAS JUST MADE A MISTAKE BY ASKING THIS QUESTION!
ANOTHER MISTAKE HAS JUST BEEN ADDED TO MY LIFE!
PLEASE EXCUSE MY MISTAKEN QUESTION!
I'LL CORRECT IT!
EACH OF YOU, COME UP WITH TEN MISTAKES IN YOUR LIFE.
THE REQUEST HASN'T CHANGED MUCH.

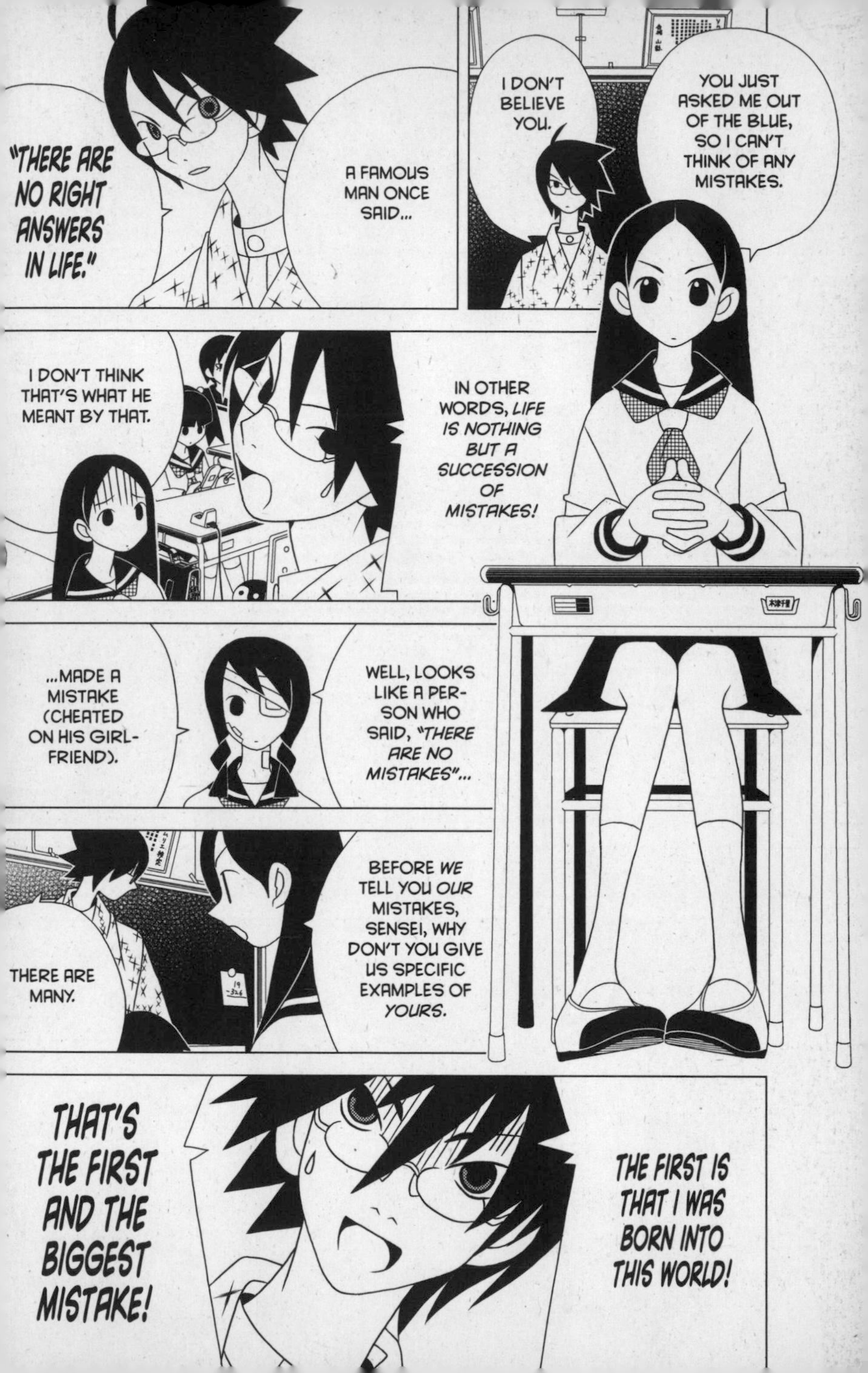
YOU JUST ASKED ME OUT OF THE BLUE, SO I CAN'T THINK OF ANY MISTAKES.
I DON'T BELIEVE YOU.
A FAMOUS MAN ONCE SAID...
"THERE ARE NO RIGHT ANSWERS IN LIFE."
IN OTHER WORDS, *LIFE IS NOTHING BUT A SUCCESSION OF MISTAKES!*
I DON'T THINK THAT'S WHAT HE MEANT BY THAT.
WELL, LOOKS LIKE A PERSON WHO SAID, "*THERE ARE NO MISTAKES*"...
...MADE A MISTAKE (CHEATED ON HIS GIRLFRIEND).
BEFORE *WE* TELL YOU *OUR* MISTAKES, SENSEI, WHY DON'T YOU GIVE US SPECIFIC EXAMPLES OF *YOURS*.
THERE ARE MANY.
THE FIRST IS THAT I WAS BORN INTO THIS WORLD!
THAT'S THE FIRST AND THE BIGGEST MISTAKE!

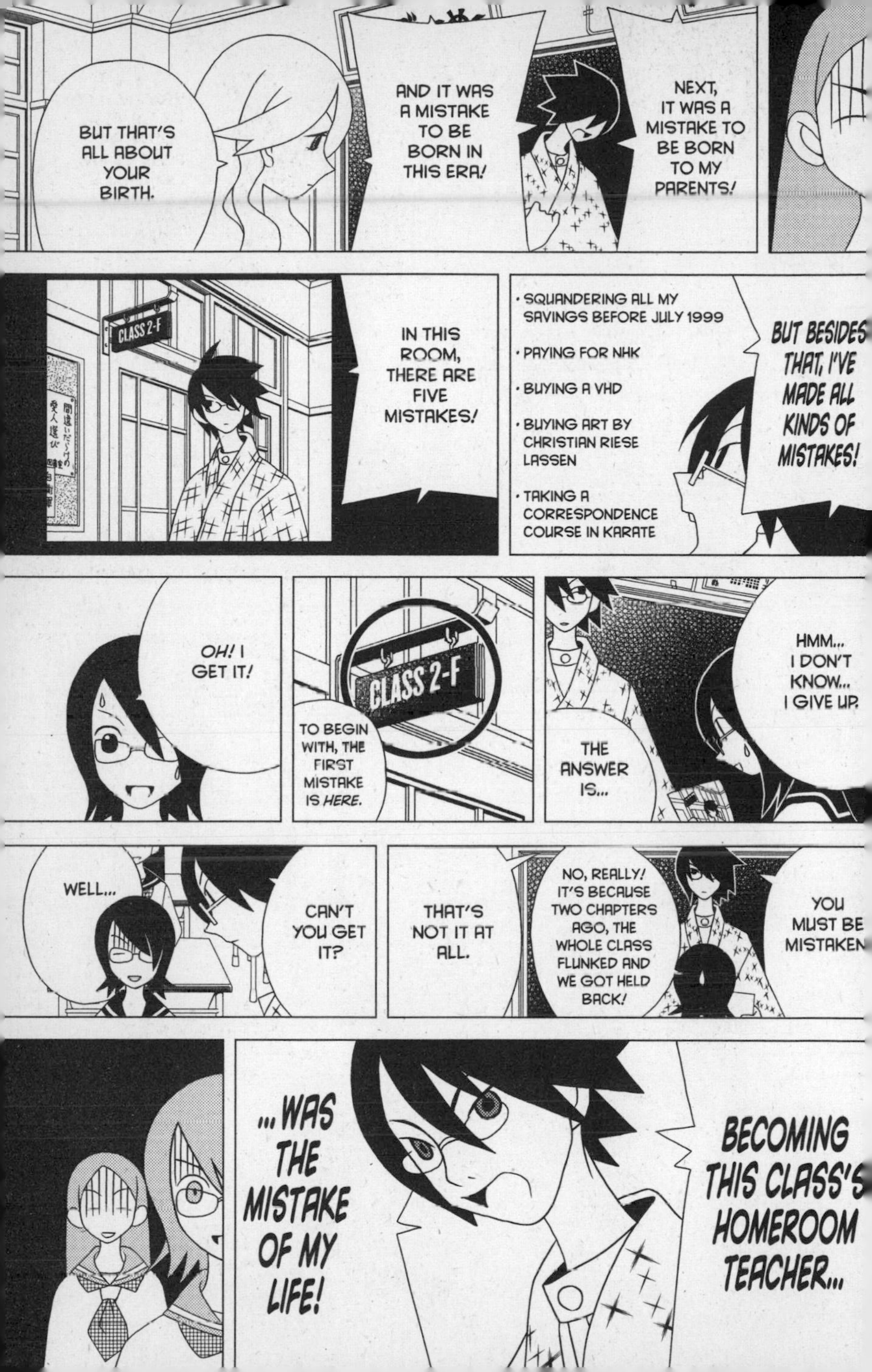
NEXT, IT WAS A MISTAKE TO BE BORN TO MY PARENTS!
AND IT WAS A MISTAKE TO BE BORN IN THIS ERA!
BUT THAT'S ALL ABOUT YOUR BIRTH.
BUT BESIDES THAT, I'VE MADE ALL KINDS OF MISTAKES!
• SQUANDERING ALL MY SAVINGS BEFORE JULY 1999
• PAYING FOR NHK
• BUYING A VHD
• BUYING ART BY CHRISTIAN RIESE LASSEN
• TAKING A CORRESPONDENCE COURSE IN KARATE
IN THIS ROOM, THERE ARE FIVE MISTAKES!
CLASS 2-F
間違いだらけの
愛人選び
HMM... I DON'T KNOW... I GIVE UP.
THE ANSWER IS...
CLASS 2-F
TO BEGIN WITH, THE FIRST MISTAKE IS *HERE*.
OH! I GET IT!
YOU MUST BE MISTAKEN
NO, REALLY! IT'S BECAUSE TWO CHAPTERS AGO, THE WHOLE CLASS FLUNKED AND WE GOT HELD BACK!
THAT'S NOT IT AT ALL.
CAN'T YOU GET IT?
WELL...
BECOMING THIS CLASS'S HOMEROOM TEACHER...
...WAS THE MISTAKE OF MY LIFE!

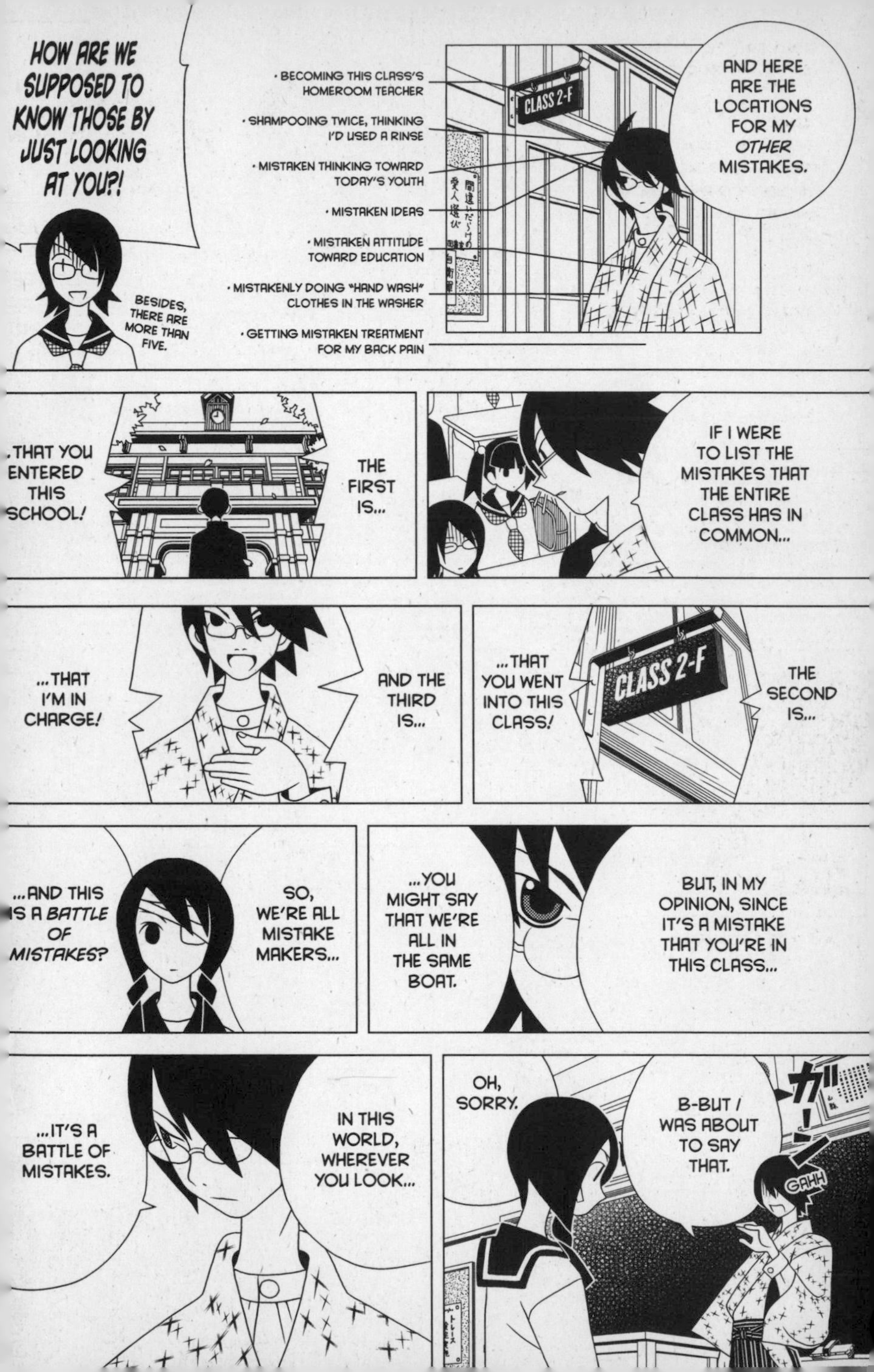
AND HERE ARE THE LOCATIONS FOR MY *OTHER* MISTAKES.
CLASS 2-F
· BECOMING THIS CLASS'S HOMEROOM TEACHER
· SHAMPOOING TWICE, THINKING I'D USED A RINSE
· MISTAKEN THINKING TOWARD TODAY'S YOUTH
· MISTAKEN IDEAS
· MISTAKEN ATTITUDE TOWARD EDUCATION
· MISTAKENLY DOING "HAND WASH" CLOTHES IN THE WASHER
· GETTING MISTAKEN TREATMENT FOR MY BACK PAIN
HOW ARE WE SUPPOSED TO KNOW THOSE BY JUST LOOKING AT YOU?!
BESIDES, THERE ARE MORE THAN FIVE.
IF I WERE TO LIST THE MISTAKES THAT THE ENTIRE CLASS HAS IN COMMON...
THE FIRST IS...
...THAT YOU ENTERED THIS SCHOOL!
THE SECOND IS...
...THAT YOU WENT INTO THIS CLASS!
CLASS 2-F
AND THE THIRD IS...
...THAT I'M IN CHARGE!
BUT, IN MY OPINION, SINCE IT'S A MISTAKE THAT YOU'RE IN THIS CLASS...
...YOU MIGHT SAY THAT WE'RE ALL IN THE SAME BOAT.
SO, WE'RE ALL MISTAKE MAKERS...
...AND THIS IS A *BATTLE OF MISTAKES*?
B-BUT *I* WAS ABOUT TO SAY THAT.
GAHH
OH, SORRY.
IN THIS WORLD, WHEREVER YOU LOOK...
...IT'S A BATTLE OF MISTAKES.

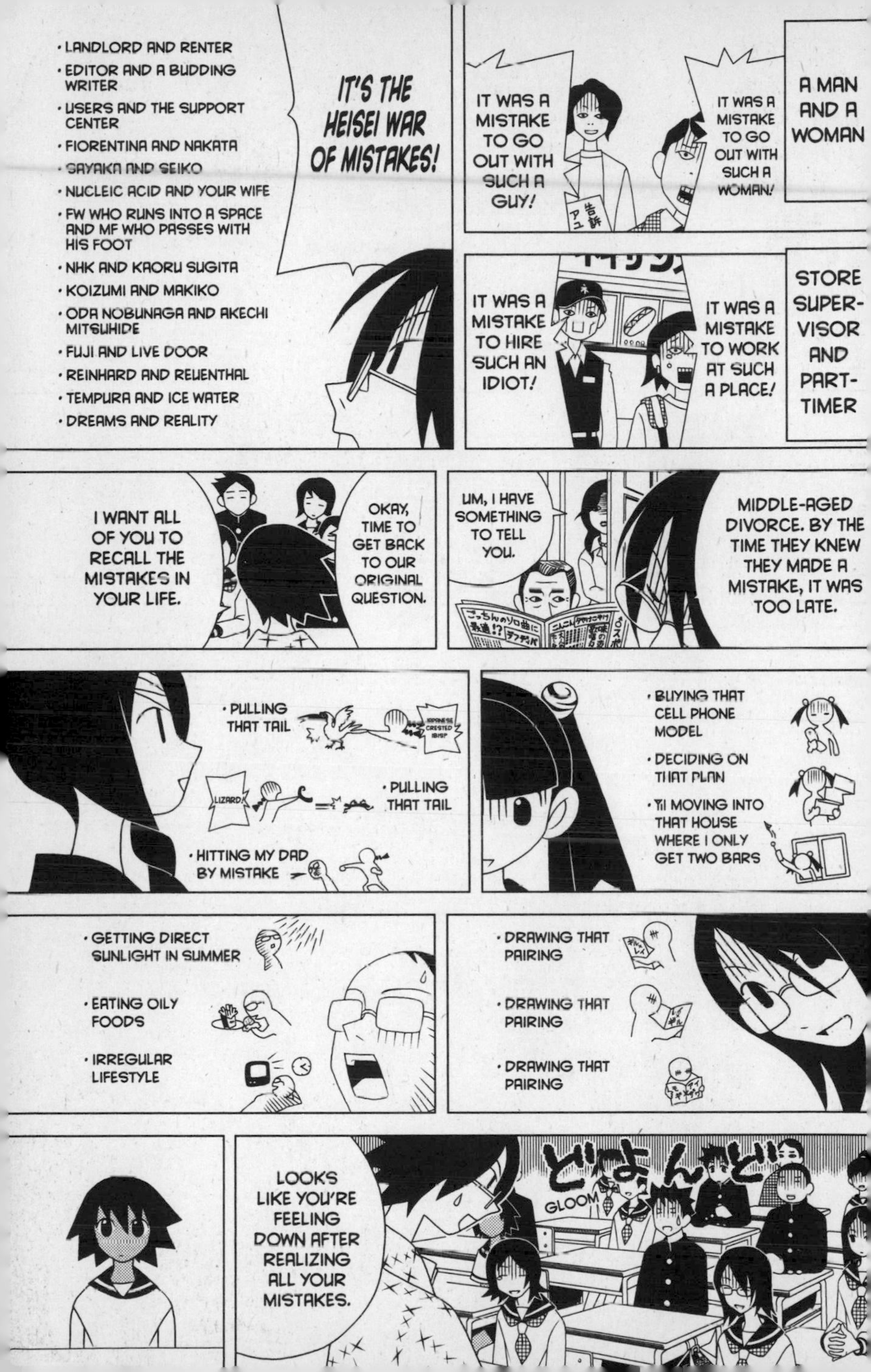
A MAN AND A WOMAN
IT WAS A MISTAKE TO GO OUT WITH SUCH A WOMAN!
IT WAS A MISTAKE TO GO OUT WITH SUCH A GUY!
STORE SUPERVISOR AND PART-TIMER
IT WAS A MISTAKE TO WORK AT SUCH A PLACE!
IT WAS A MISTAKE TO HIRE SUCH AN IDIOT!
IT'S THE HEISEI WAR OF MISTAKES!
• LANDLORD AND RENTER
• EDITOR AND A BUDDING WRITER
• USERS AND THE SUPPORT CENTER
• FIORENTINA AND NAKATA
• SAYAKA AND SEIKO
• NUCLEIC ACID AND YOUR WIFE
• FW WHO RUNS INTO A SPACE AND MF WHO PASSES WITH HIS FOOT
• NHK AND KAORU SUGITA
• KOIZUMI AND MAKIKO
• ODA NOBUNAGA AND AKECHI MITSUHIDE
• FUJI AND LIVE DOOR
• REINHARD AND REUENTHAL
• TEMPURA AND ICE WATER
• DREAMS AND REALITY
MIDDLE-AGED DIVORCE. BY THE TIME THEY KNEW THEY MADE A MISTAKE, IT WAS TOO LATE.
UM, I HAVE SOMETHING TO TELL YOU.
OKAY, TIME TO GET BACK TO OUR ORIGINAL QUESTION.
I WANT ALL OF YOU TO RECALL THE MISTAKES IN YOUR LIFE.
• BUYING THAT CELL PHONE MODEL
• DECIDING ON THAT PLAN
• MOVING INTO THAT HOUSE WHERE I ONLY GET TWO BARS
• PULLING THAT TAIL
JAPANESE CRESTED IBIS?
LIZARD?
• PULLING THAT TAIL
• HITTING MY DAD BY MISTAKE
• DRAWING THAT PAIRING
• DRAWING THAT PAIRING
• DRAWING THAT PAIRING
• GETTING DIRECT SUNLIGHT IN SUMMER
• EATING OILY FOODS
• IRREGULAR LIFESTYLE
GLOOM
LOOKS LIKE YOU'RE FEELING DOWN AFTER REALIZING ALL YOUR MISTAKES.

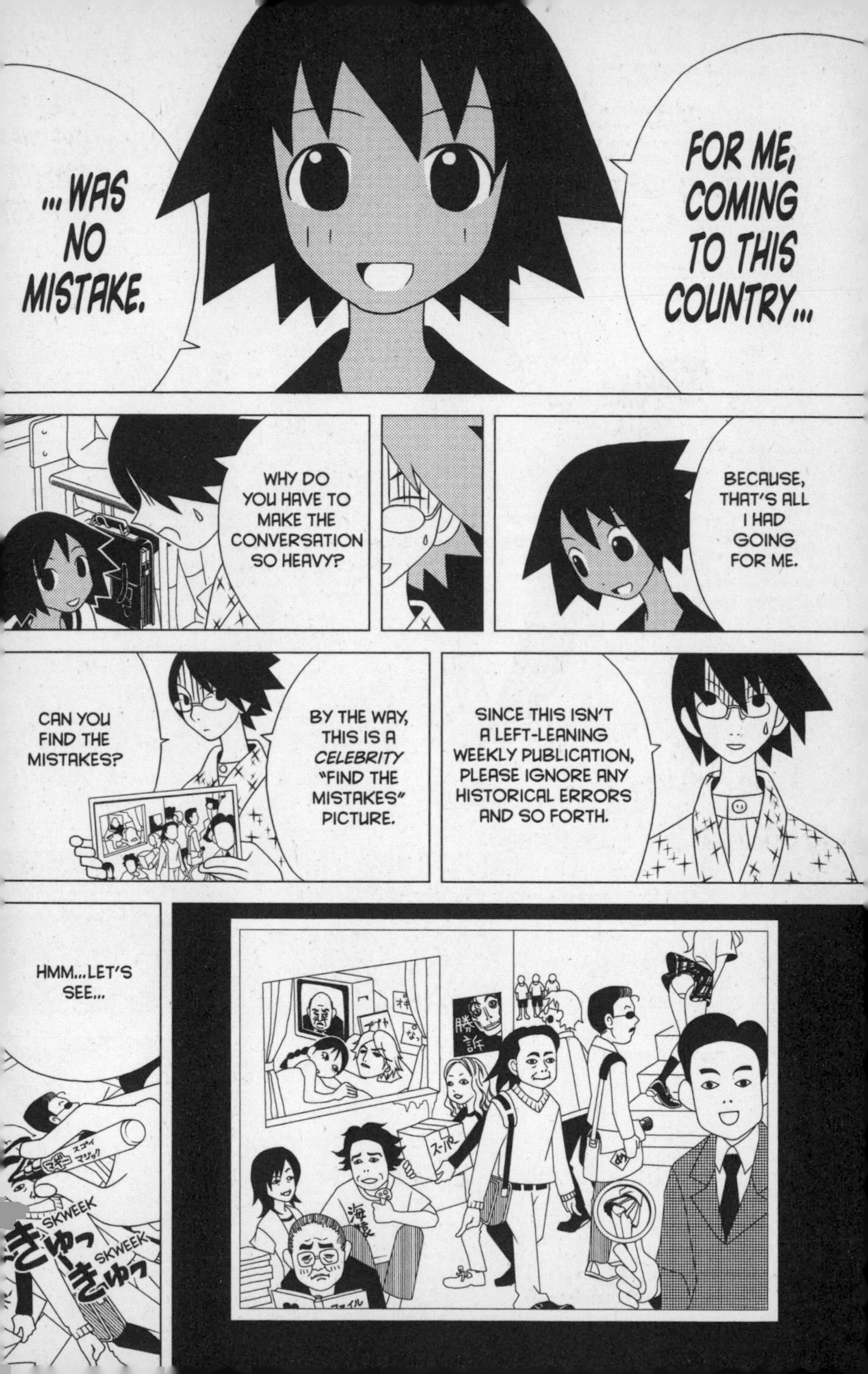
FOR ME, COMING TO THIS COUNTRY...
...WAS NO MISTAKE.
BECAUSE, THAT'S ALL I HAD GOING FOR ME.
WHY DO YOU HAVE TO MAKE THE CONVERSATION SO HEAVY?
SINCE THIS ISN'T A LEFT-LEANING WEEKLY PUBLICATION, PLEASE IGNORE ANY HISTORICAL ERRORS AND SO FORTH.
BY THE WAY, THIS IS A *CELEBRITY* "FIND THE MISTAKES" PICTURE.
CAN YOU FIND THE MISTAKES?
勝訴
スーパー
HMM...LET'S SEE...
SKWEEK きゅっ
SKWEEK きゅっ

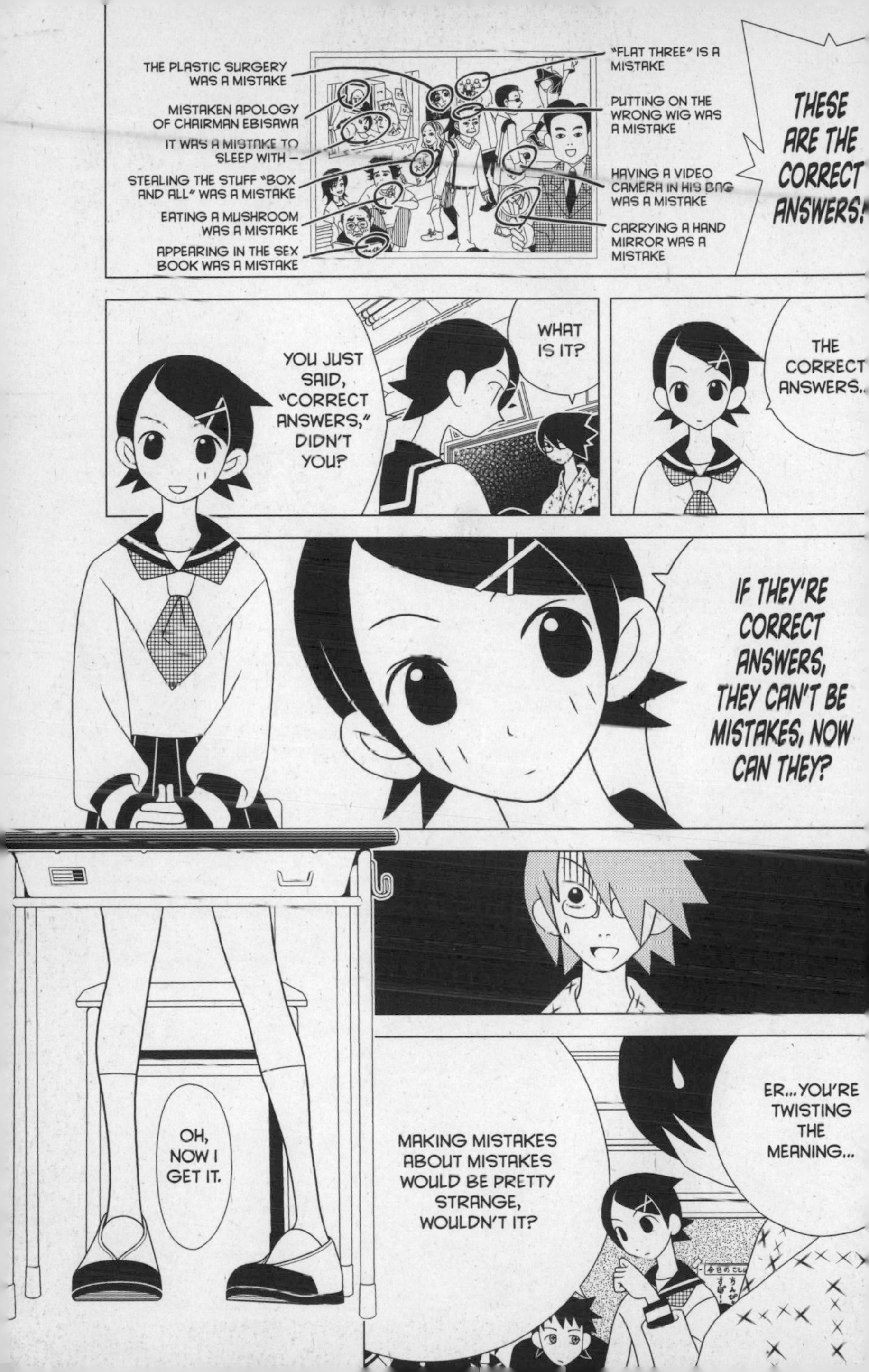
THESE ARE THE CORRECT ANSWERS!
"FLAT THREE" IS A MISTAKE
PUTTING ON THE WRONG WIG WAS A MISTAKE
HAVING A VIDEO CAMERA IN HIS BAG WAS A MISTAKE
CARRYING A HAND MIRROR WAS A MISTAKE
THE PLASTIC SURGERY WAS A MISTAKE
MISTAKEN APOLOGY OF CHAIRMAN EBISAWA
IT WAS A MISTAKE TO SLEEP WITH —
STEALING THE STUFF "BOX AND ALL" WAS A MISTAKE
EATING A MUSHROOM WAS A MISTAKE
APPEARING IN THE SEX BOOK WAS A MISTAKE
THE CORRECT ANSWERS..
WHAT IS IT?
IF THEY'RE CORRECT ANSWERS, THEY CAN'T BE MISTAKES, NOW CAN THEY?
ER...YOU'RE TWISTING THE MEANING...
MAKING MISTAKES ABOUT MISTAKES WOULD BE PRETTY STRANGE, WOULDN'T IT?
YOU JUST SAID, "CORRECT ANSWERS," DIDN'T YOU?
OH, NOW I GET IT.

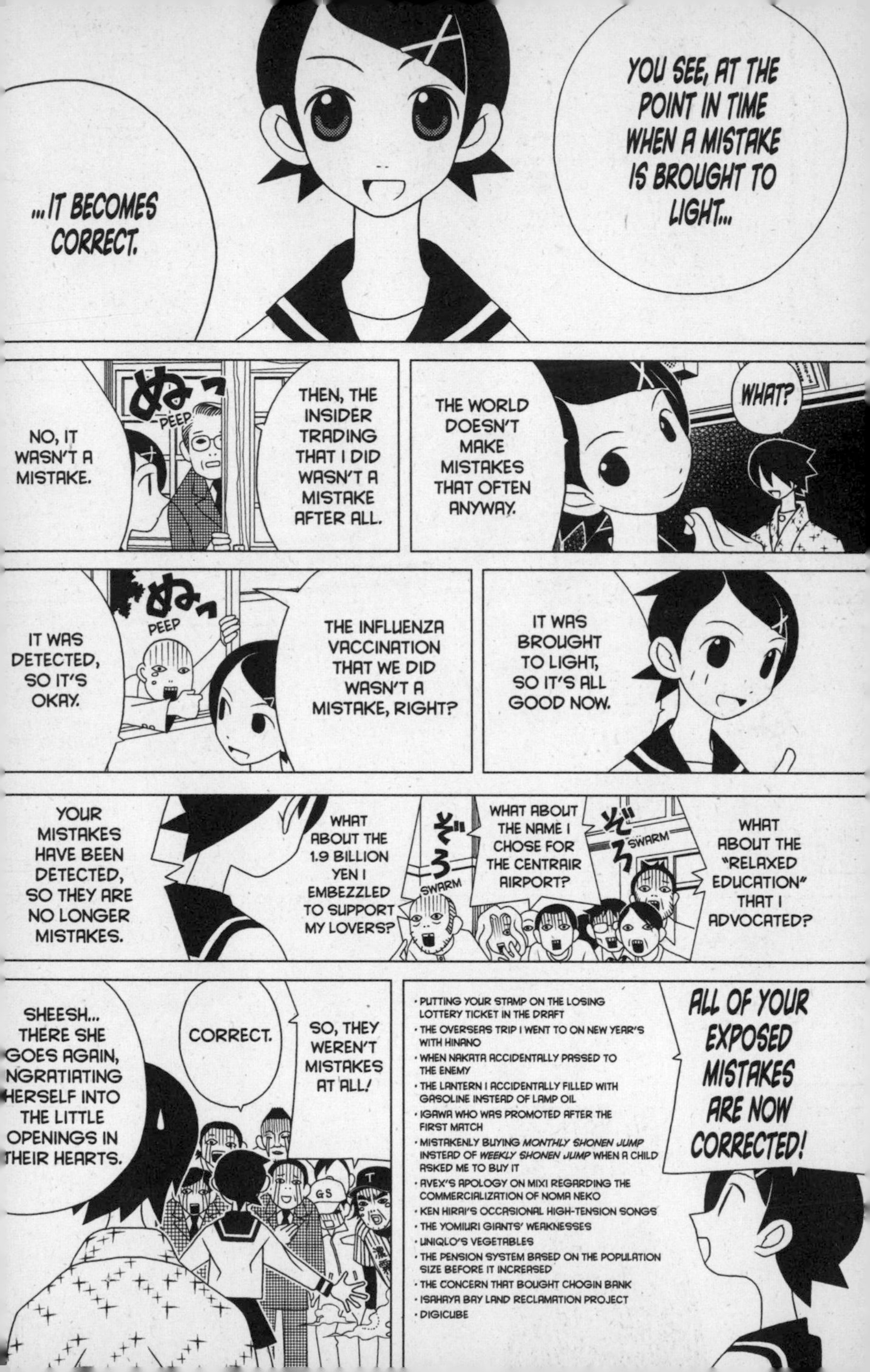
YOU SEE, AT THE POINT IN TIME WHEN A MISTAKE IS BROUGHT TO LIGHT...
...IT BECOMES CORRECT.
WHAT?
THE WORLD DOESN'T MAKE MISTAKES THAT OFTEN ANYWAY.
THEN, THE INSIDER TRADING THAT I DID WASN'T A MISTAKE AFTER ALL.
ぬっ
PEEP
NO, IT WASN'T A MISTAKE.
IT WAS BROUGHT TO LIGHT, SO IT'S ALL GOOD NOW.
THE INFLUENZA VACCINATION THAT WE DID WASN'T A MISTAKE, RIGHT?
ぬっ
PEEP
IT WAS DETECTED, SO IT'S OKAY.
WHAT ABOUT THE "RELAXED EDUCATION" THAT I ADVOCATED?
ぞろ
SWARM
WHAT ABOUT THE NAME I CHOSE FOR THE CENTRAIR AIRPORT?
ぞろ
SWARM
WHAT ABOUT THE 1.9 BILLION YEN I EMBEZZLED TO SUPPORT MY LOVERS?
YOUR MISTAKES HAVE BEEN DETECTED, SO THEY ARE NO LONGER MISTAKES.
ALL OF YOUR EXPOSED MISTAKES ARE NOW CORRECTED!
• PUTTING YOUR STAMP ON THE LOSING LOTTERY TICKET IN THE DRAFT
• THE OVERSEAS TRIP I WENT TO ON NEW YEAR'S WITH HINANO
• WHEN NAKATA ACCIDENTALLY PASSED TO THE ENEMY
• THE LANTERN I ACCIDENTALLY FILLED WITH GASOLINE INSTEAD OF LAMP OIL
• IGAWA WHO WAS PROMOTED AFTER THE FIRST MATCH
• MISTAKENLY BUYING *MONTHLY SHONEN JUMP* INSTEAD OF *WEEKLY SHONEN JUMP* WHEN A CHILD ASKED ME TO BUY IT
• AVEX'S APOLOGY ON MIXI REGARDING THE COMMERCIALIZATION OF NOMA NEKO
• KEN HIRAI'S OCCASIONAL HIGH-TENSION SONGS
• THE YOMIURI GIANTS' WEAKNESSES
• UNIQLO'S VEGETABLES
• THE PENSION SYSTEM BASED ON THE POPULATION SIZE BEFORE IT INCREASED
• THE CONCERN THAT BOUGHT CHOGIN BANK
• ISAHAYA BAY LAND RECLAMATION PROJECT
• DIGICUBE
SO, THEY WEREN'T MISTAKES AT ALL!
CORRECT.
GS
SHEESH... THERE SHE GOES AGAIN, NGRATIATING HERSELF INTO THE LITTLE OPENINGS IN THEIR HEARTS.

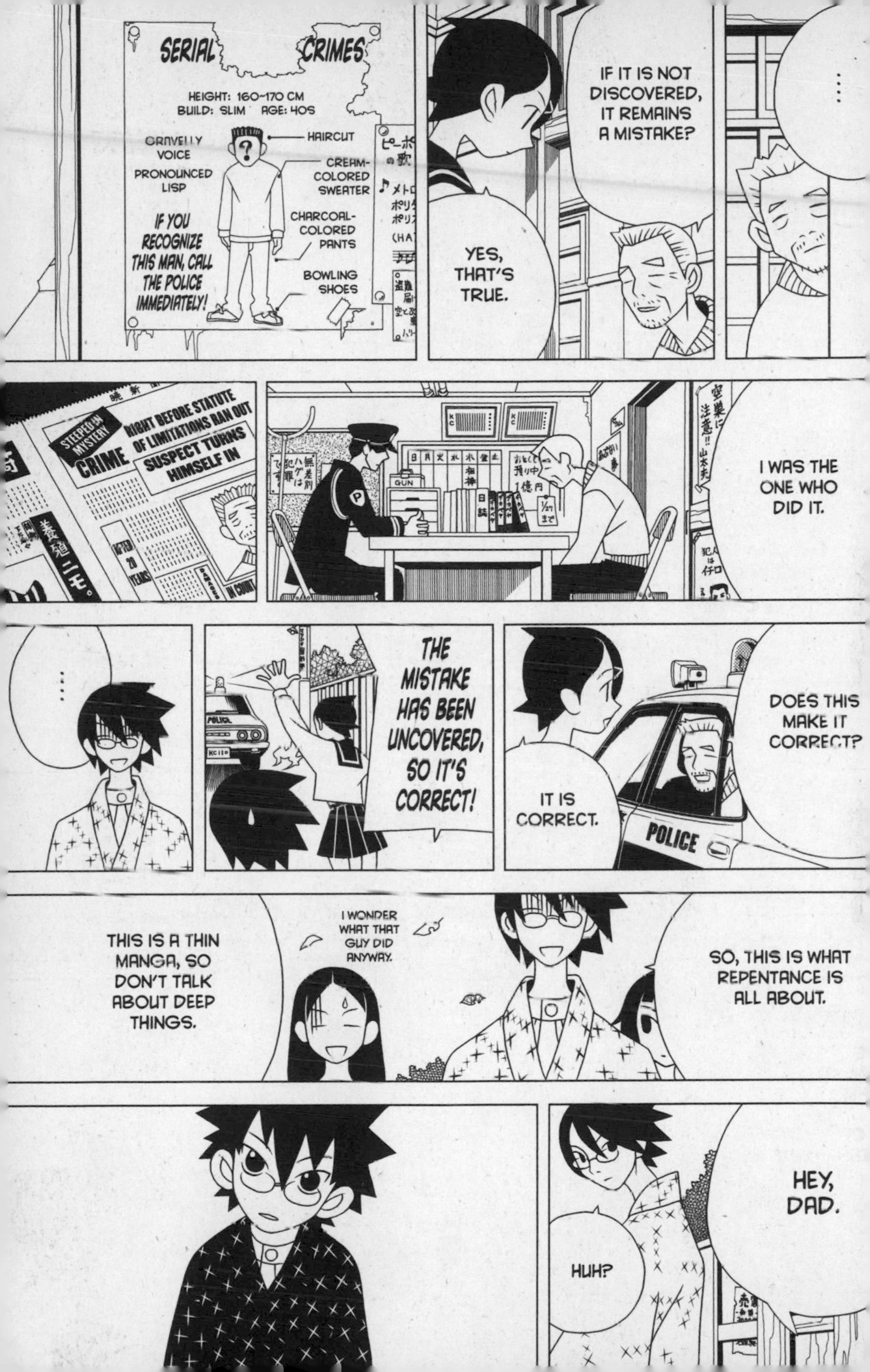
....
IF IT IS NOT DISCOVERED, IT REMAINS A MISTAKE?
YES, THAT'S TRUE.
SERIAL CRIMES
HEIGHT: 160~170 CM
BUILD: SLIM AGE: 40S
HAIRCUT
GRAVELLY VOICE
PRONOUNCED LISP
CREAM-COLORED SWEATER
CHARCOAL-COLORED PANTS
BOWLING SHOES
IF YOU RECOGNIZE THIS MAN, CALL THE POLICE IMMEDIATELY!
I WAS THE ONE WHO DID IT.
空巣に注意!!
GUN
STEEPED IN MYSTERY
CRIME
RIGHT BEFORE STATUTE OF LIMITATIONS RAN OUT
SUSPECT TURNS HIMSELF IN
AFTER 20 YEARS
IN COURT
DOES THIS MAKE IT CORRECT?
IT IS CORRECT.
POLICE
THE MISTAKE HAS BEEN UNCOVERED, SO IT'S CORRECT!
....
SO, THIS IS WHAT REPENTANCE IS ALL ABOUT.
I WONDER WHAT THAT GUY DID ANYWAY.
THIS IS A THIN MANGA, SO DON'T TALK ABOUT DEEP THINGS.
HEY, DAD.
HUH?

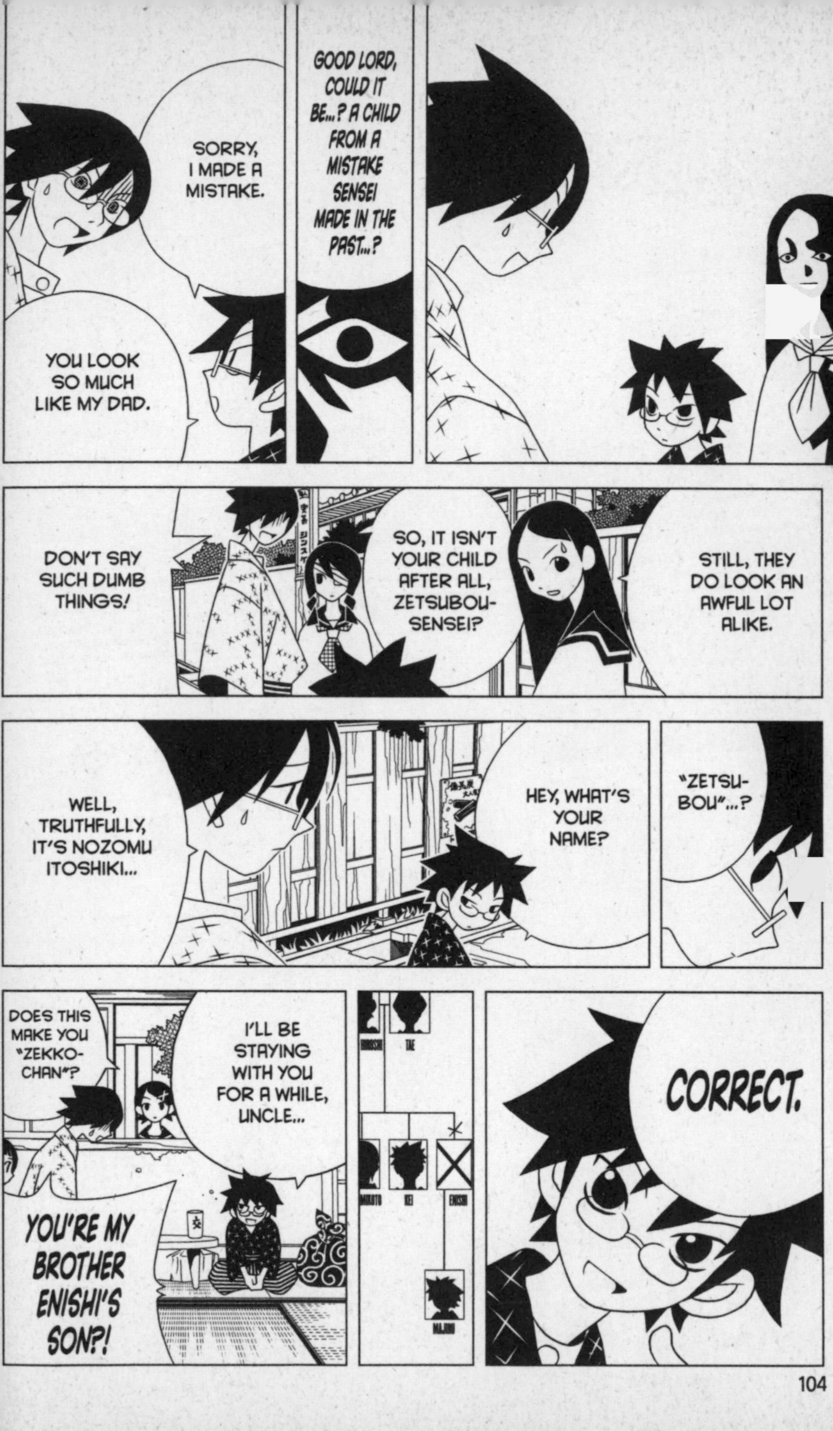
GOOD LORD, COULD IT BE...? A CHILD FROM A MISTAKE SENSEI MADE IN THE PAST...?
SORRY, I MADE A MISTAKE.
YOU LOOK SO MUCH LIKE MY DAD.
STILL, THEY DO LOOK AN AWFUL LOT ALIKE.
SO, IT ISN'T YOUR CHILD AFTER ALL, ZETSUBOU-SENSEI?
DON'T SAY SUCH DUMB THINGS!
"ZETSU-BOU"...?
HEY, WHAT'S YOUR NAME?
WELL, TRUTHFULLY, IT'S NOZOMU ITOSHIKI...
CORRECT.
HIROSHI
TAE
MIKOTO
KEI
ENISHI
MAJIRO
I'LL BE STAYING WITH YOU FOR A WHILE, UNCLE...
DOES THIS MAKE YOU "ZEKKO-CHAN"?
YOU'RE MY BROTHER ENISHI'S SON?!

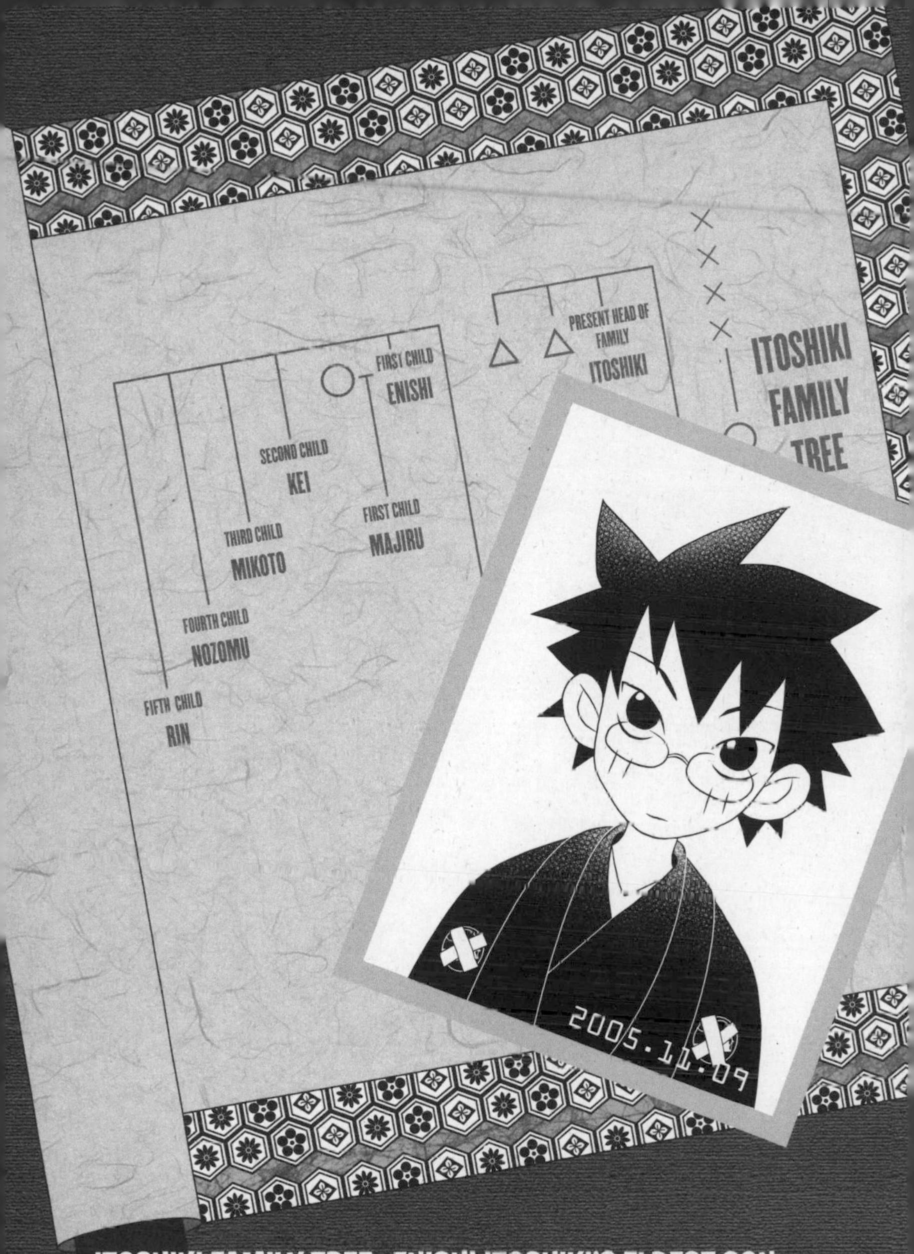
ITOSHIKI FAMILY TREE
PRESENT HEAD OF FAMILY
ITOSHIKI
FIRST CHILD
ENISHI
SECOND CHILD
KEI
THIRD CHILD
MIKOTO
FOURTH CHILD
NOZOMU
FIFTH CHILD
RIN
FIRST CHILD
MAJIRU
2005.11.09

ITOSHIKI FAMILY TREE- ENISHI ITOSHIKI'S ELDEST SON

MAJIRU ITOSHIKI

NOZOMU ITOSHIKI'S RESIDENT PARASITE

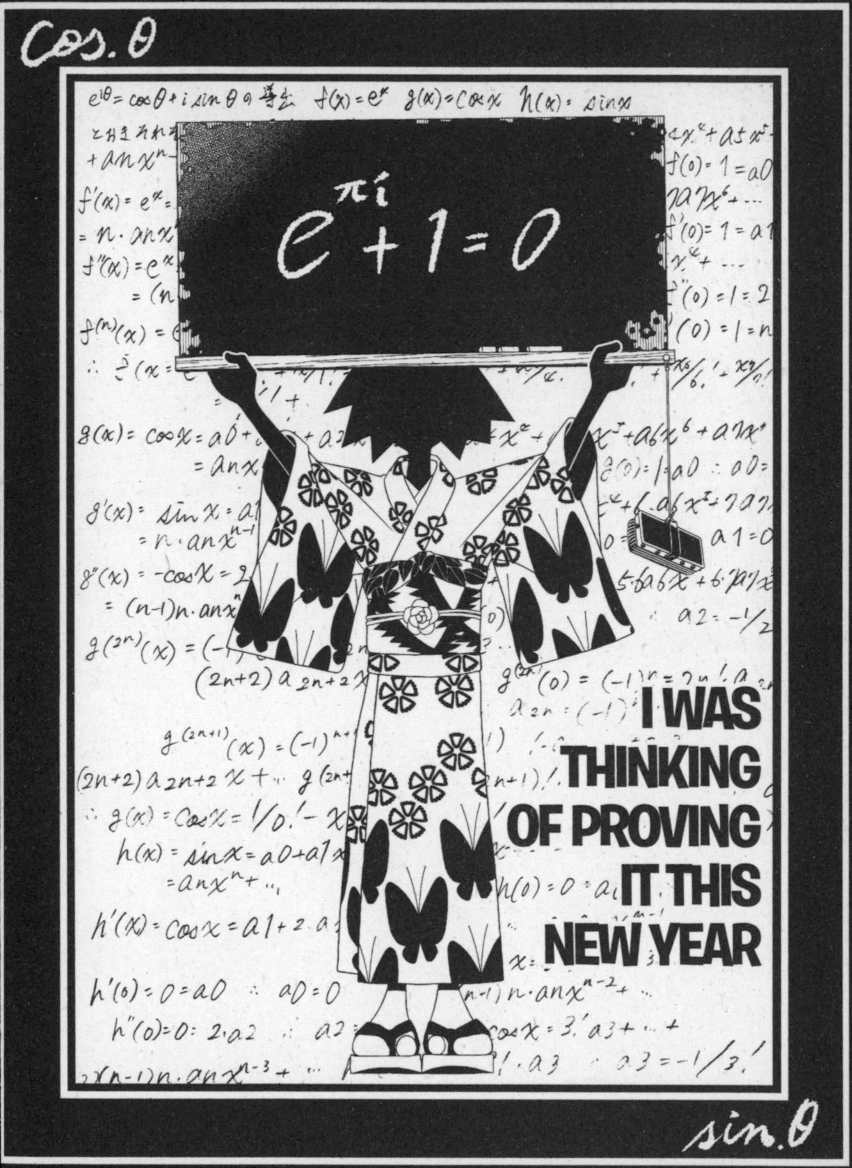
Cos. θ
e^{πi} + 1 = 0
I WAS THINKING OF PROVING IT THIS NEW YEAR
sin. θ

CHAPTER 28

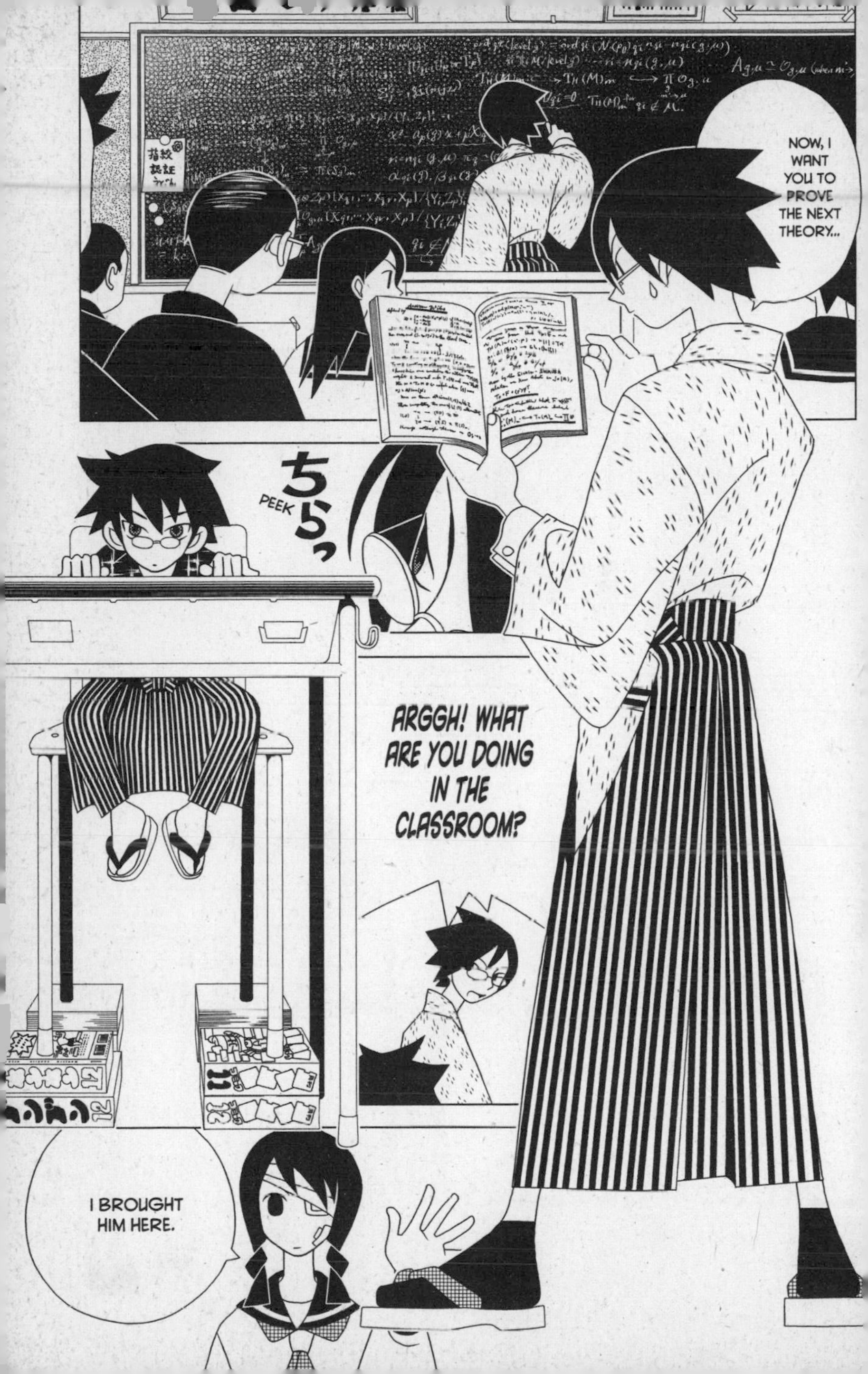
NOW, I WANT YOU TO PROVE THE NEXT THEORY...
ちらっ
PEEK
ARGGH! WHAT ARE YOU DOING IN THE CLASSROOM?
I BROUGHT HIM HERE.

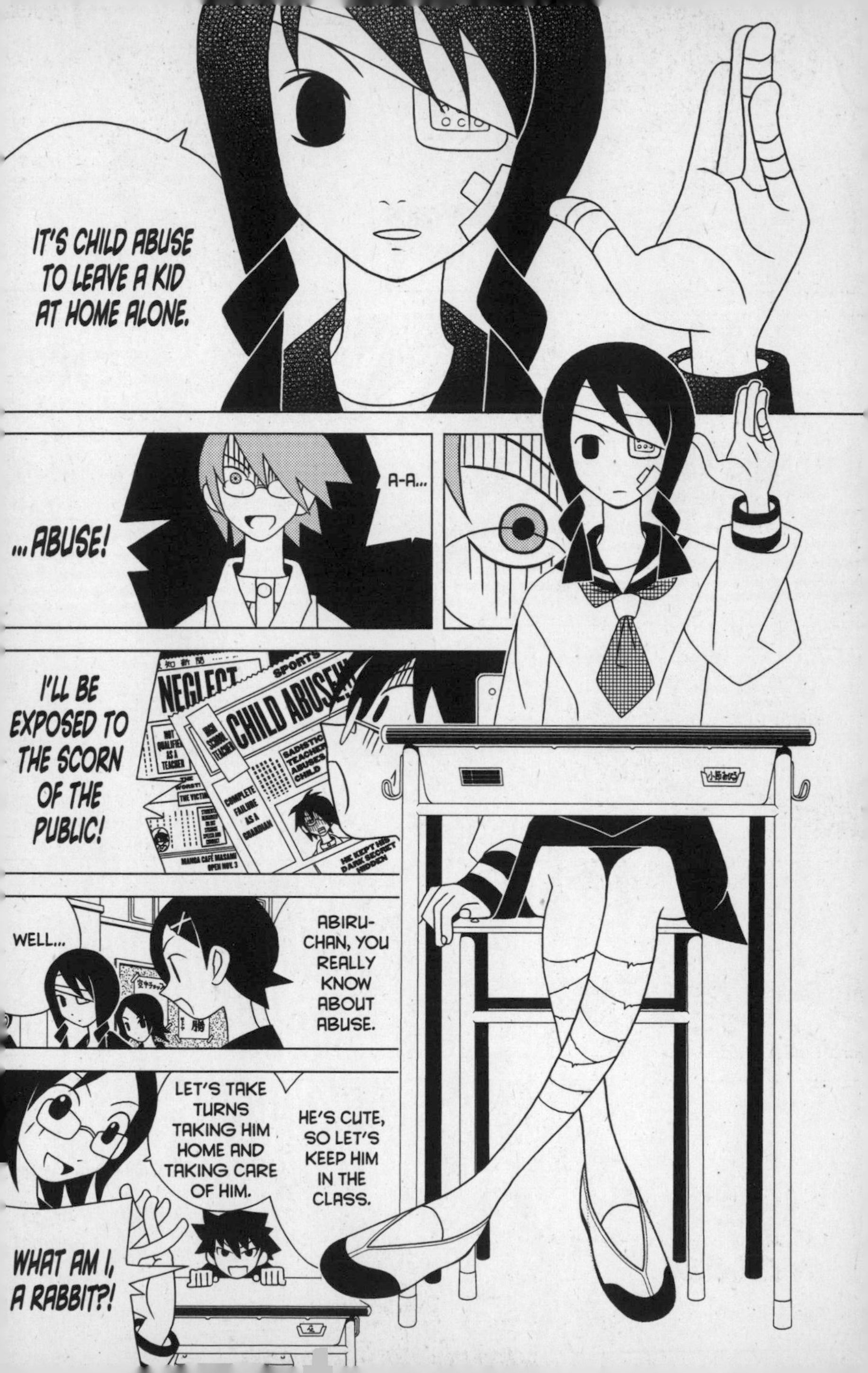
IT'S CHILD ABUSE TO LEAVE A KID AT HOME ALONE.
A-A...
...ABUSE!
I'LL BE EXPOSED TO THE SCORN OF THE PUBLIC!
NEGLECT
SPORTS
CHILD ABUSE
HIGH SCHOOL TEACHER
SADISTIC TEACHER ABUSES CHILD
NOT QUALIFIED AS A TEACHER
COMPLETE FAILURE AS A GUARDIAN
HE KEPT HIS DARK SECRET HIDDEN
MANGA CAFÉ MASAMI OPEN NOV. 3
ABIRU-CHAN, YOU REALLY KNOW ABOUT ABUSE.
WELL...
HE'S CUTE, SO LET'S KEEP HIM IN THE CLASS.
LET'S TAKE TURNS TAKING HIM HOME AND TAKING CARE OF HIM.
WHAT AM I, A RABBIT?!

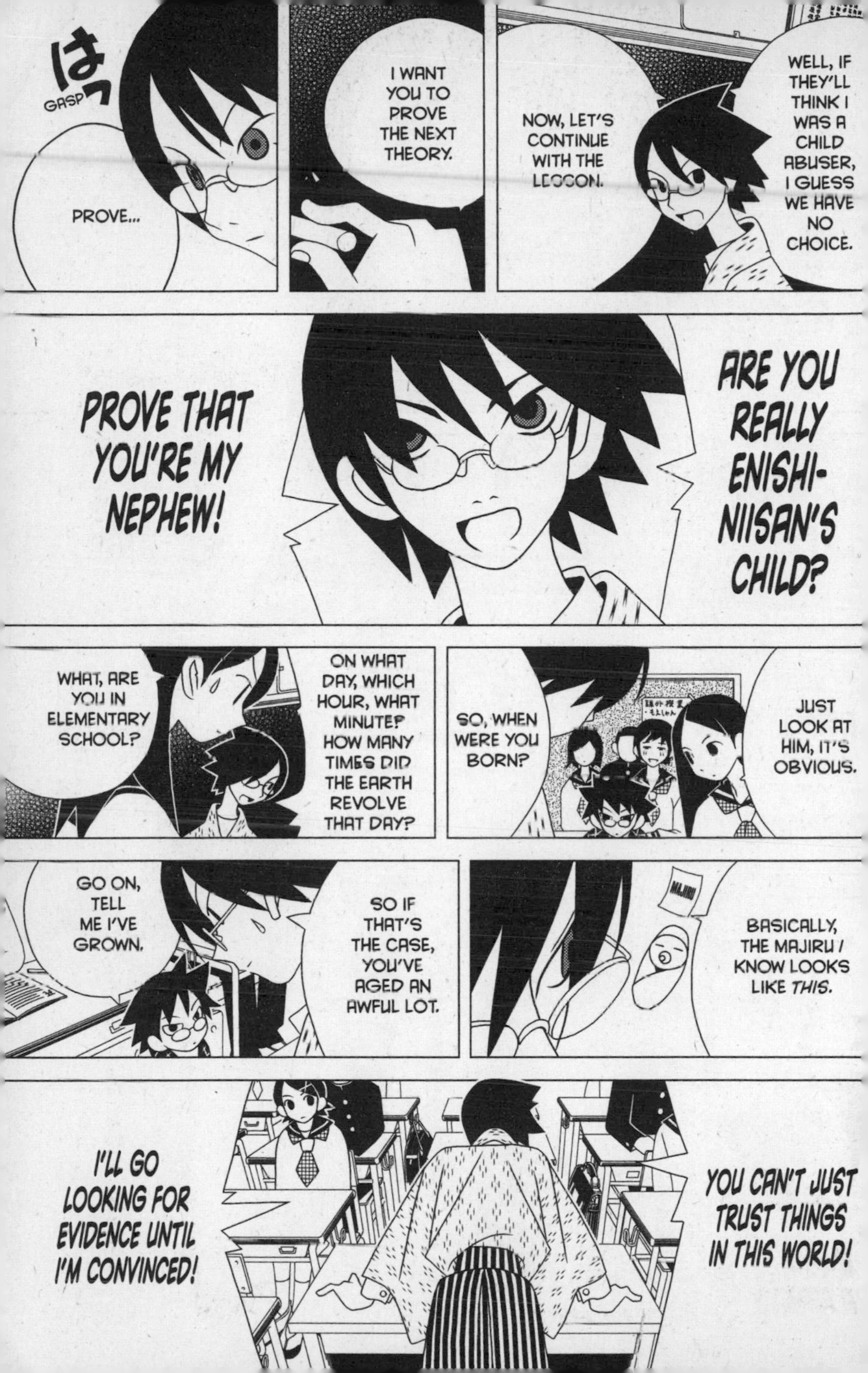
WELL, IF THEY'LL THINK I WAS A CHILD ABUSER, I GUESS WE HAVE NO CHOICE.
NOW, LET'S CONTINUE WITH THE LESSON.
I WANT YOU TO PROVE THE NEXT THEORY.
はっ
GASP
PROVE...
ARE YOU REALLY ENISHI-NIISAN'S CHILD?
PROVE THAT YOU'RE MY NEPHEW!
JUST LOOK AT HIM, IT'S OBVIOUS.
SO, WHEN WERE YOU BORN?
ON WHAT DAY, WHICH HOUR, WHAT MINUTE? HOW MANY TIMES DID THE EARTH REVOLVE THAT DAY?
WHAT, ARE YOU IN ELEMENTARY SCHOOL?
MAJIRU
BASICALLY, THE MAJIRU I KNOW LOOKS LIKE *THIS*.
SO IF THAT'S THE CASE, YOU'VE AGED AN AWFUL LOT.
GO ON, TELL ME I'VE GROWN.
YOU CAN'T JUST TRUST THINGS IN THIS WORLD!
I'LL GO LOOKING FOR EVIDENCE UNTIL I'M CONVINCED!

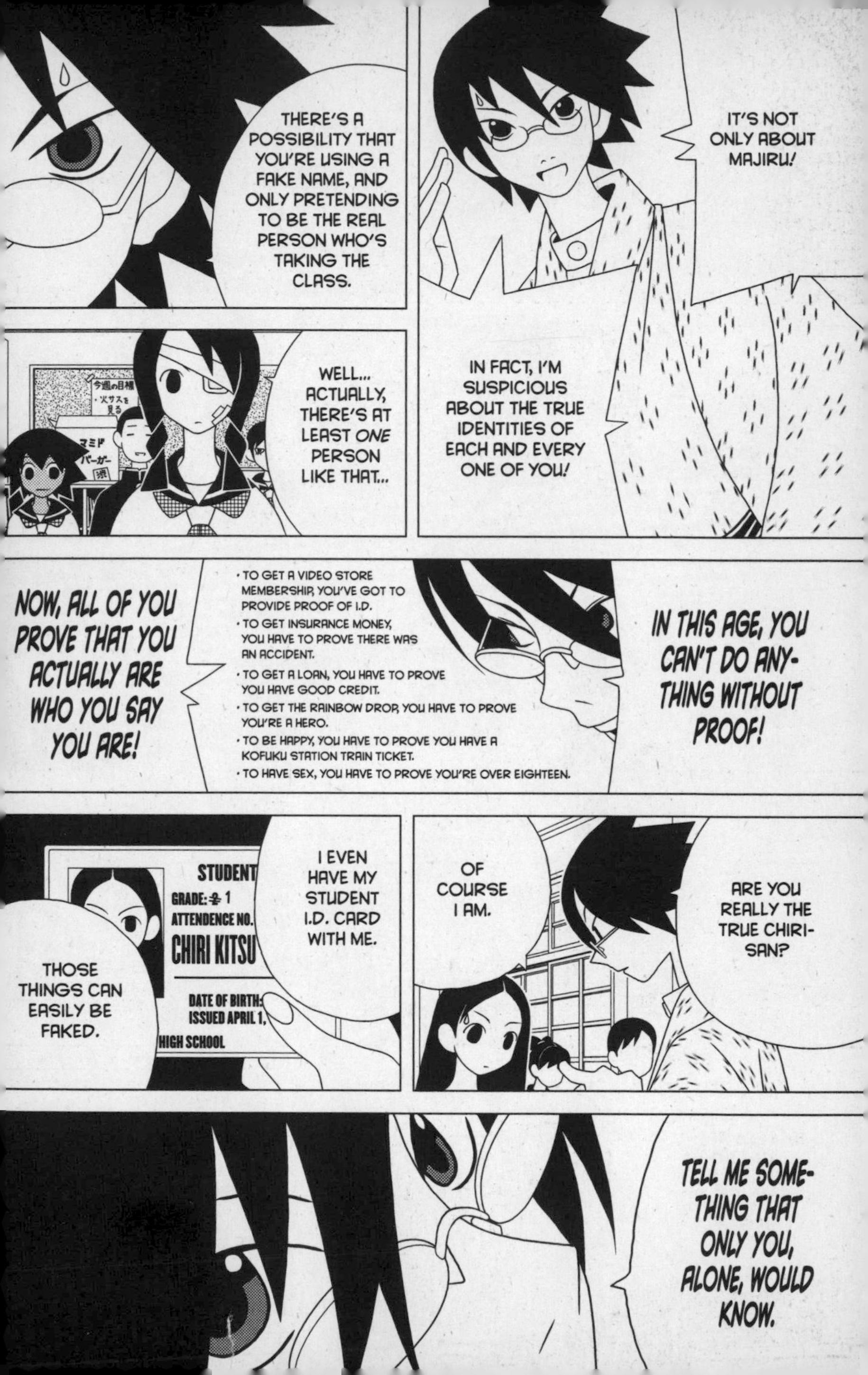
IT'S NOT ONLY ABOUT MAJIRU!
IN FACT, I'M SUSPICIOUS ABOUT THE TRUE IDENTITIES OF EACH AND EVERY ONE OF YOU!
THERE'S A POSSIBILITY THAT YOU'RE USING A FAKE NAME, AND ONLY PRETENDING TO BE THE REAL PERSON WHO'S TAKING THE CLASS.
WELL... ACTUALLY, THERE'S AT LEAST *ONE* PERSON LIKE THAT...
IN THIS AGE, YOU CAN'T DO ANYTHING WITHOUT PROOF!
• TO GET A VIDEO STORE MEMBERSHIP, YOU'VE GOT TO PROVIDE PROOF OF I.D.
• TO GET INSURANCE MONEY, YOU HAVE TO PROVE THERE WAS AN ACCIDENT.
• TO GET A LOAN, YOU HAVE TO PROVE YOU HAVE GOOD CREDIT.
• TO GET THE RAINBOW DROP, YOU HAVE TO PROVE YOU'RE A HERO.
• TO BE HAPPY, YOU HAVE TO PROVE YOU HAVE A KOFUKU STATION TRAIN TICKET.
• TO HAVE SEX, YOU HAVE TO PROVE YOU'RE OVER EIGHTEEN.
NOW, ALL OF YOU PROVE THAT YOU ACTUALLY ARE WHO YOU SAY YOU ARE!
ARE YOU REALLY THE TRUE CHIRI-SAN?
OF COURSE I AM.
I EVEN HAVE MY STUDENT I.D. CARD WITH ME.
STUDENT
GRADE: 1
ATTENDENCE NO.
CHIRI KITSU
DATE OF BIRTH:
ISSUED APRIL 1,
HIGH SCHOOL
THOSE THINGS CAN EASILY BE FAKED.
TELL ME SOMETHING THAT ONLY YOU, ALONE, WOULD KNOW.

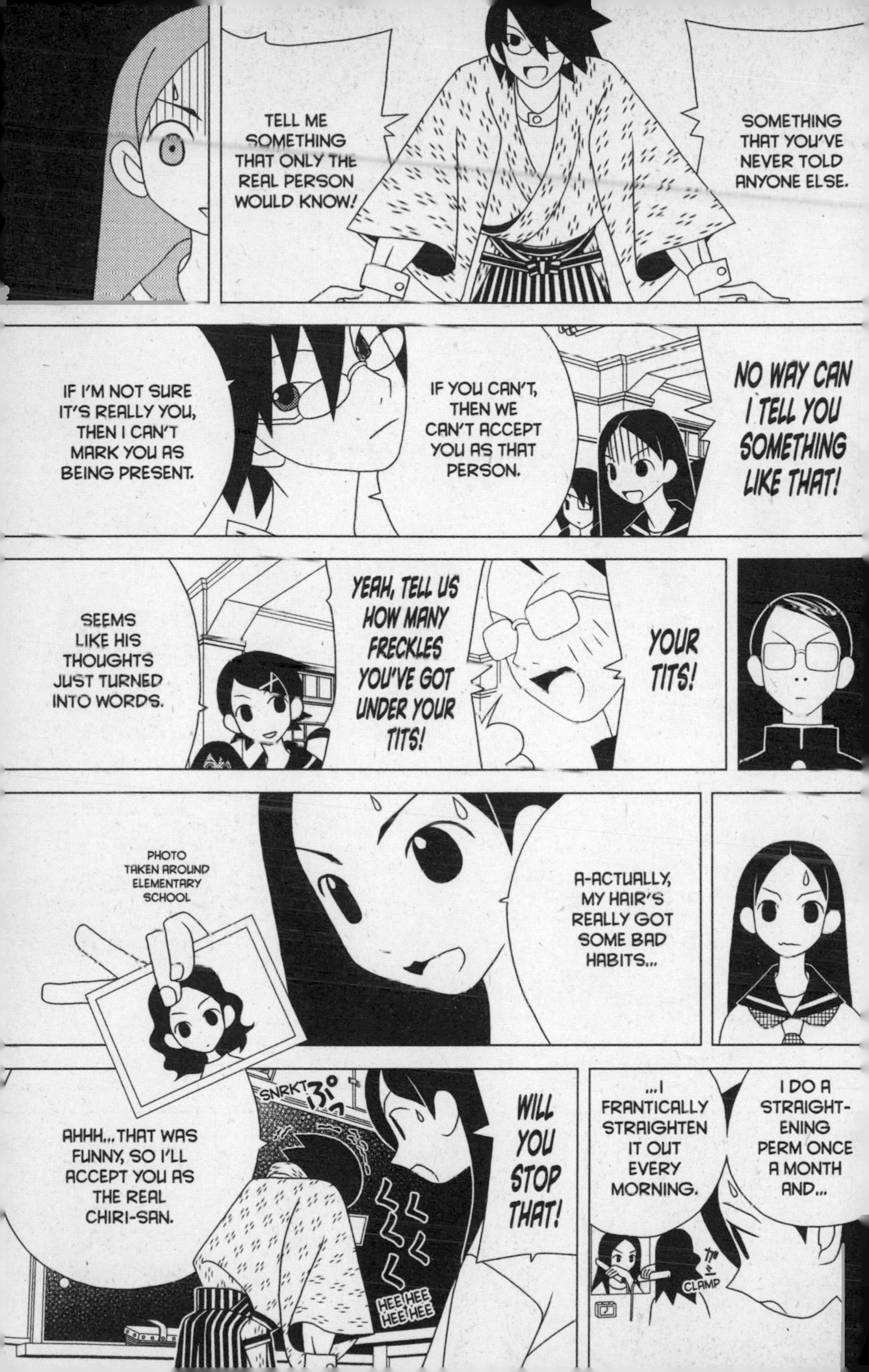
SOMETHING THAT YOU'VE NEVER TOLD ANYONE ELSE.
TELL ME SOMETHING THAT ONLY THE REAL PERSON WOULD KNOW!
NO WAY CAN I TELL YOU SOMETHING LIKE THAT!
IF YOU CAN'T, THEN WE CAN'T ACCEPT YOU AS THAT PERSON.
IF I'M NOT SURE IT'S REALLY YOU, THEN I CAN'T MARK YOU AS BEING PRESENT.
YOUR TITS!
YEAH, TELL US HOW MANY FRECKLES YOU'VE GOT UNDER YOUR TITS!
SEEMS LIKE HIS THOUGHTS JUST TURNED INTO WORDS.
A-ACTUALLY, MY HAIR'S REALLY GOT SOME BAD HABITS...
PHOTO TAKEN AROUND ELEMENTARY SCHOOL
I DO A STRAIGHT-ENING PERM ONCE A MONTH AND...
...I FRANTICALLY STRAIGHTEN IT OUT EVERY MORNING.
CLAMP
WILL YOU STOP THAT!
SNRKT
HEE HEE HEE HEE
AHHH...THAT WAS FUNNY, SO I'LL ACCEPT YOU AS THE REAL CHIRI-SAN.

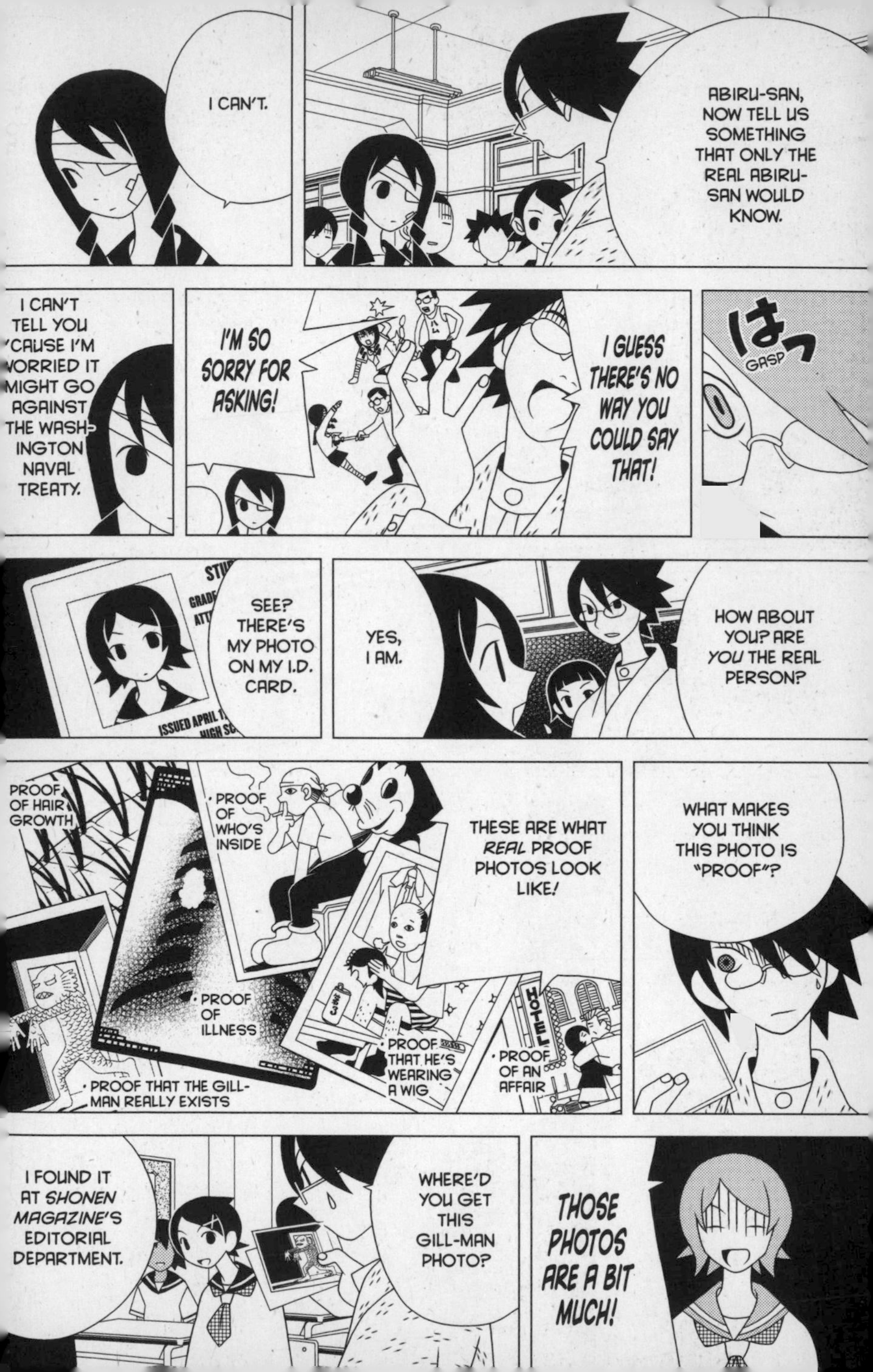
ABIRU-SAN, NOW TELL US SOMETHING THAT ONLY THE REAL ABIRU-SAN WOULD KNOW.
I CAN'T.
はっ
GASP
I GUESS THERE'S NO WAY YOU COULD SAY THAT!
I'M SO SORRY FOR ASKING!
I CAN'T TELL YOU 'CAUSE I'M WORRIED IT MIGHT GO AGAINST THE WASHINGTON NAVAL TREATY.
HOW ABOUT YOU? ARE *YOU* THE REAL PERSON?
YES, I AM.
SEE? THERE'S MY PHOTO ON MY I.D. CARD.
WHAT MAKES YOU THINK THIS PHOTO IS "PROOF"?
THESE ARE WHAT *REAL* PROOF PHOTOS LOOK LIKE!
• PROOF OF WHO'S INSIDE
PROOF OF HAIR GROWTH
HOTEL
• PROOF OF AN AFFAIR
• PROOF THAT HE'S WEARING A WIG
• PROOF OF ILLNESS
• PROOF THAT THE GILL-MAN REALLY EXISTS
THOSE PHOTOS ARE A BIT MUCH!
WHERE'D YOU GET THIS GILL-MAN PHOTO?
I FOUND IT AT *SHONEN MAGAZINE*'S EDITORIAL DEPARTMENT.

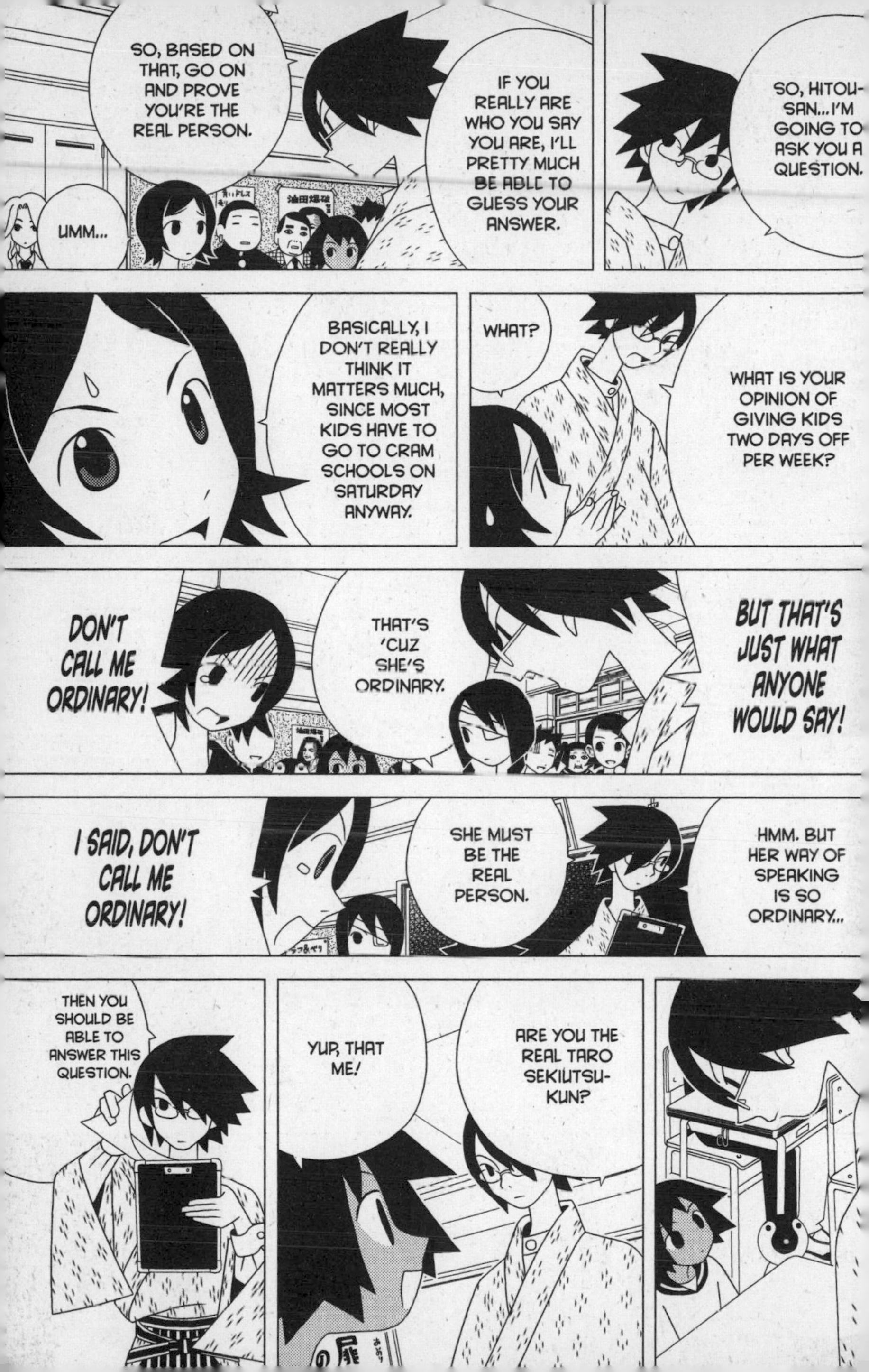
SO, HITOU-SAN...I'M GOING TO ASK YOU A QUESTION.
IF YOU REALLY ARE WHO YOU SAY YOU ARE, I'LL PRETTY MUCH BE ABLE TO GUESS YOUR ANSWER.
SO, BASED ON THAT, GO ON AND PROVE YOU'RE THE REAL PERSON.
UMM...
WHAT IS YOUR OPINION OF GIVING KIDS TWO DAYS OFF PER WEEK?
WHAT?
BASICALLY, I DON'T REALLY THINK IT MATTERS MUCH, SINCE MOST KIDS HAVE TO GO TO CRAM SCHOOLS ON SATURDAY ANYWAY.
BUT THAT'S JUST WHAT ANYONE WOULD SAY!
THAT'S 'CUZ SHE'S ORDINARY.
DON'T CALL ME ORDINARY!
HMM. BUT HER WAY OF SPEAKING IS SO ORDINARY...
SHE MUST BE THE REAL PERSON.
I SAID, DON'T CALL ME ORDINARY!
ARE YOU THE REAL TARO SEKIUTSU-KUN?
YUP, THAT ME!
THEN YOU SHOULD BE ABLE TO ANSWER THIS QUESTION.

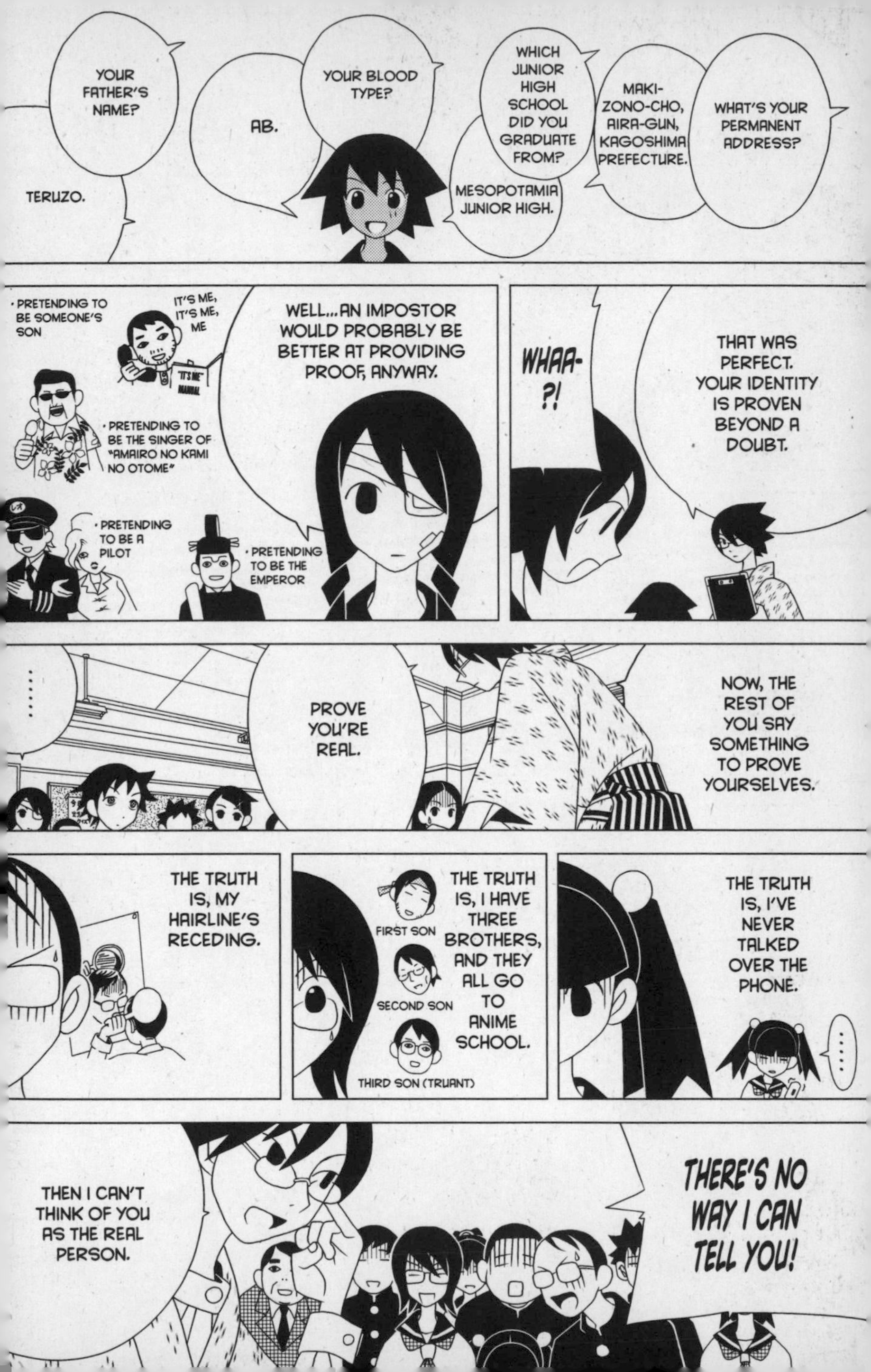
WHAT'S YOUR PERMANENT ADDRESS?
MAKI-ZONO-CHO, AIRA-GUN, KAGOSHIMA PREFECTURE.
WHICH JUNIOR HIGH SCHOOL DID YOU GRADUATE FROM?
MESOPOTAMIA JUNIOR HIGH.
YOUR BLOOD TYPE?
AB.
YOUR FATHER'S NAME?
TERUZO.
THAT WAS PERFECT. YOUR IDENTITY IS PROVEN BEYOND A DOUBT.
WHAA-?!
WELL...AN IMPOSTOR WOULD PROBABLY BE BETTER AT PROVIDING PROOF, ANYWAY.
IT'S ME, IT'S ME, ME
• PRETENDING TO BE SOMEONE'S SON
"IT'S ME" MANUAL
• PRETENDING TO BE THE SINGER OF "AMAIRO NO KAMI NO OTOME"
• PRETENDING TO BE A PILOT
• PRETENDING TO BE THE EMPEROR
NOW, THE REST OF YOU SAY SOMETHING TO PROVE YOURSELVES.
PROVE YOU'RE REAL.
......
THE TRUTH IS, I'VE NEVER TALKED OVER THE PHONE.
.....
THE TRUTH IS, I HAVE THREE BROTHERS, AND THEY ALL GO TO ANIME SCHOOL.
FIRST SON
SECOND SON
THIRD SON (TRUANT)
THE TRUTH IS, MY HAIRLINE'S RECEDING.
THERE'S NO WAY I CAN TELL YOU!
THEN I CAN'T THINK OF YOU AS THE REAL PERSON.

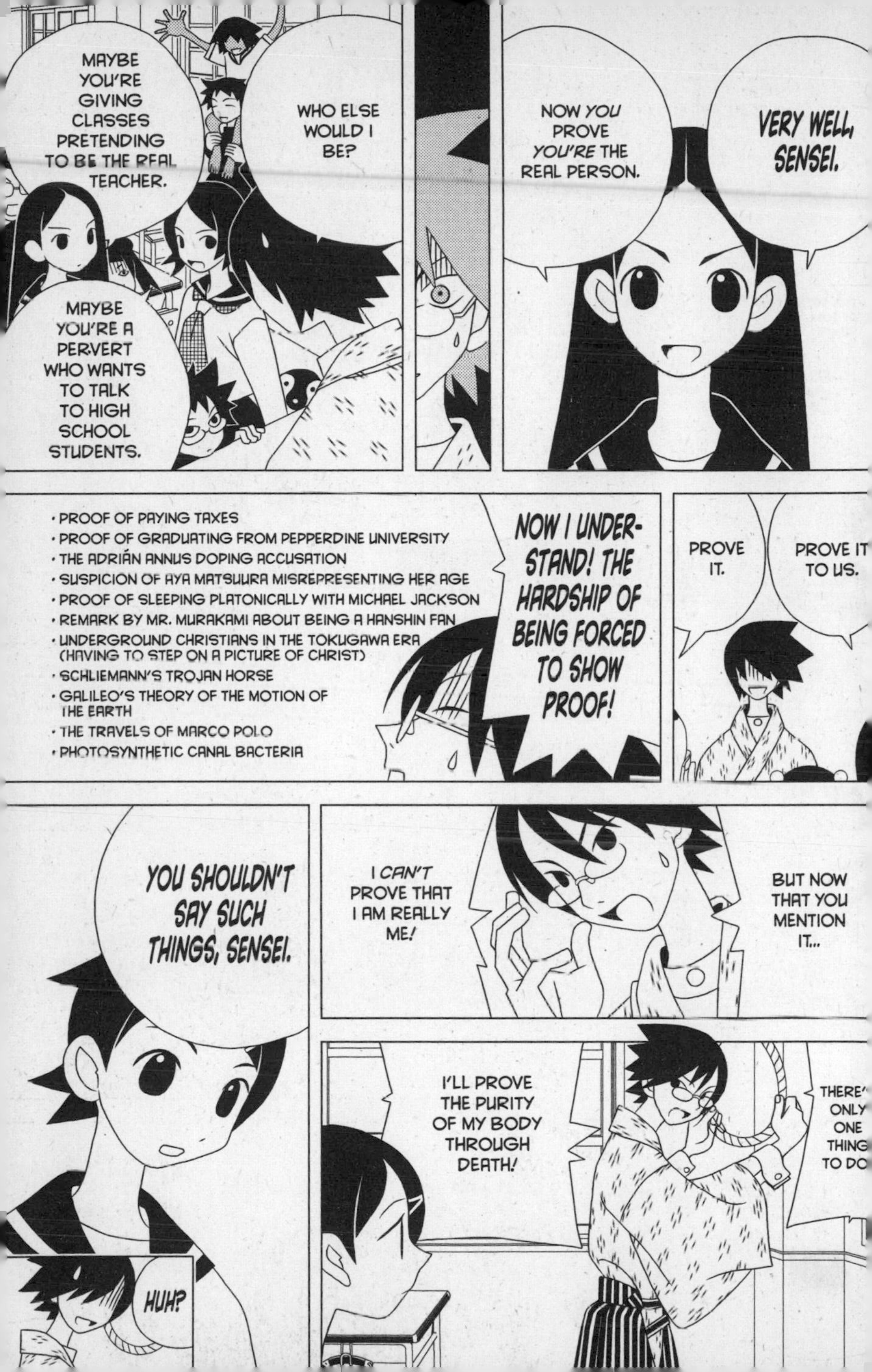
VERY WELL, SENSEI.
NOW *YOU* PROVE *YOU'RE* THE REAL PERSON.
WHO ELSE WOULD I BE?
MAYBE YOU'RE GIVING CLASSES PRETENDING TO BE THE REAL TEACHER.
MAYBE YOU'RE A PERVERT WHO WANTS TO TALK TO HIGH SCHOOL STUDENTS.
PROVE IT TO US.
PROVE IT.
NOW I UNDERSTAND! THE HARDSHIP OF BEING FORCED TO SHOW PROOF!
• PROOF OF PAYING TAXES
• PROOF OF GRADUATING FROM PEPPERDINE UNIVERSITY
• THE ADRIÁN ANNUS DOPING ACCUSATION
• SUSPICION OF AYA MATSUURA MISREPRESENTING HER AGE
• PROOF OF SLEEPING PLATONICALLY WITH MICHAEL JACKSON
• REMARK BY MR. MURAKAMI ABOUT BEING A HANSHIN FAN
• UNDERGROUND CHRISTIANS IN THE TOKUGAWA ERA (HAVING TO STEP ON A PICTURE OF CHRIST)
• SCHLIEMANN'S TROJAN HORSE
• GALILEO'S THEORY OF THE MOTION OF THE EARTH
• THE TRAVELS OF MARCO POLO
• PHOTOSYNTHETIC CANAL BACTERIA
BUT NOW THAT YOU MENTION IT...
I *CAN'T* PROVE THAT I AM REALLY ME!
THERE' ONLY ONE THING TO DO
I'LL PROVE THE PURITY OF MY BODY THROUGH DEATH!
YOU SHOULDN'T SAY SUCH THINGS, SENSEI.
HUH?

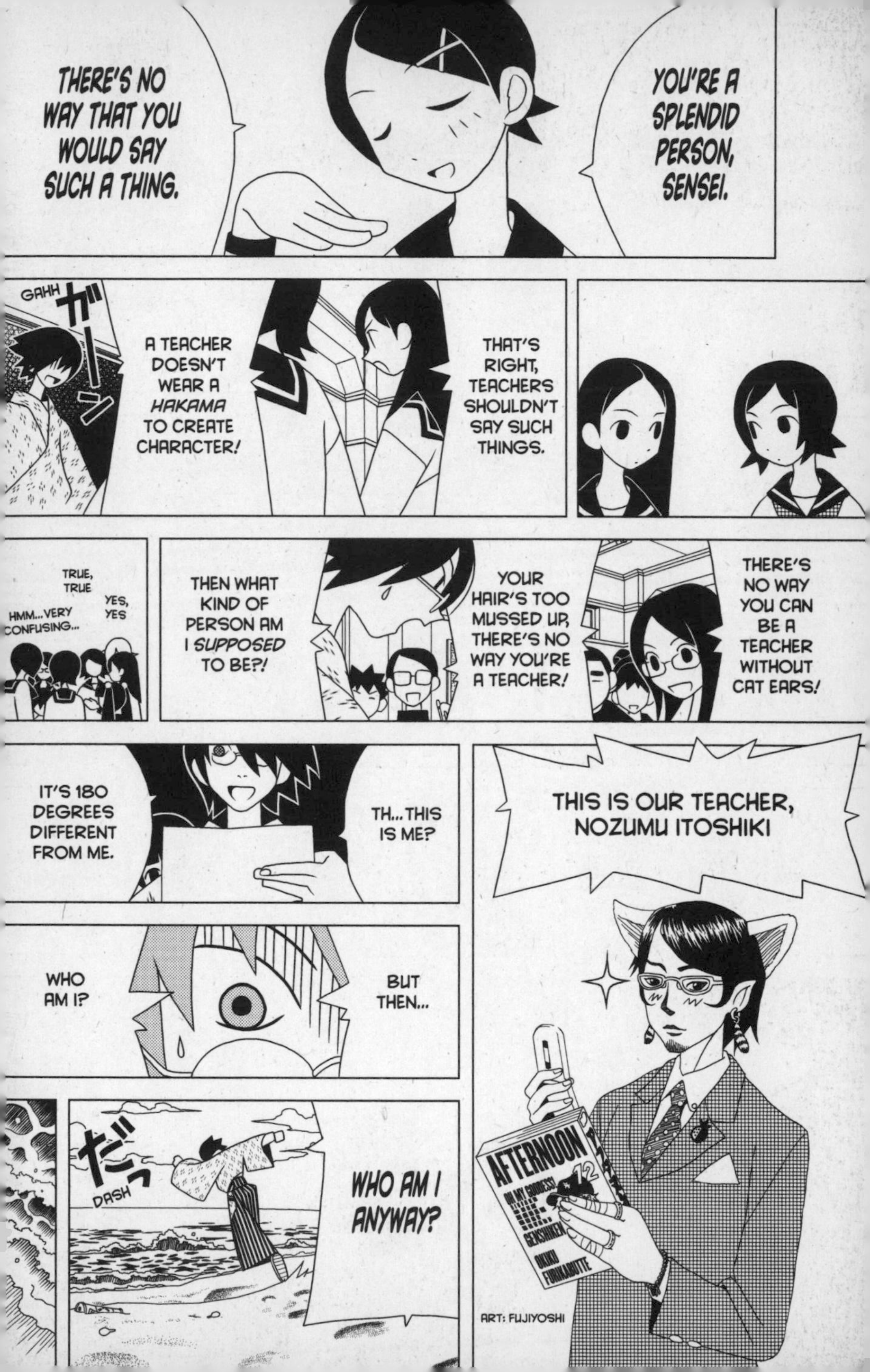
YOU'RE A SPLENDID PERSON, SENSEI.
THERE'S NO WAY THAT YOU WOULD SAY SUCH A THING.
THAT'S RIGHT, TEACHERS SHOULDN'T SAY SUCH THINGS.
A TEACHER DOESN'T WEAR A *HAKAMA* TO CREATE CHARACTER!
GAHH
THERE'S NO WAY YOU CAN BE A TEACHER WITHOUT CAT EARS!
YOUR HAIR'S TOO MUSSED UP, THERE'S NO WAY YOU'RE A TEACHER!
THEN WHAT KIND OF PERSON AM I *SUPPOSED* TO BE?!
YES, YES
TRUE, TRUE
HMM...VERY CONFUSING...
THIS IS OUR TEACHER, NOZUMU ITOSHIKI
AFTERNOON
12
OH MY GODDESS!
GENSHIKEN
ART: FUJIYOSHI
TH...THIS IS ME?
IT'S 180 DEGREES DIFFERENT FROM ME.
BUT THEN...
WHO AM I?
WHO AM I ANYWAY?
DASH

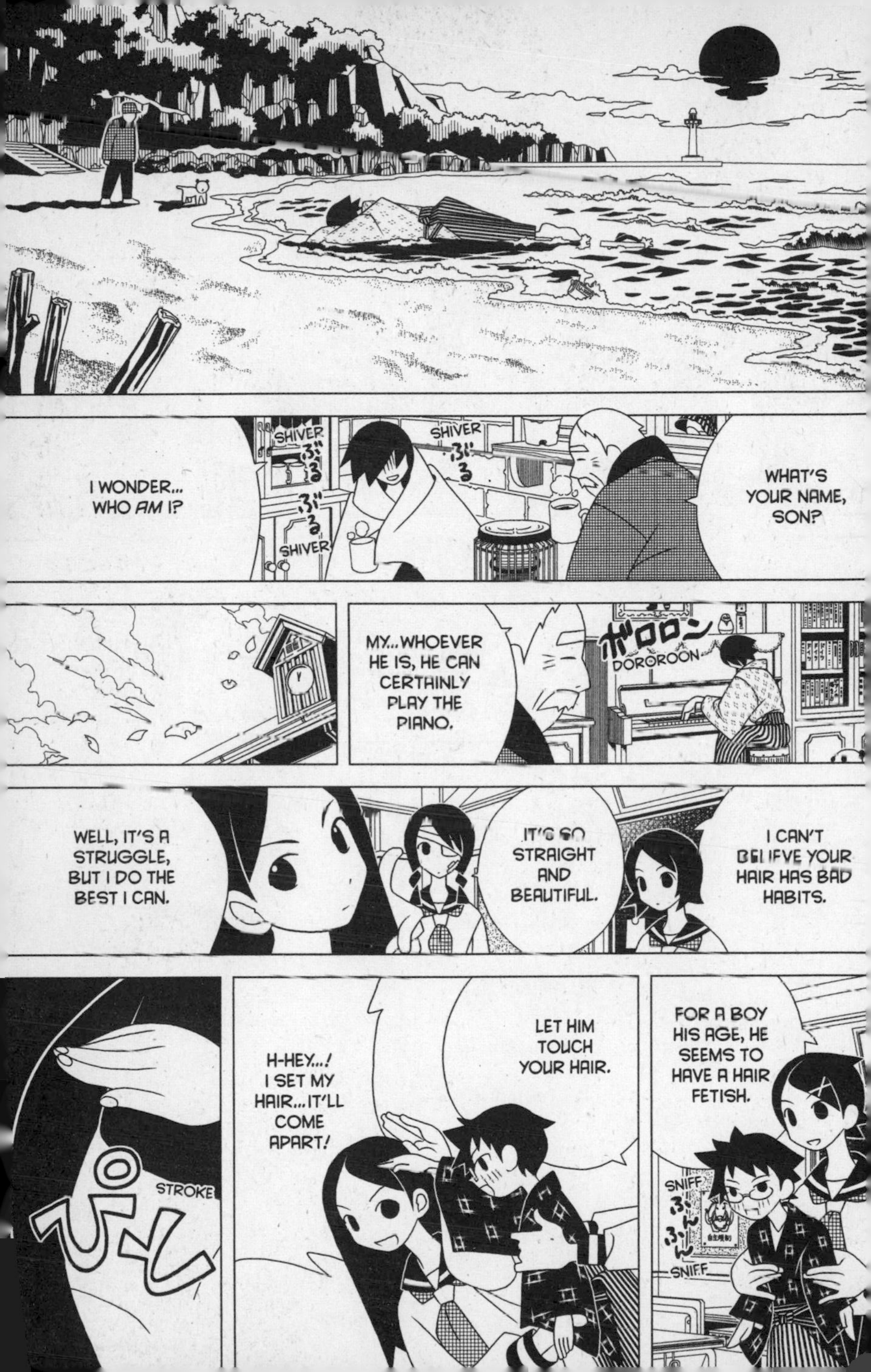
WHAT'S YOUR NAME, SON?
SHIVER
ぶる
SHIVER
ぶる
ぶる
I WONDER... WHO AM I?
ボロロン
DOROROON
MY... WHOEVER HE IS, HE CAN CERTAINLY PLAY THE PIANO.
I CAN'T BELIEVE YOUR HAIR HAS BAD HABITS.
IT'S SO STRAIGHT AND BEAUTIFUL.
WELL, IT'S A STRUGGLE, BUT I DO THE BEST I CAN.
FOR A BOY HIS AGE, HE SEEMS TO HAVE A HAIR FETISH.
SNIFF
ふん
ふん
SNIFF
LET HIM TOUCH YOUR HAIR.
H-HEY...! I SET MY HAIR... IT'LL COME APART!
STROKE
ぴと

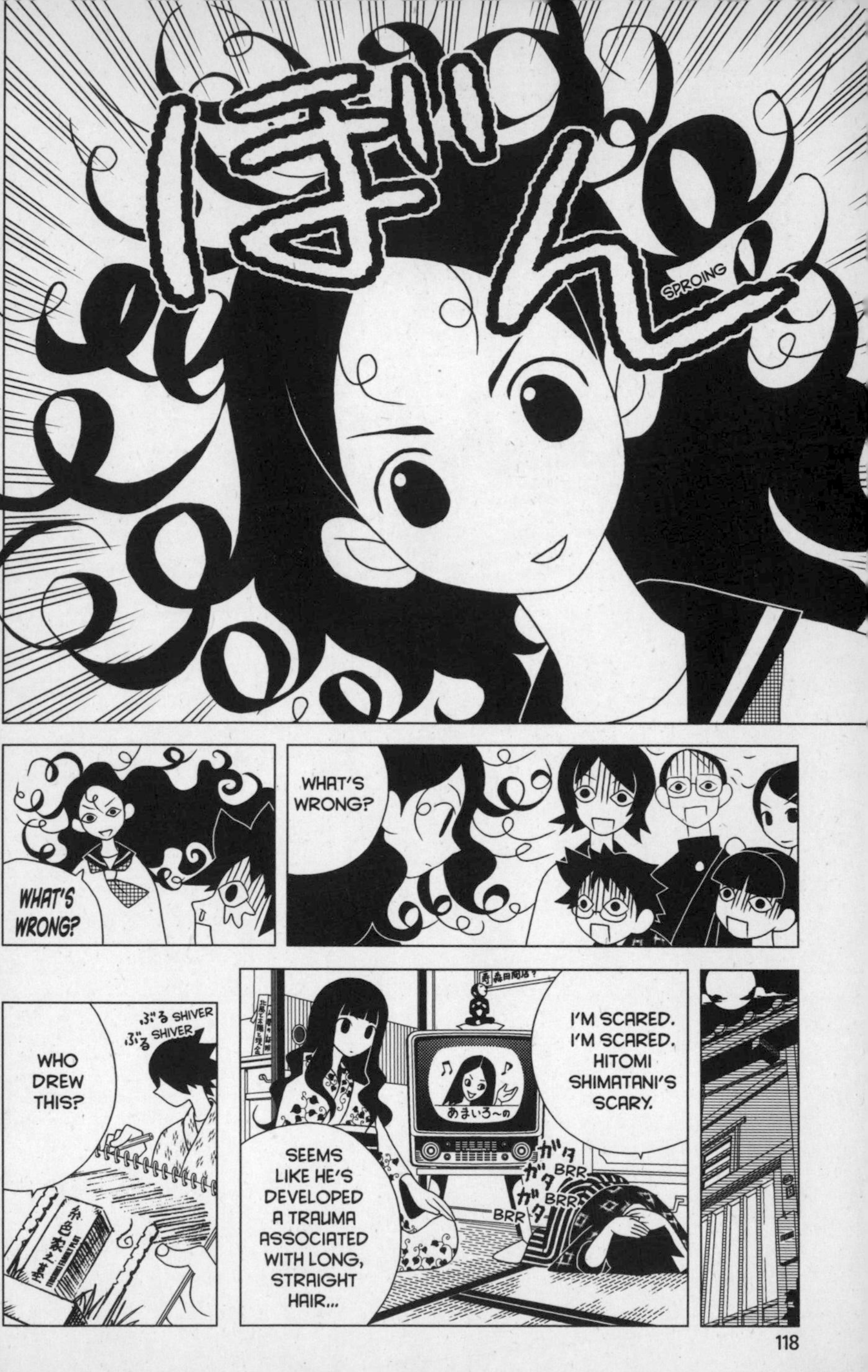
ぼいん
SPROING
WHAT'S WRONG?
WHAT'S WRONG?
I'M SCARED. I'M SCARED. HITOMI SHIMATANI'S SCARY.
あまいろ～の
ガタ BRR
ガタ BRR
ガタ BRR
SEEMS LIKE HE'S DEVELOPED A TRAUMA ASSOCIATED WITH LONG, STRAIGHT HAIR...
ぶる SHIVER
ぶる SHIVER
WHO DREW THIS?

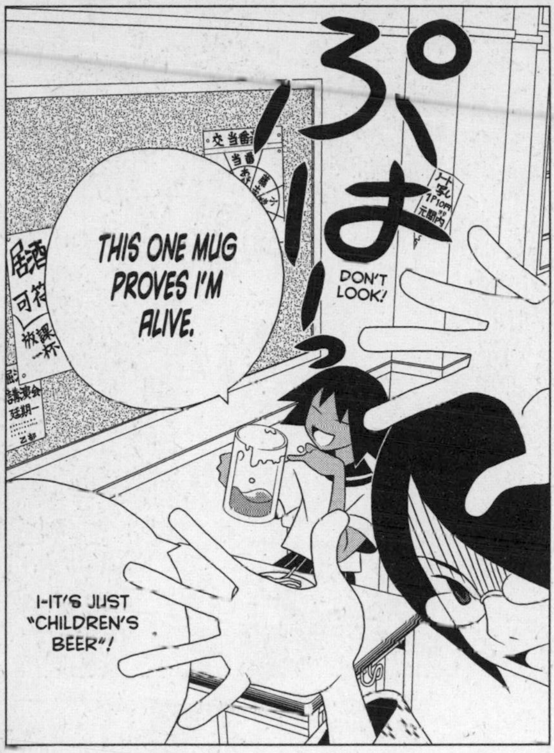
ぷはーっ
THIS ONE MUG PROVES I'M ALIVE.
DON'T LOOK!
I-IT'S JUST "CHILDREN'S BEER"!

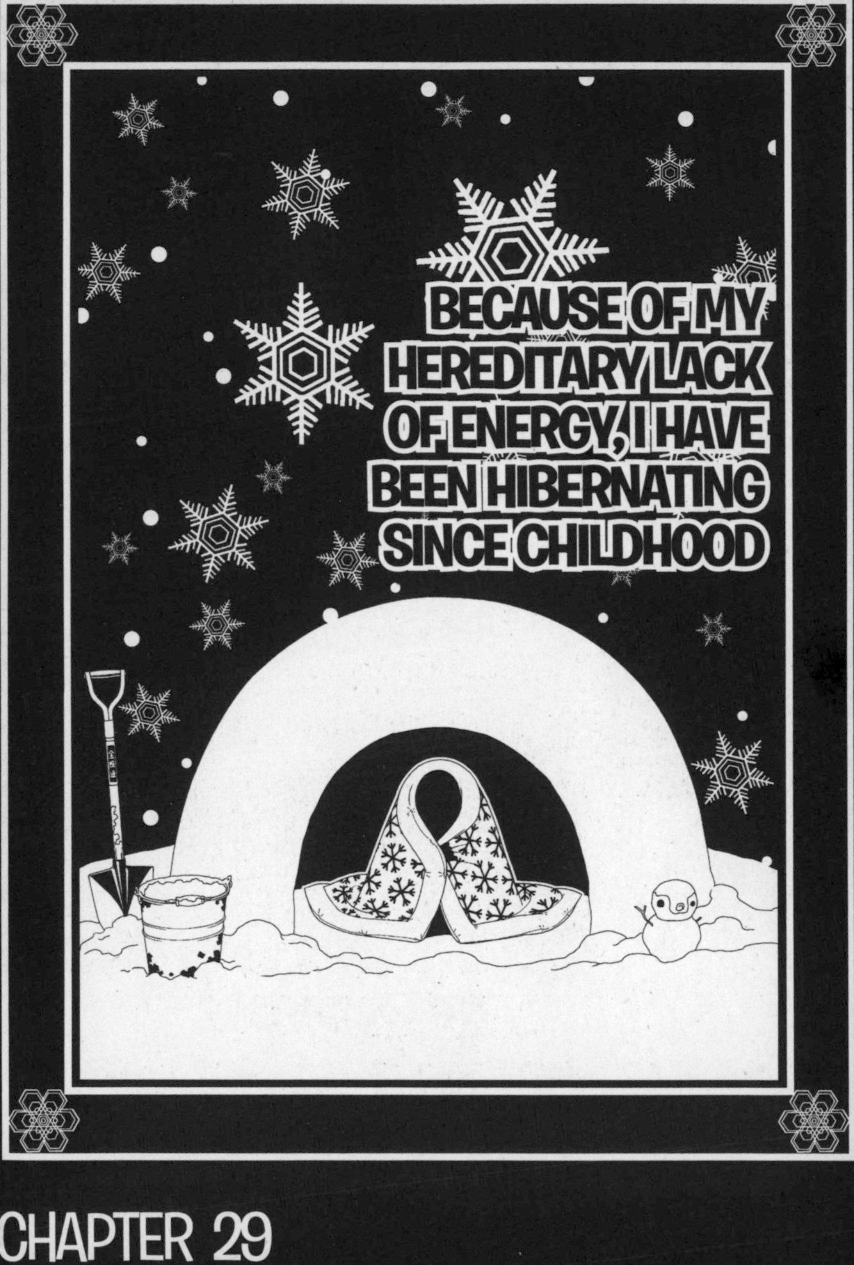
BECAUSE OF MY HEREDITARY LACK OF ENERGY, I HAVE BEEN HIBERNATING SINCE CHILDHOOD

CHAPTER 29

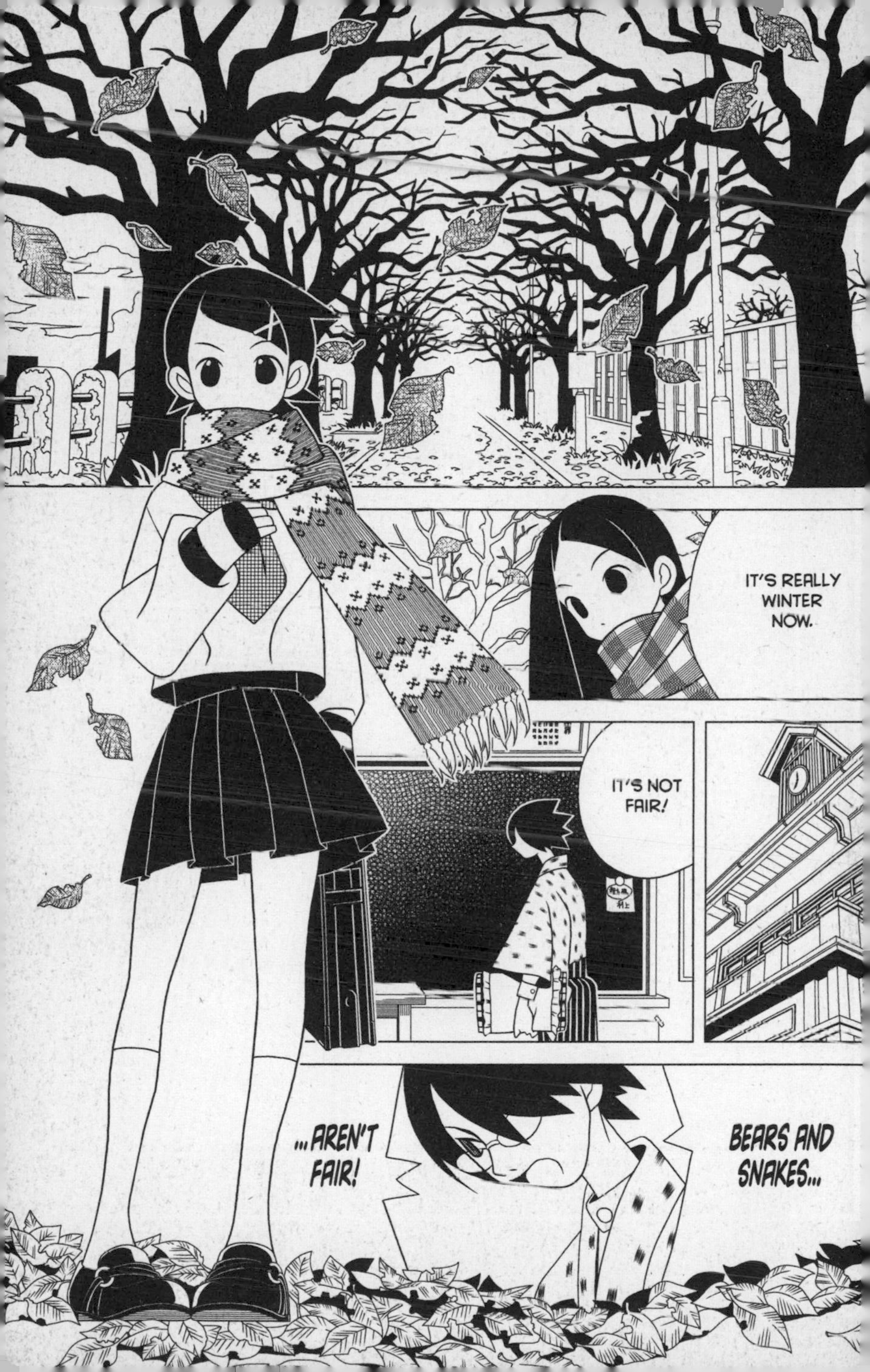
IT'S REALLY WINTER NOW.
IT'S NOT FAIR!
BEARS AND SNAKES...
...AREN'T FAIR!

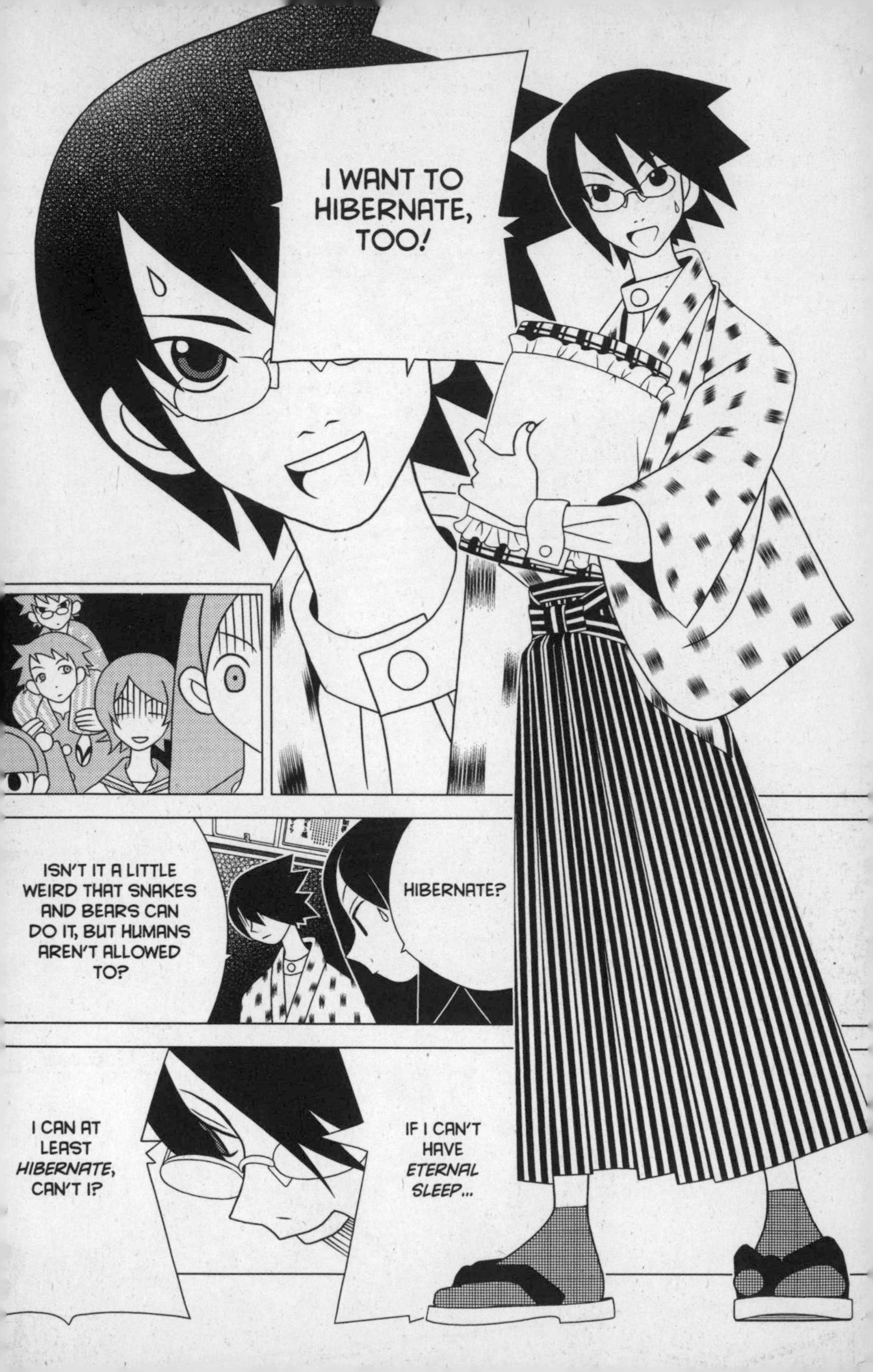
I WANT TO HIBERNATE, TOO!
HIBERNATE?
ISN'T IT A LITTLE WEIRD THAT SNAKES AND BEARS CAN DO IT, BUT HUMANS AREN'T ALLOWED TO?
IF I CAN'T HAVE *ETERNAL SLEEP*...
I CAN AT LEAST *HIBERNATE*, CAN'T I?

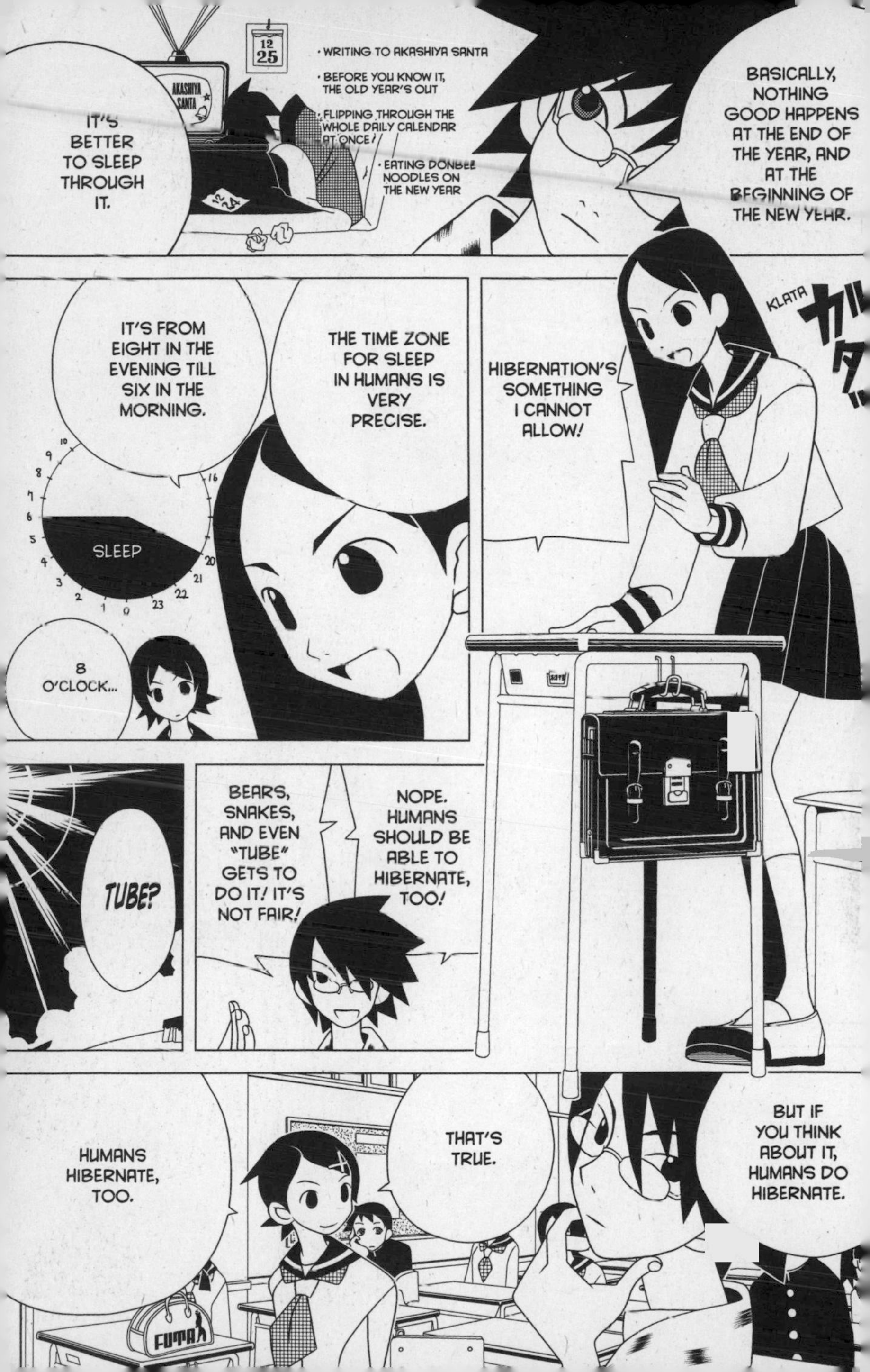
BASICALLY, NOTHING GOOD HAPPENS AT THE END OF THE YEAR, AND AT THE BEGINNING OF THE NEW YEAR.
12 25
AKASHIYA SANTA
• WRITING TO AKASHIYA SANTA
• BEFORE YOU KNOW IT, THE OLD YEAR'S OUT
• FLIPPING THROUGH THE WHOLE DAILY CALENDAR AT ONCE!
• EATING DONBEE NOODLES ON THE NEW YEAR
IT'S BETTER TO SLEEP THROUGH IT.
KLATA
HIBERNATION'S SOMETHING I CANNOT ALLOW!
THE TIME ZONE FOR SLEEP IN HUMANS IS VERY PRECISE.
IT'S FROM EIGHT IN THE EVENING TILL SIX IN THE MORNING.
SLEEP
8 O'CLOCK...
NOPE. HUMANS SHOULD BE ABLE TO HIBERNATE, TOO!
BEARS, SNAKES, AND EVEN "TUBE" GETS TO DO IT! IT'S NOT FAIR!
TUBE?
BUT IF YOU THINK ABOUT IT, HUMANS DO HIBERNATE.
THAT'S TRUE.
HUMANS HIBERNATE, TOO.
FUTA

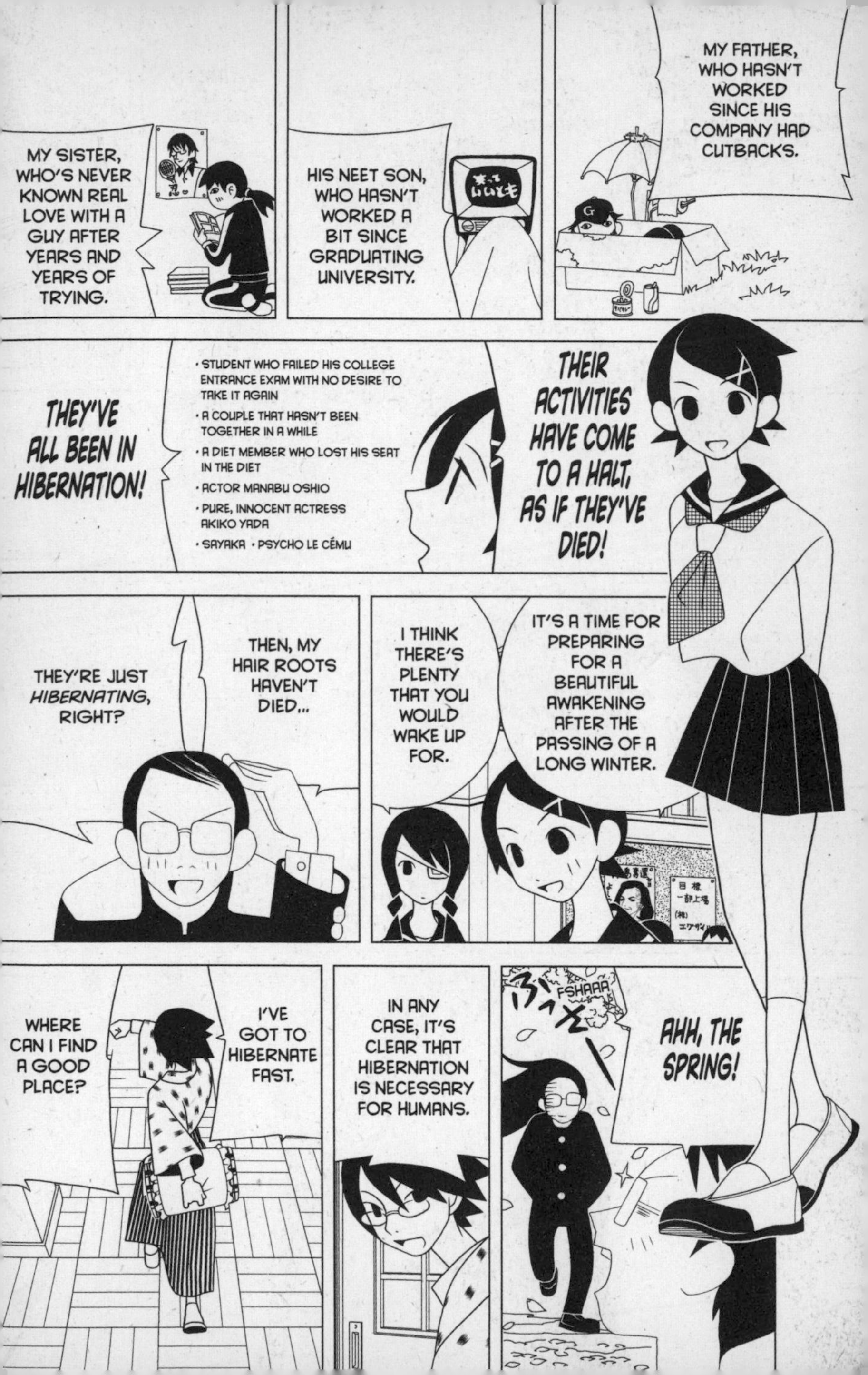
MY FATHER, WHO HASN'T WORKED SINCE HIS COMPANY HAD CUTBACKS.
HIS NEET SON, WHO HASN'T WORKED A BIT SINCE GRADUATING UNIVERSITY.
MY SISTER, WHO'S NEVER KNOWN REAL LOVE WITH A GUY AFTER YEARS AND YEARS OF TRYING.
THEIR ACTIVITIES HAVE COME TO A HALT, AS IF THEY'VE DIED!
• STUDENT WHO FAILED HIS COLLEGE ENTRANCE EXAM WITH NO DESIRE TO TAKE IT AGAIN
• A COUPLE THAT HASN'T BEEN TOGETHER IN A WHILE
• A DIET MEMBER WHO LOST HIS SEAT IN THE DIET
• ACTOR MANABU OSHIO
• PURE, INNOCENT ACTRESS AKIKO YADA
• SAYAKA • PSYCHO LE CÉMU
THEY'VE ALL BEEN IN HIBERNATION!
IT'S A TIME FOR PREPARING FOR A BEAUTIFUL AWAKENING AFTER THE PASSING OF A LONG WINTER.
I THINK THERE'S PLENTY THAT YOU WOULD WAKE UP FOR.
THEN, MY HAIR ROOTS HAVEN'T DIED...
THEY'RE JUST HIBERNATING, RIGHT?
AHH, THE SPRING!
FSHAAA
IN ANY CASE, IT'S CLEAR THAT HIBERNATION IS NECESSARY FOR HUMANS.
I'VE GOT TO HIBERNATE FAST.
WHERE CAN I FIND A GOOD PLACE?

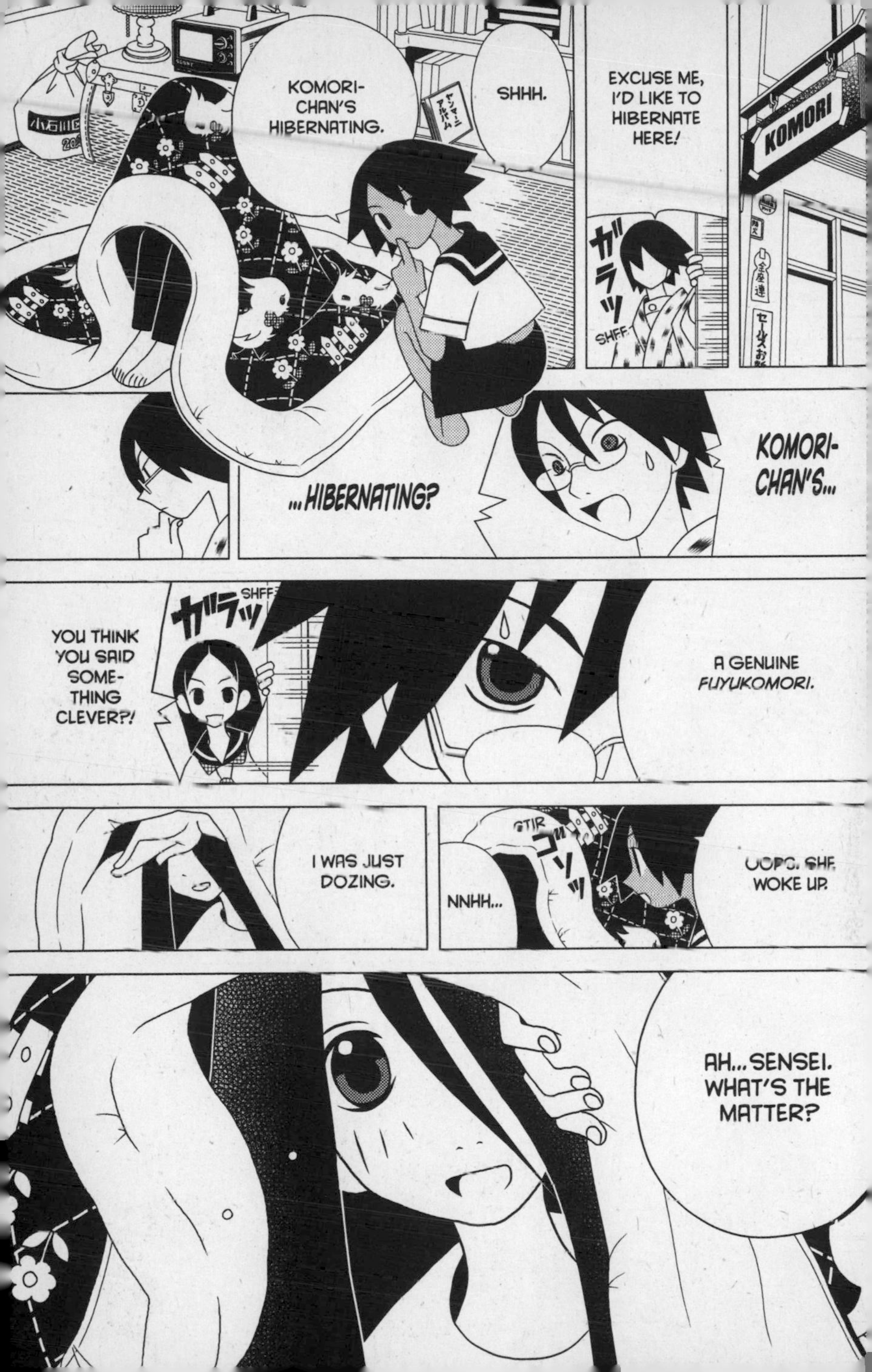
KOMORI
EXCUSE ME, I'D LIKE TO HIBERNATE HERE!
ガラッ
SHFF
SHHH.
KOMORI-CHAN'S HIBERNATING.
KOMORI-CHAN'S...
...HIBERNATING?
A GENUINE FUYUKOMORI.
ガラッ
SHFF
YOU THINK YOU SAID SOME-THING CLEVER?!
OOPS. SHE WOKE UP.
ゴソッ
STIR
NNHH...
I WAS JUST DOZING.
AH...SENSEI. WHAT'S THE MATTER?

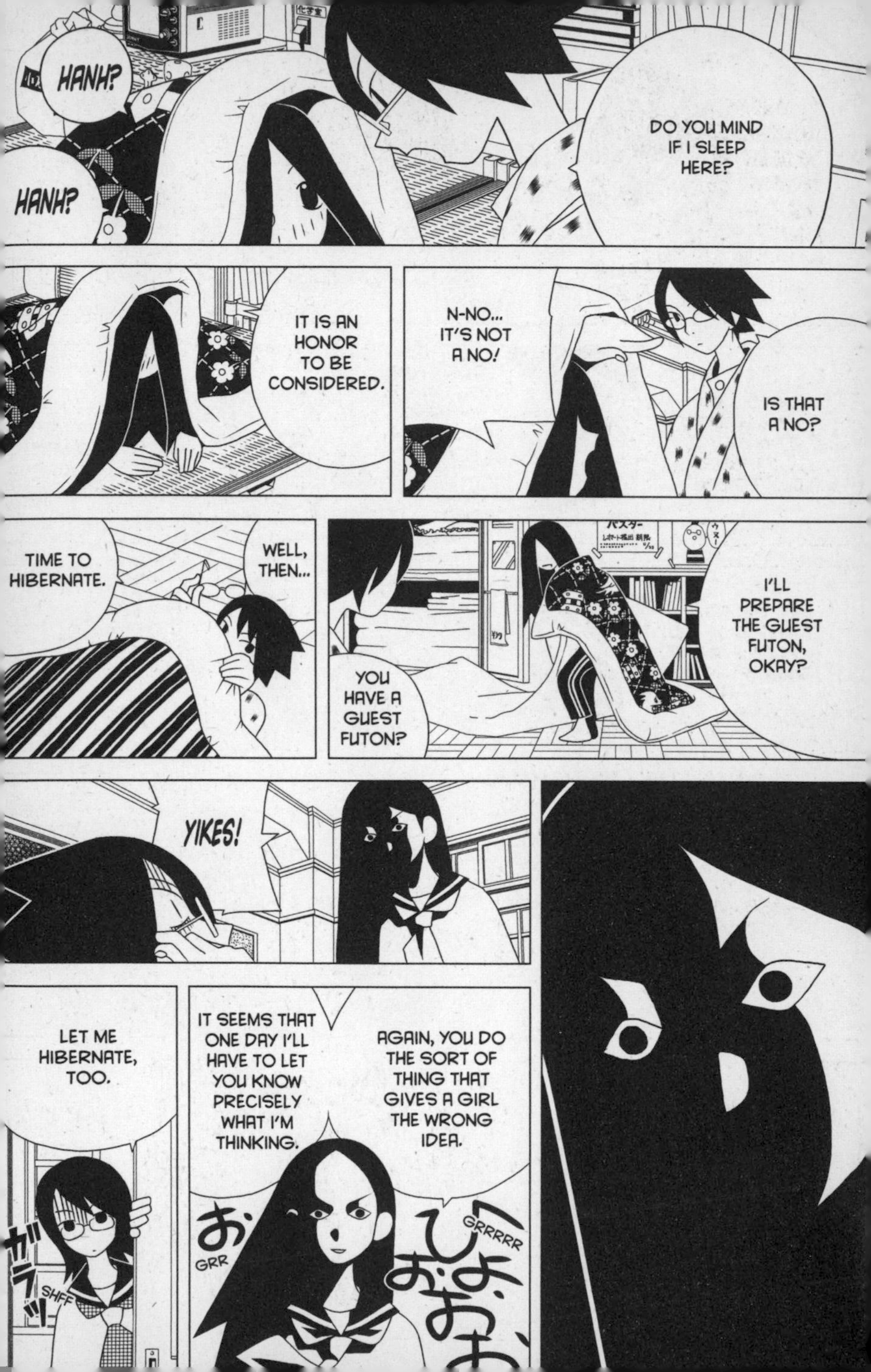
DO YOU MIND IF I SLEEP HERE?
HANH?
HANH?
IS THAT A NO?
N-NO... IT'S NOT A NO!
IT IS AN HONOR TO BE CONSIDERED.
I'LL PREPARE THE GUEST FUTON, OKAY?
YOU HAVE A GUEST FUTON?
WELL, THEN...
TIME TO HIBERNATE.
YIKES!
AGAIN, YOU DO THE SORT OF THING THAT GIVES A GIRL THE WRONG IDEA.
GRRRRR
IT SEEMS THAT ONE DAY I'LL HAVE TO LET YOU KNOW PRECISELY WHAT I'M THINKING.
GRR
LET ME HIBERNATE, TOO.
SHFF

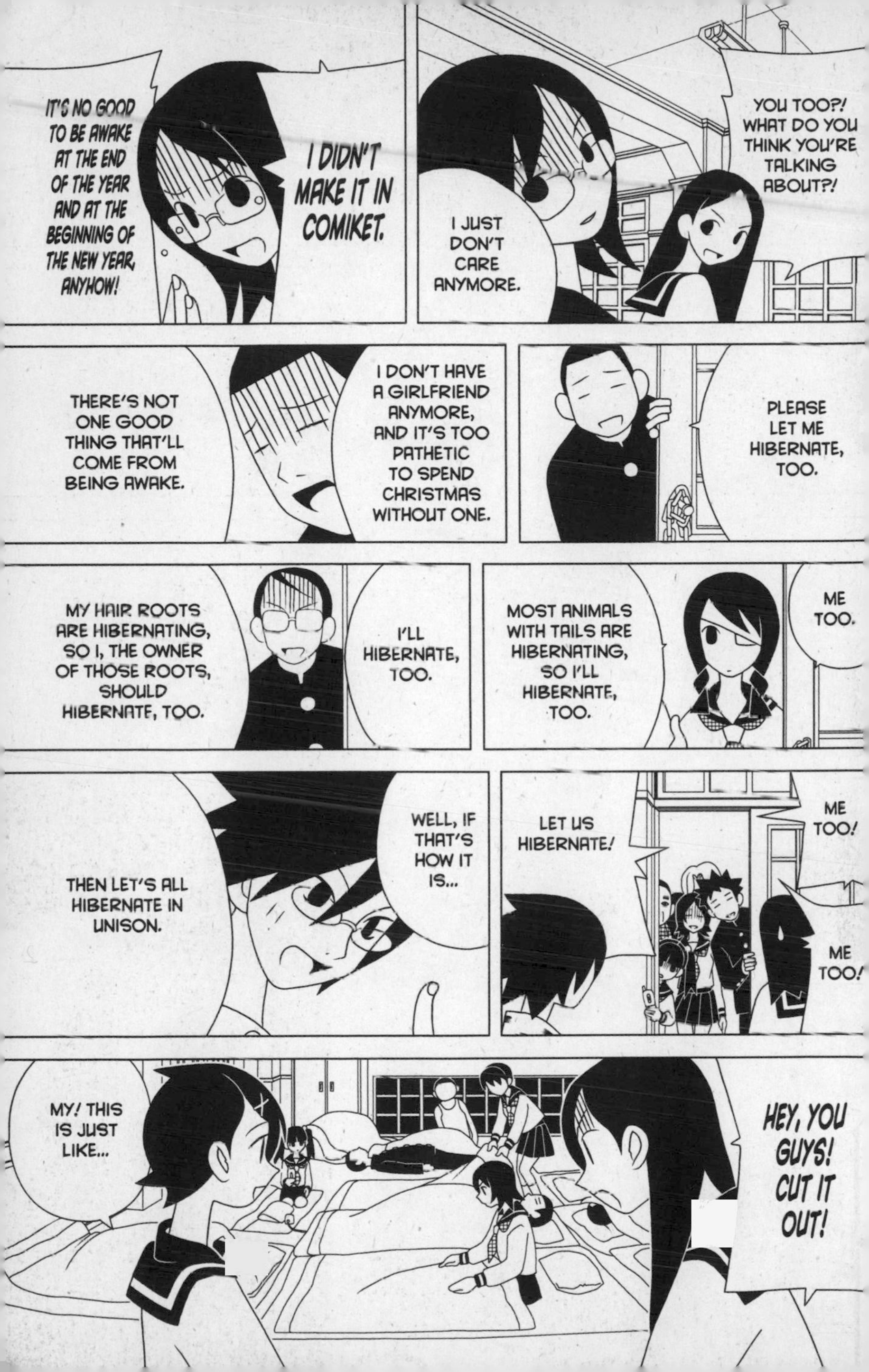
YOU TOO?! WHAT DO YOU THINK YOU'RE TALKING ABOUT?!
I JUST DON'T CARE ANYMORE.
I DIDN'T MAKE IT IN COMIKET.
IT'S NO GOOD TO BE AWAKE AT THE END OF THE YEAR AND AT THE BEGINNING OF THE NEW YEAR, ANYHOW!
PLEASE LET ME HIBERNATE, TOO.
I DON'T HAVE A GIRLFRIEND ANYMORE, AND IT'S TOO PATHETIC TO SPEND CHRISTMAS WITHOUT ONE.
THERE'S NOT ONE GOOD THING THAT'LL COME FROM BEING AWAKE.
ME TOO.
MOST ANIMALS WITH TAILS ARE HIBERNATING, SO I'LL HIBERNATE, TOO.
I'LL HIBERNATE, TOO.
MY HAIR ROOTS ARE HIBERNATING, SO I, THE OWNER OF THOSE ROOTS, SHOULD HIBERNATE, TOO.
ME TOO!
LET US HIBERNATE!
ME TOO!
WELL, IF THAT'S HOW IT IS...
THEN LET'S ALL HIBERNATE IN UNISON.
HEY, YOU GUYS! CUT IT OUT!
MY! THIS IS JUST LIKE...

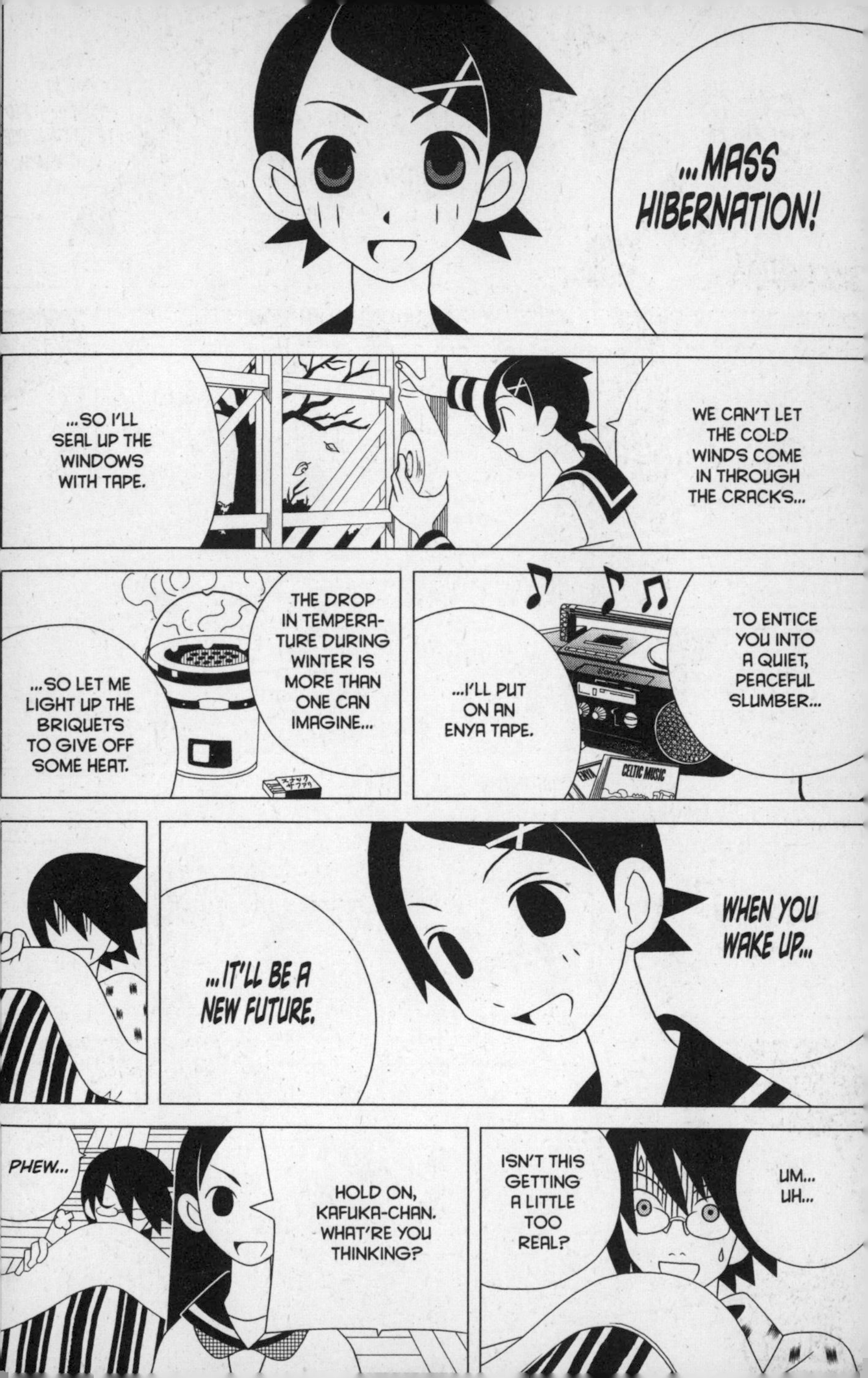
...MASS HIBERNATION!
WE CAN'T LET THE COLD WINDS COME IN THROUGH THE CRACKS...
...SO I'LL SEAL UP THE WINDOWS WITH TAPE.
TO ENTICE YOU INTO A QUIET, PEACEFUL SLUMBER...
...I'LL PUT ON AN ENYA TAPE.
ENYA
CELTIC MUSIC
THE DROP IN TEMPERATURE DURING WINTER IS MORE THAN ONE CAN IMAGINE...
...SO LET ME LIGHT UP THE BRIQUETS TO GIVE OFF SOME HEAT.
WHEN YOU WAKE UP...
...IT'LL BE A NEW FUTURE.
UM... UH...
ISN'T THIS GETTING A LITTLE TOO REAL?
HOLD ON, KAFUKA-CHAN. WHAT'RE YOU THINKING?
PHEW...

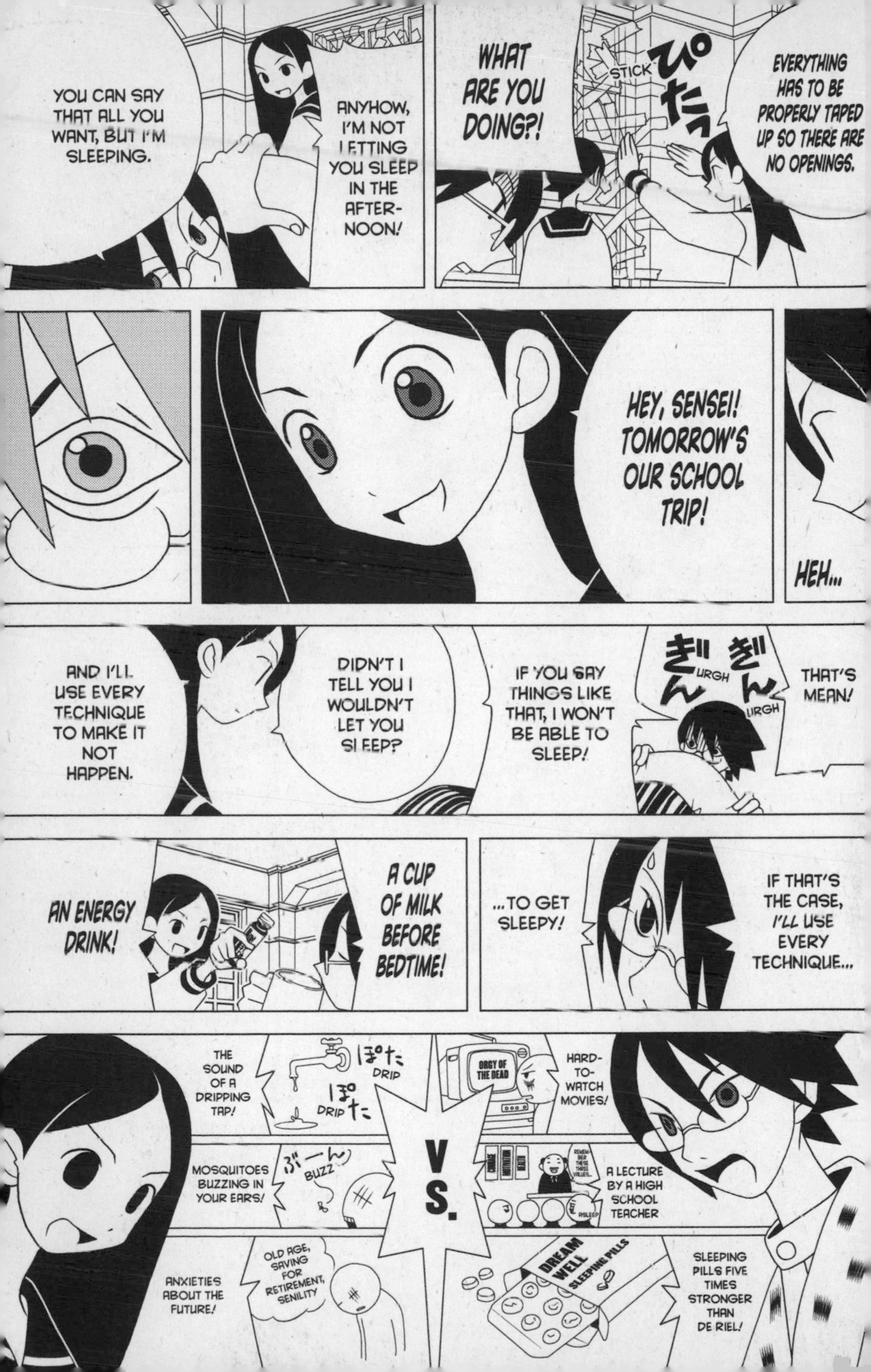

EVERYTHING HAS TO BE PROPERLY TAPED UP SO THERE ARE NO OPENINGS.
ぴたっ
STICK
WHAT ARE YOU DOING?!
ANYHOW, I'M NOT LETTING YOU SLEEP IN THE AFTERNOON!
YOU CAN SAY THAT ALL YOU WANT, BUT I'M SLEEPING.
HEH...
HEY, SENSEI! TOMORROW'S OUR SCHOOL TRIP!
THAT'S MEAN!
ぎん
URGH
ぎん
URGH
IF YOU SAY THINGS LIKE THAT, I WON'T BE ABLE TO SLEEP!
DIDN'T I TELL YOU I WOULDN'T LET YOU SLEEP?
AND I'LL USE EVERY TECHNIQUE TO MAKE IT NOT HAPPEN.
IF THAT'S THE CASE, I'LL USE EVERY TECHNIQUE...
...TO GET SLEEPY!
A CUP OF MILK BEFORE BEDTIME!
AN ENERGY DRINK!
HARD-TO-WATCH MOVIES!
ORGY OF THE DEAD
THE SOUND OF A DRIPPING TAP!
ぽたっ
DRIP
ぽたっ
DRIP
V.S.
A LECTURE BY A HIGH SCHOOL TEACHER
COURAGE
MOTIVATION
HEALTH
REMEMBER THESE THREE VALUES...
ASLEEP
MOSQUITOES BUZZING IN YOUR EARS!
ぶーん
BUZZ
SLEEPING PILLS FIVE TIMES STRONGER THAN DE RIEL!
DREAM WELL
SLEEPING PILLS
OLD AGE, SAVING FOR RETIREMENT, SENILITY
ANXIETIES ABOUT THE FUTURE!

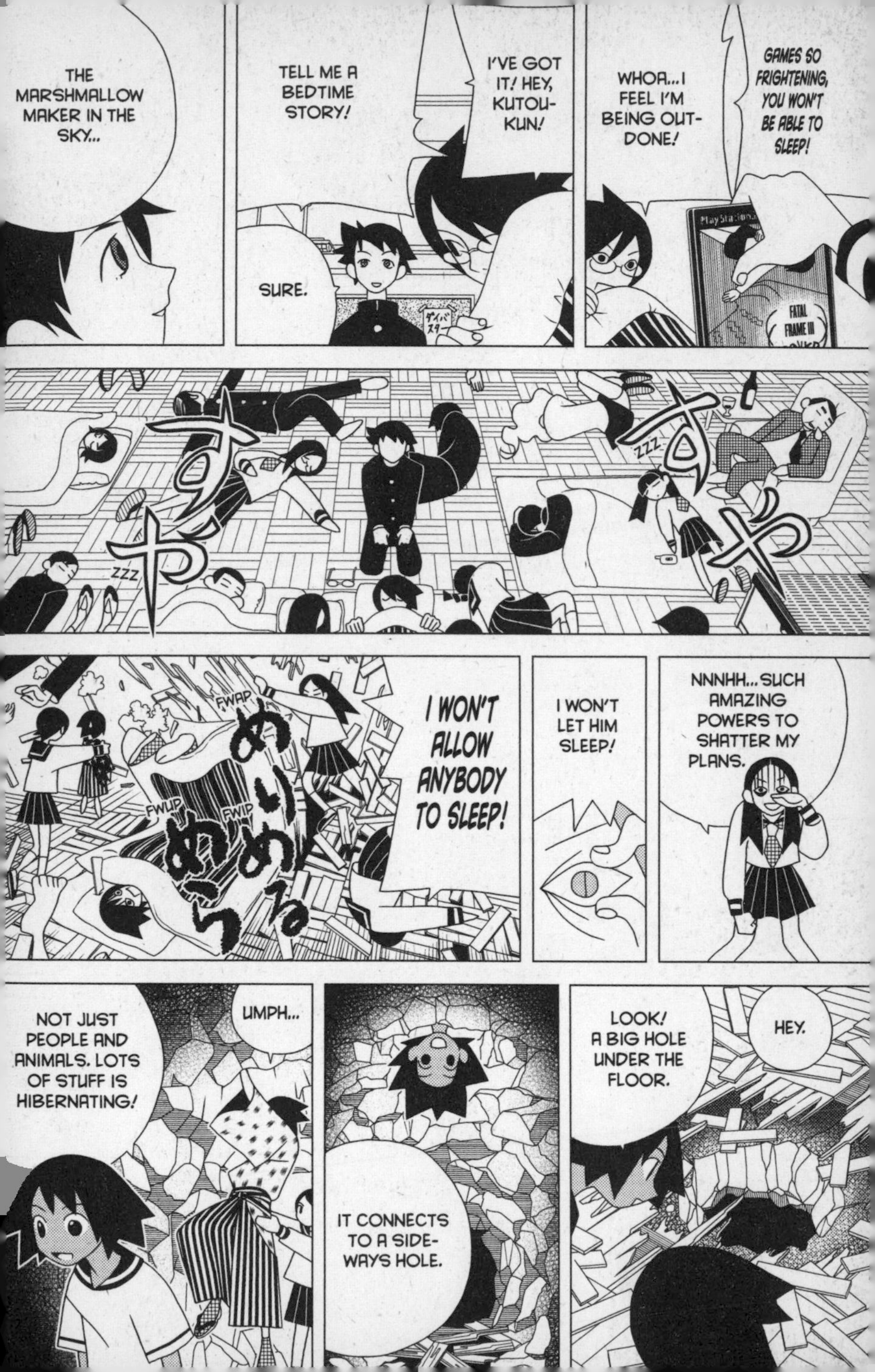
GAMES SO FRIGHTENING, YOU WON'T BE ABLE TO SLEEP!
WHOA...I FEEL I'M BEING OUT-DONE!
PlayStation2
FATAL FRAME III
I'VE GOT IT! HEY, KUTOU-KUN!
TELL ME A BEDTIME STORY!
SURE.
THE MARSHMALLOW MAKER IN THE SKY...
ZZZ
ZZZ
NNNHH... SUCH AMAZING POWERS TO SHATTER MY PLANS.
I WON'T LET HIM SLEEP!
I WON'T ALLOW ANYBODY TO SLEEP!
FWAP
FWIP
FWUP
HEY.
LOOK! A BIG HOLE UNDER THE FLOOR.
IT CONNECTS TO A SIDE-WAYS HOLE.
UMPH...
NOT JUST PEOPLE AND ANIMALS. LOTS OF STUFF IS HIBERNATING!

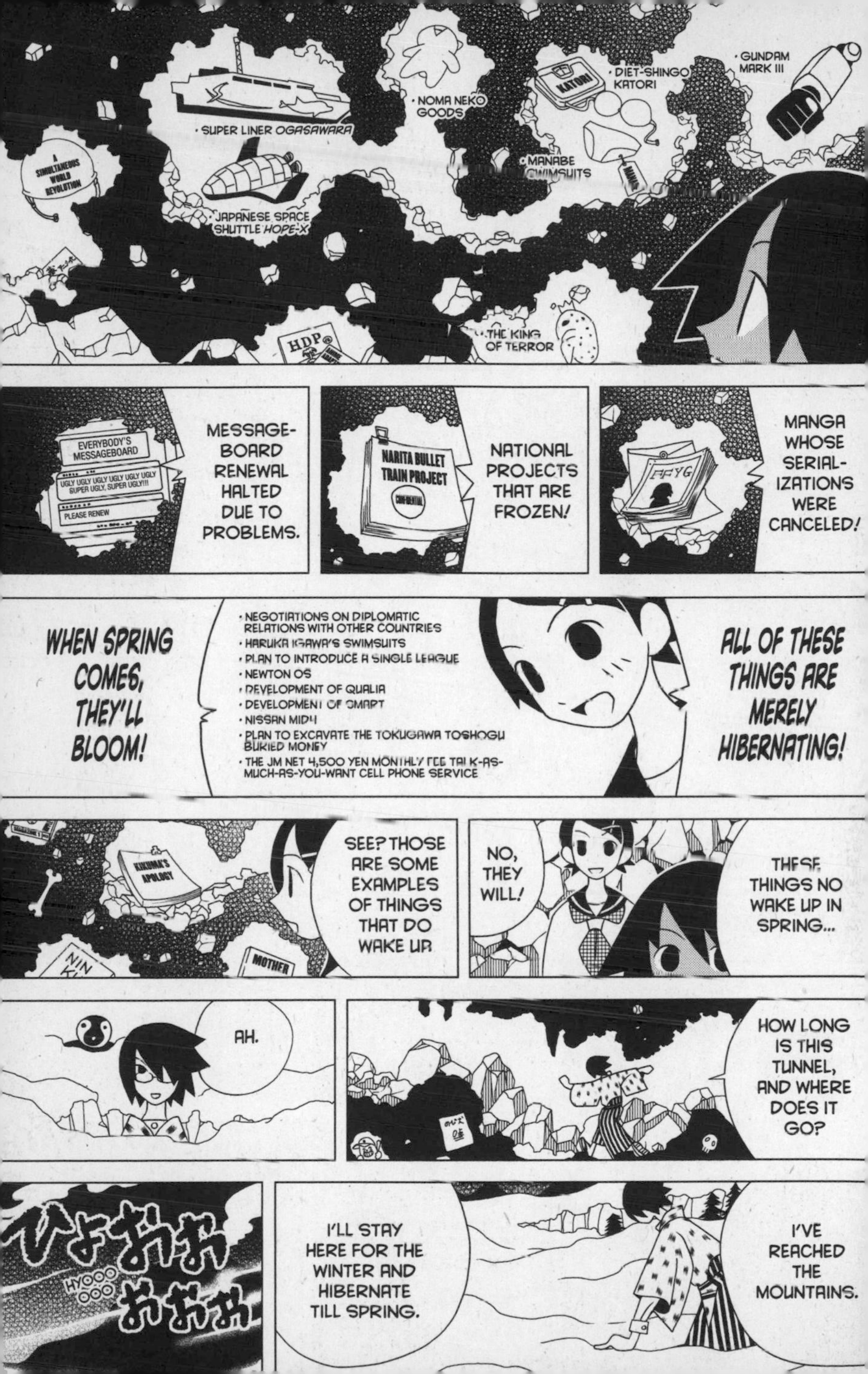

GUNDAM MARK III
DIET-SHINGO KATORI
KATORI
NOMA NEKO GOODS
MANABE SWIMSUITS
SUPER LINER OGASAWARA
A SIMULTANEOUS WORLD REVOLUTION
JAPANESE SPACE SHUTTLE HOPE-X
THE KING OF TERROR
HDP
MANGA WHOSE SERIAL-IZATIONS WERE CANCELED!
FFYG
NATIONAL PROJECTS THAT ARE FROZEN!
NARITA BULLET TRAIN PROJECT
CONFIDENTIAL
MESSAGE-BOARD RENEWAL HALTED DUE TO PROBLEMS.
EVERYBODY'S MESSAGEBOARD
UGLY UGLY UGLY UGLY UGLY UGLY SUPER UGLY, SUPER UGLY!!!
PLEASE RENEW
ALL OF THESE THINGS ARE MERELY HIBERNATING!
· NEGOTIATIONS ON DIPLOMATIC RELATIONS WITH OTHER COUNTRIES
· HARUKA IGAWA'S SWIMSUITS
· PLAN TO INTRODUCE A SINGLE LEAGUE
· NEWTON OS
· DEVELOPMENT OF QUALIA
· DEVELOPMENT OF SMAPT
· NISSAN MID4
· PLAN TO EXCAVATE THE TOKUGAWA TOSHOGU BURIED MONEY
· THE JM NET 4,500 YEN MONTHLY FEE TALK-AS-MUCH-AS-YOU-WANT CELL PHONE SERVICE
WHEN SPRING COMES, THEY'LL BLOOM!
THESE THINGS NO WAKE UP IN SPRING...
NO, THEY WILL!
SEE? THOSE ARE SOME EXAMPLES OF THINGS THAT DO WAKE UP.
KIKUMA'S APOLOGY
MOTHER
HOW LONG IS THIS TUNNEL, AND WHERE DOES IT GO?
AH.
I'VE REACHED THE MOUNTAINS.
I'LL STAY HERE FOR THE WINTER AND HIBERNATE TILL SPRING.
ひょおお おおお
HYOOOOOO

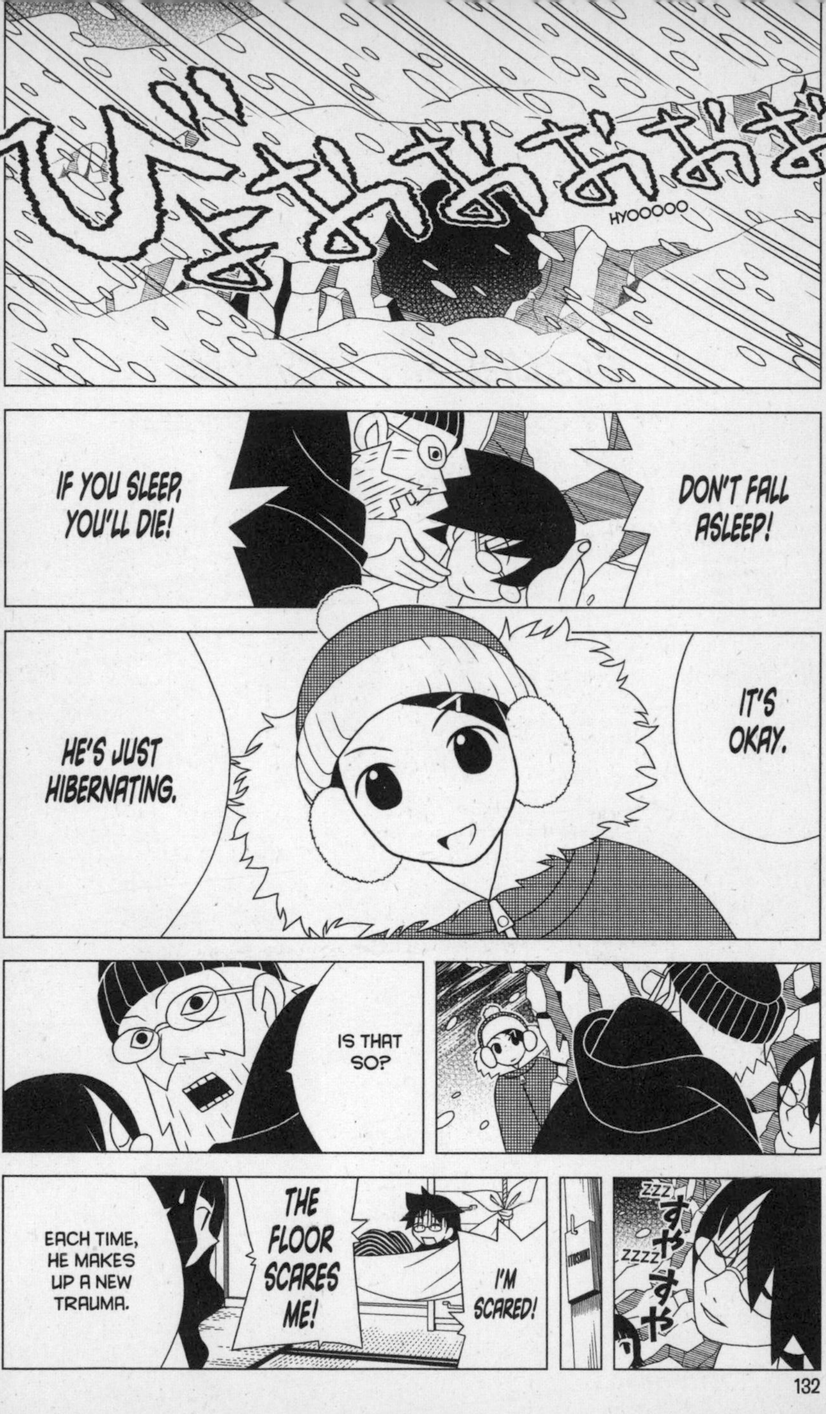
ひゅおおおお
HYOOOOO
DON'T FALL ASLEEP!
IF YOU SLEEP, YOU'LL DIE!
IT'S OKAY.
HE'S JUST HIBERNATING.
IS THAT SO?
ZZZ すや
ZZZZ すや
ITOSHIKI
I'M SCARED!
THE FLOOR SCARES ME!
EACH TIME, HE MAKES UP A NEW TRAUMA.

SEXUAL AWAKENING

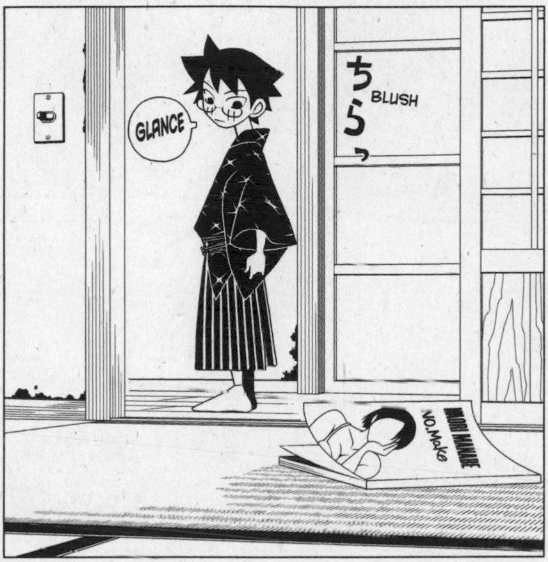
ちらっ
BLUSH
GLANCE
NO.Make

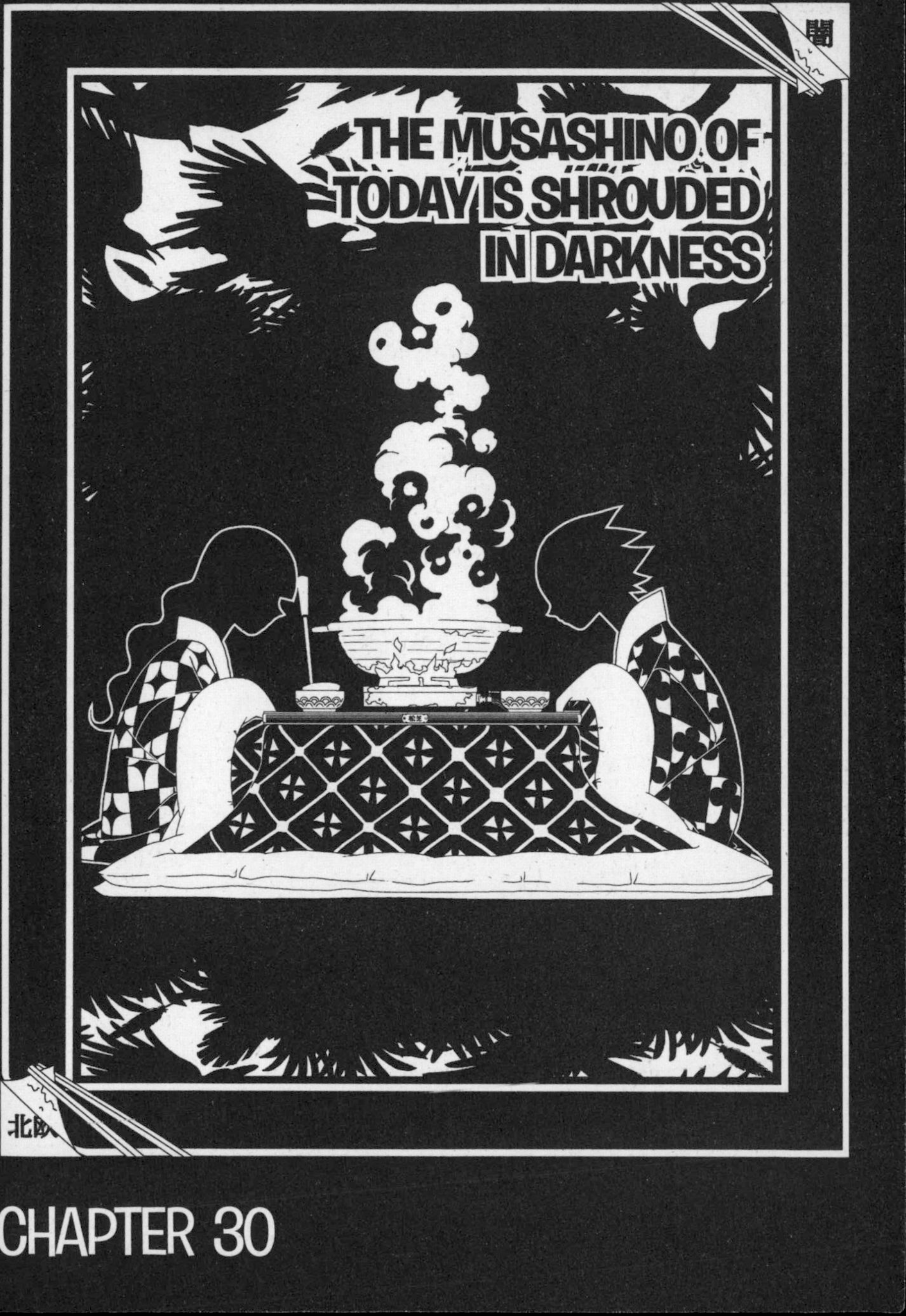
闇
THE MUSASHINO OF TODAY IS SHROUDED IN DARKNESS
北欧

CHAPTER 30

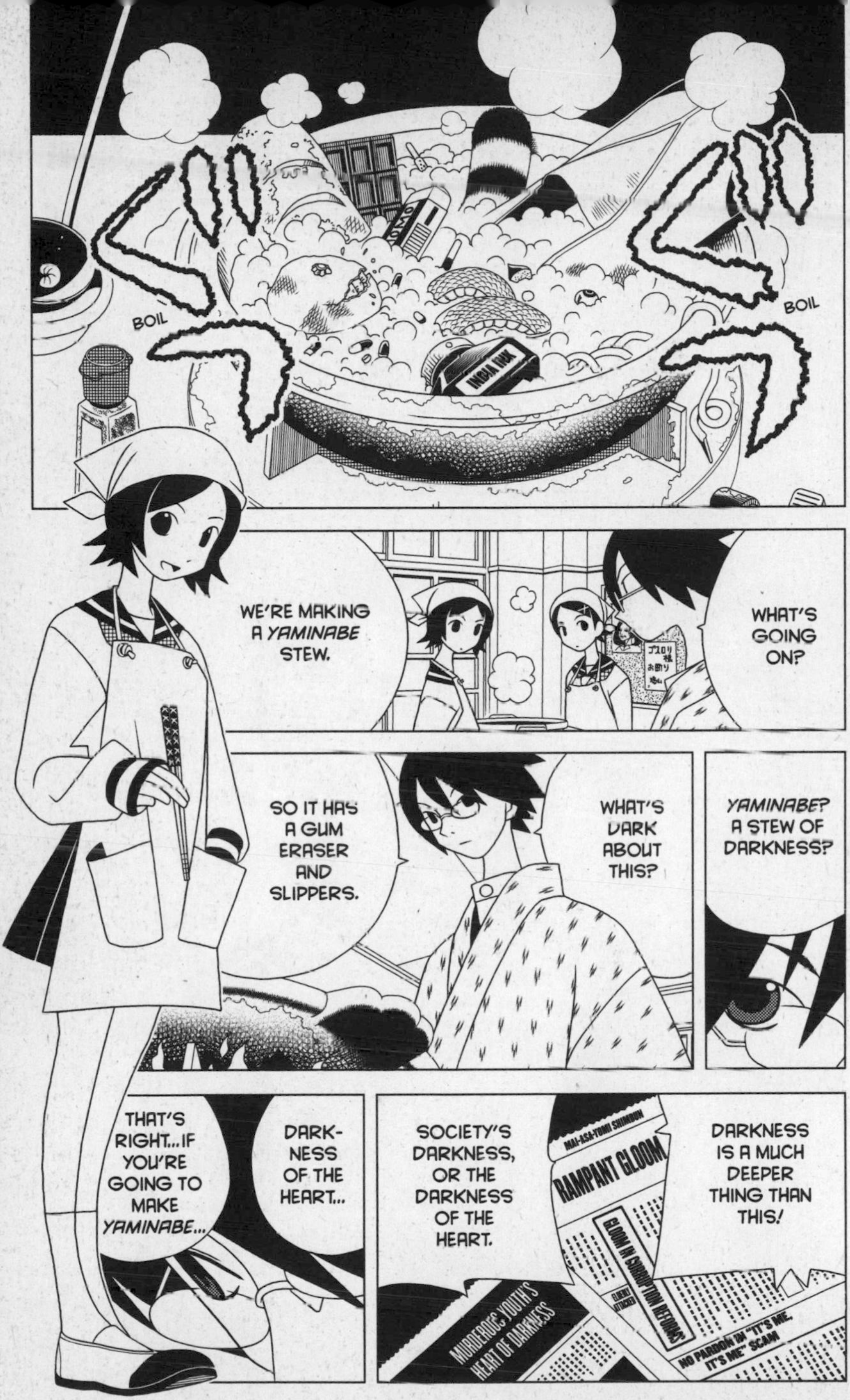
BOIL
BOIL
INDIA INK
WHAT'S GOING ON?
WE'RE MAKING A *YAMINABE* STEW.
YAMINABE? A STEW OF DARKNESS?
WHAT'S DARK ABOUT THIS?
SO IT HAS A GUM ERASER AND SLIPPERS.
DARKNESS IS A MUCH DEEPER THING THAN THIS!
SOCIETY'S DARKNESS, OR THE DARKNESS OF THE HEART.
MAI-ASA-YOMI SHIMBUN
RAMPANT GLOOM
GLOOM IN CORRUPTION REFORMS
ELDERLY ATTACKED
NO PARDON IN "IT'S ME. IT'S ME" SCAM
MURDEROUS YOUTH'S HEART OF DARKNESS
DARKNESS OF THE HEART...
THAT'S RIGHT...IF YOU'RE GOING TO MAKE *YAMINABE*...

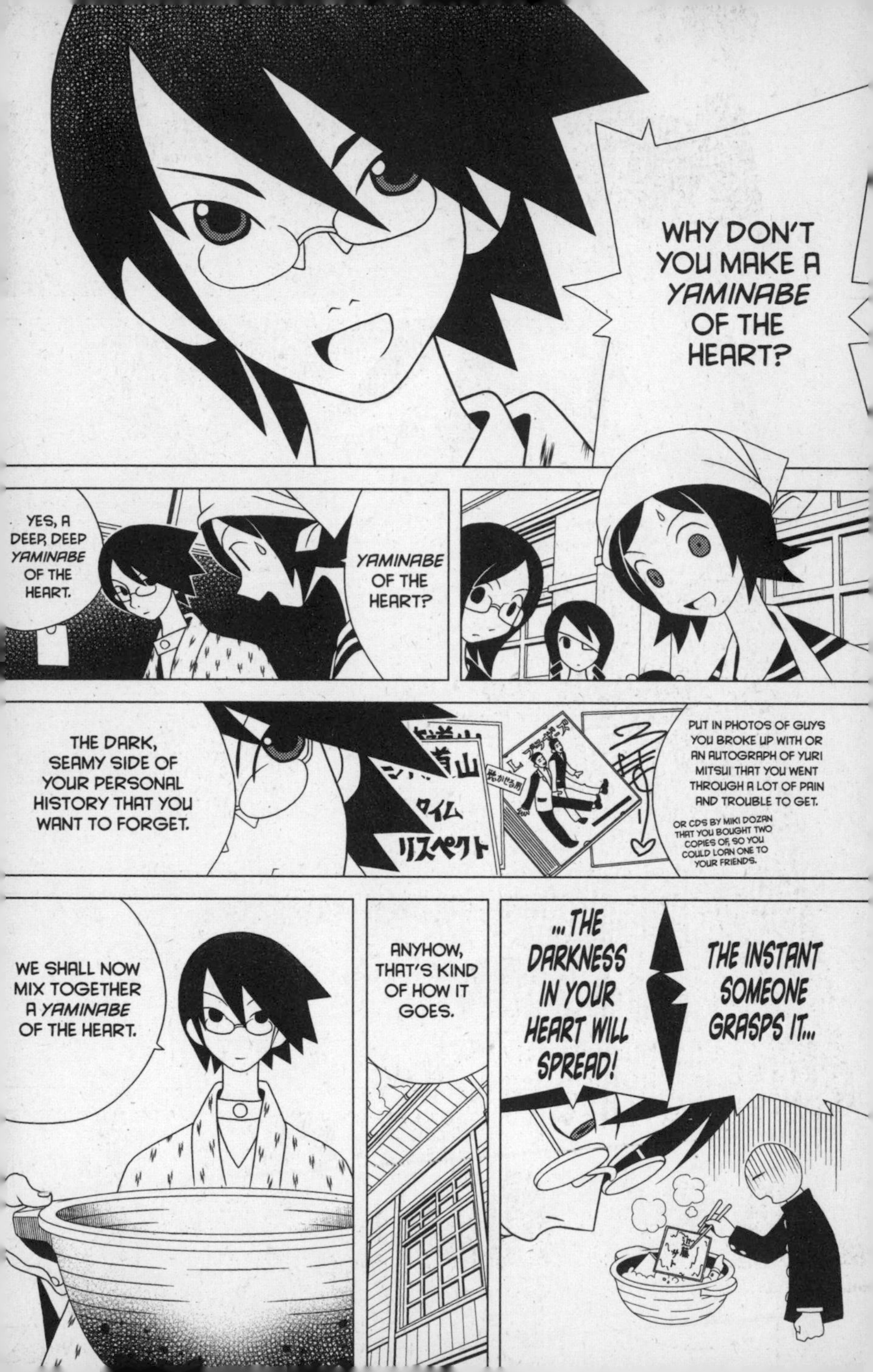
WHY DON'T YOU MAKE A *YAMINABE* OF THE HEART?
YAMINABE OF THE HEART?
YES, A DEEP, DEEP *YAMINABE* OF THE HEART.
PUT IN PHOTOS OF GUYS YOU BROKE UP WITH OR AN AUTOGRAPH OF YURI MITSUI THAT YOU WENT THROUGH A LOT OF PAIN AND TROUBLE TO GET.
OR CDS BY MIKI DOZAN THAT YOU BOUGHT TWO COPIES OF, SO YOU COULD LOAN ONE TO YOUR FRIENDS.
THE DARK, SEAMY SIDE OF YOUR PERSONAL HISTORY THAT YOU WANT TO FORGET.
THE INSTANT SOMEONE GRASPS IT...
...THE DARKNESS IN YOUR HEART WILL SPREAD!
ANYHOW, THAT'S KIND OF HOW IT GOES.
WE SHALL NOW MIX TOGETHER A *YAMINABE* OF THE HEART.

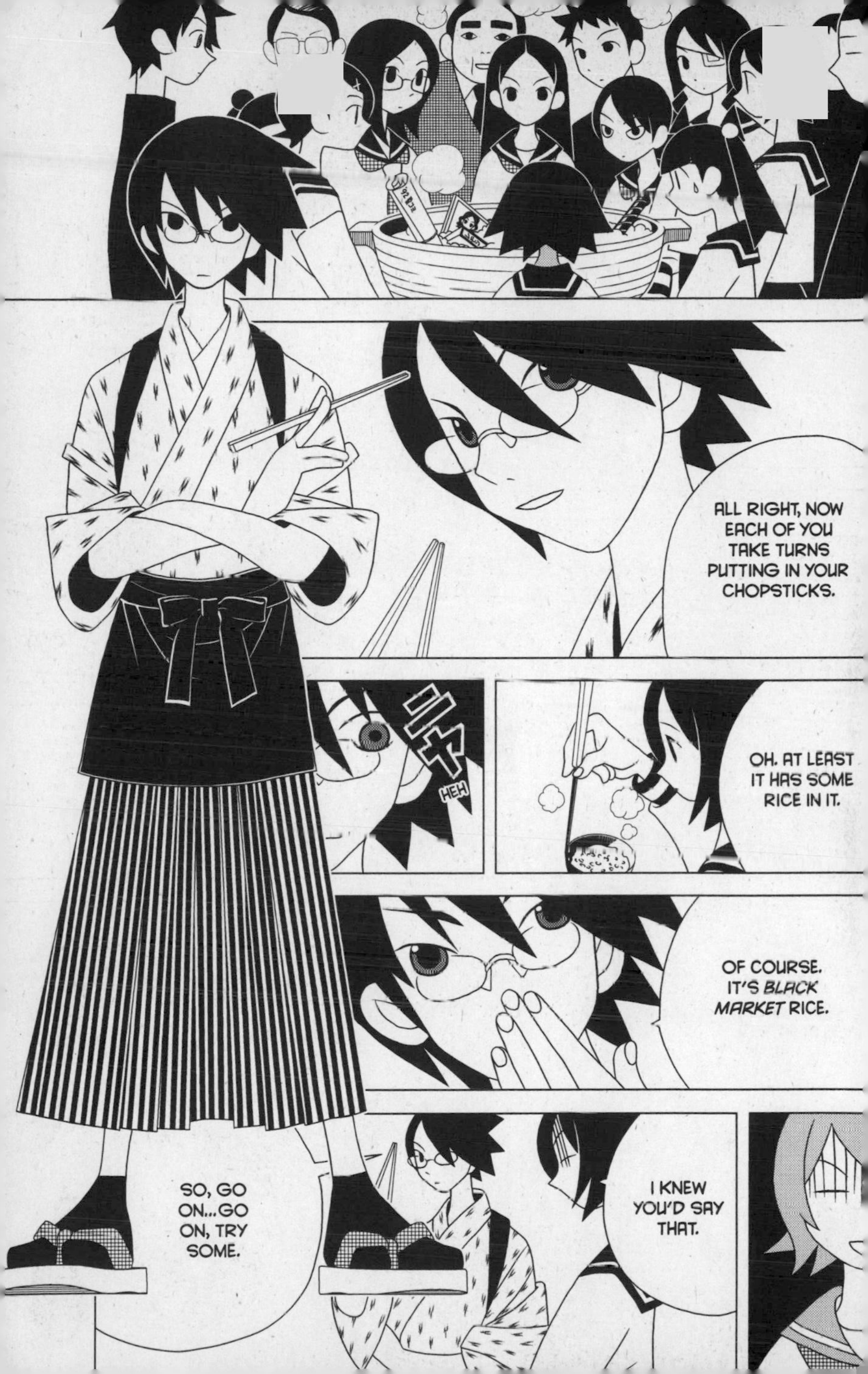
ALL RIGHT, NOW EACH OF YOU TAKE TURNS PUTTING IN YOUR CHOPSTICKS.
OH. AT LEAST IT HAS SOME RICE IN IT.
HEH
OF COURSE. IT'S *BLACK MARKET* RICE.
I KNEW YOU'D SAY THAT.
SO, GO ON...GO ON, TRY SOME.

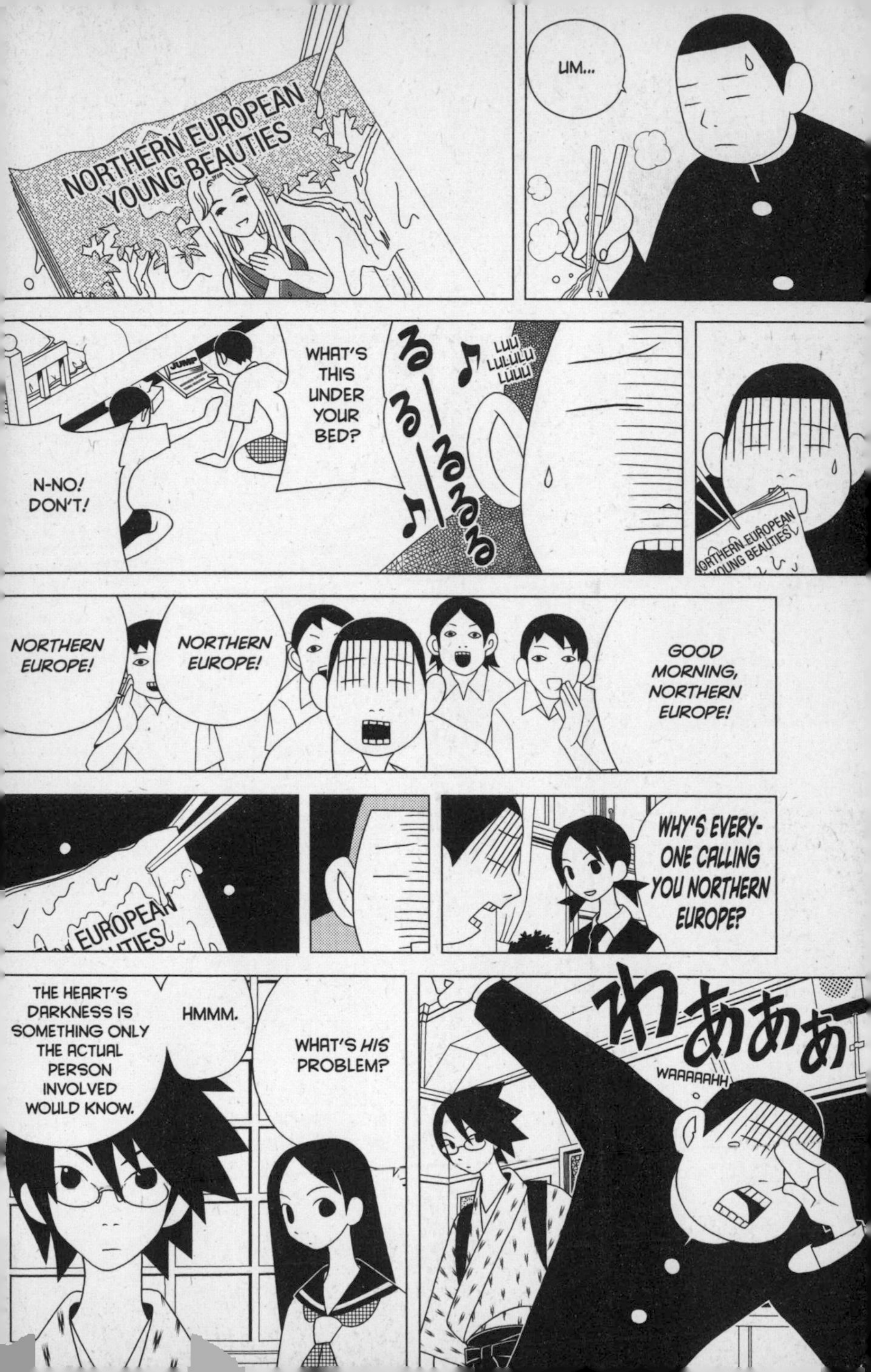
UM...
NORTHERN EUROPEAN YOUNG BEAUTIES
NORTHERN EUROPEAN YOUNG BEAUTIES
LUU LULULU LUUU
るーるーるるるる
WHAT'S THIS UNDER YOUR BED?
N-NO! DON'T!
GOOD MORNING, NORTHERN EUROPE!
NORTHERN EUROPE!
NORTHERN EUROPE!
WHY'S EVERY-ONE CALLING YOU NORTHERN EUROPE?
EUROPEAN
わあああ
WAAAAAAHH
WHAT'S *HIS* PROBLEM?
HMMM.
THE HEART'S DARKNESS IS SOMETHING ONLY THE ACTUAL PERSON INVOLVED WOULD KNOW.

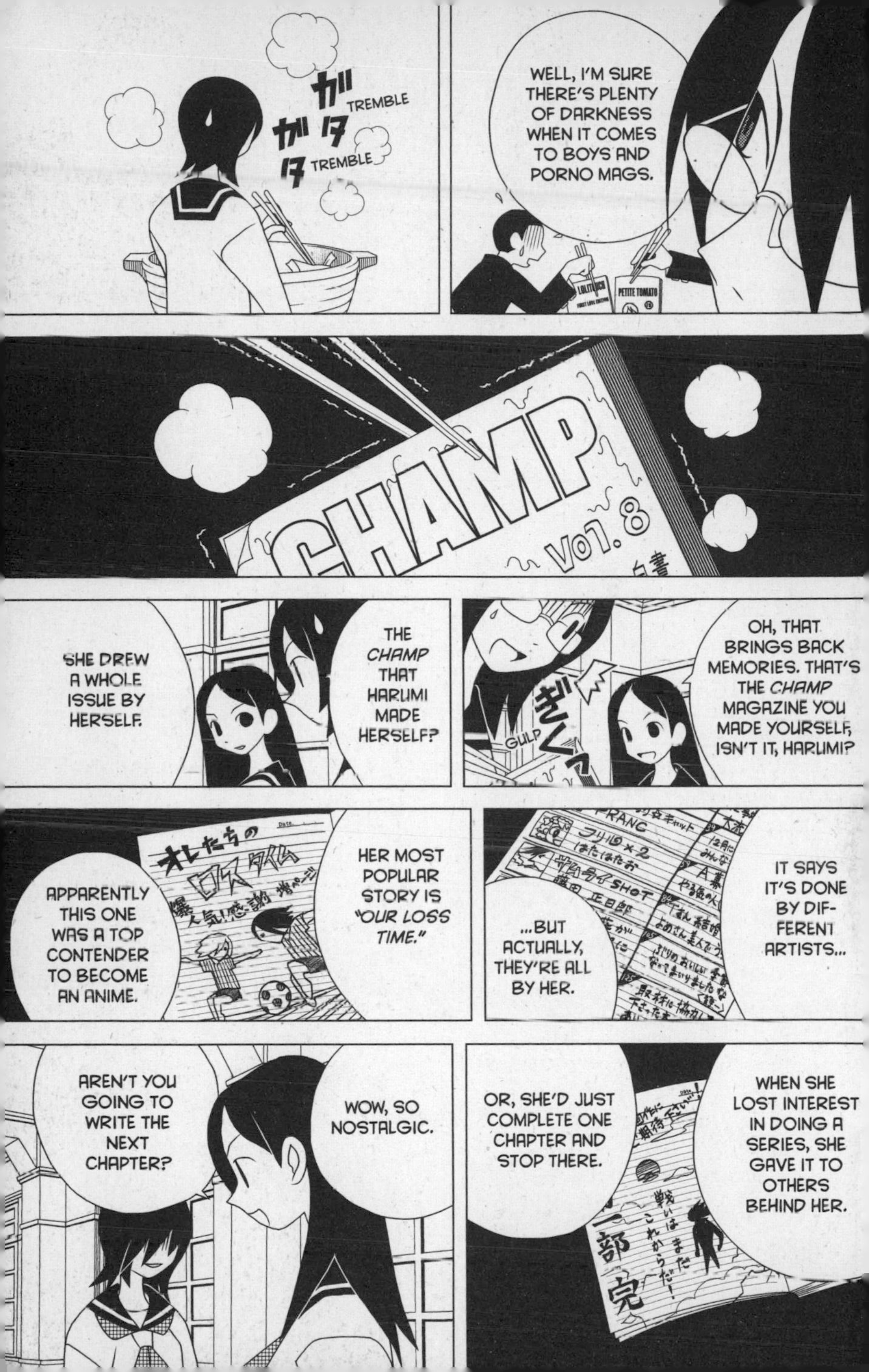
WELL, I'M SURE THERE'S PLENTY OF DARKNESS WHEN IT COMES TO BOYS AND PORNO MAGS.
PETITE TOMATO
ガタ TREMBLE
ガタ TREMBLE
CHAMP Vol. 8
白書
OH, THAT BRINGS BACK MEMORIES. THAT'S THE *CHAMP* MAGAZINE YOU MADE YOURSELF, ISN'T IT, HARUMI?
ぎくっ GULP
THE *CHAMP* THAT HARUMI MADE HERSELF?
SHE DREW A WHOLE ISSUE BY HERSELF.
IT SAYS IT'S DONE BY DIFFERENT ARTISTS...
...BUT ACTUALLY, THEY'RE ALL BY HER.
HER MOST POPULAR STORY IS *"OUR LOSS TIME."*
オレたちのロスタイム
APPARENTLY THIS ONE WAS A TOP CONTENDER TO BECOME AN ANIME.
WHEN SHE LOST INTEREST IN DOING A SERIES, SHE GAVE IT TO OTHERS BEHIND HER.
OR, SHE'D JUST COMPLETE ONE CHAPTER AND STOP THERE.
戦いはまだこれからだ!
一部完
WOW, SO NOSTALGIC.
AREN'T YOU GOING TO WRITE THE NEXT CHAPTER?

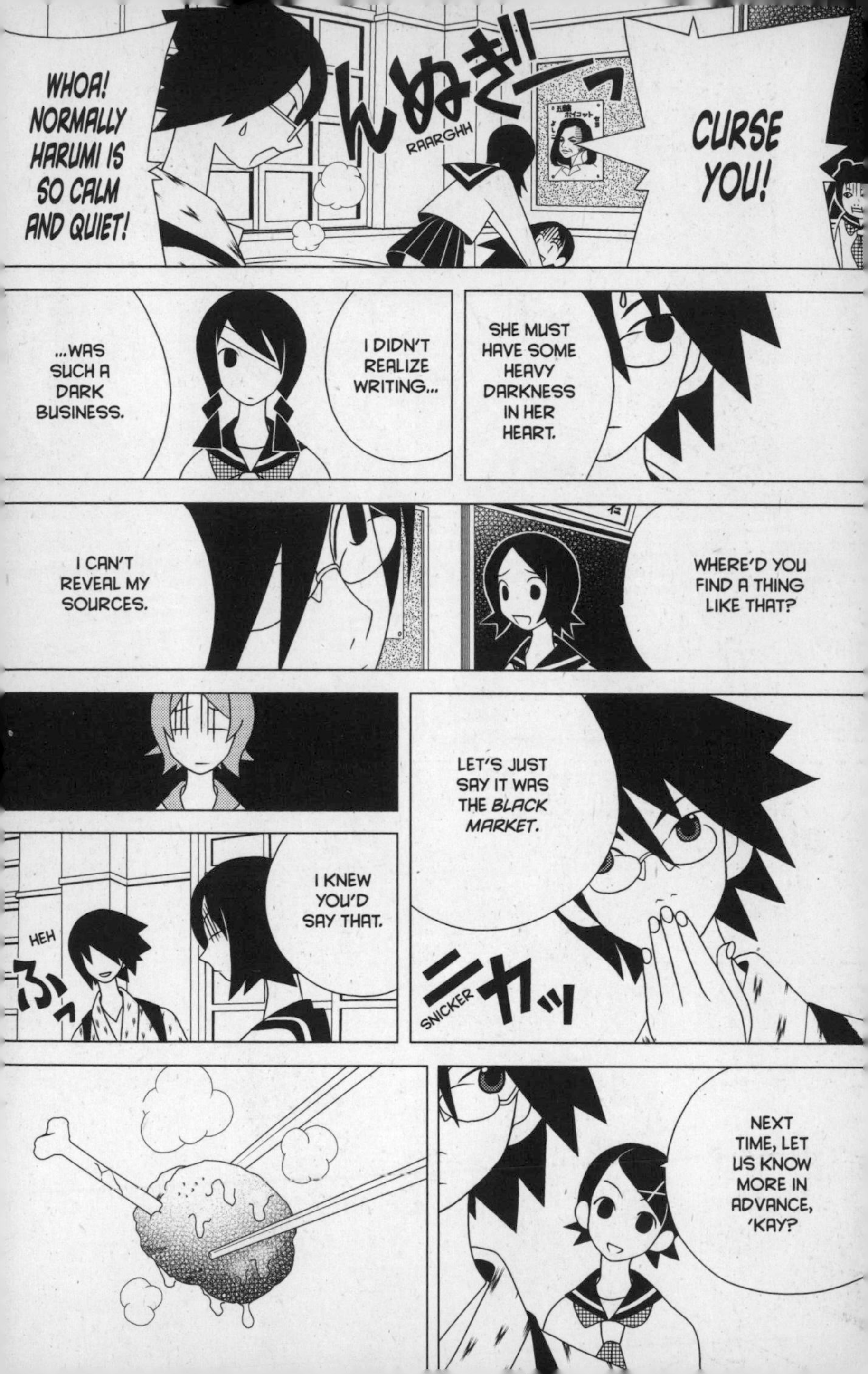
CURSE YOU!
んぬぎーっ
RAARGHH
WHOA! NORMALLY HARUMI IS SO CALM AND QUIET!
SHE MUST HAVE SOME HEAVY DARKNESS IN HER HEART.
I DIDN'T REALIZE WRITING...
...WAS SUCH A DARK BUSINESS.
WHERE'D YOU FIND A THING LIKE THAT?
I CAN'T REVEAL MY SOURCES.
LET'S JUST SAY IT WAS THE *BLACK MARKET*.
ニヤッ
SNICKER
I KNEW YOU'D SAY THAT.
ふっ
HEH
NEXT TIME, LET US KNOW MORE IN ADVANCE, 'KAY?

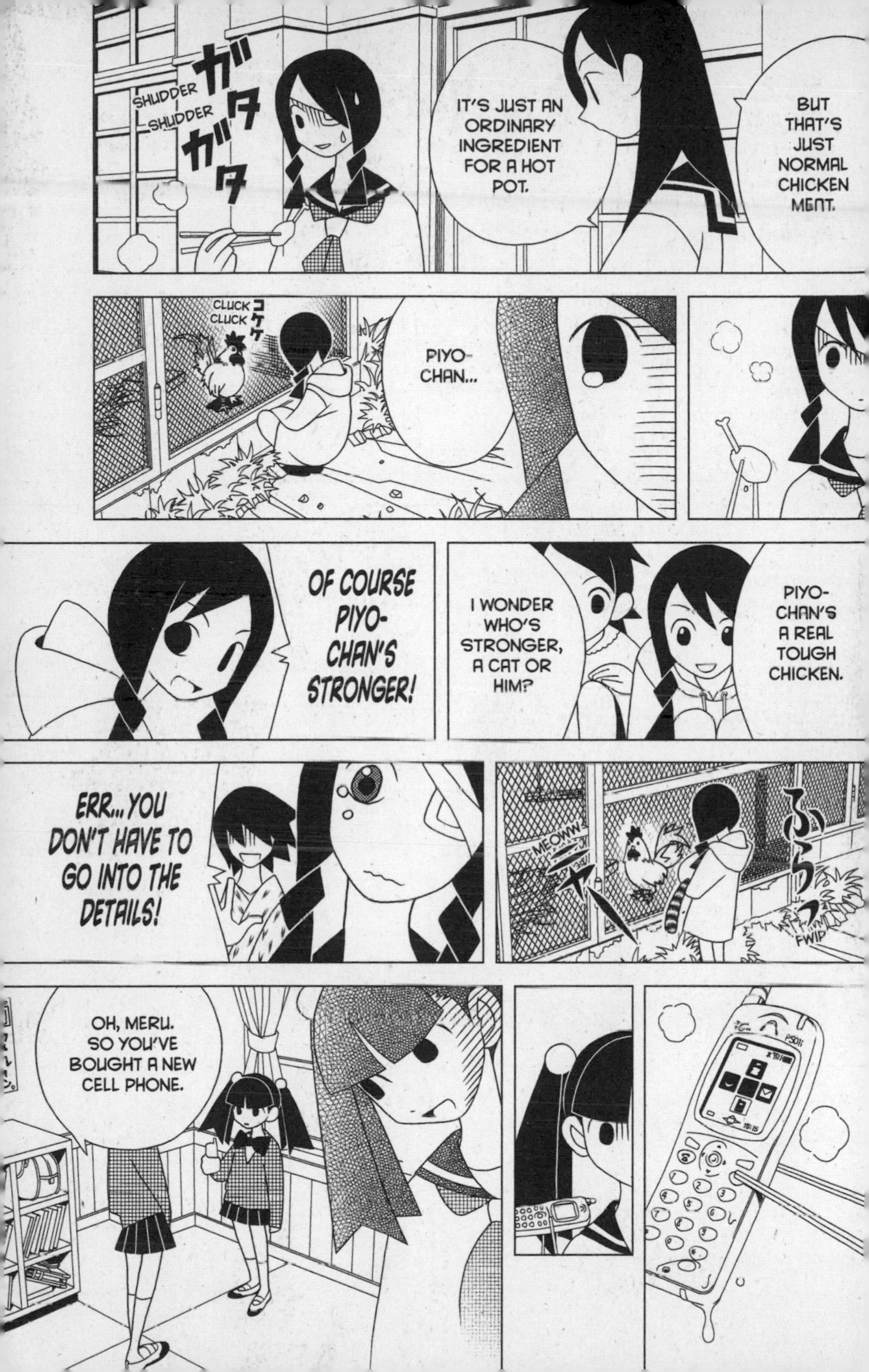
BUT THAT'S JUST NORMAL CHICKEN MEAT.
IT'S JUST AN ORDINARY INGREDIENT FOR A HOT POT.
SHUDDER SHUDDER
ガタガタ
PIYO-CHAN...
CLUCK CLUCK
コケ
PIYO-CHAN'S A REAL TOUGH CHICKEN.
I WONDER WHO'S STRONGER, A CAT OR HIM?
OF COURSE PIYO-CHAN'S STRONGER!
ふらっ
FWIP
MEOWW
ERR... YOU DON'T HAVE TO GO INTO THE DETAILS!
OH, MERU. SO YOU'VE BOUGHT A NEW CELL PHONE.

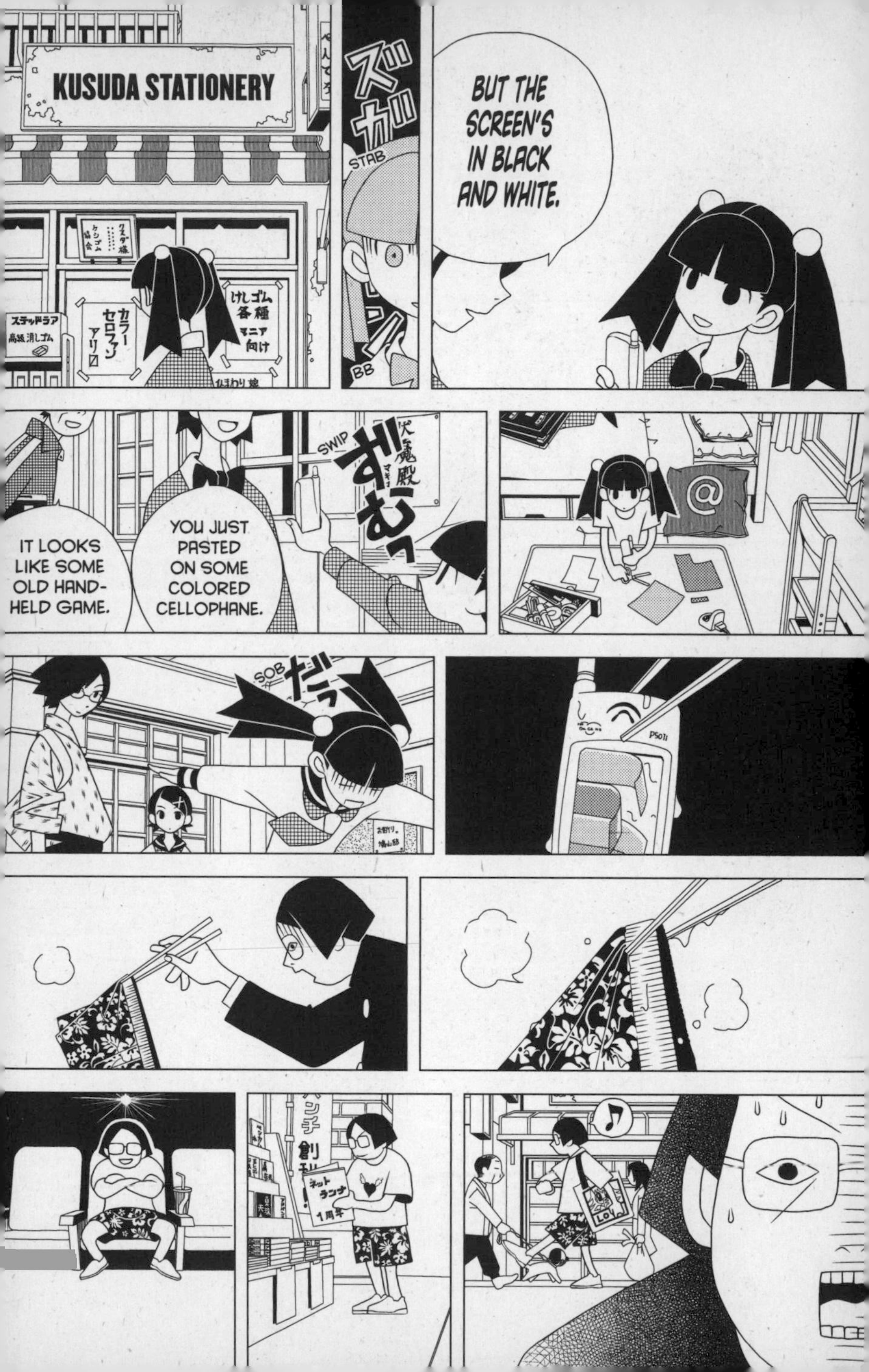
BUT THE SCREEN'S IN BLACK AND WHITE.
STAB
BB
KUSUDA STATIONERY
SWIP
YOU JUST PASTED ON SOME COLORED CELLOPHANE.
IT LOOKS LIKE SOME OLD HAND-HELD GAME.
P501i
SOB

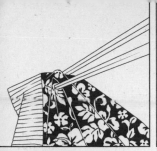

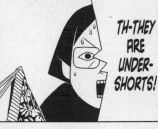

MAN, THOSE AREN'T SHORTS, THEY'RE UNDER-SHORTS.
ズゴァアン
KA-BOINNG
TH-THEY ARE UNDER-SHORTS!
ぬあああぁあぁあぁ
WAAAHHHH
THERE'S PLENTY TO GO AROUND.
SO COME ON, ALL OF YOU.
AN EMPTY CAPSULE DIPPED IN MUD THAT WAS FORCED BACK INTO THE MACHINE FROM THE BOTTOM.
A MOVIE TICKET FOR A MOVIE I SAW WITH MY PARENTS AND FELT UNCOMFORTABLE BEING AT.
PANT PANT
ハァハァ
AN INKED-UP SHIRT—I WANTED A NEW SHIRT SO BADLY, I SPILLED INK OVER MY CLOTHES SO THEY'D BUY ME ONE.
A "DRIVING SAFETY" POSTER THAT I WON A SCHOOL AWARD FOR—BUT MY PARENTS ACTUALLY DREW IT FOR ME.
DANGER!
賞
AND THIS CARDBOARD? I WANTED AN ASIMO SO BADLY, I MADE MY BROTHER WEAR A CARDBOARD COSTUME!
ASIMO

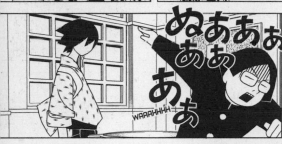

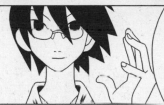

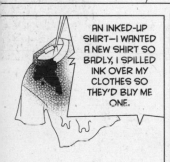

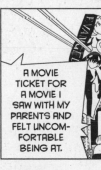

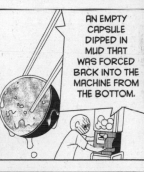

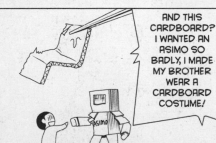

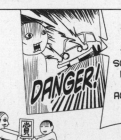

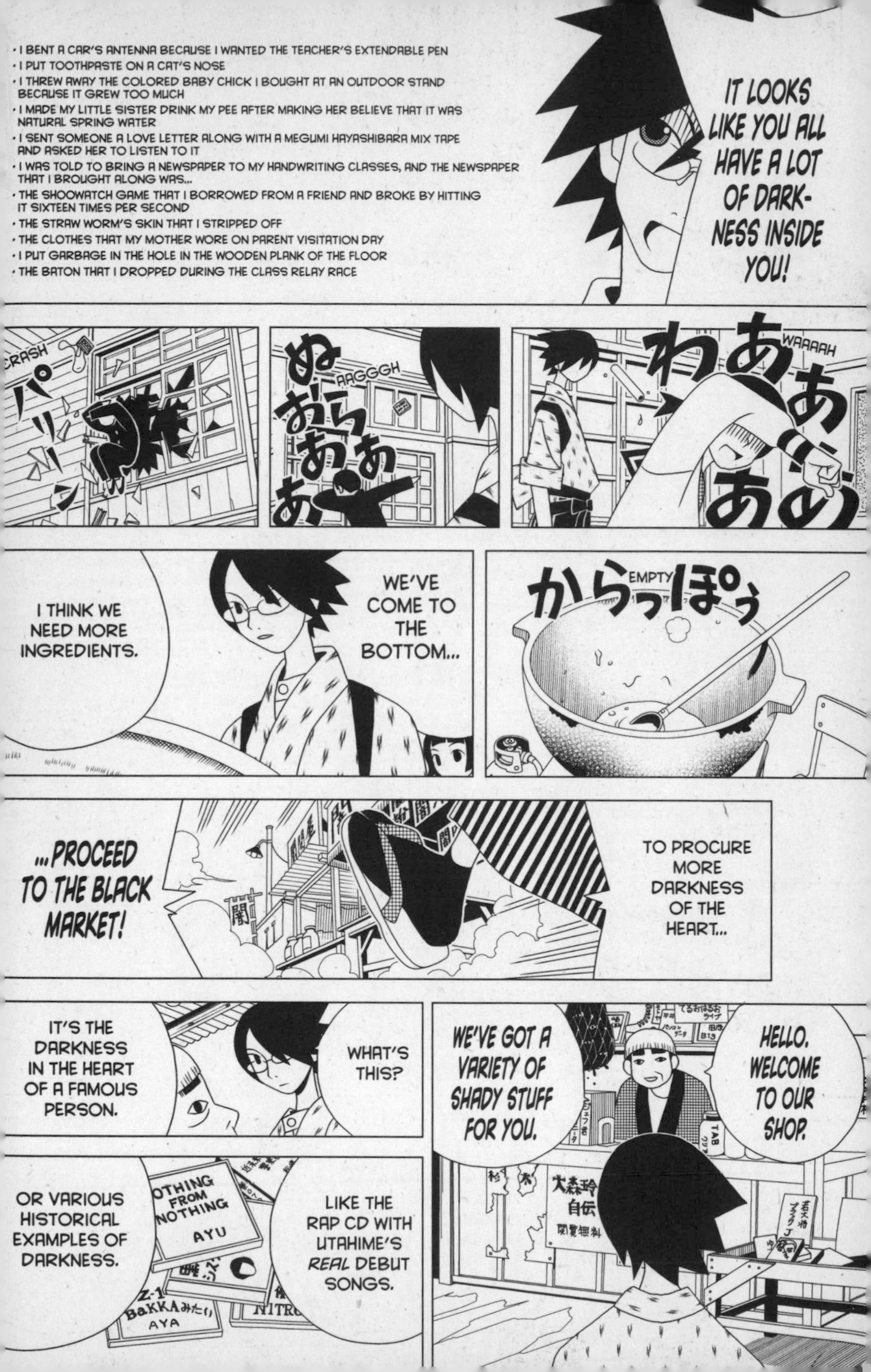

IT LOOKS LIKE YOU ALL HAVE A LOT OF DARK-NESS INSIDE YOU!
• I BENT A CAR'S ANTENNA BECAUSE I WANTED THE TEACHER'S EXTENDABLE PEN
• I PUT TOOTHPASTE ON A CAT'S NOSE
• I THREW AWAY THE COLORED BABY CHICK I BOUGHT AT AN OUTDOOR STAND BECAUSE IT GREW TOO MUCH
• I MADE MY LITTLE SISTER DRINK MY PEE AFTER MAKING HER BELIEVE THAT IT WAS NATURAL SPRING WATER
• I SENT SOMEONE A LOVE LETTER ALONG WITH A MEGUMI HAYASHIBARA MIX TAPE AND ASKED HER TO LISTEN TO IT
• I WAS TOLD TO BRING A NEWSPAPER TO MY HANDWRITING CLASSES, AND THE NEWSPAPER THAT I BROUGHT ALONG WAS...
• THE SHOOWATCH GAME THAT I BORROWED FROM A FRIEND AND BROKE BY HITTING IT SIXTEEN TIMES PER SECOND
• THE STRAW WORM'S SKIN THAT I STRIPPED OFF
• THE CLOTHES THAT MY MOTHER WORE ON PARENT VISITATION DAY
• I PUT GARBAGE IN THE HOLE IN THE WOODEN PLANK OF THE FLOOR
• THE BATON THAT I DROPPED DURING THE CLASS RELAY RACE
わああああ
WAAAAH
ぬおらあああ
AAGGGH
パリーン
CRASH
からっぽう
EMPTY
WE'VE COME TO THE BOTTOM...
I THINK WE NEED MORE INGREDIENTS.
TO PROCURE MORE DARKNESS OF THE HEART...
...PROCEED TO THE BLACK MARKET!
HELLO. WELCOME TO OUR SHOP.
WE'VE GOT A VARIETY OF SHADY STUFF FOR YOU.
大森玲 自伝 閲覧無料
WHAT'S THIS?
IT'S THE DARKNESS IN THE HEART OF A FAMOUS PERSON.
LIKE THE RAP CD WITH UTAHIME'S *REAL* DEBUT SONGS.
OR VARIOUS HISTORICAL EXAMPLES OF DARKNESS.
OTHING FROM NOTHING
AYU
Z-1
BaKKAみたい
AYA

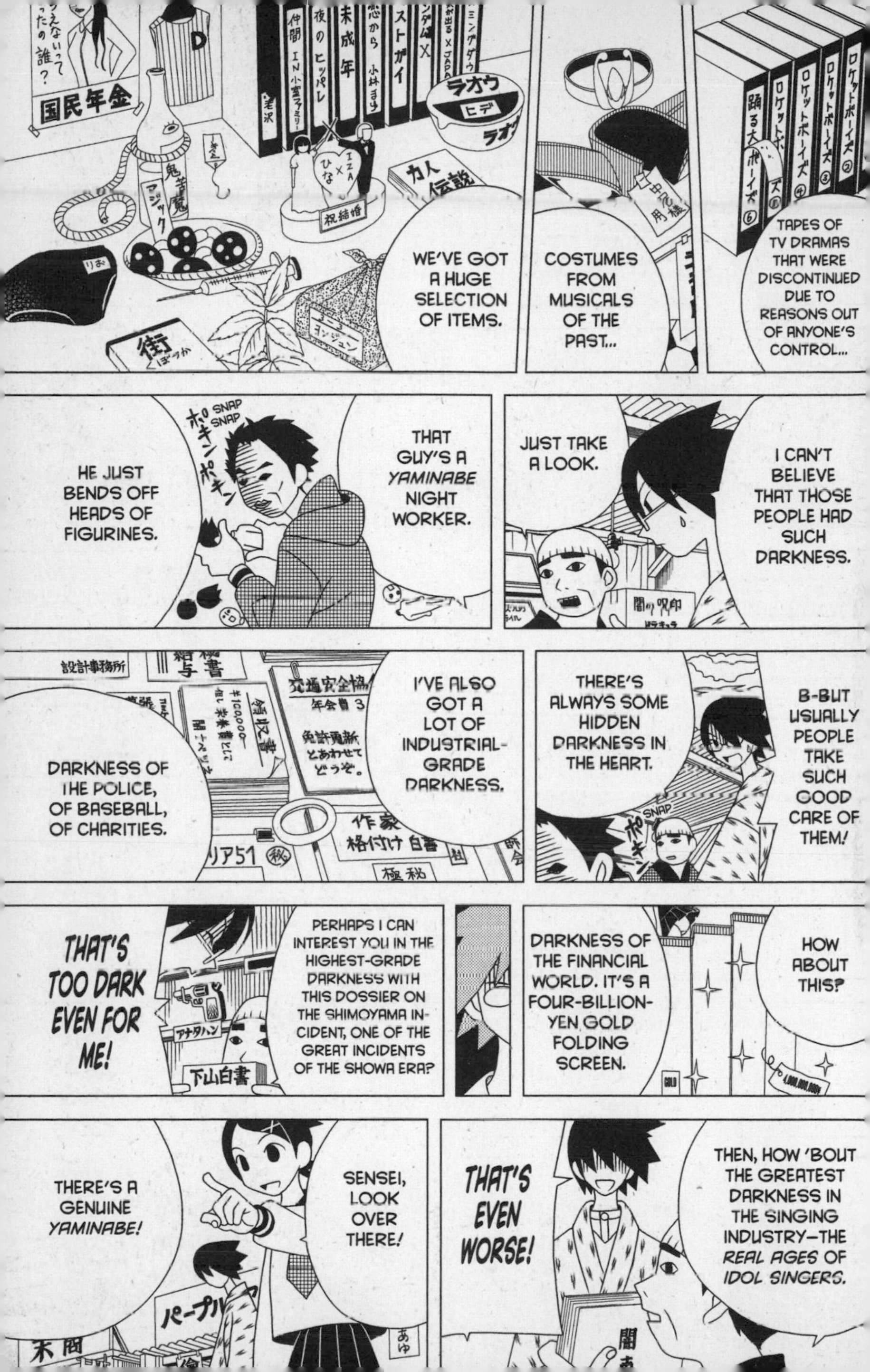

TAPES OF TV DRAMAS THAT WERE DISCONTINUED DUE TO REASONS OUT OF ANYONE'S CONTROL...
COSTUMES FROM MUSICALS OF THE PAST...
WE'VE GOT A HUGE SELECTION OF ITEMS.
I CAN'T BELIEVE THAT THOSE PEOPLE HAD SUCH DARKNESS.
JUST TAKE A LOOK.
THAT GUY'S A *YAMINABE* NIGHT WORKER.
SNAP SNAP
HE JUST BENDS OFF HEADS OF FIGURINES.
B-BUT USUALLY PEOPLE TAKE SUCH GOOD CARE OF THEM!
THERE'S ALWAYS SOME HIDDEN DARKNESS IN THE HEART.
SNAP
I'VE ALSO GOT A LOT OF INDUSTRIAL-GRADE DARKNESS.
DARKNESS OF THE POLICE, OF BASEBALL, OF CHARITIES.
HOW ABOUT THIS?
DARKNESS OF THE FINANCIAL WORLD. IT'S A FOUR-BILLION-YEN GOLD FOLDING SCREEN.
PERHAPS I CAN INTEREST YOU IN THE HIGHEST-GRADE DARKNESS WITH THIS DOSSIER ON THE SHIMOYAMA INCIDENT, ONE OF THE GREAT INCIDENTS OF THE SHOWA ERA?
THAT'S TOO DARK EVEN FOR ME!
THEN, HOW 'BOUT THE GREATEST DARKNESS IN THE SINGING INDUSTRY—THE *REAL AGES OF IDOL SINGERS.*
THAT'S EVEN WORSE!
SENSEI, LOOK OVER THERE!
THERE'S A GENUINE *YAMINABE!*

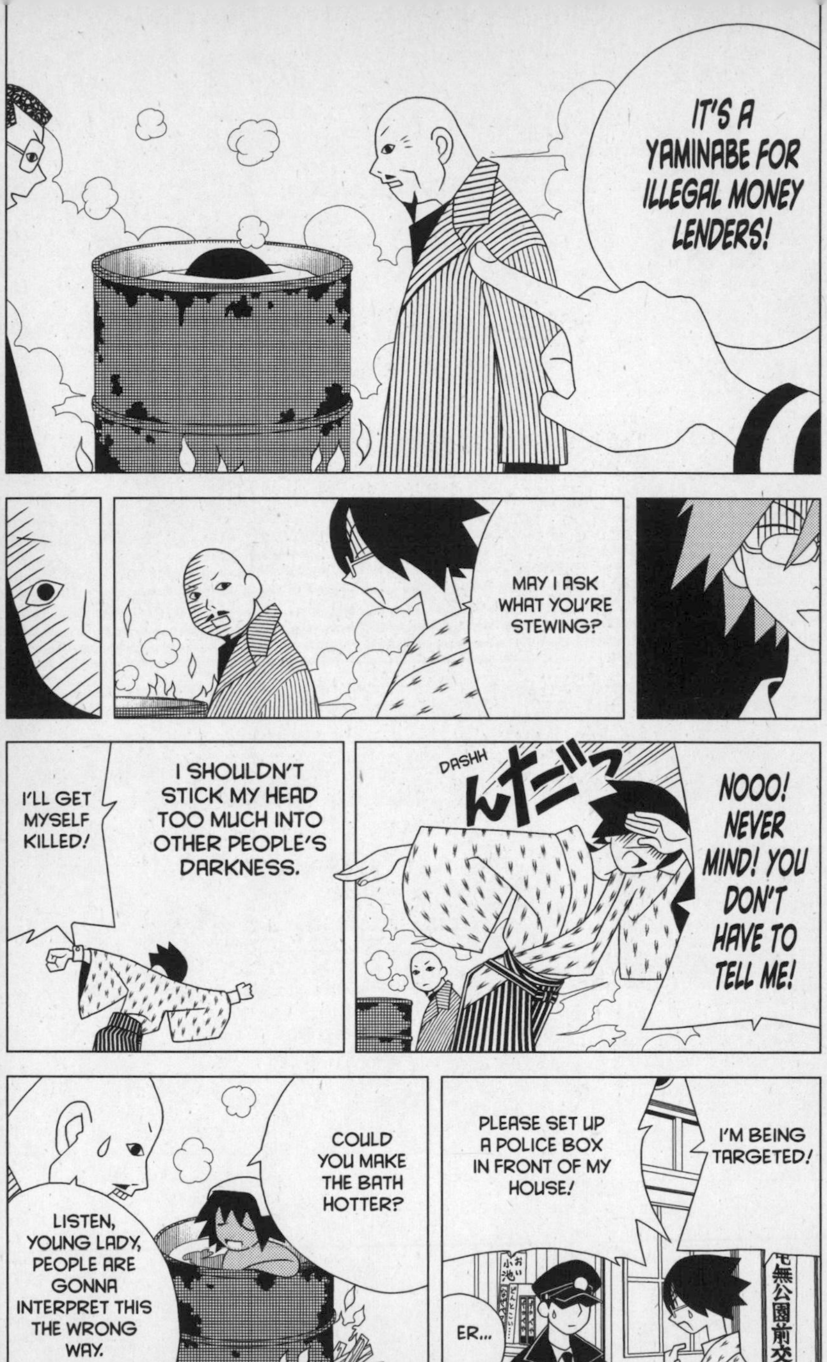
IT'S A YAMINABE FOR ILLEGAL MONEY LENDERS!
MAY I ASK WHAT YOU'RE STEWING?
NOOO! NEVER MIND! YOU DON'T HAVE TO TELL ME!
んだっ
DASHH
I SHOULDN'T STICK MY HEAD TOO MUCH INTO OTHER PEOPLE'S DARKNESS.
I'LL GET MYSELF KILLED!
I'M BEING TARGETED!
PLEASE SET UP A POLICE BOX IN FRONT OF MY HOUSE!
ER...
COULD YOU MAKE THE BATH HOTTER?
LISTEN, YOUNG LADY, PEOPLE ARE GONNA INTERPRET THIS THE WRONG WAY.

THE PRESENT-DAY BLACK MARKET

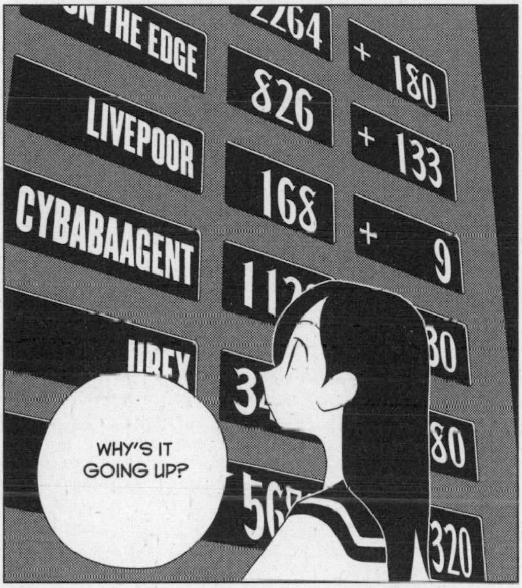
WHY'S IT GOING UP?
2264
+ 180
826
LIVEPOOR
+ 133
168
CYBABAAGENT
+ 9
320

CURRENT CHARGES FROM THIS ISSUE

LETTER OF ACCUSATION

PLAINTIFF:
  OCCUPATION: STUDENT
  NAME: KAERE KIMURA

(OFFICIAL SEAL) DEFENDANT:
  OCCUPATION: STUDENT
  NAME: TARO SEKIUTSU

DATE: OCTOBER 5
ATTN: CHIEF OF POLICE

- PURPOSE OF ACCUSATION
THE ACTS BY THE DEFENDANT AS STATED BELOW ARE CONSIDERED TO FALL UNDER
CRIMINAL LAW, ARTICLE 230 (CRIME OF DEFAMATION OF CHARACTER) AND ARTICLE 233
(CRIME OF OBSTRUCTION OF BUSINESS) AND THIS COMPLAINT IS MADE TO PURSUE SE-
VERE PUNISHMENT TO BE HANDED OUT TO THE DEFENDANT.

- FACTS OF THE ACCUSATION
AT ABOUT 3:30 PM, WHILE I WAS REHEARSING WITH THE BAND IN PREPARATION FOR THE
CULTURAL FESTIVAL, THE DEFENDANT CALLED OUT, "THIS SONG IS NO GOOD!" THEN SHE
GRIMACED, AND MADE A GESTURE TO ATTEMPT TO PERSUADE WITNESSES TO AGREE
WITH HER.

AT THAT TIME, I WAS UNAWARE OF WHAT HAD HAPPENED, SINCE I WAS SO ABSORBED IN MY
MUSIC, BUT DUE TO THIS MALICIOUS BEHAVIOR ON THE PART OF THE DEFENDANT, THE REP-
UTATION OF MY SINGING AND THE BAND WERE SERIOUSLY DAMAGED. FURTHERMORE,
IT PREJUDICED THE AUDIENCE WHO WAS LISTENING TO MY SONG, AND ALTHOUGH MY
SPECTACULAR DEBUT IN THE ENTERTAINMENT WORLD WAS PRACTICALLY GUARANTEED,
THIS INCIDENT CAUSED MY CAREER TO GO BACK TO A BLANK SLATE.

THE AFOREMENTIONED ACTS ARE CONSIDERED TO FALL UNDER CRIMINAL LAW, ARTICLE
230 (CRIME OF DEFAMATION OF CHARACTER) AND ARTICLE 233 (CRIME OF OBSTRUCTION
OF BUSINESS) AND IN ORDER FOR THE DEFENDANT TO BE GIVEN STRICT PUNISHMENT, I
HEREBY MAKE MY CHARGES.

TESTIMONY
1. WITNESS: NOZOMU ITOSHIKI
2. WITNESS: NAMI HITOU

PAPER BLOGS

FOREWORD | CREEPY THINGS DARE | READING | CULTURAL FESTIVAL | PREVIEWING

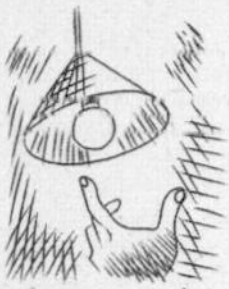

I CHANGED THE LIGHTBULB IN MY TOILET TO THE LOWEST WATTAGE.

A DARK ROOM IS CALMING. EVEN LATE AT NIGHT, TOKYO IS BRIGHT, AND THAT DOESN'T SUIT ME. EVEN THOUGH IT'S BRIGHT, ONCE I SLIPPED AND FELL ON A PIECE OF ICE THE SIZE OF A LARGE PAPERBACK BOOK. WE HAD ANOTHER SEVERE WINTER THIS YEAR. I GOT FREEZER BURNS FROM MY TOILET SEAT. WHEN I TURNED MY COAT POCKETS INSIDE OUT, MECHANICAL PENCIL LEADS THAT HAD TURNED INTO POWDER SCATTERED EVERYWHERE. SOGGY POCKET WARMERS CAME OUT OF MY WASHING MACHINE. WHAT DOES IT SAY ABOUT MY MENTAL STATE WHEN I DREAM OF TAKAKO MATSU, WHO I DON'T LIKE MUCH?

FOREWORD | **CREEPY THINGS DARE** | READING | CULTURAL FESTIVAL | PREVIEWING

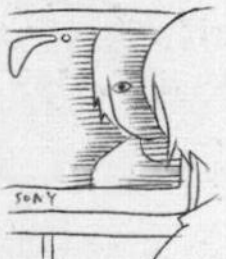
SONY

I THINK I'M CREEPY. I JUST CAN'T STAND ANY PART OF MYSELF. IF I WENT TO A PICNIC AND SAW MY UGLY FACE REFLECTED IN THE LAKE, I'D JUST JUMP INTO IT. IF I WENT SHOPPING AND SAW MY UGLY FIGURE REFLECTED IN THE SHOW WINDOW, I'D BANG MY HEAD AGAINST THE GLASS AND CUT MY THROAT WITH A FRAGMENT. MY TV IS ALWAYS ON. THAT'S BECAUSE IF I TURNED IT OFF, I'D SEE MY UGLY REFLECTION. ON SUNNY DAYS, I HAVE NO DESIRE TO LEAVE THE HOUSE. EVEN MY SHADOW IS UGLY. I'M AN UGLY MANGA CHILD WHO'LL NEVER SEE THE DAY WHEN I BECOME A SWAN.

I CHANGED THE LIGHTBULB OVER MY SINK TO THE LOWEST WATTAGE.

FOREWORD | CREEPY THINGS DARE | **READING** | CULTURAL FESTIVAL | PREVIEWING

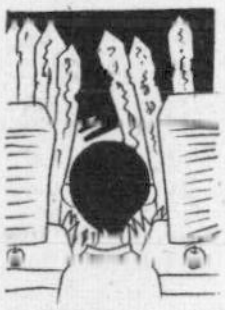

I WAS A KID WHO SUFFERED A LOT. I WAS OFTEN TOLD TO READ OUT LOUD IN FRONT OF THE CLASS. THE TEACHER ALWAYS TOLD ME, "YOU READ IN A REAL ROD-STRAIGHT MONOTONE, DON'T YOU." I RESENTED THAT, SO THOUGHT I'D GO AND REALLY READ RODS. THERE WERE THESE WOODEN RODS THAT ARE AT THE BACK OF GRAVESTONES. BUT THE KANJI ON THEM WERE TOO DIFFICULT, SO I COULDN'T READ THEM. I FAILED AT READING RODS. AS A PERSON WHO COULDN'T EVEN READ RODS, I SHOULD'VE JUST CRAWLED STRAIGHT UNDER THAT STONE. I WAS A KID WHO SUFFERED A LOT. I NEVER WON A POPSICLE, SO I COULDN'T READ WHAT WAS ON A POPSICLE STICK. THAT'S BECAUSE THERE'S NOTHING WRITTEN ON IT.

I CHANGED THE LIGHTBULB IN MY KITCHEN TO THE LOWEST WATTAGE.

FOREWORD | CREEPY THINGS DARE | READING | **CULTURAL FESTIVAL** | PREVIEWING

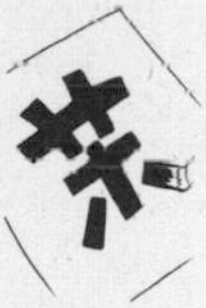

I DON'T LIKE FESTIVALS THAT GO FROM MIDNIGHT TO MORNING. I DISLIKE CULTURAL FESTIVALS IN GENERAL. THAT'S BECAUSE THEY DEMAND CULTURE OF UNCULTURED PERSONS LIKE ME. CULTURAL WORK ISN'T MY THING. FOR OUR CULTURAL FESTIVAL, OUR CLASS PUT ON A TEA SHOP. I WAS GIVEN THE RESPONSIBILITY OF PAINTING THE CHARACTER FOR "TEA" *(OCHA)* FOR THE SIGN. I DON'T LIKE VIRIDIAN PAINT. YOU CAN PAINT, AND PAINT, BUT IT ALWAYS COMES OUT UNEVEN. I'M SO UNCULTURED THAT I CAN'T EVEN PAINT THE WORD "TEA" PROPERLY. SO, DON'T TRY TO GET ME TO DO ANY HIGH-CULTURE THINGS. I DON'T UNDERSTAND RUSSIAN ANIMATION, OR 800 YEN MANGA, OR 326, OR HIROMIX. DON'T CALL MANGA THE "CULTURAL PRIDE OF JAPAN TO THE WORLD," BECAUSE THERE ARE PLENTY OF MANGA IN THIS COUNTRY THAT AREN'T LIKE THAT.

I CHANGED THE LIGHTBULB OVER THE STAIRWAY TO THE LOWEST WATTAGE.

FOREWORD | CREEPY THINGS DARE | READING | CULTURAL FESTIVAL | **PREVIEWING**

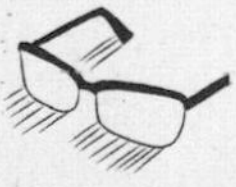

I DON'T HAVE CLOTHES TO WEAR TO GO OUT AND BUY CLOTHES. THOUGH I WANT TO GO AND CHECK OUT FASHIONABLE CLOTHES TO BUY, THERE ARE NO CLOTHES TO PREVIEW BEFORE I BUY THEM. I HAVE TO GO AND PREVIEW CLOTHES THAT I HAVE TO PREVIEW. PEOPLE WHO ARE TIMID STRUGGLE TO GO AND CHECK THINGS OUT IN ADVANCE. WHEN I WEAR OLD CLOTHES THAT I FORCED MYSELF TO BUY, I REALLY LOOK LIKE I'M WEARING RAGGEDY DUDS. A PAIR OF GLASSES THAT I THOUGHT LOOKED TRENDY ENDED UP BEING CALLED "ANEHA GLASSES" AND PEOPLE MADE FUN OF ME. ONE DAY I WANTED A CAT, SO I WENT TO THE PET SHOP TO PREVIEW SOME OF THEM. I PREVIEWED THE SAME CAT OVER AND OVER AGAIN. AFTER I HAD PREVIEWED IT SEVERAL TIMES, I WENT TO THE STORE AND IT WASN'T THERE ANYMORE. OF COURSE, IT WAS BOUGHT UP BY SOMEONE ELSE. BEFORE I EVEN BOUGHT IT, I SUFFERED PET-LOSS SYNDROME.

I CHANGED THE LIGHTBULB IN MY ENTRYWAY TO THE LOWEST WATTAGE POSSIBLE.

AMAKUDARI | OMIKOSHI | FINDING MISTAKES | PROOF | HIBERNATION | YAMINABE

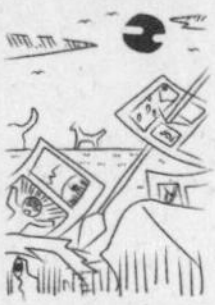

MANGA ARTISTS NEVER GET CUSHY JOBS THROUGH *AMAKUDARI*. I'LL PROBABLY BE UNHAPPY IN MY NEXT LIFE. NO, MAKE THAT DEFINITELY UNHAPPY. I WON'T HAVE SAVINGS TO LIVE OFF OF, NOR WILL I HAVE WORK. THE ONLY THING I CAN DO IS TO TRY BEING USEFUL TO SOCIETY THROUGH MANGA. FOR INSTANCE, I WENT ON A SOJOURN IN THE URURUN WORLD. I WENT TO A REMOTE PART OF AFRICA TO TEACH DISADVANTAGED CHILDREN HOW TO DRAW MANGA. WHEN I CONFIDENTLY DREW MY BEST MANGA, THE CHILDREN UNANIMOUSLY SAID, "YOU'RE PLAGIARIZING *DRAGON BALL*. THIS IS PLAGIARISM." THE SON OF THE HEAD OF THE VILLAGE GOT MAD AND CRITICIZED ME BITTERLY. "THE ART STYLE LOOKS OLD, THE STORIES ARE CLICHÉD, AND THE SUBJECT MATTER ISN'T APPROPRIATE FOR A *SHONEN MAGAZINE*." AND SO, I TEARFULLY DEPARTED. WITH AN INJURED HEART, I VOWED NEVER TO RETURN. I COULDN'T EVEN CONTRIBUTE TO SOCIETY.

I CHANGED THE LIGHTBULB AT MY DESK TO THE LOWEST WATTAGE.

AMAKUDARI | **OMIKOSHI** | FINDING MISTAKES | PROOF | HIBERNATION | YAMINABE

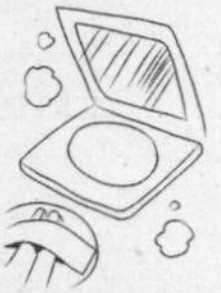

THE *FUNDOSHI* THAT I WAS FORCED TO WEAR WAS NOTHING MORE THAN AN EXERCISE IN HUMILIATING MASOCHISM. IT WAS FOR THE *OMIKOSHI* FOR THE VILLAGE ASSOCIATION. AT THAT TIME, MY MONGOLIAN BLUE SPOT WAS STILL THERE AND I REALLY, REALLY DIDN'T LIKE IT. WHEN I TOLD PEOPLE IN MY CLASS, I WAS TEASED HORRIBLY, SO I HAD NO CHOICE BUT TO TRANSFER TO A NEW SCHOOL, RIGHT? I HAD TO KEEP HIDING IT. I APPLIED MY MOM'S FOUNDATION ON MY BUTT. IT WAS THE FIRST TIME I'D EVER USED MAKEUP. I STARTED FEELING A LITTLE UNCOMFORTABLE HALFWAY THROUGH WHILE PUTTING IT ON. BUT I WANTED TO HIDE IT WELL, SO I APPLIED THE MAKEUP METICULOUSLY. MY FRIENDS WHO CAME TO PICK ME UP TEASED ME, SAYING, "YOU SMELL LIKE YOUR MOM." BUT I DIDN'T CARE. IT WAS BETTER THAN LETTING PEOPLE SEE MY MONGOLIAN BLUE SPOT. THAT WAS THE FIRST AND LAST TIME THAT I PUT FOUNDATION ON MY BUTT. EVEN NOW, WHEN I SMELL CHEAP WOMEN'S FOUNDATION, I FEEL UNCOMFORTABLE. LATELY, I'M SURE FOUNDATIONS HAVE REALLY BECOME ADVANCED, SO KIDS CAN FEEL ALL RIGHT ABOUT NOT APPLYING IT TOO THICKLY.

I CHANGED THE LIGHTBULB IN MY LIVING ROOM TO THE LOWEST WATTAGE.

AMAKUDARI | OMIKOSHI | **FINDING MISTAKES** | PROOF | HIBERNATION | YAMINABE

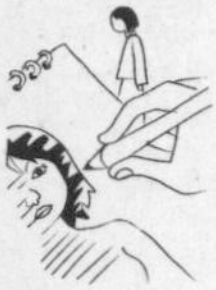

MY LIFE HAS BEEN FULL OF MISTAKES, AND I'M SURE IT WILL CONTINUE TO BE FILLED WITH MISTAKES. PEOPLE OFTEN POINT MY MISTAKES OUT TO ME. EVEN IF I ACKNOWLEDGE MY MISTAKE AND APOLOGIZE, I'M TOLD THAT IT'S A MISTAKE TO ACKNOWLEDGE MY MISTAKE SO EASILY. THAT'S ME, I CAN ONLY MAKE MISTAKEN EXPRESSIONS OF LOVE. DURING JUNIOR HIGH, WHEN I LIKED A GIRL, I CHECKED OUT HER ADDRESS, MADE HESITANT PHONE CALLS (IT SEEMS THAT SOCIETY CALLS THEM "CREEPY PHONE CALLS WHERE THE CALLER DOESN'T SAY ANYTHING"), AND DREW A REALISTIC PORTRAIT OF HER. ACTUALLY, IT WASN'T JUST HER FACE THAT I DREW. SINCE I WAS THE KIND OF KID WHO'D DRAW NIPPLES IN JUMP MANGA WHEN THE CHARACTERS DIDN'T HAVE ANY NIPPLES, I DID AT LEAST THAT. IT WAS A MISTAKEN EXPRESSION OF LOVE. I'M SORRY. IN THE END, I DIDN'T TALK TO HER EVEN ONCE DURING THE THREE YEARS OF SCHOOL.

I CHANGED THE LIGHTBULB IN MY PENLIGHT TO THE LOWEST WATTAGE.

AMAKUDARI | OMIKOSHI | FINDING MISTAKES | **PROOF** | HIBERNATION | YAMINABE

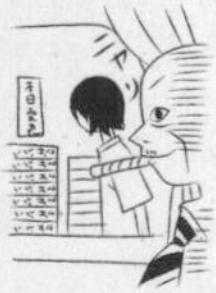

EVERY ONCE IN A WHILE I GET UNEASY. I WONDER IF THE THINGS I DRAW ARE ACTUALLY BEING PRINTED IN MAGAZINES, AND IF PEOPLE ARE ACTUALLY READING THEM. I'M SHY, SO I DON'T HAVE A PROBLEM WITH THEM NOT BEING READ, BUT SOMETIMES I THINK THAT IT'S SOME RICH PERSON'S HOBBY, AND THAT I'M BEING DUPED. MAYBE THEY'RE INTENTIONALLY CHOOSING A TALENTLESS AUTHOR LIKE ME TO WRITE THESE STORIES, AND THEY MAKE ME *THINK* THAT THE MAGAZINES ARE BEING PUBLISHED, BUT MEANWHILE THAT PERSON'S LOOKING AT THEM AND LAUGHING... THE REALLY INGENIOUS, GRANDIOSE SHOCKER IS THAT PERHAPS THE NEIGHBORHOOD CONVENIENCE STORES AND BOOKSTORES ARE IN ON THE JOKE, AND THEY'RE PUTTING FAKE COPIES OF *SAYONARA, ZETSUBOU-SENSEI* WHERE MY EYES WILL SEE THEM... NO, THAT'S GOT TO BE IT. IT'S JUST TOO BIZARRE TO THINK THAT I'M BEING PUBLISHED IN *SHONEN MAGAZINE* AND HAVING BOOKS PUBLISHED. ARE MY MANGA BEING SOLD IN YOUR TOWN...? I DIDN'T THINK SO... THIS MANUSCRIPT COULDN'T EVEN GET TO YOUR TOWN, SO THERE'S NO WAY I COULD PROVE IT. EVERY DAY MY SUSPICIONS ARE GETTING CLOSER TO BEING CONFIRMED.

I CHANGED THE LIGHTBULB IN MY STORAGE SHED TO THE LOWEST WATTAGE.

AMAKUDARI | OMIKOSHI | FINDING MISTAKES | PROOF | **HIBERNATION** | YAMINABE

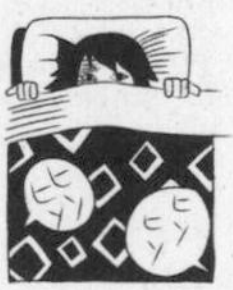

I ENVY HIBERNATION. FOR THE LAST SEVERAL YEARS, THERE HASN'T BEEN A DAY WHEN I'VE SLEPT DEEPLY, OR FOR A LONG STRETCH. EVEN WHEN I TRIED DRINKING MILK BEFORE BED, I GOT SICK IN THE MIDDLE OF THE NIGHT AND ENDED UP RUNNING TO THE TOILET. WHEN I SLEEP LIGHTLY, I'LL HEAR THE ASSISTANTS' CONVERSATIONS FROM THE NEXT ROOM, AND THEY ALL SOUND LIKE THEY'RE CRITICIZING ME. NO, BUT OF COURSE, THEY ARE CRITICIZING ME. LIKE, "FOR AN ADULT, HE'S SHAMEFUL," OR "HE HAS NO PRESENCE," OR "I'M NOT LEARNING ANYTHING BEING HERE." THERE ARE LIMITS TO MAKING FUN OF SOMEBODY. THE WHOLE WORLD IS SAYING BAD THINGS ABOUT ME. SALESPEOPLE AT CONVENIENCE STORES, PASSENGERS ON THE BUS, FANS OF *GINTAMA*—THEY'RE ALL SPEAKING ILL OF ME. AND FINALLY, I HEARD THIS. THE PLAN TO KILL KUMETA. A PERFECT PLAN TO DUMP MY BODY IN THE CAR, ROLL THE CAR INTO THE LAKE, AND MAKE IT LOOK LIKE A SUICIDE. I'VE GOT TO KILL BEFORE I GET KILLED.

I'VE CHANGED THE LIGHTBULB IN MY BATHROOM TO THE LOWEST WATTAGE.

AMAKUDARI | OMIKOSHI | FINDING MISTAKES | PROOF | HIBERNATION | **YAMINABE**

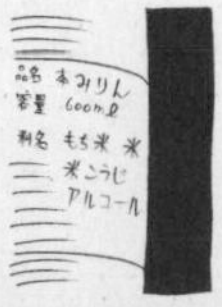
品名 本みりん
容量 600mℓ
もち米 米
米こうじ
アルコール

BASICALLY, WHEN YOU'RE HAVING AN OFFICIAL *YAMINABE*, THE TENSION OF THE DARK MYSTERY ALREADY GETS LOST. WHEN YOU DO A HOT POT STEW BY YOURSELF, IT'S CLOSER TO BEING A *YAMINABE*. WHEN I LOOK AT THE INGREDIENTS LIST FOR THE SEASONING *MIRIN*, THIS IS WHAT I FIND LISTED. INGREDIENTS: GLUTINOUS RICE, RICE, MALTED RICE. IT KIND OF FEELS LIKE I'M BEING MADE FUN OF IN THE WORST WAY. KOJI KUMETA, ALL ALONE, HAVING A HOT POT WITH RICE. IF YOU WANT TO LAUGH, GO AHEAD AND LAUGH. I'M JUST NOTHING BUT BLACK MALTED RICE, MADE FROM BLACK MARKET RICE. THE INTERIOR OF MY HEART IS PITCH-BLACK DARKNESS, AND THE DARKNESS IN MY HEART IS SO DEEP, IT'S BOTTOMLESS. AS A KID, THE COLOR BLACK IN MY PAINT SET WOULD BE THE FIRST TO GO. I BECAME A MANGA ARTIST WITH FEW COLOR PAGES.

I CHANGED THE LIGHTBULB IN MY LIGHT BOX TO THE LOWEST WATTAGE.

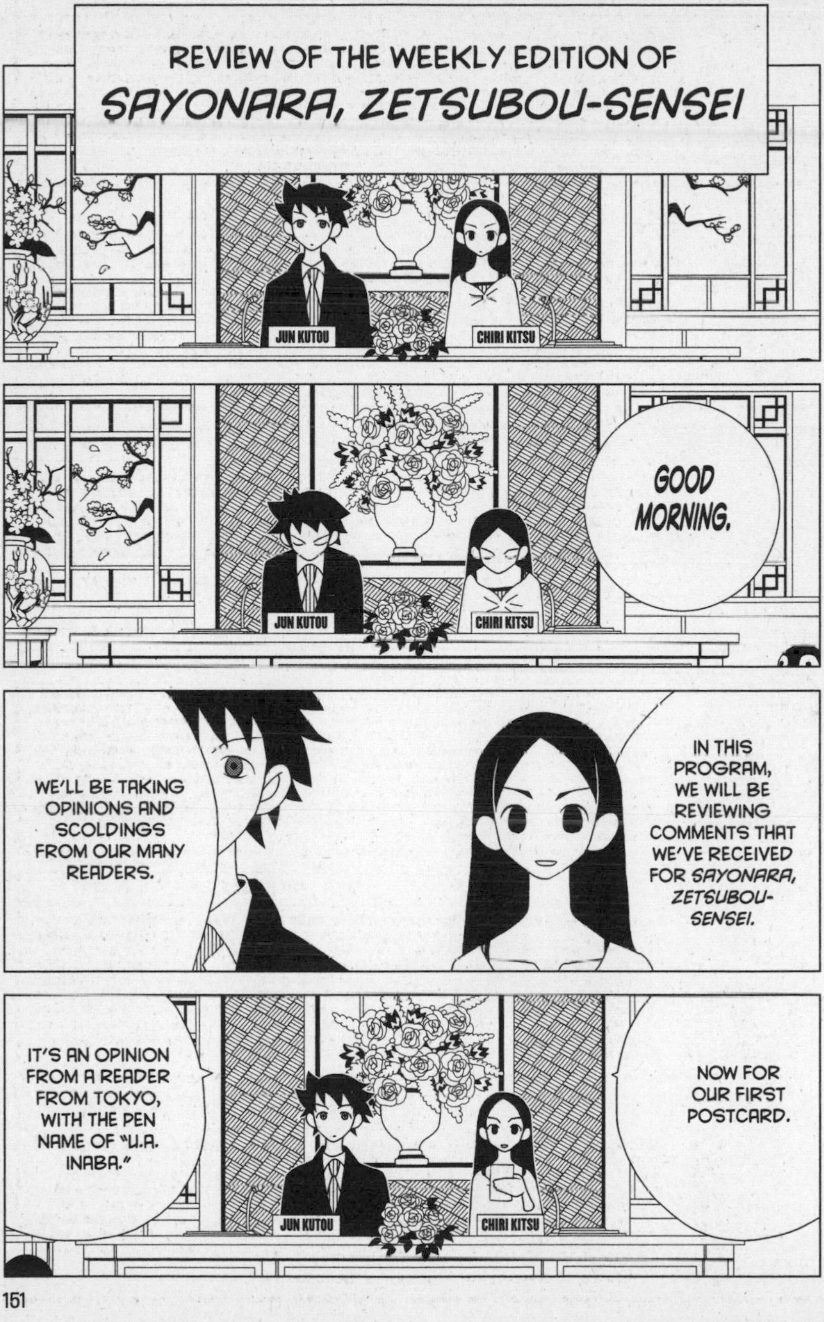
REVIEW OF THE WEEKLY EDITION OF *SAYONARA, ZETSUBOU-SENSEI*
JUN KUTOU
CHIRI KITSU
GOOD MORNING.
IN THIS PROGRAM, WE WILL BE REVIEWING COMMENTS THAT WE'VE RECEIVED FOR *SAYONARA, ZETSUBOU-SENSEI.*
WE'LL BE TAKING OPINIONS AND SCOLDINGS FROM OUR MANY READERS.
NOW FOR OUR FIRST POSTCARD.
IT'S AN OPINION FROM A READER FROM TOKYO, WITH THE PEN NAME OF "U.A. INABA."

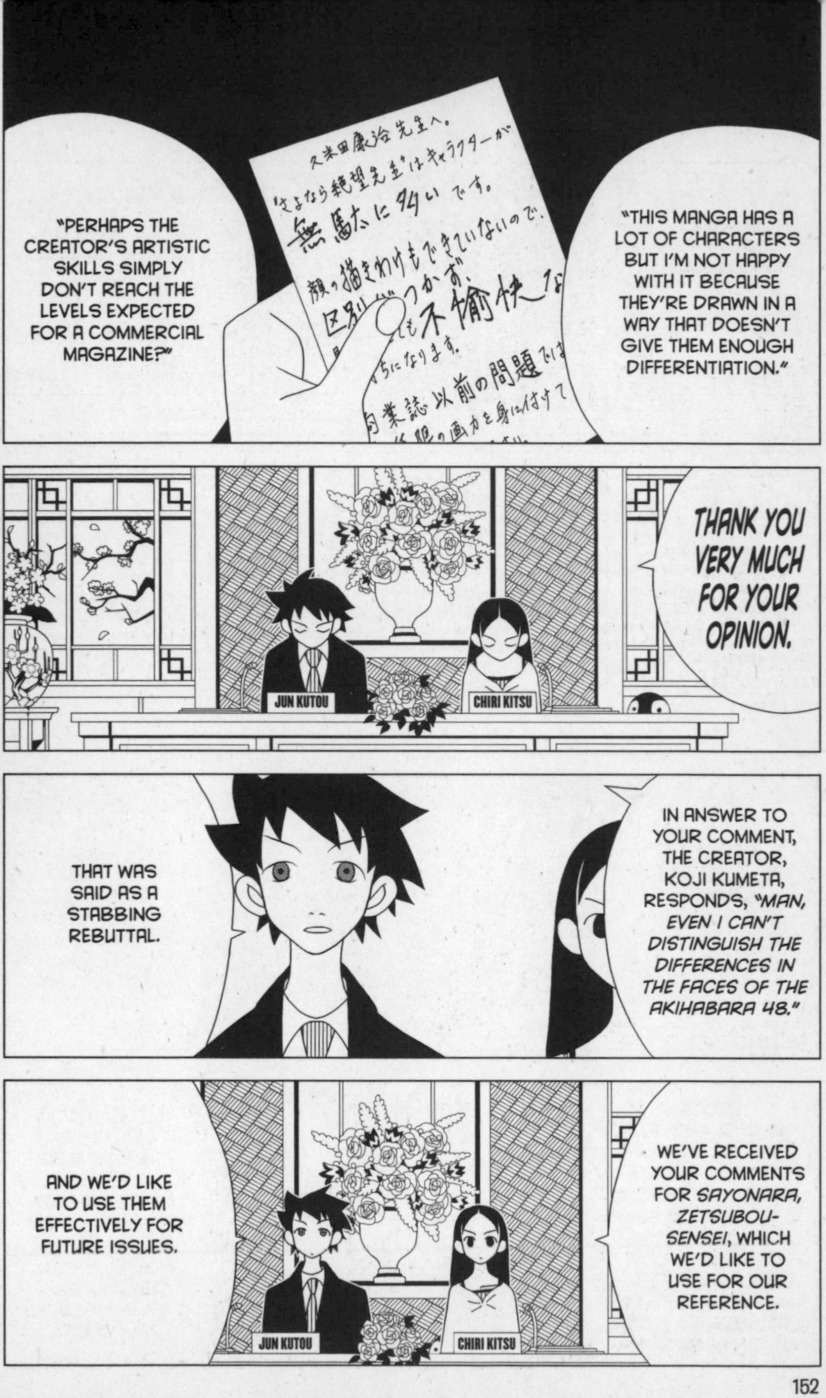

"THIS MANGA HAS A LOT OF CHARACTERS BUT I'M NOT HAPPY WITH IT BECAUSE THEY'RE DRAWN IN A WAY THAT DOESN'T GIVE THEM ENOUGH DIFFERENTIATION."
久米田康治先生へ。
さよなら絶望先生はキャラクターが
無駄に多いです。
顔の描きわけもできていないので、
区別がつかず、
"PERHAPS THE CREATOR'S ARTISTIC SKILLS SIMPLY DON'T REACH THE LEVELS EXPECTED FOR A COMMERCIAL MAGAZINE?"
THANK YOU VERY MUCH FOR YOUR OPINION.
JUN KUTOU
CHIRI KITSU
IN ANSWER TO YOUR COMMENT, THE CREATOR, KOJI KUMETA, RESPONDS, "MAN, EVEN I CAN'T DISTINGUISH THE DIFFERENCES IN THE FACES OF THE AKIHABARA 48."
THAT WAS SAID AS A STABBING REBUTTAL.
WE'VE RECEIVED YOUR COMMENTS FOR SAYONARA, ZETSUBOU-SENSEI, WHICH WE'D LIKE TO USE FOR OUR REFERENCE.
AND WE'D LIKE TO USE THEM EFFECTIVELY FOR FUTURE ISSUES.
JUN KUTOU
CHIRI KITSU

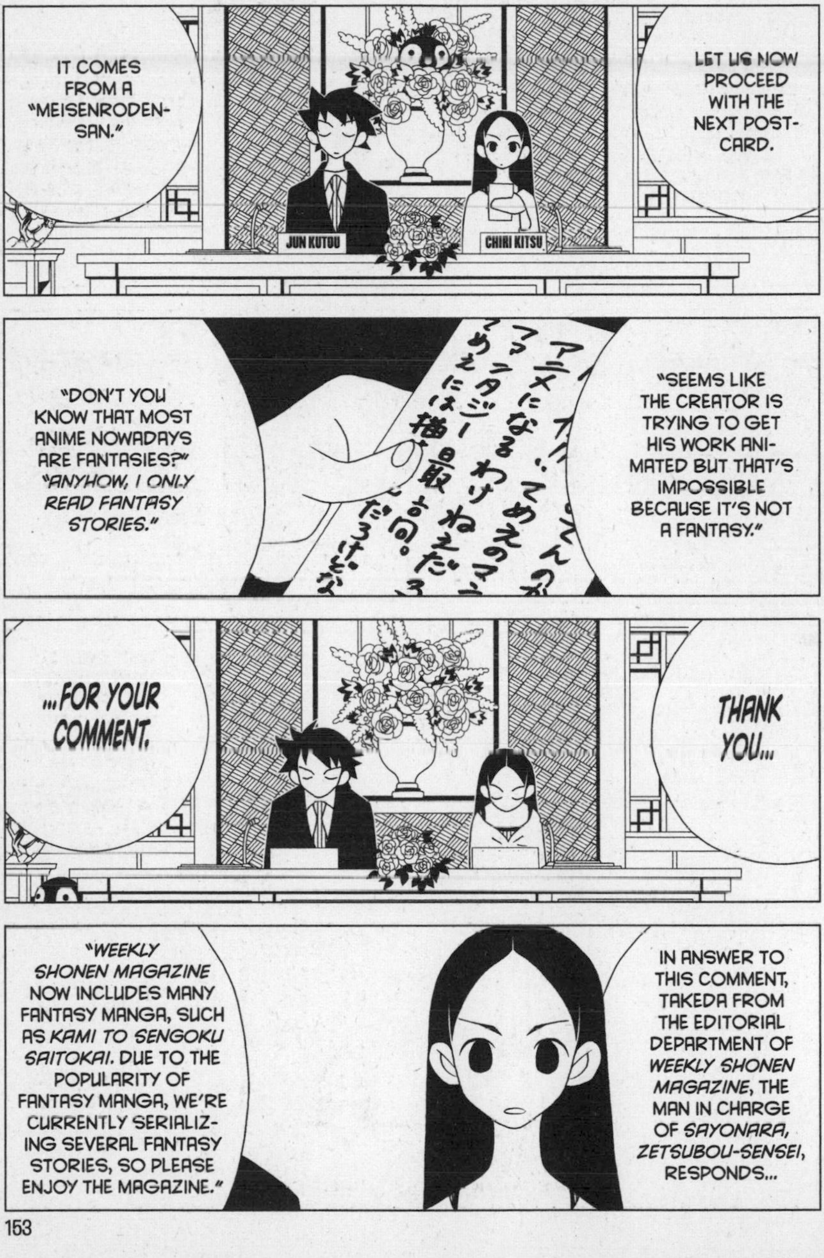
LET US NOW PROCEED WITH THE NEXT POST-CARD.
IT COMES FROM A "MEISENRODEN-SAN."
CHIRI KITSU
JUN KUTOU
"SEEMS LIKE THE CREATOR IS TRYING TO GET HIS WORK ANI-MATED BUT THAT'S IMPOSSIBLE BECAUSE IT'S NOT A FANTASY."
"DON'T YOU KNOW THAT MOST ANIME NOWADAYS ARE FANTASIES?" *"ANYHOW, I ONLY READ FANTASY STORIES."*
THANK YOU...
...FOR YOUR COMMENT.
IN ANSWER TO THIS COMMENT, TAKEDA FROM THE EDITORIAL DEPARTMENT OF *WEEKLY SHONEN MAGAZINE*, THE MAN IN CHARGE OF *SAYONARA, ZETSUBOU-SENSEI*, RESPONDS...
"*WEEKLY SHONEN MAGAZINE* NOW INCLUDES MANY FANTASY MANGA, SUCH AS *KAMI TO SENGOKU SAITOKAI*. DUE TO THE POPULARITY OF FANTASY MANGA, WE'RE CURRENTLY SERIALIZ-ING SEVERAL FANTASY STORIES, SO PLEASE ENJOY THE MAGAZINE."

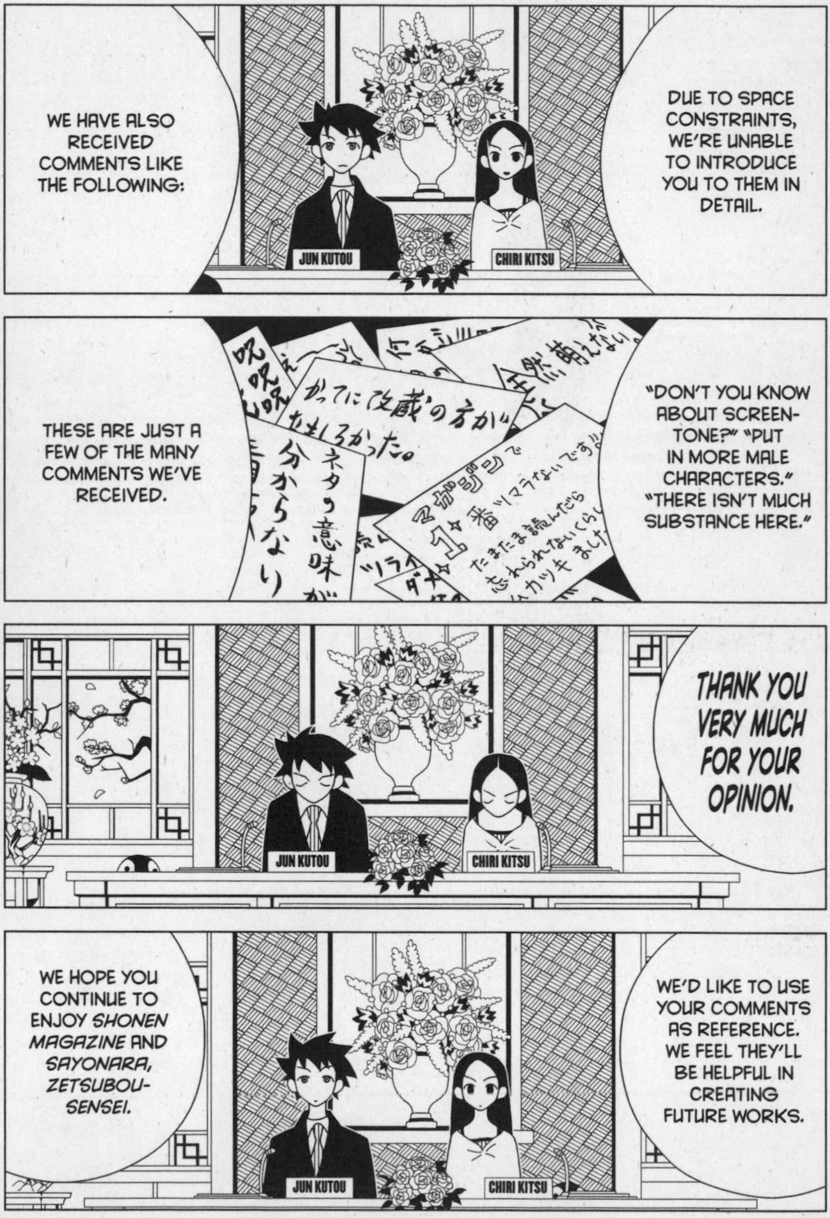
DUE TO SPACE CONSTRAINTS, WE'RE UNABLE TO INTRODUCE YOU TO THEM IN DETAIL.
WE HAVE ALSO RECEIVED COMMENTS LIKE THE FOLLOWING:
JUN KUTOU
CHIRI KITSU
"DON'T YOU KNOW ABOUT SCREEN-TONE?" "PUT IN MORE MALE CHARACTERS." "THERE ISN'T MUCH SUBSTANCE HERE."
かってに改蔵の方がおもしろかった。
THESE ARE JUST A FEW OF THE MANY COMMENTS WE'VE RECEIVED.
THANK YOU VERY MUCH FOR YOUR OPINION.
JUN KUTOU
CHIRI KITSU
WE'D LIKE TO USE YOUR COMMENTS AS REFERENCE. WE FEEL THEY'LL BE HELPFUL IN CREATING FUTURE WORKS.
WE HOPE YOU CONTINUE TO ENJOY *SHONEN MAGAZINE* AND *SAYONARA, ZETSUBOU-SENSEI.*
JUN KUTOU
CHIRI KITSU

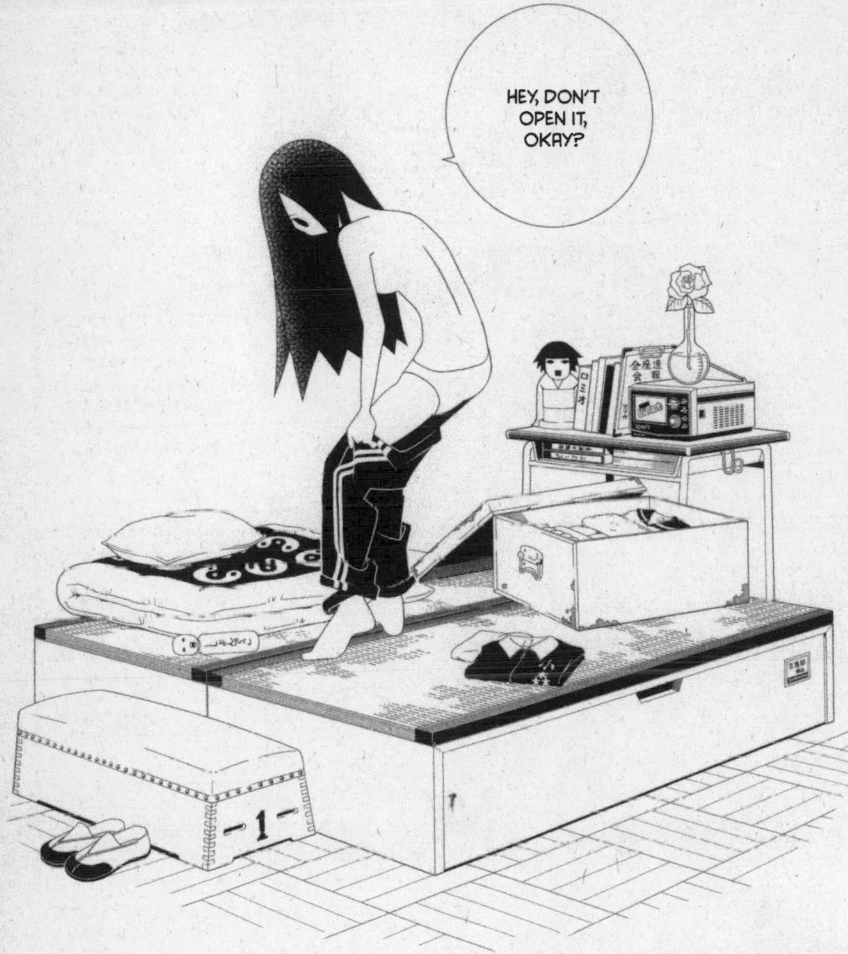
HEY, DON'T OPEN IT, OKAY?

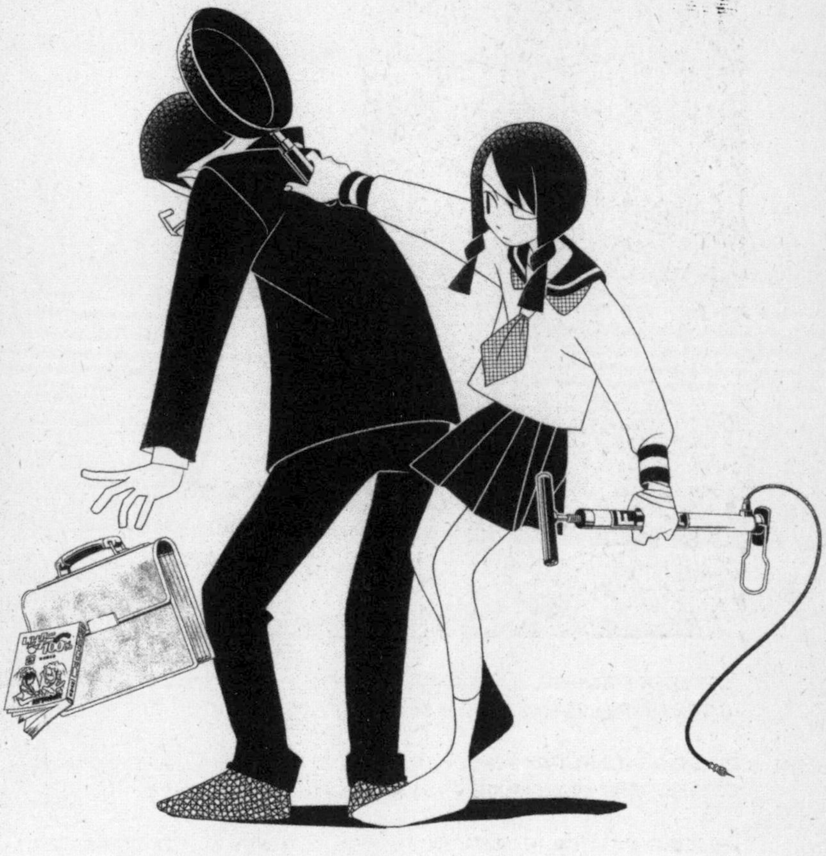

ZETSUBOU LITERARY COMPILATION

BOTCHAN

JUST LIKE HIS PARENTS, HE WAS A BOY WHO WANTED TO DIE, AND EVER SINCE HE WAS A LITTLE CHILD, HE'D ALWAYS THINK OF WAYS TO KILL HIMSELF.

DURING HIS ELEMENTARY SCHOOL DAYS, HE ATTEMPTED SUICIDE BY JUMPING OUT OF THE SECOND STORY WINDOW, BUT HE COULDN'T DIE.

THE FOLLOWING YEAR, HE TRIED CUTTING HIS WRISTS WITH A LETTER OPENER BUT, AGAIN, HE COULDN'T DIE.

THEN THE YEAR AFTER THAT, HE ATTEMPTED SUICIDE BY HANGING HIMSELF WITH A TWISTED PAPER ROPE, AND HE TRIED TO POISON HIMSELF WITH ASPARAGUS GAS BUT, AGAIN, HE COULDN'T DIE.

THAT WAS HIS LIFE.

Translation Notes

Japanese is a tricky language for most Westerners, and translation is often more art than science. In the case of a text-dense manga like *Sayonara, Zetsubou-sensei*, it's a delicate art indeed. Although most of the jokes are universal, Koji Kumeta is famous for filling his manga with references to Japanese politics, entertainment, *otaku* culture, religion, and sports. Unless you're a true Japanophile, it's difficult to understand it all without some serious background knowledge of current events at the time the manga was running. Kumeta also uses references to foreign literature and politics, so even Japanese readers probably don't get all the humor. For your reading pleasure, here are notes on some of the more obscure references and difficult-to-translate jokes in *Sayonara, Zetsubou-sensei*.

General Notes

Sayonara, Zetsubou-sensei (title)

The title *Sayonara, Zetsubou-sensei* literally translates to "Goodbye, Mr. Despair." It's a possible reference to James Hilton's 1934 novel of a beloved teacher, *Goodbye, Mr. Chips* (known in Japan as *Chips-sensei, Sayonara*). The Del Rey edition preserves the original Japanese title, with "The Power of Negative Thinking" as a subtitle to express Itoshiki's philosophy. (The English subtitle is itself a reference to Norman Vincent Peale's 1952 self-help book *The Power of Positive Thinking*.)

Signs

Koji Kumeta's highly detailed and realistic renderings of modern Japanese life present one special challenge to the letterer. Kumeta fills his panels with all the ephemera of everyday life—street signs, product labels, magazine covers, newspaper pages, and so on. It's difficult to replace this text with English lettering without interfering with the integrity of the original illustrations. Out of respect for Kumeta's unique artwork, many signs have retained their original Japanese lettering.

Page Notes

It's Way Too Gross in This Sad Town, page 4

Sayonara, Zetsubou-sensei's chapter titles are usually references to Japanese fiction, generally classics from the prewar period (in keeping with Zetsubou-sensei's old-fashioned clothes). This particular title is a reference to Osamu Dazai's 1935 short story *Doke no Hana* ("Flowers of Buffoonery"), which includes the line "Beyond this place is a sad town."

Gross-out test, page 7

This chapter involves the traditional Japanese game of *kimo-dameshi* ("test of courage"), in which people dare one another to walk through creepy places like graveyards, while other people lurk in the shadows to jump out and scare them. However, Zetsubou-sensei and his sister turn it into a game of *kimoi-dameshi* ("test of gross-ness"). Summer is the season of ghosts in Japan, so *kimo-dameshi*—either in professional "ghost houses" or just with your friends—is a traditional way to get the chills on hot, spooky summer nights. However, this story was originally printed in Japan in the autumn, not the summer, so the game is a little out of season—hence Chiri's comment.

Kira Yoshikage's collection of nail clippings, page 10

Kira Yoshikage is a character from Hirohiko Araki's long-running manga, *JoJo's Bizarre Adventure*. A serial killer obsessed with the human hand, he kept a collection of his own fingernail clippings, sorted by year.

Nonburnables day, page 11

In Japan, people separate their garbage into different types, such as burnable and nonburnable. Garbage disposal crews collect specific types of garbage on specific days, and may complain to the residents if the garbage is unsorted or left out on the wrong day.

Assorted references, page 13

The long-haired baseball player is a reference to Kei Igawa (1979–), a Japanese pitcher who famously declared that he wouldn't cut his hair as long as his team kept winning. "Gil" and "Rey" are Gilbert Durandal and Rey Za Burrel, characters from the 2004 anime series *Gundam SEED Destiny*. Fujiyoshi is a connoisseur of *yaoi dojinshi*, in which fans draw imaginary relationships between male characters from mainstream manga and anime, but evidently the thought of these two getting together is too much even for her. Otome Road ("Maiden Road") is a nickname for a street in Tokyo's Ikebukuro district famous for its many businesses aimed at nerdy young women, such as the manga and *dojinshi* store K-Books. The Saibamen (known as Cultivars in the VIZ manga translation) are plant-based life forms from Akira Toriyama's *Dragon Ball Z*. "Imprisoned prince" refers to an infamous incident in Japan in which a man imprisoned a woman in his apartment for two weeks in 2001. He received a suspended sentence, then in 2004, he imprisoned another woman for three months until she escaped, keeping her on a dog collar and referring to her by the pet name *oji* ("prince"). After he was arrested the second time, numerous "human pet"–themed adult video games were confiscated from his apartment. "Fuyuhiko-san" is an adult man with an extremely creepy Oedipus complex from the 1992 TV drama *Zuto Anata ga Suki Datta* ("I've Always Loved You").

Assorted references, page 15

Kimokawa is a Japanese combo word made from *kimoi* (gross, disgusting) and *kawaii* (cute). Yoshiaki Murakami is the founder of the briefly famous investment management company M&A Consulting, aka the "Murakami Fund"; in 2006, after this manga was first published, he was indicted in an insider trading scandal and sentenced to two years in prison. (Koji Kumeta presumably thinks Murakami is *kimokawa* because of his goofy, boyish appearance.) *Kuraki Papa* is a Japanese TV show. "Yamahira's sex book" refers to Japanese politician Taku Yamasaki (1936–), who was publicly shamed when a former bar hostess, Kanako Yamada, wrote a graphic book about their ten-year-long affair during which she had two abortions. 326 is the pen name of Mitsuru Nakamura (1978–), a book illustrator and author (or, as he puts it, an "illust-writer") with a distinctively funky art style.

I've Read Books Full of Shame, page 18

This title is a reference to Osamu Dazai's 1948 novel, *Ningen Shikkaku* ("No Longer Human"), which includes the line "I've lived a life full of shame."

Reading, page 19

This chapter plays with the Japanese verb *yomu* ("read"), which can be used in the sense not just of reading a book, but also "reading" a person's expression and attitude, or predicting the future, the weather, etc. Most of the books and library signs which appear in this chapter are just normal signs and children's book titles.

"You're planning to read what's in my heart, aren't you?" page 20

In the original Japanese, Zetsubou-sensei uses the word *kokoro*, which means "heart," not usually in an anatomical sense but in the sense of one's inner self. An alternate translation in this instance might be "mind" (as in "read my mind"), but other parts of this chapter use *kokoro*, in a sense closer to the English "heart," so there is no one perfect translation.

Shonen Magazine, page 21

Weekly Shonen Magazine is the magazine in which *Sayonara, Zetsubou-sensei* appears in Japan. As to whether its page count has been decreasing, as Zetsubou-sensei suggests, you'd have to read it to find out.

Aoi Hiiragi and Seiji Amasawa, page 22

Aoi Hiiragi (1962–) is a shojo manga artist best known for *Mimi wo Sumaseba* ("If You Listen Closely"), which was adapted into the Studio Ghibli animated film *Whisper of the Heart*. The book titles, from *Hono no Tatakai* ("Battle of Flames") to *Tokagemori no Ruu* ("Roo of the Lizard Forest"), are made-up children's book titles. However, "Seiji Amasawa" is a character from *Mimi wo Sumaseba*, whose plot hinges on a library checkout card filled out in Amasawa's name.

Assorted references, page 23

Katsuya Nomura (1935–) is a famous Japanese baseball player and manager. The Masters Tournament is an international championship golf tournament. Sakura Yokomine (1985–) is a Japanese golfer. Her father, Yoshihiro Yokomine (1960–), is a Japanese politician and former radio personality who was accused of making large sums of money betting on golf games. Katsuya Okada (1953–) is a member of the House of Representatives of Japan, and former president of the Japanese minority party, the Democratic Party of Japan (DPJ). After the unexpected landslide victory of the Liberal Democratic Party (LDP) in the 2005 general elections, which delivered a severe blow to the DPJ, Okada resigned as president.

Yumi Adachi and Arthur Kuroda, page 24

Yumi Adachi (1981–) is a Japanese actress, model and singer. From 2002 to 2005 she dated Arthur Kuroda, an actor more than twenty years her senior. In May 2005 they broke up, and in September 2005 she announced her marriage to comedian Jun Itoda. At the time of her marriage she also announced that she was two months pregnant, causing Zetsubou-sensei to be skeptical about the exact timing of the breakup and pregnancy. (However, after this manga was first printed in Japan, Adachi gave birth on April 2006, more or less on schedule.)

Book in panel 2, page 31

The title of the book in panel 2 is *Fubuki no Anata* ("You are a Snowstorm"), a parody of *Fubuki no Ashita* ("Yesterday's Snowstorm"), one of Yoichi Kimura and Hiroshi Abe's series of children's books. Could it be a reference to Zetsubou-sensei's stormy emotions and frosty demeanor?

A Cultured Man Was Waiting for the Rain to Stop Under the Rashomon Gate, page 34

This title is a reference to Ryunosuke Akutagawa's 1914 short story *Rashomon* (no direct relationship to the Japanese movie of the same name), which includes the line "A lowly man was waiting for the rain to stop under the Rashomon gate."

Cultural festival, page 35

Bunka sai ("Cultural festivals") are annual events held at most schools in Japan. At culture festivals, students set up dances, concerts, plays, food stalls, and so forth, displaying their artistic and academic skills and learning to work as a group. Campus clubs like the manga club often sponsor specific events, and parents and people from other schools are invited to come by and see what kind of work the students have been doing. But how exactly is it "cultural"? Good question. This chapter plays with the idea of "cultural" vs. "noncultural," a distinction sort of like "highbrow" vs. "lowbrow" or "intellectual" vs. "dumbed down."

Blackboard text, page 37

Written on the blackboard are the names of various celebrities, entertainers and artists, including Sofia Coppola, Yuriko Nakamura, Ai Iijima, and Horiemon (Takafumi Horie).

"That's *my* job!" page 39

Usui is chagrined because, although technically he is class chairman, everyone always forgets about his existence and assumes that Chiri is the chairman. (See volume 2, page 58.) In Japanese schools the *iincho*, literally "chairman" or "representative," performs functions similar to an American school's class president. (In fact, the word is often translated as "class president.")

Tatsuya Uesugi and Minami Asakura, page 39

Judging from the names, the class is performing a theatrical version of Mitsuru Adachi's classic 1981 romantic comedy manga *Touch*.

Assorted references, page 40

Takeshi Kaneshiro (1973–) is an actor/singer of mixed Taiwanese and Japanese ancestry. Haruo Mizuno (1931–2008) was a Japanese movie producer, director, and critic, who introduced films for a long-running Japanese TV program.

Assorted references, page 41

Ryo Tamura (1972–), together with Atsushi Tamura, is one of the members of the Japanese comedy duo London Boots ("Lonboo" for short). "Nakai-kun" refers to Masahiro Nakai (1972–), a TV celebrity and the lead member of the Japanese idol group SMAP. The Birdman Rally is a homemade glider and human-powered flight competition. *Manzai* is a type of Japanese stand-up comedy which revolves around puns and gags. Though Chiri performs alone, *manzai* usually involves two performers; London Boots is a *manzai* act.

"This is the part that divides the winners from the losers," pages 42–43

The original Japanese reads *Koko ga shobu no wakarame yon* ("This is the turning point of the battle/match/ contest"). *Wakarame*, "turning point," also means "dividing line," and could refer to the part in Chiri's hair. It's an intentionally corny gag.

Mataro, page 44

Mataro is a nickname for Maria, whose full name, after all, is Taro Maria Sekiutsu.

Assorted references, pages 44–45

"Nocchi dessssu!" was the catchphrase of Nozomu Sato (1965–), aka Nocchi, a Japanese comedian. In 2008, Sato changed his image to "Japan's official Obama comedian," focusing on impersonations of Barack Obama and continually using Obama's new catchphrase "Yes, we can!" "Ishii-chan dessssu" was the catchphrase of Kouta Ishii (1975–), a comedian from the Japanese comedy duo Yarusenasu. "Kusanagi-kun" is Tsuyoshi Kusanagi (1974–), an actor and member of the Japanese idol group SMAP, who's also well known for being a lousy visual artist. East End x Yuri was a short-lived band. "Nacchi" is Natsumi Abe (1981–), a J-pop singer and actress, who was accused of plagiarizing poetry she included in some of her photo books. Yassy-kun the mountain goat was the campaign mascot of Yasuo Tanaka (1956–), the governor of Nagano Prefecture from 2000 to 2006. Masayuki Kakefu (1955–) is a balding baseball commentator and former professional baseball player. Junichi Ishida (1954–) is an actor/director who once scandalously told entertainment reporters that "culture and arts sometimes come from illicit love affairs." This was reported in the media as "immortality (or illicit love affairs) is culture."

Kishidan, page 46

Kishidan ("The Knights") is a comedic Japanese pop group that affects the retro style of 1980s *bosozoku* motorcycle gangs. The joke refers to the auto-correct features on Japanese search engines and cell phones; Zetsubou-sensei's cell phone auto-corrects the neutral *hiragana* characters "ki-shi-dan" to the kanji characters used in the band's name, while Meru's outdated cell phone converts the same *hiragana* characters to a meaningless phrase with the same pronunciation.

Cultural knife, page 46

A *bunkabocho* ("cultural knife") is an old-fashioned advertising term for a stainless steel kitchen knife that could cut through anything, a bit like Ginsu knives in the United States. The word *bunka* ("cultural") and the phrase *bunka ichi* ("No. 1 culture") were common superlatives in Japanese advertising dating back to the 1950s, and were also parodied for humor purposes, as in the title of the 1987 manga/anime *All Purpose Cultural Cat Girl Nuku Nuku*.

The *Namayatsuhashi* Must Be Burned, page 50

Yatsuhashi is a Japanese delicacy made from rice flour, sugar, and cinnamon. It's served either baked and crispy or raw and chewy—the raw form is called *namayatsuhashi* ("raw yatsuhashi"). It's a regional specialty of Kyoto, so it makes sense in the title of a chapter about a trip to Kyoto.

Preview, page 52

The Japanese word for preview used throughout this chapter is *shitami*. It's a word used for preliminary inspections, such as visiting a college before you decide to go there.

Assorted references, page 53

Bubuzuke is a Kyoto specialty food that's served over rice. It seems it is also a polite way to say you've over-stayed your welcome. "Letdown Travel Agency" was originally *Gakkari Kanko* ("Disappointing/Discouraging Travel Agency"). The papers in Zetsubou-sensei's hands in panel 7 are a list of suspicious "entertainment expenses" paid to the school principal, the PTA, etc., to the amount of 80,000 yen (about $862) each.

"So Mirai-san wasn't doing a love preview," page 55

Sleggar Law (aka Slegger) and Maria Yashima are characters from the 1979 anime series *Mobile Suit Gundam*.

AB Road, page 56

AB Road (www.ab-road.net) is a Japanese travel and tourism magazine.

Fureizu Mortuary, page 60

The original Japanese reads *Fureizu Kaikan* ("Phrase Assembly Hall"), a pun on the title of Mayu Shinjo's 1997 shojo manga *Kaikan Fureizu* ("Sensual Phrase"). The Japanese words for "assembly hall" and "sensual" sound the same, although they are written with different kanji characters.

Ryuzaki Family Plot, page 61

"Ryuzaki family plot" may be a reference to the character "L" in the manga *Death Note*. (The name Ryuzaki is one of L's aliases.)

I Am *Amakudari*. I Still Don't Have Any Work to Do, page 64

This title is a reference to Natsume Soseki's 1905–1906 novel *I Am a Cat*, which begins with the line "I am a cat. I still don't have a name."

Amakudari, page 66

This Japanese word literally means "descent from heaven." It's a practice in Japan where senior bureaucrats retire to cushy, high-profile positions in the private and public sectors. It often leads to corruption and collusion among colleagues in business, as *amakudari* employees are paid well with taxpayer's money, and there's less oversight by public agencies. Two Japanese prime ministers made policy changes aimed at eliminating *amakudari*, in 2002 and again in 2007, but it's unclear how much effect they had.

Currency conversion, page 67

800,000 yen is approximately $8,620. Thirty million yen is approximately $322,000.

Assorted references, pages 70–71

"Makenaide" ("Don't Lose") is an "inspiring" Japanese pop song. The line about Sakamoto refers to Ryoma Sakamoto (1835–1867), the Meiji Era hero who negotiated a secret alliance between the Choshu and Satsuma clans as part of an attempt to create a modern Japanese government. Hachioji is a suburb of Tokyo, over twenty miles from the city center. Manabu Oshio (1978–) is a Japanese actor/singer who, in 2005, announced that he was giving up acting to focus on his music career with an indie label. "Aoba University Troop 2" is a reference to Akio Chiba's 1972 baseball manga *Captain*. "Musashinomori School" is a reference to Daisuke Higuchi's 1998 soccer manga *Whistle!* "Madame Dewi" refers to Dewi Sukarno (1940–), formerly Naoko Nemoto, a Japanese woman who married Sukarno (1901–1970), the first president of Indonesia. After Sukarno was overthrown in a 1967 coup and died three years later, Dewi became a wealthy international socialite. Kaoklai Kaennorsing (1983–) is a K-1 champion Muay Thai kickboxer.

Kyabetsu Taro, page 72

Kyabetsu Taro ("cabbage taro") is a Japanese snack. Ironically, it contains no cabbage.

Itoshiki-kun, page 73

When Zetsubou-sensei starts acting like a high school student, Chiri starts calling him "Itoshiki-kun." She can add the "kun" because her teacher is now acting as if he's her age. Chiri couldn't call him that if he were still her superior.

Sportop, page 73

Sportop is a Japanese energy drink.

As Gregor Samsa Awoke One Morning He Found Himself Carrying a *Mikoshi*, page 78

This title is a reference to Franz Kafka's 1915 short story *The Metamorphosis*, which opens with the line "As Gregor Samsa awoke one morning from uneasy dreams he found himself transformed in his bed into a gigantic insect."

Omikoshi or *mikoshi*, page 79

A *mikoshi* (or, in more respectful language, *omikoshi*) is a portable Shinto shrine that serves as a vehicle of a divine spirit. It is beautifully ornate with carvings and gilding, and borne on the shoulders by *mikoshi* carriers by means of two poles. During festivals, a *mikoshi* is carried around the neighborhood and down the main streets and the excitement can get intense.

Assorted references, page 81

"Kaoru-hime" refers to volleyball player Kaoru Sugayama (1978–), often called Kaoru-hime ("Princess Kaoru") or *shiroi yosei* ("white fairy") because of her good looks. "Todai's Seiko-chan" refers to politician Satsuki Katayama (1959–), a graduate of prestigious Todai University. Due to her looks, she has been compared to singer/songwriter Seiko Matsuda (1962–). "Sakurai Misuchiru" is short for Kazutoshi Sakurai (1970–), a Japanese musician most famous for his band Mr. Children. Mirai Moriyama (1984–) is a Japanese actor and model. Yawara is the title character of Naoki Urasawa's 1986 sports manga *Yawara! A Fashionable Judo Girl*. When real-life Japanese teenager Ryoko Tamura won a silver medal for judo at the 1992 Barcelona Olympics, she was nicknamed "Yawara-chan" after the character.

Assorted references, page 82

"Tama-chan," aka "Tamao Nishi," was the name given to an Arctic bearded seal who took up residence in various Japanese rivers in 2002. When he moved to a river in Yokohama, the amused locals of Yokohama's Nishi ward registered him as a citizen. Later, a small pup seal appeared in Japan's Isatomae River, where it was nicknamed "Uta-chan" by the residents of nearby Utatsu-cho. "It stands!" refers to Futa-kun, a red panda at the Chiba Zoo who became a big attraction due to his ability to stand on his hind legs.

"If a person just dies in a novel..." page 83

This is a reference to a tear-jerking Japanese romance, Kyoichi Katayama's *Socrates in Love*, published in 2001. A massive bestseller, it was adapted into manga, a TV drama, and a live-action film.

Assorted references, page 85

Junichiro Koizumi (1942–) was the prime minister of Japan from 2001 to 2006, during which time he became known as an economic reformer. "The piano man" refers to Andreas Grassl (1984–), a German man found wandering the streets in England in April 2005, who remained unidentified for more than four months due to his refusal to communicate apart from drawing and playing the piano. Actor Yuya Yagira (1990–) became the youngest person ever to receive the Best Actor Award at the Cannes Film Festival for his role in the 2004 film *Nobody Knows*. The Seakagoke Spider (*seakagoke gumo*) was a poisonous spider that became the focus of a public health scare when it was discovered to have extended its habitat around Osaka Bay. "Minus Ion" devices, also known as "negative ion" devices, are a type of air purifiers that are supposed to cause health benefits by ionizing air molecules. Naniwa Ward is a neighborhood in Osaka, Japan. Japanese department stores are famous for selling food in their basements, often in high-class restaurants with famous chefs, and the competition among stores is intense. "Ramen Wars" refers to a 2005 incident in Japan when a jealous ramen shop owner kidnapped and beat a former business partner who had founded a more successful ramen shop by himself. The "Korean Wave" refers to a huge surge in the popularity of South Korean pop culture throughout Japan and the rest of Asia in the 1990s; some Japanese people reacted against this with expressions of anti-Korean sentiment. The Roppongi Hills Zoku, or "Hills Tribe," is a nickname for the flashy, new-money tenants of Tokyo's Roppongi Hills business megacomplex, opened in 2003. Agaricus is a mushroom known for its purported medical properties. "Suicup" is a nickname for Eri Furuse, a former NHK newscaster known for her large breasts (*suika* means "watermelon"). Odaiba and Shiodome are trendy neighborhoods built on reclaimed land in Tokyo Bay.

Assorted references, page 86

The Avex Group is a music label and entertainment company in Japan, known for repackaging fading stars' music, such as with the 2005 group Cutie Mommy, made up of three idol singers from the eighties. *Corocoro Comic* is a manga magazine aimed at elementary school kids, featuring many toy and video game manga. *Hakkutsu! Aruaru Daijiten* ("Excavate! An Encyclopedia of Facts") was a 1996–2007 TV infotainment program. In 2007 it was canceled when it was discovered that they had fabricated data about the health benefits of *natto* (fermented soybeans).

Moe boom, page 86

Moe (literally meaning "budding" or "sprouting") is Japanese slang for a fetish or a great love for characters in manga, anime, and video games. In a broad sense, it can mean any beloved hobby, but the original context is of male *otaku* who obsess over cute big-eyed anime girls. On page 87, the *otaku* vainly attempts to popularize *hore* ("fascinating") as a replacement for *moe*, a term which has been overused by the mainstream media.

Evening Primroses on Mt. Fuji Are a Mistake, page 92

This title is a reference to Osamu Dazai's 1939 short story collection *Fugaku Hyakkei* ("One Hundred Views of Mt. Fuji"), which includes the line "Evening primroses are suited to Mt. Fuji."

Assorted references, page 96

Zetsubou-sensei's quote ("There are no right answers in life") is a combination of quotes from the French aviator/author Antoine de Saint Exupéry ("There are no solutions in life. There is only the energy to advance forward") and Japanese anatomist/philosopher Takeshi Yoro ("For the problems we face in our lives, there are no right answers. But in the meantime, there are answers"). Abiru's quote ("There are no mistakes") is possibly a reference to a book of the same name by Japanese entertainer Hidekazu Nagai (1970–), who has been embroiled in various scandals involving women.

Assorted references, page 97

July 1999 was the month in which, according to the prophecies of Nostradamus, the "King of Terror" was supposed to appear, ushering in the end of the world. "Paying for NHK" refers to the Japanese law that each household with a working television must pay monthly fees to NHK, Japan's national public broadcasting system. However, there is no penalty for not paying, so many (possibly most) people don't pay anything, and the system is sort of a national joke. VHD ("Video High Density") was a failed Japanese videodisc format launched in 1978.

Heisei, page 99

When Nozomu declares, "It's the Heisei war of mistakes!" it's a play on words. The Heisei Era is the name of the current Japanese era, which began in 1989, but the name Heisei also means "peace everywhere," so it's an ironic name for a war.

Assorted references, page 99

Hidetoshi Nakata (1977–) is a former Japanese professional soccer player. His soccer playing started to go downhill when he joined Fiorentina, an Italian soccer club, in 2004, and he retired in 2006. J-pop star Sayaka Kanda (1986–), also known as simply Sayake, is the daughter of Japanese singer-songwriter Seiko Matsuda (1962–). In 2005, the mother and daughter had a much-publicized falling-out, and Seiko's management agency "retired" Sayaka from show business, reportedly due to Seiko's disapproval of Sayaka's boyfriends. In Japanese, "nucleic acid and your wife" is a pun (*kakusan* and *okusan*). Kaoru Sugita (1964–) is a Japanese actress who was supposed to appear in an NHK TV drama, but they couldn't agree to her scheduling and pay demands so she was bumped off the series. Makiko Tanaka (1944–) is a Japanese politician who was kicked out of the ruling Liberal Democratic Party after she made remarks critical of then-prime minister Junichiro Koizumi. She later successfully ran as an independent. MF (midfielder) and FW (winger) are soccer terms. Akechi Mitsuhide (1528–1582) was a samurai and general under the great daimyo Oda Nobunaga (1534–1582), who later betrayed Nobunaga and forced him to commit *seppuku*. Fuji TV and Livedoor are Japanese media corporations that fought a highly publicized battle for control of the radio station NBS (Nippon Broadcasting System) in 2005. Reinhard von Lohengramm and Oskar von Reuenthal are characters in the classic science fiction manga/anime/novel series *Legend of the Galactic Heroes*.

Assorted references, pages 100–101

All the people depicted are Japanese (or global) celebrities. The guy with the video camera is Masashi Tashiro (1956–), a former Japanese TV performer and musician who was arrested in 2000 for filming up women's skirts. The guy with the hand mirror is Kazuhide Uekusa, a former professor at Waseda University who was arrested in 2004 for using a mirror to peep under girls' skirts at a train station. The guy on the TV is Katsuji Ebisawa, president of NHK TV, who stepped down from his post and publicly apologized following a series of embezzlement scandals in 2005. The "flat three" refers to the three-man backline defensive strategy used by French soccer coach Philip Troussier when he was coaching the Japanese national team from 1998 to 2002. (It wasn't successful.) The guy with the mushroom is Hideaki Ito (1975–), a Japanese actor who was hospitalized in 2001 after eating a magic mushroom. (His T-shirt advertises his 2006 film *Limit of Love: Umizaru*.) The man in the corner reading a book is Taku Yamasaki (1936–), a Japanese politician who was publicly humiliated in 2003 when his ex-mistress wrote a sexually explicit book about their ten-year-long affair. The text on the poster of Michael Jackson reads "Lawsuit won!"

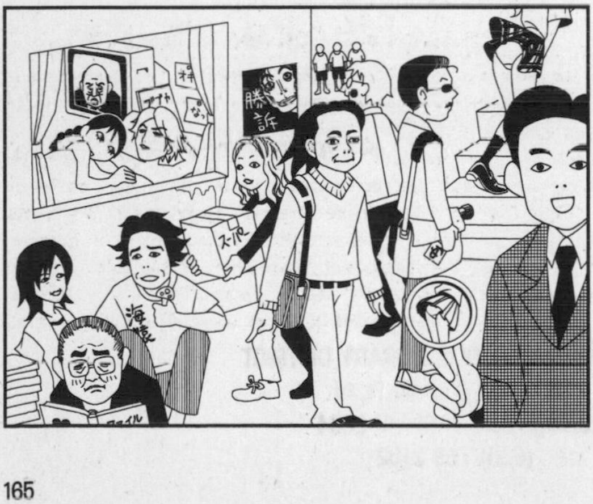
勝訴
スーパー
ファイル

Assorted references, page 102

Yutori Kyoiku ("relaxed education") is a 2002 education initiative aimed at reducing stress in students and giving them more outlets for self-expression by reducing the Japanese school week from six days to five days (see page 113), reducing workload, and offering more electives. Some people blame it for a decline in Japanese academic abilities. The Chubu Centrair International Airport was opened in Japan in 2005. Fifty-six-year-old Masaaki Matsubayashi became infamous for embezzling more than 1.9 billion yen to pay for his extravagant lifestyle which included seventeen mistresses. The "lottery ticket" line refers to the lottery that, except for a brief period from 2002 to 2005, was used to determine the draft of Japanese high school students into professional baseball. Koji Nakata (1979–) is a Japanese soccer player who accidentally passed to the opposing team in a 2005 match against Latvia. Kei Igawa (see page 12) is a Japanese baseball player whose performance declined in 2004–2005. Noma Neko is a cat mascot character created in 2005 by Avex for a music video. When Noma Neko first appeared, users of the Japanese community site 2channel noticed a strong similarity to the fan-created 2channel cat mascot, Mona, and cried foul, prompting massive criticism of Avex. Avex eventually released an apology on the networking site Mixi, and canceled plans to obtain a trademark on the character. Ken Hirai (1972–) is a singer who releases work fairly infrequently. Uniqlo is Japan's leading clothing retail chain, who at one point attempted selling groceries (vegetables, etc.) through a subsidiary. The attempt was a failure and the subsidiary was dissolved in 2004. Chogin Bank, aka LTCB, was one of Japan's top-ranked long-term credit banks, until it collapsed under bad-loan losses in 2000. The Isahaya Bay land reclamation project, which began in 1997 in an attempt to drain wetlands and convert them into agricultural land, was an environmental fiasco which devastated the local fishing industry. DigiCube was a subsidiary of Square founded in 1996 for the purpose of selling entertainment software in convenient stores. It filed for bankruptcy in 2003.

I Was Thinking of Proving It This New Year, page 106

This title is a reference to Osamu Dazai's short story *Ha* ("Leaf"), which includes the line "I was thinking of dying this New Year."

Rainbow Drop, page 110

The Rainbow Drop is an item in the very first Dragon Quest (aka Dragon Warrior) video game.

Kofuku, page 110

Kofuku Eki ("Happiness Station") is an unusually-named train station in Hokkaido. When it appeared in a 1973 TV documentary, "happy tickets" from the station became popular souvenirs. The station closed in 1987.

Washington Naval Treaty, page 112

The Washington Naval Treaty, an attempt to limit place limits on battleships and other naval power, was signed between Japan, Britain, the United States, France, and Italy in 1922.

Impostors, page 114

Calling someone over the phone and pretending to be their son, in order to get them to wire you money, is an old scam in Japan. The second example refers to a man who moved to the Japanese village of Miyota-machi and briefly passed himself off as 1960s pop singer Michio Shimizu, judging a karaoke competition and singing the song *Amairo No Kami No Otome* ("The Maiden with the Flaxen Hair"). "Pretending to be a pilot" refers to the movie *Catch Me If You Can*, in which Leonardo DiCaprio plays a talented impostor. "Pretending to be the Emperor" refers to a 2003 scam in which a man pretended to be Prince Arisugawa, a relative of the Japanese royal line, and invited guests to his "wedding" with a female conspirator. About 360 wedding guests were bilked out of a total of 13 million yen in cash gifts.

Assorted references, page 115

Adrián Annus (1973–) is a Hungarian hammer thrower who was stripped of his gold medal at the 2004 Summer Olympic Games for a doping violation. Aya Matsuura (1986–) is a Japanese idol singer accused in the past of lying about her age. In 2005, Yoshiaki Murakami's "Murakami Fund" bought a 38 percent stake in Hanshin Electric Railway (the owner of the Hanshin Tigers baseball team), sparking many buyout rumors, although the fund said at the time it had no intention of controlling the company. "Photosynthetic canal bacteria" was a junk-science cure-all term associated with a fake health supplement, Shinkogen, sold by Next Century Farm Research Institute, a natural foods lab in Japan's Gifu prefecture. In 2005, a junior high girl died at the lab, prompting a government investigation of their foods and a huge scandal.

Hakama, page 116

The *hakama* is part of the traditional Japanese clothing worn by Zetsubou-sensei.

Top four panels, page 117

This scene is a reference to the case of Andreas Grassl (see notes for page 85).

Hitomi Shimatani, page 118

Hitomi Shimatani (1980–) is a Japanese J-pop singer who (sometimes) wears her hair parted in the middle.

Children's beer, page 119

Kodomo beer ("children's beer") is a type of nonalcoholic beer marketed toward children in Japan.

Because of My Hereditary Lack of Energy, I Have Been Hibernating Since Childhood, page 120

This title is a reference to Natsume Soseki's 1906 novel *Botchan*, which begins with the line "Because of a hereditary recklessness, I have been playing always a losing game since my childhood."

Assorted references, page 123

Every Christmas Eve, Fuji TV puts on a live TV show called *Akashiya Santa's Greatest Christmas Present Show in History*. The hosts call viewers who submitted postcards in advance, and the viewers tell their sob stories on the air; the people with the most interesting stories win prizes. Soba (buckwheat noodles) are a traditional good-luck food eaten on the New Year, and Donbee is a brand of instant noodles. Tube was a Japanese rock band who generally only released CDs during the summer.

Assorted references, page 124

NEET stands for "Not currently engaged in Employment, Education, or Training," a term often applied to unemployed adults still living with their parents. Akiko Yada (1978–) is an actress and the wife of actor/musician Manabu Oshio (see the notes for page 70–71). For Sayaka, see the notes for page 99. Psycho le Cému was an all-male Japanese "visual rock" band active from 1999 to 2005, when their lead singer, Daishi, was arrested for failing a drug test. The band went "on hiatus," their tour was canceled, and their merchandise was removed from store shelves.

Fuyukomori, page 125

This is a pun using the verb *komori* ("to confine"). Kiri Komori is a *hikikomori* (a shut-in, someone who "confines" themselves indoors) and something that hibernates is a *fuyukomori* (literally, something that is "confined" during the winter).

Assorted references, page 127

Comiket, short for Comic Market, is Japan's biggest *dojinshi* (self-publishing/fanzine) convention, which takes place twice a year in Tokyo. In Japan, Christmas is considered a "romantic holiday for couples," so like Valentine's Day, it's a depressing day to be single.

Orgy of the Dead, page 129

Orgy of the Dead (in Japanese *Shiryo no Bon Odori*, "Bon Festival of the Dead") is an infamously horrible 1965 movie directed by Ed Wood.

De Riel, page 129

De Riel, from SSP Co., Ltd., is a relatively mild brand of Japanese sleeping pills.

Assorted references, pages 130-131

Fatal Frame is a survival-horror video game series. "Gundam Mark III" refers to any one of several obscure *mecha* from the Mobile Suit Gundam franchise, generally a variant design that appeared in toys or model magazines but never in the anime. Shingo Katori (1977–) is a member of the J-pop group SMAP who underwent a crash diet and wrote a book based on his experiences. Kaori Manabe (1981–) is a TV personality and swimsuit model. "HDP" refers to the magazine *Hot-Dog Press*, a young men's magazine published by Kodansha from 1979 to 2004. The "Super Liner Ogasawara" was a giant cruise liner, planned but never built, which was intended to ferry passengers to and from Japan's remote Ogasawara islands. HOPE-X was an experimental Japanese space plane, first proposed in the 1980s and finally canceled in 2003. For the "King of Terror" and "Noma Neko," see the notes for page 97 and 102. Haruka Igawa (1976–) is a Japanese "talent" and swimsuit model. Japan has two major professional leagues, the Pacific League and the Central League; with pro baseball's popularity floundering in Japan, there have been plans to switch to a one-league system. Smart, formerly Smart GmbH, is a canceled microcar brand of the automobile manufacturer Daimler AG. The ultra-maneuverable, 4WD Nissan MID4 was shown in prototype at the Frankfurt auto show in 1985, but never went into production. In September 2005, the communications company JM Net announced an "all you can talk" cell phone plan for 4500 yen a month (about $49). The plan was impossible, but the announcement temporarily drove up stock prices, allowing the company executive to sell at a massive profit before he was arrested for violating the Securities and Exchange Law. JM Net then went bankrupt. *Ninku* is a manga by Koji Kiriyama and *Mother* is a Japanese RPG series (known as *Earthbound* in the United States); both went on extremely long hiatuses between installments. Yukino Kikuma (1972–) is a Fuji TV announcer who wrote a formal apology for drinking alcohol when she was a minor.

The Musashino of Today Is Shrouded in Darkness, page 134

This title is a reference to Doppo Kunikida's 1901 short story collection *Musashino*, which includes the phrase "Musashino of long ago..." Musashino, a rural farming village during the time of Kunikida's life (1871–1908), eventually became urbanized and is now a suburb of Tokyo.

Yaminabe, page 135

Yaminabe literally means "dark hot pot." It's something of a potluck stew; friends come together and put mysterious ingredients in a big pot and cook the stew in the dark. Then each participant takes something from the pot with chopsticks, and once everyone has something, the light is turned (or kept) off and they eat what they took. Rules vary from place to place, but it's all done for laughs and thrills.

Assorted References, page 136

Yuri Mitsui (1968–) is an actress, model, and race car driver. Miki Dozan (1970–) is a musician and reggae DJ.

Champ magazine, page 139

The hand-drawn manga magazine is a parody of the Japanese magazines *Shonen Champion* and *Shonen Jump*. With the dedication of a true fangirl, the young Fujiyoshi has painstakingly recreated the contents page, enthusiastic title pages, and cliff-hanger endings of an actual manga magazine.

Assorted references, page 144

Megumi Hayashibara (1967–) is a popular Japanese voice actress and singer. Shoowatch, short for "Shooting Watch," is a handheld game by Hudson where you try to push the button as many times as possible in ten seconds.

Shimoyama Incident, page 145

On July 5, 1949, the dismembered body of Japan National Railways president Sadanori Shimoyama was found on a railway track. The case was never solved.

Black market, page 147

The names on the left are parodies of actual Japanese companies, such as LiveDoor, Avex, and CyberAgent.

Assorted references, page 149

Takako Matsu (1977–) is an actress/singer/songwriter. Hiromix (1976–) is a Japanese photographer. Hidetsugu Aneha (1957–) is a former Japanese architect sentenced to five years in prison for falsifying data on earthquake safety. He wore quirky glasses.

Mongolian blue spot, page 150

The "Mongolian blue spot" is a benign birthmark above the buttocks, most common among East Asians and Turks.

Koji Kumeta, page 150

The ingredient names for the seasoning mirin are made with glutinous rice, rice, and malted rice. The manga artist's first name, Koji, is a synonym for "malted rice" (although the characters are different) and his last name, Kumeta, has the character "rice" in it. So, he's sort of eating a yaminabe with a lot of himself in it.

Pile of mail, page 154

The letters are all hate mail with text like "It's the No. 1 Most Boring!," "I don't understand the stories," and "I just happened to read it but I can't forget how sick it made me."

Manga cover, page 156

The manga cover is a parody of Strawberry 100%.

Botchan, page 157

Botchan is a famous novel written by Natsume Soseki (see notes for page 120). Botchan is a nickname given to privileged or wealthy young boys. However, Koji Kumeta writes the word "Botchan" with words that sound the same, but it has a totally different meaning—"dead little one."

TOMARE!

STOP

You're going the wrong way!

MANGA IS A COMPLETELY DIFFERENT TYPE OF READING EXPERIENCE.

TO START AT THE **BEGINNING**, GO TO THE **END**!

That's right!

Authentic manga is read the traditional Japanese way—from right to left, exactly the *opposite* of how American books are read. It's easy to follow: Just go to the other end of the book and read each page—and each panel—from right side to left side, starting at the top right. Now you're experiencing manga as it was meant to be!